TRANSCENDENCE

Philosophy, Literature, and Theology
Approach the Beyond

TRANSCENDENCE

Philosophy, Literature, and Theology
Approach the Beyond

Edited by
Regina Schwartz

ROUTLEDGE
NEW YORK AND LONDON

Published in 2004 by
Routledge
29 West 35th Street
New York, NY 10001
www.routledge-ny.com

Published in Great Britain by
Routledge
11 New Fetter Lane
London EC4P 4EE
www.routledge.co.uk

Routledge is an imprint of the Taylor & Francis Group.

Library of Congress Cataloging-in-Publication Data

Transcendence : philosophy, literature, and theology approach the beyond / edited by Regina Schwartz.
     p. cm.
Includes bibliographical references and index.
   ISBN 0-415-96703-1 (alk. paper) — ISBN 0-415-96704-X (pbk. : alk. paper)
   1. Transcendence of God.   2. Transcendence (Philosophy)   3. Transcendence (Philosophy) in literature.   I. Schwartz, Regina M.
   BT124.5.T73 2004
   212'.7—dc22
       2003022832

Contents

Introduction

Transcendence: Beyond . . .

All I could see from where I stood were three long mountains and a wood.
 I turned and looked the other way,
 And saw three islands in a bay.
 And I could touch them, almost, with my hand,
 And reaching out my hand to try
I screamed to feel it touch the sky
I screamed, and lo, infinity came down to settle over me. . . .
     —"Renascence" Edna St. Vincent Millay

Why a volume on "transcendence" now? Ironically, while transcendence signals what is beyond—beyond what can be known, represented, or experienced—it has also been linked to unfashionable concepts like presence, being, power, an argument without recourse, an authority beyond reason, the tyranny of the most excellent, the hegemony of the west, and of course, a totalitarian deity, and its fate has suffered with theirs. How transcendence acquired this unsavory reputation is not difficult to figure: crimes have been committed in the name of transcendent principles—principles held beyond question, beyond critique—and even in the name of a transcendent God. When, in the wake of the phenomenological turn in philosophy, the postmodern turn in linguistics, and the multi-in cultural studies, so many disciplines have, each in their own way, argued that transcendence is a relic of former mistakes—why are so many strong thinkers turning to transcendence again?

As the following essays attest, the current interest in transcendence is very far from an effort to rehabilitate the transcendence of logos or authority. Instead, they demonstrate the energy and commitment with which that category is being re-conceived. Far from the ground of oppression, transcendence is now conceived as the ground of humility: epistemological, ethical, aesthetic, and political. In philosophy, phenomenology has been one context of this renewal of interest, where the transcendent means the irreducibility of the other, carrying the ethical consequence of responsibility (as in Levinas), or givenness, where the transcendent breaks in upon us through "saturated phenomena" (as in Marion)—phenomena that exceed our intuition, and certainly exceed our conceptual control. While the philosophical line that runs from Spinoza to Deleuze stands for absolute immanence, the failures of philosophies of absolute immanence are exposed (by Zizek and by Milbank). In theology, transcendence has resurfaced as mystical theology—beyond all names, defying predication; it is the transcendence that eludes idolatry, both our grasp of the other and the other's grasp of us. In literature and literary theory, transcendence points to "that within representation that nonetheless exceeds representation"[1] (as Ward, Dolar, and Hart show). While we have been told that there is no otherness that cannot be domesticated; nonetheless, these essays show that the dimension of transcendence is reintroduced as a crack in immanence, a resistance to it, a primordial inconsistency, a resistance to symbolization. Even those who claim to be radical materialists rediscover transcendence in new guises: the postmodern notion of transgression, the phenomenological notion of the other, the scientific notion of the impenetrable mystery of an infinite universe, the aesthetic notion of excess, the psychoanalytic notion of subjectivity, the political notion of revolutionary ecstasy.

Taylor establishes many of the questions this volume engages, tracing how "pre-modern societies were founded in a transcendent reality, in eternity" while modern states were founded in secular time, in a finite space and time in which human beings assume responsibility once accorded the transcendent. He describes the result: "Disenchantment on the one side, and the splintering of spirituality on the other, have contributed to the eviction of transcendence from the public sphere. At the same time, the new cosmic imaginary that places us in an abyssal universe renders the presence of God in the world, in nature, in the physical reality around us, problematic and uncertain. This distancing of God is completed by the development of an immanent-humanist option."[2] And this leads him to the penetrating question: "How have human beings been able, after the centuries and millennia during which moral life was inconceivable without God or another transcendent reality, to conceive of their entire existence only in terms of immanence?"[3] Kosky's essay charts the moment when transcendence vanished, seemingly without a trace, from the world of modern man, suggesting that Nietzsche's announcement of the death of God signaled total immanence. But the contributors to this volume demonstrate that pure immanence is not the only recourse. Instead they show that transcendence has been reconceived, sometimes radically. Transcendence does not only refer to the indefinite, infinite, beyond, for it is also the ground of ethics. For Levinas, "To be good is a deficit, waste and foolishness in a being; to be good is excellence and elevation beyond being. Ethics is not a moment of being; it is otherwise and better than being, the very possibility of the beyond."[4] In my own work, I am eager to reconceive justice under the horizon of transcendence, a justice that is beyond procedural and formal categories to be infused with charity. Transcendence also structures subjectivity, for the beyond is within the subject; as Jean Wahl put it, "Man is always beyond himself. But that beyond-oneself must eventually be conscious of the fact that it is himself that is the source of transcendence."[5]

Historically, the separation between immanence and transcendence has inspired various responses: Hegel understood the Incarnation to reconcile God and man as he sought to reconcile Christian revelation with reason through a philosophy of religion; Feuerbach understood God as man alienated from himself, and wanted earth-bound man to reclaim his projected heavens. Milbank describes the "sundering of the sublime from the beautiful and the consequent substitution of sublimity for transcendence" and critiques those gestures, recovering the relation between the sublime and the beautiful. By Kant, the "beautiful can only be a sign of the moral if it is purged of its contamination by desire," but Milbank would restore eros to the beautiful and both to transcendence. Sheppard shows that Emerson and Whitman respond to the Kantian dilemma of transcendence by fiat—the excess of poetic inspiration—even as relying on that excess courts the risk of delirium. Our contributors cite different factors in the split—among them, the Protestant Reformers, Spinoza, Kant, and the Enlightenment *philosophes*—and they propose different responses to heal it: access to the beyond through desire (Milbank's erotic sublime, Carlson's mystical theology, Marion's love), through the visible (Carlson's account of Fra Angelico, Horner's account of Marion's icon), through the literary (Sheppard, Hart), through silence (Ward) through ethics (Levinas, Schwartz), through the freedom of the subject (Dolar), through the crack, or gap in the Real itself (Zizek). But in each, the urgency of interest in transcendence is an outcome of postmodern thinking. No longer confident in reason's capacities to know and to master, no longer believing that representation "presents" the signified, no longer trying to possess the other as the object of knowledge, no longer positing a self-present idealist subject, and no longer preoccupied with definitions of God, they turn to what? Transcendence, but without proposing "a return or recovery of previous figures of transcendence."[6]

While the contributors to this volume are drawn from the disciplines of philosophy, theology, and literature, they share the common view that the split between the concepts of the transcendent and the immanent, the infinite and finitude, is regrettable, for once they are radically separated, the transcendent becomes radically inaccessible, abstract, even empty, and in this view, only immanence is available to us, through reason and through experience. For Hegel, the gap between immanence and transcendence is an effect of the gap within immanence, and this is the sense of transcendence that renders the individual responsible: "The fact that we cannot ever 'fully know' reality is not a sign of the limitation of our knowledge, but the sign that reality itself is 'incomplete,' open, an actualization of the underlying virtual process of becoming." Zizek shows how this perspective of radical immanence can lead to ontology without ethics, an "is" without "ought." If, for Spinoza, full knowledge can allow you to dispense with the ought, the deontic, for Kant, it is the opposite: in order to open up a space for ethics, you to need to limit knowledge; that is, the gap between the phenomenal and noumenal domains is essential for his ethics. Ward sees modernity's retention of transcendence as taking two forms: either complete presence, the absolute contact with the object, as in the aesthetics of the sublime, or complete absence, utter meaninglessness: the aesthetics of kitsch which "announces that though the sign is bankrupt, such emptiness can be entertaining . . ."[7] These are in turn caught up in the binaries of language and silence, the silence of full presence and the silence of the void. Ward offers a theological understanding of silence that refuses the dualism of immanence and transcendence. Carlson sees the most radical repudiation of transcendence in contemporary culture's omnivorous images: within the culture of image today . . . transcendence can seem to "appear" only through its negation or, even more, through its sheer absence—as that which is so thoroughly lost that few actually miss it or even see it as absent. Such a culture would seem to be a culture of absolute immanence, a culture lacking any reference beyond itself—lacking, indeed, any beyond at all, and hence any possibility of transcendence.[8] So it would seem; but it is not, for the image is not always a conspicuous sign of the absence of transcendence; rather, "the overwhelming immanence of visuality ever signals, without reaching, the invisible."[9] It can suggest "the mystery of invisibility made visible," as Horner demonstrates in the work of Marion, and as it does in Fra Angelico where transcendence "assumes body in the very matter of painting," and in this way, the image can overcome the dualisms of complete presence or kitsch and absence as Ward argues. Blanchot offers the dark side, as Hart explains, "Rather than consoling us with the thought that the real and the image are distinct and stable orders, that we can measure the truth of an image against the reality it represents . . . as Blanchot likes to put it, that the distance between a thing and its image is always and already *within* the thing."[10] Blanchot's concept of the "le pas au-delà", meaning both "the step beyond" and "the step not beyond" has two implications: on the one hand, each and every move beyond immanence returns us to a new, expanded sense of the immanent. On the other hand, in its struggle with immanence, transcendence always wins, even if only negatively.

Clearly, "transendence" is an overdetermined word with a long complex history; nonetheless, we can discern distinguishable meanings in currency. One includes the old contrast of transcendence with immanence. A "vertical transcendence" suggests leaving the immanent world, leaving the phenomenal, for another world, either in a transascendence to the heights or a transdescendence to the depths. But to understand transcendence as a negation of immanence, as beyond this world, is fraught with contradiction. Hegel offers a critique of this in his *Phemonenology of the Spirit*, "the bad infinity" that is only a negation of immanence rather the coinciding of them. If we "transcend" this world for another world and then reach it, it becomes immanent, hence, transcendence is not beyond the world; rather, is a passage from one world to another. Levinas further exposed the transcendence of negativity as not opening to a reality infinitely distant from my own, but only defined by my own, in opposition: "This mode of negating while taking refuge in what one negates delineates the same or the I."[11]

The second sense of transcendence would be "horizontal." On the one hand, this is the project of self-transcendence, the understanding that we are incomplete, thrusting ourselves into an incomplete future. Our encounter with our death is such a transcendence, the heroic grasping of the last possibility. Horizontal transcendence also includes the rethinking of transcendence in the context of ethics: here, the subject is less the self-transcendence of the ego than the relation to the transcendent other embedded in social life: "The other metaphysically desired is not "other" like the bread I eat, the land in which I dwell, the landscape I contemplate, like, sometimes, myself for myself. I can "feed" on these realities and to a very great extent satisfy myself, as though I had simply been lacking them. . . . The metaphysical desire tends toward *something else entirely*, toward the *absolutely other*."[12] Of course, these categories— vertical and horizontal—are heuristic distinctions that ultimately break down, for the vertical inflects the horizontal, and vice versa; "There can be no 'knowledge' of God separated from the relationship with men."[13] Nonetheless, these essays resist the reduction of transcendence to immanence: as Hart writes, "we distance transcendence from experience at the cost of rendering it unintelligible. More often than not, I suspect, the poets are concerned with a movement of unrest within experience, a sense of irruption within the immanent."[14] Transcendence is a delirious rupture in immanence, an erotic claim made by it, a gap in the Real, a question put to subjectivity, a realm of the impossible that breaks into possibility. As such, "beyond" also signals the character of this collection, beyond the traditional disciplinary categories of philosophy, theology and literature, not only because the topic is the purview of these disciplines, but also because it blurs their delimiting preconditions. To think about transcendence is necessarily to think beyond these and all divides.

Regina Schwartz
Evanston, 2003

Notes

1. Regina Schwartz, Ed. *Transcendence: Philosophy, Literature, and Theology Approach the Beyond* (New York: Routledge, 2004), 212.
2. Ibid., 8.
3. Ibid., 4.

4. Emmanuel Levinas, "God and Philosophy" in *Collected Philosophical Papers*, trans. Alphonso Lingis (Boston: Martinus Nijhoff, 1987), 162.
5. Jean Wahl, *Traite de Metaphysique* (Paris: Payot, 1953), 721.
6. Schwartz, *Transcendence*, 13.
7. Ibid., 133.
8. Ibid., 109.
9. Ibid., 120.
10. Ibid., 162.
11. Levinas, *Totality and Infinity: An Essay on Exteriority,* trans. Alphonso Lingis (Pittsburgh: Duquesne University Press, 1969), 40–42.
12. Ibid., 33.
13. Ibid., 79.
14. Kevin Hart, "La Poesia è scala a Dio: On Reading Charles Wright" in *Journal of Religion and the Arts*, 7, forthcoming.

1
A Place for Transcendence?

BY CHARLES TAYLOR
TRANSLATED BY DAMIAN TREFFS

I.

What is the place of transcendence in our societies today? We pose the question because we have the sense, and rightly so, that religion, instead of being at the center of society as it has been throughout the entirety of the course of human history, is often marginalized in the modern West.

We separate out three phenomena in this area that are often confused: a) Religion is no longer at the center of public life in contemporary democracies. In general, they are officially or semi-officially "secular." b) In most of these societies, many people are no longer practicing; they do not attend church, and often describe themselves as "non-believers." c) Whereas in the past it was very difficult not to believe, now it is often the reverse: for certain people, and in certain places, faith is difficult, seen as a hardly founded eccentric option.

Paul Valadier speaks of a "rupture in the transmission of faith between generations: . . . including, in many cases, the very opening to religious meaning, the minimal comprehension of what an act of faith consists in, the simple experience of the sacred, or God. . . . The understanding that faith is not pure nonsense, but rather a sensible and even exhilarating step is what is missing, and this because the transmission, not of Christian knowledge and custom alone, but of the act itself by which something is able to present itself in the religious universe, is lacking or no longer seems necessary for life and meaning."[1]

For many people, the Christian religion is a black box; they have absolutely no comprehension of what takes place inside. How have we arrived at this state of affairs? What has happened between, say, 1500 and 2000 for such a reversal to have taken place? Before locating the place or places of transcendence in the actual world, it will be necessary to attempt to explain this change. In the first part of this paper, I would like to offer some reflections on the important developments which have made this possible.

1. The first, the most striking when one looks at the history of these last centuries, is the disappearance of the "enchanted" world. This expression seems a bit odd[2]; what I intend here is the opposite of Weberian *"Entzauberung,"* a word that served as the title for Gauchet's famous work.[3] An enchanted

1

world is one in which we feel spirits, magical and spiritual forces in the things around us.

Our peasant ancestors would ring the church bells during a storm, the so-called "*carillon de tonnerre*." It was believed that lightning, which of course threatens us, is guided by spirits, or spiritual forces; that the instruments and actions of the church also carry spiritual force, positive, beneficent, those that are capable of protecting us from the bad forces inhabiting the thunder.

Beliefs such as these are not dead today. A great many people would be quite ready to admit that, in this or that specific context, they are tempted to believe in such "occult" forces. But these beliefs no longer form a system [*ne font plus système*], are no longer shared by everyone; such that it no longer goes without saying that things can come to pass in this way in the world in which we live. This kind of spiritual force is no longer, phenomenologically, part of our experience of the everyday. To the contrary, when we look at the "official history" of our civilization, that is, from the point of view of science, this type of spiritual force or influence no longer exists for us.

What relation does this process of disenchantment have to the belief in God? There is a certain kind of mentality among non-believers which says that belief in God is nothing more than a function of this vision of an enchanted world. With the disappearance of the whole, the parts are also necessarily erased. But this is false, as the historians well know. Christianity, following Judaism, has had complex, and often hostile, relations with the enchanted world. In fact, the principal motor of disenchantment across the ages has been the Jewish and then Christian religions, the later intensified during the centuries following the Protestant and Catholic Reformations.

The relation is rather that for as long as we lived in an enchanted world, as long as we made the *carillon de tonnerre* ring, we felt that we were in a world full of threats, vulnerable, so to speak, to the many forms of black magic. In this world, for the majority of believers, God was the source of a positive force capable of defeating magic. God was the principal source of counter-magic, or white magic. He was the ultimate assurance that good would triumph in this world over the legions of evil spirits and forces.

In this world, that is, being deeply submerged in it, truly believing in it, it was practically impossible not to believe in God. To reject God is to give oneself over to the devil. A negligible minority of truly exceptional, or perhaps despairing, individuals may have rejected God during that time. But for the large majority, the question was not one of knowing whether one believed in God or not; the positive force was as palpable a fact as were the threats it thwarted. The question of faith is here played out in the register of confident-belonging, rather than that of accepting certain doctrines. One was, in this sense, closer to the situation of the gospels.

Now, the enchanted world/faith relation is thus: in that world, there was a certain impossibility of not believing in God, comparable in our day to a refusal to believe in electricity. I have absolutely no doubt whatsoever that Hydro-Québec distributes electricity; that they will maintain the lines to my house, or successfully repair breakdowns, is another story. That is a question of whether I have confidence in them. But existential belief is not a problem.

Moreover, this impossibility of non-existence was a social fact. The channels of this power, its handling insofar as it was possible for human beings, passed through social institutions, primarily the church, at all levels. To make the *carillon de tonnerre* sound was an act of the parish, of its priest or the one in charge of the bells. The presence of God passed through the texture of the social, which created another form of the impossibility of non-belief: the defense against evil required the solidarity necessary for the handling of this positive force. To call on God's intervention against the lightning is an act of the parish, and everyone must go along. Abstention is treason.

2. With the disappearance of the enchanted world, an important obstacle to non-belief disappears, so to speak. But there were others. In particular, there is one that was born with disenchantment itself. Because the Reform movements which dispelled the ancient world of spirits and forces were animated by a Christian faith, or, later, a deist vision, that governed a new world order that they instituted, this order followed God's design, and made God present in another way. If He was no longer essential as a power in the field of forces and spirits, He became even more unavoidable as the architect, the guarantor, the designer of the cosmic as much as the social order. I will turn to the cosmic aspect shortly, but here let us look at the foundation of the United States in order to understand this new form of presence in society. For many of the founders, at issue was a new form of political society that would realize God's plan. In this they followed the Puritan tradition which had viewed the new American colonies as opportunities to bring to fulfillment the will of God. The new Jerusalem would be "a city on a hill," radiating all around, a source of light in the darkness.

For the leaders of the Revolution, divine Providence had foreseen a certain order of things. The famous words of the Declaration of Independence attest to this: "We hold these truths to be self-evident, that all men are created equal, [and] that they are endowed by their Creator with certain inalienable rights." It was a matter of building a society that would put this into practice, and for the first time. It was a decidedly Protestant, or even Deist, milieu. For these individuals, God was not present in the sacraments, not to speak of relics, places of pilgrimage, or sacred gatherings. But He was incontestably present as the Will that they followed, and the moral force that made possible their obedience. He was no longer there in the Sacred, that is, as the intra-worldly concentration of divine power in certain particular objects (relics), actions (consecration), places (Jerusalem, St. James of Compostela), or times (Christmas, Easter); but He was present as the designing Will of the order in which they lived.

Now, it is possible to misunderstand this new form of presence because we are now in the habit of identifying revolution with a form of communal action for which human beings claim complete responsibility and where, therefore, there is no longer a place for God. Yet, while it is true that human responsibility is an integral part of the context of modernity, this does not necessarily exclude God.

If one compares the new American republic with a monarchy with its roots in the Middle Ages, in France, for example, the difference is apparent. Monarchy is never founded solely in the communal actions of its subjects; it is prior to them, and makes their actions possible. However, this framework itself supposes more than human activity. The kingdom is also a "mystical body"; the concrete actual king does not exhaust the kingdom. He is the representative of a superior reality that does not exist in profane, "secular" time, but in another more elevated time. This is the doctrine of the "king's two bodies."[4]

One could say that pre-modern societies were founded in a transcendent reality, in eternity or at least a superior time, beyond profane time, while modern states are founded through common actions in secular time, such as the Declaration of Independence, the Philadelphia Congress, and so forth. In this sense, humans have full responsibility. But this does not exclude God insofar as the plan that we follow in these actions comes from Him.

On the contrary, modernity has opened a new niche for the social presence of God. A society founded on a common action, such as a revolution or constituent assembly, requires a common definition anchored in a social imaginary. One could call this definition the political identity of a society. Yet, this identity can include an essential reference to God, such as in the case of the new American republic. We become "one nation under God." God is thus anchored in the social imaginary. This constitutes a rather widespread phenomenon in the modern world. The national sentiment of a people, for example, can define itself in relation to a certain confessional membership; the Catholic church, the Polish, Irish, and French Canadians of long ago come to mind.

3. But these loyalties are not sempiternal; the case of the Quebecois brings this point forcefully home. In order to understand the actual world, it is necessary to see what has undermined this second form of the social presence of God. I would like to quickly evoke here three important changes.

First, the creation of an exclusive humanism, humanism excluding the transcendent. Very soon after the American Revolution, the French Revolution gave us the spectacle of a state's founding on a plan that was no longer (for some at least) attributed to God, but to "Nature." The transcendent was expressly excluded.

We are accustomed to taking this development for granted; for some, the simple unveiling of the truth of the human, for others, simple apostasy. But, to my mind, it has to do with an extraordinary turn, a surprising and, in certain respects, admirable, realization. How have human beings been able, after the centuries and millennia during which moral life was inconceivable without

God or another transcendent reality, to conceive of their entire existence only in terms of immanence?

Without fully discussing this important question here, I do want to say that this realization comprises two facets. First, it was necessary to conceive a human good radically cut off from transcendence. What filled this role in the first place is the conception of a human moral order, derived from Locke and the modern Natural Law thinkers. Human beings pursue life, liberty, and happiness, each for himself. But God (or later, Nature) had fashioned humans to live together. They must associate in order to live well, but their association, fundamentally egalitarian and non-hierarchical, must be constructed such that one's search for happiness causes no harm and is seen to contribute to the happiness of others. This vision of things is also at the root of our actual conception of universal human rights.

The second facet was more difficult still. It was necessary to reconceive human motivation in order to attribute to us the power to follow this morality without any help from a transcendent source. It is not merely divine grace which is excluded here; the Platonic recourse to the Idea of the Good, the Stoic reference to the divine Logos in us, each become redundant. The sources of morality, and even of the most exalted altruistic sacrifice, are found entirely within the realm of immanence.

The most important immanent sources of morality were: (a) Reason: as the ability to reach the level of universality, to distance itself from our relation to particularity, it allows us to conceive the universal, impartial good, and that gives us the power to realize it. Consider the importance accorded to the concept of the "impartial spectator" in Hutcheson, Adam Smith, and, later, the Utilitarians.

(b) Sympathy: an innate tendency, nature's endowment, that pushes us to help our fellows, and that makes us fit to live spontaneously in the moral order discussed above. Rousseau is the great inspiration of this line of thought.

Now, what is surprising is not so much that we were able to invent *theories* of this kind, but that human beings became capable of building their lives out of these sources of morality. This is the extraordinary achievement. Though these sources, in the final analysis, proved to be inadequate, as any believer will admit, one would not deny that this is a difficult and admirable feat.

In any case, the creation of this exclusive humanism changes the entire situation. Henceforth, the social imaginaries of new societies can form themselves around these immanent points of reference. It might have to do with a metaphysical conception of "nature" as with the Jacobins; or we could even attempt to define political identity solely as a function of common interests, concrete and ideal. For individuals as well, a moral life without transcendental reference becomes a clear option.

4. The second important transformation—that is, the second in time—is the passage from the cosmos to the universe. To live in a cosmos is to exist in a world that is limited and structured by a plan, whether the framework is of Plato's Ideas, or of Creation as described in the Bible (or, obviously, both, as ordinarily they are found together). In spite of our confusion and our ignorance of details, in spite of local appearances of disorder, one knows that the structure is there, holding up, and that arriving at the limit, one could touch it. Now, these are moral structures; that is, the plan is founded in the Good. The cosmos is related to our ethical life. Its message is profoundly positive.

The last two centuries have seen the effacing of this consciousness of the cosmos which has been replaced by the universe. This latter is vast, without imaginable limits, and does not immediately present itself as resting on a plan. If there is a structure, it would seem rather denuded of moral relevance. This universe seems above all indifferent to human life and its little drama that unfolds on the surface of a little planet, around an average star, situated in a galaxy like thousands of others.

We are dealing here with a change of theory, but again it involves more than just that. It is a change of imaginary, this time cosmic, that has come about in our civilization for a century or two. It is not merely that we know that the universe is many millions of years old, instead of the 6000 that our ancestors inferred—a bit hastily—from the Bible. It is also that we sense, when contemplating old rocks or glaciers, that it goes back to time immemorial. We sense that there is behind us what Buffon called "the dark abyss of time."[5] The abyss of time is dark because one cannot see to the bottom, that is, the beginning, as our ancestors thought they could, thanks to a Biblical account of creation taken in a spirit of naïve literalism. The early limit of their world, in a sense, was for them bathed in light. For us it is lost in darkness. And with this, it is also our genesis, from the non-human, or even the non-living, that is lost in the twilight.

This new cosmic imaginary plays in both senses in the struggle between belief and non-belief. On the one hand, it is clear that for many, the theory of evolution, for example, has discredited the Bible, and seems even to be a proof of materialism. But it moves also in another direction to the extent that it reintroduces mystery into the world. If one refers this to the apologetics of the Classical Age, those of Newton for instance, demonstrating the existence of God and his goodness with respect to the form of the universe and its advantages for men, one sees that they postulated a world ruled by strict and invariable laws, perfect and comprehensible, where there was no place for mystery. All that surpassed our understanding was found in the designs of God who had presided over the creation, therefore beyond the limits of the world. There was no intra-cosmic mystery.

But our universe, opening onto an unfathomable abyss, place of our dark genesis, awakens a sentiment of mystery, even among non-believers. A sense of wonder is seen in the writings of many an atheist thinker, such as the following from over two centuries ago from the pen of Diderot:

> What is our length of time compared to the eternity of time? . . . An indefinite succession of animalcules in the fermenting atom, the same indefinite succession in the other atom which we call the Earth. Who knows the races of animals which came before us? Who knows the races of animals that will succeed us?[6]

Rather paradoxically, one finds a strange alliance in current debates between "fundamentalist" Protestants in the United States and the most pure and hard-line materialists who challenge anything that smacks of mystery, in contrast to non-believers in the line of Diderot who cannot help but experience profound emotions of humility and wonder before that which exceeds us immeasurably. This universe evokes for us what the eighteenth century called "the sublime," that which led Kant to compare the vault of the heavens with the moral law. [7]

5. The last of the three changes are more recent. It has come about over the last fifty years, or perhaps more recently. I have spoken above of the two ways that God can be present in the public sphere, in the sacred or in political identity. In either case, the transcendent is bound up with social relations. These societies are "Durkheimian" in this limited sense.[8]

But in our time there have developed forms of spirituality radically decoupled from social ties. This is obviously the case with those forms that one often groups under the rubric "The New Age." But this phenomenon is rather more widespread. One should almost speak here of a post-Durkheimian age. And for the relation to God anchored in the sacred, and for that which passes as identity politics, there is necessarily a certain solidarity in spiritual life. It can be either through belonging to a church (the Catholic model) or to be sure, through belonging "to the church of one's choice," that is, a mutually recognized group of denominations (the "Protestant" model as seen in the United States).

But these ties of solidarity line up less and less well with the expressivist culture of our times, imbued with an ethic of authenticity. Above all, it is a matter of being true to one's own spiritual direction. That does not prevent a relation to transcendence, far from it, nor an aspiration to self-overcoming; but it does create a climate in which adhering to a form of spirituality that does not speak to us, because it is part of "our" tradition, or "our" identity, has less and less meaning for a growing number of people. One might not necessarily go as far as a speaker at a New Age festival in England, for whom the watchword is: "Only accept what rings true to your own inner Self."[9] But the primacy of personal inspiration is becoming more and more apparent. We live a fractured spirituality.

It is clear that this changes the situation, and not merely for religions, for the Christian churches for example; it also undermines forms of secular political identity, as in France, where there has been ingrained for some time a certain metaphysic of "republican" allegiance.

II.

All of this has led to what I call an eclipse of God in our civilization. By this I mean that God is no longer present in our world in a clear and evident way as hitherto. Disenchantment on the one side, and the splintering of spirituality on the other, have contributed to the eviction of transcendence from the public sphere. At the same time, the new cosmic imaginary that places us in an abyssal universe renders the presence of God in the world, in nature, in the physical reality around us, problematic and uncertain. This distancing of God is completed by the development of an immanent-humanist option that is strong and, in certain respects, plausible.

All of this leaves us with a world where truths of faith are both far from being in evidence and strongly contested. One must add to this that non-belief is, for reasons that we cannot examine here, particularly strong among intellectuals, academics, journalists, in brief, the cultured. And this non-belief is at the same time multifaceted and intellectually solid. Having done a certain, say materialist, reading of the abyssal universe, for instance, one can remain content in an unshakable refusal of faith, often as satisfying and free from inquietude as the devout worshippers of times past.

How can one live in this condition if one is a believer? There are two main types of reaction. Some would undo the eclipse, go back to the source, and recreate a world where God is present as previously. This aspiration takes different forms. For example, on the Protestant side, the "fundamentalist" Americans who would refuse the abyssal universe, would censor science in the name of a certain reading of the Bible, and above all avoid the intra-cosmic mystery of the genesis of the human being from nature. From the Catholic side, one has often been tempted by the project to reconstitute Christendom, that is to say, a new society that would be in solidarity with the Church, where all of culture would be impregnated with evangelical values. But if I am right about the developments that I have discussed above, these two attempts are doomed to failure in advance, and cannot but sow destruction.

The other response would take the eclipse as a point of departure. It would be a matter of refinding the paths to God that this new condition makes available to us. Instead of wishing to rest in the eclipse, one tries to go beyond it. This is the path that more and more Christians are taking these days.

What does all this mean? I will finish by examining some examples taken from different dimensions of our actual condition.

First, there are the core loci, so to speak, the points of crisis in our world today. For example, humanitarianism. I don't think that it is an exaggeration to say that no previous civilization has accepted the obligation to help human beings, wherever and against all, as our contemporaries have. There are campaigns, fund-raising committees, and international operations against hunger, illness, natural disasters; inter-state actions for preventing genocide; and so on and so forth. All of this might seem meager in the face of the needs, dangers, and the crimes effectively committed. But we are the first generation of humanity to take on the tasks, at least to the extent that we perceive them.

But we sense that all is not well within the immense humanitarian "industry." For example, we maintain enormous flows of contributions with the help of often irresponsibly used media images. Spectacular events, affecting images, keep the money rolling in, but there are often more pressing needs elsewhere, and we have to either re-allocate the public's contributions elsewhere without telling them or inflect the priorities of action in order to follow public emotion.

But behind these concrete problems there is something more profound. We have assumed, as a culture, a morality of compassion and beneficence that is perhaps beyond our emotional capabilities. It demands a devotion, an understanding, gifts of self-overcoming that we do not possess. That is what we need in order to be ready to attend to true needs, even when we are not immediately drawn to them.

Stated differently, what we are missing is a love for the human being as he/she is, with all its imperfections, weaknesses, idiocy, ugliness. But in the end, it is that which Christians claim to find in *agape,* the love that God has for human beings, and that Christ had shown us; or that the Buddhists identify with the *mahakaruna.* A place where transcendence can appear in the world, beyond the eclipse, would emerge if those individuals close to God come to make this love live again among us. One can think, among other possible examples, of Mother Teresa or of Jean Vanier.[10]

To be sure, these exceptional individuals do not offer us a political "solution" to our humanitarian dilemmas. The irony, of course, is that the work of Mother Teresa is a source of sentimental and unrealistic new images in the deforming mirror of the media. But if contact between humans and God is renewed, this will be no small thing.

A second central locus: the search for meaning. In our civilization, the problem of meaning has been posed for the last two centuries. We ask ourselves the question of the meaning of life. That is, people feel that meaning could be missing. This is new. In an era where one fears being damned, the question of meaning cannot be asked. The meaning of things is fixed; the big question is what side one will fall on. The preoccupation with meaning is a phenomenon of the world of the eclipse. In a recent work, Luc Ferry poses this problem. Almost always, our lives have an immediate meaning, we have projects, routines, tasks. But if we stop ourselves to place these projects, these routines, in question, we risk noting that "the 'meaning of meaning'—the ultimate significance of all particular significations—is lacking."[11] Ferry searches for a meaning of the sacred that would be entirely immanent. I do not think that this is a viable project. But neither do I have a solution to offer. I note simply that this gap in meaning is another place where transcendence can enter into our world.

I pass quickly to another dimension, that of the new spaces that the eclipse has opened up. The effacing of the cosmos, the contestation of faith, has rendered null and void the traditional languages of art. It has taken from us an ensemble of references of which the meaning was well fixed and known: the correspondences, the biblical narratives, and so on. But poetry, music, and much later, painting have created others, "the subtler languages," to use Shelley's expression made famous by Earl Wasserman. These are the languages which evoke their unique references in their very constitution, from the resonances that they awaken in the author and the reader. The "angels" of Rilke are not those of tradition, of the Bible and theology. They emerge in the space created by his poems, they constitute new significations.[12] These languages are not constitutively tied to an ontology, nor to transcendence or immanence. One can consider this as a loss when compared to the long tradition of Christian art. Or, one can see here an occasion to explore new paths to God, as did Hopkins and Eliot, for example. If we choose this second way, we see new places where transcendence can reappear.

A third dimension: the modern subject. Through all of these developments, we have become different. The modern subject is no longer open to the universe as were those that lived in an enchanted world. Spiritual significations no longer reside in things, but an impassable membrane separates the realm of the spirit—interior—from that of physical reality—exterior. This membrane is further reinforced by an attitude of disengagement and the discipline of modern rationality.[13] This kind of subject does not find God by the same methods and ways as before. It is for this reason that the modern world endlessly produces new forms of spirituality. We have already seen this mechanism at work at a previous stage of early modernity. Seventeenth-century France, the location of a new interiorized subject, produced a flowering of spiritual and devotional practices, such as the treatise on the love of God of Saint Francis de Sales, and the "theocentrism" of Bérulle.[14]

I have quickly reviewed some examples of the possible sites of transcendence beyond the eclipse in three realms. What arises from this discussion is that all these steps can be pursued in a spiritually fractured world like ours. I consider this fracturing to be, in effect, irreversible; religious institutions will be forced to work within the limits of this condition of dispersal.

Still, for their adherents, there is another, a fourth dimension for intervention: prophecy. But this requires that one invent new forms in a situation of post-Christendom.[15]

Notes

This essay has been adapted from "Une place pour la transcendance?", in Pierre Gaudette, ed., *Mutations culturelles et transcendance*, Québec: Laval Théologique, 2000.

1. In *Esprit*, no. 233, June, 1997, 39–40.
2. *"La disparition du monde 'enchanté."*
3. Marcel Gauchet, *Le désenchantement du Monde*, (Paris: Gallimard, 1985).
4. See E. Kantorowicz, *The King's Two Bodies*, (Princeton University Press, 1957).
5. See Paolo Rossi, *The Dark Abyss of Time*, (University of Chicago Press, 1984), 99.108–9.
6. Denis Diderot, *Le Rêve de d'Alembert*, in *Oeuvres*, 299.
7. "Zwei Dinge erfüllen das Gemüth mit immer neuer und zunehmender Bewunderung und Ehrfurcht, je öfter und anhaltender sich das Nachdnken damit beschäftigt: *der bestirnte Himmel über mir und das moralische Gesetz in mir." Kritik der praktischen Vernunft*, Berlin Academy Edition, (Berlin: Walter Gruyter 1968) 161. ["Two things fill the mind with ever new and increasing admiration and awe, the oftener and the more steadily we reflect on them: *the starry heavens above and the moral law within."*]
8. I am not espousing the strong Durkheimian thesis according to which the transcendent, the sacred, *is* society.
9. Sir George Trevelyan, during a conference of the Festival for Mind, Body and Spirit, cited in Paul Heelas, *The New Age Movement*, (Oxford: Blackwell's 1996), 21. One might be tempted to believe that this slogan is attractive only to New Agers. But Heelas maintains (chapter 6) that there is here a certain affinity here with attitudes shared by a great many people. For example, a 1978 Gallup Poll found that 80 percent of Americans agreed that "an individual should arrive at his or her own religious beliefs independent of any churches or synagogues." Heelas, 164; also cited in Robert Bellah et al., *Habits of the Heart*, Berkeley: University of California Press 1985, 228.
10. I have discussed this question at greater length in *A Catholic Modernity?* (New York: Oxford University Press, 1999).
11. Luc Ferry, *L'Homme-Dieu ou le sens de la vie*, (Paris: Grasset, 1996), 19.
12. I have developed this argument at greater length in *Sources of the Self*, (Cambridge, Mass.: Harvard University Press, 1989), chapter 21. I have learned much from Earl Wasserman's *The Subtler Language*, (Baltimore: Johns Hopkins University Press, 1968).
13. See Norbert Elias, *Über den Prozess der Zivilization*, (Frankfurt: Suhrkamp, 1978).
14. See Henri Bremond, *L'Histoire du Sentiment religieux en France*.
15. The discussion of José Casanova in his recent work is a good point of departure: José Casanova, *Public Religions in the Modern World*, (University of Chicago Press, 1994).

2

The Birth of the Modern Philosophy of Religion and the Death of Transcendence

BY JEFFREY L. KOSKY

Writing about transcendence today, as the twentieth century has come to a close, I cannot escape the thought that I will be suspected as the rear guard of an already vanquished troop defending an already forgotten cause. It seems that this task, to write on transcendence, runs counter to every dominant movement and voice of twentieth-century culture. I remind myself that we, the inhabitants of the century that has just ended, have witnessed the progressive realization of what Max Weber, at the beginning of the century, called the "disenchantment of the world." With this phrase, Weber described the world view upon which modern culture was premised: the assumption that the world is fully knowable, fully calculable, fully open to the probing of the scientific mind and reason. In such a world where all is potentially if not yet actually available for man, what place is left for transcendence, for something, or something that is not at all a thing, which might transcend the grasping mind or hand of modern man? The fact that fewer and fewer authors and scholars today even think or discuss "disenchantment" only indicates how illuminating Weber's vision has proven to be; for to forget that the world is disenchanted is precisely the spell cast by disenchantment. Transcendence is so far lost that we don't even know it is gone.

In this essay I will not propose a return or recovery of previous figures of transcendence; such a task would deny the historical and cultural horizon within which thought has its life. Others in this collection will have shown how, even without following the path of such a return, it might be possible within the contemporary horizon to catch a glimpse of transcendence flickering ambiguously amidst the images which have cast us in their net. What I propose to do instead is to mark the moment when transcendence vanished from the modern world, with or without a trace being a question undecided here. More specifically, I am interested in how this vanishing of transcendence has been expressed in one particular, indeed academic, faculty: namely, the philosophy of religion. Concerned as it is with the loftiest of man's aspirations— namely religion, the one dimension of human existence where transcendence might be expected to retain its meaning—the philosophy of religion would seem to be the place where the meaning of transcendence would remain alive and well. In fact, this has not been the case, and it is this paradox that I want to explore through a reading of the birth of the modern philosophy of religion.

Few will doubt that the modern philosophy of religion was born at the dawn of the nineteenth century. Born with Kant and the Kantians, the discipline came of age, like so much of modernity, in Hegel and Nietzsche. They therefore define the horizon within which philosophy of religion operated in modernity. What is this horizon? What are the conditions under which philosophy of religion emerged and so operates? Perhaps ironically, readings of Kant, Hegel, and Nietzsche confirm a close connection between the birth of the philosophy of religion and the realization of total immanence announced in the sentence "God is dead!" For subsequent philosophy of religion, then, one phenomenon in particular has posed a nearly insurmountable difficulty—divine transcendence.

The death of God received its first philosophical articulation in Hegel's philosophy. "God is dead" appears in Hegel's writings for the first time in *Faith and Knowledge* (1802) where he writes, "Formerly, the infinite grief existed historically in the formative process of culture. It existed in the feeling that "God Himself is dead."[1] Even if Hegel's first statement of the death of God thus claims that this is "the feeling upon which the *religion* of more recent times rests," it is important to note that this statement is part and parcel of a critique of *philosophy* as represented by the leading philosophies of Hegel's time, the reflective philosophies of subjectivity found in Kant, Jacobi, and Fichte. Thoroughly entrenched in nineteenth-century Enlightenment culture, modern philosophy, as represented by these authors, conceptualized what existed historically as "the feeling that 'God Himself is dead.'" The Enlightenment God is a dead God, according to Hegel, since "spirit that does not manifest itself or reveal itself is something dead" (LPR, 102). The God of the Enlightenment was precisely a God who does not manifest himself in knowledge and so a God totally abstract and unrelated to life—dead.

On Hegel's reading, modern philosophy's flight from the transcendent began when Luther and his Reformation followers instituted an unbridgeable separation between finite human existence and transcendent or infinite divine existence. Fearing that mediating structures such as icons and the sacraments would pose a crisis for the faithful asked to believe, for instance, that the (finite) bread and wine experienced at the eucharist are in fact (divine, infinite) body and blood, Protestantism banished the infinite from the intuitable, perceptible finite. Protestantism located religion in subjectivity and feeling, but a subject still separated from God by the infinite abyss of sin such that divinity remained an object of longing and desire. For the Protestant, on Hegel's reading,

> beauty and truth present themselves in feelings and persuasions, in love and intellect [understanding]. Religion builds its temples and altars in the heart of the

individual. In sighs and prayers, he seeks for the God whom he denies to himself in intuition, because of the risk that the intellect will cognize what is intuited as a mere thing, reducing the sacred grove to mere timber (FK, 57).

According to Hegel, then, the unbridgeable gap between sighing subjectivity and the God for whom it longs was established in order to ward off the risk that knowledge, in the act of comprehending its object, will reduce God to the level of man—or worse, that of a mere thing. God was removed from finitude so that his transcendence might be preserved. Religion, on the other hand, was located in the finite, more precisely in a finite and limited subjectivity yearning for the infinite that transcends its grasp. "Religion, as this longing, is subjective; but what it seeks and what is not given to it in intuition, is the Absolute and the eternal" (FK, 58).

What Luther instituted as a prophylaxis of sorts—aiming to prevent debasing the divinity of God in and through the act of reducing him to finitude and immanence—backfires in its very functioning, according to Hegel, and leaves an abstract, unknowable God. In short, Protestantism succeeded all too well in its attempt to preserve transcendence and the absolute distinction between God and man.[2] Frustrated by the impossibility of satisfying its yearning for the infinite, sighing subjectivity reconciles itself with the finitude to which it is confined and admits no reality beyond empirical existence and the ordinary, everyday world of science and the understanding. Hegel writes,

> The infinite longing that yearns beyond body and world, reconciled itself with existence. But the reality with which it became reconciled, the objective sphere acknowledged by subjectivity, was in fact merely empirical existence, the ordinary world and ordinary matters of fact (*Wirklichkeit*). Hence this reconciliation did not itself lose the character of absolute opposition implicit in beautiful longing. Rather it flung itself upon the other pole of the antithesis, the empirical world (FK, 59).

Subjectivity puts its longing to rest by absolutizing the position of finitude and empirical reality—one might say, simply by forgetting what it could not know and then forgetting this forgetting. This forsaking of transcendence in the distance that was meant to protect it results in and belongs to the good conscience of a subject "allowed to confide in ordinary life and surrender to it without sin" tarnishing its clean conscience (FK, 59). God, the infinite, or the transcendent has no experienceable relation to this finite reality, and this absence is not even noted in a possible trace left in sin and the disturbed conscience. Such a God is not alive in this world or for this subject. This is at least one of the things Hegel means when he writes that "the religion of more recent times rests" on "the feeling that God Himself is Dead."

According to Hegel, this "formative process of culture" has established the subjective standpoint which determines Enlightenment philosophy. Even though by the time of Kant, Enlightenment philosophy no longer absolutized empirical reality, according to Hegel, it nevertheless had absolutized subjective experience. Knowledge was confined to the phenomenal realm where the activity of the finite, human mind contributed to the experience made.

> The fixed standpoint which the all-powerful culture of our time has established for philosophy is [one where] philosophy cannot aim at the cognition of God, but only at what is called the cognition of man. This so-called man and his humanity conceived as a rigidly, insuperable finite sort of Reason form philosophy's absolute standpoint. Man is not a glowing spark of eternal beauty, or a spiritual focus of the universe, but an absolute sensibility.[3] He does, however, have the faculty of faith so that he can touch himself up here and there with a spot of alien supersensuousness (FK, 65).

Like the Protestant culture in which it was rooted, Enlightened philosophy absolutized the distinction between the finite and infinite, man and God, and took man as its absolute standpoint—a man, moreover, determined by finitude and sensibility and so a man incapable of elevating himself to the eternal and absolute.

Confined to the finite and the limits of sensible intuition, Kantian philosophy employed reason in the critical project of reflecting on itself and thereby removed God from the sphere of its applicability. For Kant, as is well known, reason turns in on itself in order to analyze itself and discover its own limits. This critical turn was meant to secure the possibility of knowledge by specifying the a priori structures of the mind which make knowledge and experience possible. Knowledge was possible so long as it was confined to the phenomenal realm of experience where the mind is active; but when the mind attempts to extend knowledge beyond the realm of experience and make a claim to know things-in-themselves, it falls into illusion. Prey to what Kant called the transcendental illusion, finite man mistakes the structures of thought for structures of reality. In the case of God, reason is particularly susceptible to this. The so-called proofs for the existence of God, for instance, rest on the illusory supposition that the principle of causality applies outside the field of our understanding, that is on the supposition that causality is not a category of the understanding but a category of being. To infer from our experience of the world that the world must have a cause outside it (named, God) is "a judgment of purely speculative reason, since the object which we are inferring is not an object of possible experience," and therefore this cause is not a possible object of knowledge.[4] Kant's critique of pure reason secured knowledge from its skeptical attackers, but only at the price of removing God from this well-defended fortress.

Having removed God from a knowledge confined to the limits of sensible experience, Kant believed that he had actually made room for faith, as he wrote famously in the "Preface to the Second Edition" of *The Critique of Pure Reason*:

"I have therefore found it necessary to deny *knowledge*, in order to make room for *faith*" (CPR, 29). What knowledge gave up, faith found, but this faith could not know what it nevertheless held as its own. Knowledge had surrendered God to faith with the express purpose of preserving and protecting God from the threat knowledge itself posed. On Hegel's reading, this striving for a place beyond the limited and finite place established for knowledge (a place called faith) represents both what is most noble about Kantian philosophy and its ultimate betrayal of philosophy. Hegel writes,

> The torment of a nobler nature subjected to this limitation, this absolute opposition [between the finite and infinite], expresses itself in yearning and striving; and the consciousness that it is a barrier which cannot be crossed expresses itself as faith in a realm beyond the barrier. But because of its perennial incapacity this faith is simultaneously the impossibility of rising above the barrier into the realm of Reason, the realm which is intrinsically clear and free of longing (FK, 64–5).

Confronted with the barrier posed by the limits of the understanding, man's better part, his nobler nature, longs for something unlimited and infinite, something beyond this barrier. This longing, however, cannot fulfill itself in knowledge, for man's knowledge is confined to finitude and the limits of the understanding, so it expresses itself in faith which can never know what it nevertheless desires.

When Kant claims that his philosophy aims to abolish knowledge in order to make room for faith, he illustrates almost to perfection what Hegel means by the death of God. Kant's God is a dead one, for Hegel, to the degree that it is apprehended in a faith which cannot know what it nevertheless talks about, believes in, and longs for. Transcendent—that is, separated from knowledge by the absolute opposition between the finite and the infinite, the God of faith must always remain abstract and dead, apart from the living world of knowledge and experience.

It is precisely in this Kantian context that the modern philosophy of religion emerged. As the eminent scholar Walter Jaeschke, one of the chief editors of Hegel's *Lectures on the Philosophy of Religion*, notes, "The first works to bear the name of philosophy of religion are written by committed Kantians. Karl Heinrich Pölitz in particular expressly took his stand in 1795 wholly on the practically grounded doctrine of God and religion."[5] While it might seem surprising that the philosophy of religion should emerge at the moment when God was being cast from knowledge to faith, it was precisely this act of banishment that opened its possibility, determined its task, and guided its future. As Jaeschke writes, "as long as it seemed as though the idea of God was not only conceivable but indispensable to theoretical philosophy, indeed, properly speaking, its central point, the philosophy of religion had only marginal importance. What first released it from this shadow existence was Kant's demonstration of the failure of traditional philosophical theology."[6] How did removing the idea of God from philosophical knowledge of God make an opening for the philosophy of religion? And what tasks belonged to this emergent philosophy of religion?

What theoretical reason gave up with Kant (namely: God) practical reason recovered. That is to say, though theoretical reason cannot have any knowledge of God, God nevertheless appears as a necessary postulate of the practical reason. In his *Critique of Practical Reason*, the idea of the moral good and the presupposition of moral experience serve as the basis on which Kant shows how such morality necessarily presupposes the a priori operation of what he calls the categorical imperative. Just as theoretical reason acts in knowledge in and through the forms of the intuition and the categories of the understanding, practical reason contributes the category of the ethical imperative to our moral life.

Now, according to Kant, along with the categorical imperative, practical reason postulates the idea of God—and it is just that, a postulate which means that it is not known, and in fact can never be known, if there is a reality corresponding to this idea. Kant's argument, however, is well known. The chief end of the moral life is virtue rewarded by happiness. To be morally virtuous we must never do the good in expectation of reward for then we act out of a motive other than love of duty and hence are not virtuous. However, Kant says, we anticipate, and even believe, that this virtue will be crowned with reward. In order that this end might be upheld, the practical form of reason operative in morality necessarily postulates three ideas: 1) freedom, since only if we can do what we ought to do will this end be realized; 2) immortality, since the infinite distance between our sinful nature and the good we desire cannot be overcome in this life; and 3) God, who assures that virtue receives its just reward by apportioning happiness according to merit. The idea of God thus belongs to the practical faith that moral behavior will receive reward, and this idea is perfectly rational insofar as it is a postulate of reason in practical form.

The place where God is found has thus been shifted from theoretical knowledge to the practical reason active in morality and in doing so Kant has "made room for faith" (CPR, 29). The man of the Enlightenment, according to Kant, "needs no speculative proofs for God's existence. He is convinced of it with certainty, because otherwise he would have to reject the necessary laws of morality which are grounded in the nature of his being. Thus he derives theology from morality, yet not from speculative but from practical evidence; not through knowledge but through faith."[7] The idea of God remains and is fully rational because it is rooted in the a priori structure of reason in its moral operation. The qualification that we are here dealing with a practical knowledge, or faith, must not be understood to imply a lesser degree of evidence; for it is delivered with all the certainty and conviction as pertains to our conviction in human freedom—which is to say, for man at that time, a great deal.[8]

Having banished the possibility of knowing God in order to save God for faith, critical philosophy faced the daunting task of deciding what to do with the traditions and dogma of the historical religions. Within the philosophical disciplines, reflection on religion thus replaced speculation on God. Making no claim to uncover knowledge of God, the philosophy of religion in Kant and especially his followers aimed to save what of religion was in accord with the activity of practical reason. Submitted to the definition of religion as the practical knowledge of our moral duties as divine commands (CPrR, 134), religion would comprise nothing more than what morality and practical reason could tolerate. With this identification, it became possible for philosophical reflection on actual, historical religions to assess the extent to which particular doctrine or dogma did and did not conform to the religion of reason. The philosophy of religion was initially charged not with knowledge of God, but a critique of the representations, positive forms, and doctrine found in historical religions.

The classic expression of Kant's philosophy of religion is *Religion Within the Limits of Reason Alone* (1793) where the historical institutions and beliefs of Christianity are evaluated and reinterpreted in light of the ethical religion of reason. To such a project, the revealed elements of religion obviously posed the largest obstacle insofar as the claims of revelation introduced a transcendence and authority beyond reason. This is evident in the Kantian reinterpretation of the Christological problem. Whereas traditional Christology sought to explain the relation between the human and divine, the finite and the infinite, the worldly and the transcendent, the Kantian Christology concerned the relation between the historical and the ideal in the person of Christ. For the Kantian philosophy of religion, the Christ of history is no longer a revelation of a transcendent God but a material example of the ethical ideal, something like a role model, that is needed because the sluggish and sensuous nature of finite man prohibits him from attaining the ideal moral behavior he should be able to reach in and through reason alone. "Thus [Hegel writes] Christ is dragged down to the level of human affairs, not to the level of the commonplace but still to that of the human" (LPR, 82).

On Hegel's reading, this project of salvaging religion was eventually renounced when victorious reason became more confident with its triumph. In Kant and his heirs, the triumph of philosophy over religion was so great that in 1802, only a decade after Kant's *Religion Within the Limits of Reason Alone*, Hegel wrote that "a philosophical struggle against the positive, against miracles and suchlike, is now regarded as obsolete and unenlightened. Kant tried to put new life into the positive form of religion with a meaning derived from philosophy, but his attempt was received poorly, not because it would have changed the meaning peculiar to these forms, but because they no longer appeared worth the bother" (FK, 55). On Hegel's reading, enlightened philosophy had won so great a victory that when its very own philosophy of religion tried to save religion its attempt seemed empty, futile, and vain.

Hegel is quick to observe, however, that philosophy had really only vanquished the positive forms of religion (FK, 55). He doubts, therefore, that this victory really defeated the foe it intended. The philosophy of religion may have emptied the religious form of its positive content, and it may have preserved whatever of this content still stood after it had passed through the tribunal of reason; but, precisely in this way, the philosophy of religion failed to capture the content of real religious faith: namely, God. The religion it won out over was not a real faith, but only a weak caricature of faith and therefore the victory is no victory at all.

The fact that faith still reached outside and above what so-called Reason could comprehend was the best sign that Reason's victory was still incomplete. Enlightened reason "acknowledges its own nothingness by placing that which is better than it in a *faith outside and above* itself, as a *beyond*" (FK, 56). Lacking its better part, Enlightenment philosophy, on Hegel's reading, was unsatisfied—and unsatisfactory—because it had won a victory over religion only by leaving what was essential to the content of religion (God) over and above Reason. Once again, Hegel is asserting that Kantian philosophy is both embedded in and the actualization of what exists in the surrounding culture as the feeling "God Himself is dead"!

Understood as the denial of knowledge of God and the supposition of a faith reaching beyond it, the death of God becomes a problem for philosophy itself. The death of God means that philosophy has failed to reconcile within itself the distinction between faith, with its transcendent God, and knowledge. Faith still reaches beyond knowledge toward a God who cannot be known, a God who is in this sense dead and whose death leaves knowledge incomplete precisely in what concerns its highest object.

The truth of the Enlightenment—"that heaven be transplanted to the earth below"[9]—was in need of assistance, according to Hegel, in that philosophy needed to recover knowledge of God. This is why Martin De Nys and Walter Jaeschke speak of Hegel as undertaking a "project which one legitimately names philosophical theology."[10] Through the resources of philosophy, they argue, Hegel hopes to develop the knowledge of God omitted from modern philosophy and thereby bring philosophy to completion. However, this project is only imperfectly grasped when one—like Jaeschke, for example (who is here unlike De Nys and also unlike Eberhard Jüngel)—does not add that this philosophical theology, this transplantation of heaven to the earth below, is propelled by the introduction of an idea that first appeared historically in a particular religious tradition: namely, the idea of the death of God that appeared in Christianity.[11] It is this Christian death of God which lets us see how Hegel was able to overcome the death of God in Enlightenment philosophy, and it is this same death of God which lets us see how the philosophy of religion emerged in Hegelian philosophy.

To understand how Hegel's appropriation of this second sense of the death of God can revoke the death of God in Enlightenment philosophy, I want to return to the important passage from the conclusion of *Faith and Knowledge* where Hegel first uses the phrase "God is dead."

> But the pure concept of infinity as the abyss of nothingness in which all being is engulfed, must signify the infinite grief [of the finite] purely as a moment of the supreme idea. Formerly, the infinite grief existed historically in the formative process of culture. It existed in the feeling that "God Himself is dead," upon which the religion of more recent times rests; the same feeling that Pascal expressed in so to speak sheerly empirical form: "la nature est telle qu'elle *marque* partout un Dieu *perdu* et dans l'homme et hors de l'homme [Nature is such that it *signifies* everywhere a *lost* God both within and outside man]. By *marking this feeling as a moment of the supreme Idea*, the pure concept must give philosophical existence to what used to be either the moral precept that we must sacrifice the empirical being (*Wesen*), or the concept of formal abstraction [e.g., the categorical imperative]. Thereby it must reestablish for philosophy the Idea of absolute freedom and along with it the absolute Passion, *the speculative Good Friday in place of the historic Good Friday. Good Friday must be speculatively reestablished in the whole truth and harshness of its God-forsakenness.* . . . The highest totality can and must achieve its resurrection solely from this harsh consciousness of loss, encompassing everything, and ascending in all its earnestness and out of its deepest ground to the most serene freedom of its shape [my emphasis] (FK, 190).

There are two important points to notice here.

(1) The first sense of the death of God is now superseded, not annihilated, by a second, according to which the first is only a moment in the unfolding of its idea. The proposition "God is dead" is no longer absolute in its first sense but is now read as a truth which belongs to God Himself. As Jüngel writes,

> By designating the feeling that "God Himself is dead" as a moment of the supreme idea, talk about the death of God gains a twofold meaning. First of all, in talk about the death of God, the situation of absolutized finitude expresses itself, which corresponds to abstract infinitude as empty negativity. Once that feeling is grasped as a moment of the supreme Idea, then the death of God is understood as an event of the *self-negation* of God, who does not desire to be "in and for himself" and does not desire to forsake the world in its finitude.[12] (GMW, 74).

What Jüngel points out is twofold: (a) on Hegel's reading, talk about the death of God gives expression to the Kantian standpoint insofar as it had absolutized finitude and correlatively posited only an abstract and empty infinite. (b) Hegel has made that death of God a moment in the procession and return of God Himself. Thus understood, the atheistic feeling of the modern age, given philosophical articulation in Kant and the Enlightenment *philosophes*, stands within the unfolding of the Absolute, not as having truth on its own but as the moment of God's self-negation, the moment when God passes over into his opposite, leaving behind the remoteness of his transcendence and infinity in order to enter finitude.

(2) By philosophically interpreting an idea given in revealed religion, in particular, the Christian religion, it becomes possible to overcome the atheistic feeling of modern times. Hegel's task, as Jüngel says, was to reconcile faith and knowledge, heaven and earth, "against the apparently satisfied Enlightenment, by recapturing philosophically the content of faith. Philosophy had to grasp that in revealed religion heaven itself *has come* to earth. Philosophy had to reconcile Christianity with the Enlightenment. To do that, it needed and used the dark statement, the Death of God" (GMW, 89). In Christianity, as interpreted by Hegel the philosopher, the death of God means that the abstract and unknowable God has descended into finitude, even to the point of death, in order to be known by man. The process begun by the Incarnation is thus completed in the death of God on the Cross. The Christian proclamation "God is dead" means that heaven has been emptied and indeed come to earth, that the truths of faith are not in heaven but fully revealed in and for the finite world—precisely as the truth of the Enlightenment had wished. The feeling "God is dead," which arises for the modern mind of the Enlightened because of its absolute separation from God, is indeed true in its feeling that the heavens are empty; but if it is to realize its truth and complete the project of reconciling heaven and earth, this feeling must be reinterpreted in light of the Christian tradition where the heavens are empty precisely because they have emptied themselves kenotically in their revelation here on earth. Only in and through its acceptance of the Christian sense of the death of God will philosophy achieve its final satisfaction in the knowledge of a wholly immanent totality.

If the death of God is a truth belonging to God, or if the wisdom of the heavens has indeed died and descended to earth, overcoming the separation of God and man, then the so-called Hegelian philosophical theology does not find its object in the remote or abstract heavens but here on earth. Where? In religion, where the knowledge of God is actual. As Hegel himself says, "the doctrine of God is to be grasped and taught only as the doctrine of religion."[13] Hegel's philosophy of religion therefore will differ significantly from that which issued from Kant. Whereas the Kantian philosophy of religion arises precisely out of the unknowability of God, the Hegelian belongs to and serves the knowledge of God. Jaeschke will speak of Hegel's philosophical theology "passing over into philosophy of religion, or vice versa: the philosophy of religion is for Hegel only one part of philosophical theology, that part in which philosophical theology reaches its conclusion."[14] In recovering knowledge of God, not just reflecting on the positive forms of religion, Hegel's philosophy of religion revokes the death of God which had been instituted in Kant's philosophy. In so doing, it reconciles the last distinction within itself, overcomes the last transcendence resisting it, and realizes the death of God taught in Christianity. The Hegelian philosophy of religion at once presupposes the death of God and completes it.

This interpretation of the death of God as a fundamentally Christian truth about God is closely related to Hegel's description of Christianity as "the revealed religion." For a religion to be revelatory, according to Hegel, means precisely that its God can be known or cognized by the finite, human subject.

> Those who say that Christianity is not revelatory do not speak from the standpoint of the Christian religion at any rate, for the Christian religion is called the revealed religion. Its content is that God is revealed to human beings, that they know what God is. Previously they did not know this; but in the Christian religion there is no longer any secret—a mystery certainly, but not in the sense that it is not known. For consciousness at the level of understanding or for sensible cognition it is a secret, whereas for reason it is something manifest (LPR, 130).

The secret of the mystery having been removed by God's revelation in and as the Christian religion, consciousness can know God completely and unreservedly. The mystery being known, the secret no longer a secret, Hegel's philosophy of religion realizes the conquest, or the descent, of the heavens by comprehending the religious consciousness where the knowledge of God is actual.

The revelatory character of Christianity stems from the determination of God not as substance but as spirit. Whereas substance consists entirely in remaining in itself and needing no other for its existence, spirit is itself by manifesting itself in and for an other. "Spirit is an absolute manifesting. Its manifesting is a positing of determination and a being for an other. 'Manifesting' means 'creating an other,' and indeed the creating of subjective spirit for which the absolute is" (LPR, 129). The determination of God as spirit means that God is not God if he does not manifest himself, does not leave his abstract and empty infinitude to manifest himself in and as the finite. If God as infinite spirit has emptied himself into finite spirit, the finite knowledge of God is not simply a relation of the finite to the infinite, but the infinite's self-relatedness back to itself. The religious consciousness is not simply knowledge of God—or it is knowledge *of* God where the genitive is read as both objective and subjective. In the knowledge *of* God actual in the religious consciousness, God knows himself and thus returns to himself from his self-othering in finitude.

Religion, however, does not yet know its own consciousness as such. A philosophy of religion is therefore needed to comprehend the truth which religion already is. This is why, as Hegel says in the passage from the conclusion of *Faith and Knowledge*, "Good Friday must be speculatively reestablished" and why the "pure concept must give philosophical existence" to what previously was a historical or moral doctrine. Noting differences between the subjective perspective of religion and the speculative perspective of religion, Hegel writes, "In its concept, religion is the relation of the subject, of the subjective consciousness to God who is spirit. In its concept regarded speculatively, it is therefore spirit conscious of its own essence, conscious of its own self" (LPR, 104). The difference here noted stems from the standpoint adopted. For the understanding that starts with man, religion is a relation of two independent and external beings, a subject and object transcending one another. For speculative philosophy, by contrast, where the starting point is God as spirit, religion is the closure of the circle whereby infinite spirit realizes itself in and through the subjective consciousness of it itself.

In this way, the philosophy of religion is not simply a description of man. Likewise, the philosophy of religion is not simply an interpretation of religion in light of philosophical knowledge, salvaging what accords with it and discarding what does not. Nor is it an attempt to demonstrate the necessity of religious views. Rather, religion is of interest to Hegelian philosophy because religion is a self-relation of spirit to itself; considered in the speculative philosophy of religion, the religious consciousness of God is the return of spirit to itself. This is why the philosophy of religion completes the philosophical theology undertaken by Hegel. And, if philosophy itself remained incomplete to the degree that it failed to reconcile itself with what faith holds of God, then the philosophy of religion completes philosophy itself.

But, the philosophy of religion achieves this task only on condition that it accept the determination of God by the harsh word "God himself is dead" or else by the (equivalent) determination of God as spirit whose essence is the full manifestation of all mystery—both determinations given in the Christian religion. Though Hegel negates the Enlightenment death of God and thereby brings metaphysics to its end, he does so only by a second, Christian death of God where the first is revoked in and through its interpretation as a negative realization of the full manifestation of God as spirit. There is thus no escape from the death of God, only its being enshrined as the very essence of God grasped in a finally completed and fully revelatory immanence.

In connecting the Christian and explicitly Christological source of the death of God with the atheistic spirit of the times and in making this connection essential to philosophy's triumph over the last transcendence, Hegel opened the door for an interpretation of this connection that would emphasize the atheistic spirit of the times. It is Feuerbach who, in and through his critique of Hegel's speculative philosophy, realizes this inevitable reversal. In a reversal of Hegelian philosophy that makes its achievement explicit, Feuerbach's philosophical reflection on religion results in an immanence that no longer happens in the name of God or Spirit, but Man.

On Feuerbach's reading, Hegel intended the admirable end of thinking Christianity together with the essence of the modern era but he failed to realize this end insofar as he reinstated theology in and through the speculative concept of God *as spirit.* Hegelian immanence is in fact an immanence of the transcendent. Feuerbach will therefore object that Hegelian philosophy "is the negation of theology from the viewpoint of theology or the negation of theology that is itself again theology."[15] What Feuerbach objected to in Hegel was the fact that theology was restored in and through the Christianization of the modern atheistic moment or, in other words, the fact that the negation of Christianity was identified with Christianity itself in the "speculative Good Friday." Feuerbach, on the other hand, will dissociate the atheistic death of God from the knowledge of God by claiming that atheism leads not back to God—as in Hegel where the realization of the emptiness of the heavens is only the negative of the total presence of God in the world—but to man who, as an atheist, knows no God other than the one he himself creates in his own image. This is what Feuerbach means with the famous pronouncement, oft repeated, that "the secret of theology is anthropology." What Hegel did not know, according to Feuerbach, but what his attempt to take seriously the atheism of the modern era should have led him to see, was that "the task of the modern era was the realization and humanization of God—the transformation and dissolution of theology into anthropology" (PPF, 5). Feuerbach's atheistic humanism thus represents the inversion or mirror image of Hegel's reconciliation of the finite and infinite, man and God, in a fully immanent movement of reappropriation. This position was an inevitable outcome once the death of God was accepted into thought of God, seeing as it always remained possible to interpret this death not from the standpoint of its Christian significance but from the perspective of the other side of the Hegelian reconciliation: namely, the atheistic modern era.

Inverting the Hegelian position, Feuerbach conceives religion not as the circuit of spirit relating to itself in and out of its state of alienation, but as man's alienation from himself or his own nature. The formulae expressing this alienation are numerous: "To enrich God man must become poor;"[16] or better:

> Religion is the disuniting of man from himself; he sets God before him as the antithesis of himself. God is not what man is—man is not what God is. God is the infinite, man the finite being; God is perfect, man imperfect; God eternal, man temporal; God almighty, man weak; God holy, man sinful. . . . But in religion man contemplates his own latent nature. Hence it must be shown that this antithesis, this differencing of God and man, with which religion begins, is the differencing of man with his own nature (EC, 33).

Like Hegel, Feuerbach turned to philosophy and philosophical cognition for a therapy that would heal the tears and oppositions that divide man from the God standing over and above him in faith. Reflecting his inversion of the Hegelian starting point, however, for Feuerbach, the therapy of modernity consists in a philosophical critique that resolves or reduces[17] religion and the God of faith to their anthropological, not spiritual, essence.

For both Feuerbach and his intellectual father Hegel, the therapy consists in resolving this alienated state by removing the idea of a transcendent God— whether it be in the name of a God whose death is his very life or in the name of Man who stands in the place of the dead God. The most provocative example for understanding how Feuerbach follows from and inverts Hegel is his reading of the incarnation; for it is the incarnation that serves as the figure for the truth of all other figures of religious thought. For Hegel, as we saw, the Incarnation was in fact the truth of reconciliation shown in representational form, the reconciliation of God and Man in God as Spirit, Infinite and Finite in Infinite Spirit. On Hegel's reading, the incarnation was the first step in the process that culminated in the crucifixion. It bespoke the Christian truth overlooked by Enlightenment philosophy, that God had indeed abandoned his remote and abstract infinitude and descended to the earth where he could be known by man. For Feuerbach, the situation is the inverse: "This example clearly exhibits the distinction between the method of our philosophy and that of the old speculative philosophy. [Ours] criticizes the dogma and reduces it to its natural elements, immanent in man, to its originating and central point— love" (EC, 52). When subject to the proper form of philosophical critique, the religious doctrine of incarnation signifies in human terms. What Hegel saw as the beginning of a process starting from God is here seen as the end of a process starting with Man.

> The Incarnation is nothing else than the practical, material manifestation of the human nature of God. . . . God became man out of mercy: thus he was in himself already a human God before he became an actual man. . . . If in the Incarnation we stop short at the fact of God becoming man, it certainly appears a surprising, inexplicable, marvelous event. But the incarnate God is only the apparent manifestation of deified man; for the descent of God to man is necessarily preceded by the exaltation of man to God. Man was already in God, was already God himself, before God became man (EC, 50).

The Hegelian reconciliation is here inverted, such that God and Man are reconciled not in God or the Infinite as the origin and end of the process of alienation and reconciliation, but in Man as origin and end. It could be said that the circle of immanence opened and closed by the Hegelian death of God is here so completely immanent that it is no longer thought in terms of God, the former name of transcendence.

Even though Feuerbach never speaks expressly of the death of God, the very absence of the phrase "the death of God" would, as Jüngel notes, seem to indicate the extent to which the Christian God had been banished or killed. Once the phrase has been separated from its first, Christian sense, it is only a short step to the resurrection of this phrase where "the death of God" will signify precisely and only the death of God, that there are no gods. Opened by Feuerbach, this possibility was realized in Nietzsche. Through the mediation of Feuerbach, it falls to Nietzsche to show the conclusion of the end realized in and through the Hegelian philosophy of religion.

If Hegel enshrines the death of God in a philosophy of religion that recovers God in a positive sense, then Nietzsche does the same in a negative sense. As in Hegel's critique of Enlightenment philosophy, for Nietzsche, too, the death of God is a word directed against those who posit an unknowable, unintelligible God. When Zarathustra desires "that your conjectures should be limited by what is thinkable . . . that everything be changed into what is thinkable for man, visible for man, feelable by man," he joins Hegel in criticizing any philosophy or thinking that "recognizes something higher above itself from which it is self-excluded." Like Hegel, Zarathustra announces the death of God in order that philosophy might free itself from this willed servitude to an authority above or outside it. "If there were gods, how could I endure not to be a god! Hence there are no gods."[18] Zarathustra teaches the death of God in order that man might escape belief in or subservience to a transcendent power standing over against him.

However, whereas Hegel saw this infinite gap being overcome by a death of God which belongs to the very essence of God, Nietzsche saw it being overcome in a death of God that puts an end to the essence of God. "Hence, there are no gods." Having entered philosophy in Hegel's thought, the death of God no longer belongs to the essence of God. By the time it reaches Nietzsche, it is no longer connected to its Christian roots, and so when Nietzsche, the madman, and Zarathustra all claim "God is dead," this death is expressed in an unsurpassable way. Since it has been disconnected from the Christian context where it was a truth about God, the death of God does not mediate or reconcile the atheistic feeling of modern times and Christian faith. Divorced from its Christian roots, the death of God again means the impossibility of any philosophy or theology recovering knowledge of God.

In Nietzsche, the death of God no longer means the self-othering of spirit, but the emptiness of all talk about God that is divorced from the will to power which employs God. Thus, for Nietzsche, the death of God issues in a philosophy of religion that is not charged with the task of completing the knowledge of God but one that reduces God to the will to power. Nietzschean philosophy of religion therefore assumes its genealogical shape, in which the idea of God is related to the many forms of the will to power that have used it to preserve and enhance their own power. Thought in a philosophy that reduces all religious meanings to the form of will to power which they express and enhance, God is no longer over against thought as in the Enlightenment and he no longer lives in thought itself as for Hegel. In Nietzsche, then, the happy, Hegelian alliance of the philosophy of religion and philosophical theology is rent asunder by the thought of the death of God, the very thought which Hegel had introduced in order to join the two tasks. In accepting Hegel's introduction of the death of God into philosophy but rejecting his reading of it, Nietzsche left the twentieth century with a philosophy of religion no longer attached to the project of knowing or even overcoming an already revoked transcendence.

In terms of the story I have just told, the emergence of the philosophy of religion in the nineteenth century both presupposes and consummates the death of God and the realization of a pure and total immanence. To be sure, each of the figures in this story claimed to have retrieved the sense of God in his very death—to the benefit of practical faith in God (Kant), knowledge of God (Hegel), the expression of man's nature (Feuerbach), or to God's ultimate end (Nietzsche); but none adopted a figure of philosophy that granted significance to the sense of transcendence or to a revelation that maintained this transcendence. Even Kant, who claimed to have cleared a way for faith in the existence of a God transcending theoretical reason, did so at the price of excluding this transcendence from philosophical knowledge. This short history of the birth of the modern philosophy of religion thus identifies immanence as the horizon within which such philosophy moves, and it would appear that no subsequently post-modern philosophy of religion will have been possible without acknowledging this immanence and the death of God as the signs under which it operates. Would the test of any advance in the post-postmodern philosophy of religion be its ability to articulate the significance of transcendence? And can such a philosophy of religion do so in a thought that nevertheless moves in the sphere of immanence where philosophy operates?[19]

Notes

1. G. W. F. Hegel, *Faith and Knowledge* (Albany: SUNY Press, 1977); 190. Hereafter cited intertextually as FK.
2. While the "disenchantment" of the world was meant to protect divine transcendence, to protect against "reducing the sacred grove to mere timber," it had the opposite effect when the protected transcendence was simply forsaken and left to languish in its distance. As Hegel notes, "It is precisely through its flight from the finite and through its rigidity that subjectivity turns the beautiful into mere things—the grove into timber, the images into things that have eyes and do not see, ears and do not hear" (FK, 58). Hegel here would anticipate some of Max Weber's theses concerning unintended consequences in the life of ideas and the Protestant Reformers. See Max Weber, *The Protestant Ethic and the Spirit of Capitalism* (New York: Charles Scribner's Sons, 1958).
3. This needs to be read in contrast with Hegel's determination of man as finite spirit, that is to say as the manifestation of infinite spirit for itself. Man as finite spirit would be the self-othering of infinite spirit in and as the consciousness which knows it. Infinite spirit would thus return to itself in man's knowledge of God. See below for how this conception of finite and infinite spirit is related to the philosophy of religion.
4. Immanuel Kant, *Critique of Pure Reason* (New York: St. Martin's Press, 1965), 528. Hereafter cited intertextually as CPR.
5. "Philosophical Theology and Philosophy of Religion," in *Reason in Religion: The Foundations of Hegel's Philosophy of Religion* (Berkeley: University of California Press, 1990), 110.
6. Walter Jaeschke, *Reason in Religion: The Foundations of Hegel's Philosophy of Religion* (Berkeley: University of California Press, 1990), 4.

7. Immanuel Kant, *Lectures on Philosophical Theology* (Ithaca, N.Y.: Cornell University Press, 1978), 42. Hereafter cited intertextually as LPT.

8. I should note that Hegel's interpretation of all this could not be put better than it is expressed in the following observation from Kant himself: "We now have sufficient insight to tell that we will be satisfied from a practical standpoint, but from a speculative standpoint our reason will find little satisfaction" (LPT, 27)—and we are well aware of Hegel's attitude to dissatisfied reason.

9. G. W. F. Hegel, *Phenomenology of Spirit* (Oxford: Oxford University Press, 1977), 355.

10. Martin J. De Nys, "Philosophical Thinking and the Claims of Religion," in *New Perspectives on Hegel's Philosophy of Religion*, op. cit.; p. 19. See also Jaeschke, "Philosophical Theology and Philosophy of Religion;" 1, 6 et passim.

11. Eberhard Jüngel, in *God as the Mystery of the World* (Grand Rapids, Mich.: Wm. B. Eerdmans, 1983), writes, "The first philosophical interpretations of talk of the death of God known to us neither deny nor forget the theological origin of this expression, but rather make it very plain. It was Georg Friedrich Wilhelm Hegel who introduced talk of the death of God into philosophy and in doing so was well aware that he was using a theological expression" (63). See also Martin De Nys in "Philosophical Thinking and the Claims of Religion": "Hegel overcomes the 'death of God' that Enlightenment philosophy brings about by philosophically appropriating and maintaining the insight into the death of God that belongs to the consummate religion," namely Christianity (25).

12. Eberhard Jüngel, *God as the Mystery of the World*, op. cit., 74. Hereafter cited intertextually as GMW.

13. Cited in Jaeschke, "Philosophical Theology and Philosophy of Religion"; 8.

14. Ibid., 8.

15. Ludwig Feuerbach, *Principles of the Philosophy of the Future* (Indianapolis: Bobbs Merrill, 1966), 31. Hereafter cited intertextually as PPF.

16. Ludwig Feuerbach, *The Essence of Christianity* (Buffalo, N.Y.: Prometheus Books, 1989), 26. Hereafter cited intertextually as EC. This remark obviously had a decisive impact on Marx.

17. In speaking of Feuerbach's critique, the language of reconciliation is not appropriate as it is in the case of Hegel; for what Hegel sees as reconciliation, Feuerbach sees as insoluble contradiction. Whereas Hegelian philosophy wants to reconcile opposites, finding identity in difference and difference in identity, Feuerbach's criticism reduces opposition to one of the terms—God to man—in a movement of reappropriation.

18. Friedrich Nietzsche, *Thus Spoke Zarathustra* in *The Portable Nietzsche* (New York: Viking Penguin, 1982), 198.

19. I take up these questions in Part III of my book *Levinas and the Philosophy of Religion* (Bloomington: Indiana University Press, 2001), where I try to show how Levinas's ethical phenomenology contributes to a philosophy of religion.

3

Philosophy and Positivity[1]

BY EMMANUEL LEVINAS
TRANSLATED BY JEFFREY L. KOSKY

"We suspect that the disaster is thought."
(Maurice Blanchot, *Discours sur la patience,* in *Le Nouveau Commerce,*
30–31, 21.)[2]

"The sign *is always an* interrogative sign *enveloping the positive sign. This is why
we could say that human reality was* sign *and sign understood as an interrogation
of all forms of positivity and all forms of negativity. It is the sign to which all signs
refer and the interrogation to which all interrogations refer."*
(Jeanne Delhomme, *La pensée interrogative,* 153.)

I. Philosophy at Its Awakening

"You would not seek me if you had not already found me"—this declaration
most certainly does not imply the equivalence of seeking and possessing. It
gives voice to the anticipation that guides the seeking—grasping before the
grasp, grasping of the pre-given and, for the seeker, a project. The term sought
is present in the seeking without being present, but its absence is not a pure
void. Less than all, it is more than nothing. Seeking is, on this reading, *privation* in expectation of *possession.* Or it is the wretchedness of finitude—valued
as an evil on account of a radical impossibility of entering into possession.

But all that is so on condition that the privation which sustains the seeking
be the absence of a *term,* the absence of what can be offered to the grasp and
thus to anticipation—that is to say, the absence of an identical that would be
stability and instantiation, able to present itself and be re-presented, to stand
in a presence and be taken in hand or pointed at; the logical identity of an
atom, of a *point* or an *instant,* at one and the same time—in the same present—pure *where,* pure *when* and pin*point;* birth or extenuation of what admits
qualification and hardens in thickness; a something (*etwas überhaupt),* referred, despite its formalism, to things, to solids. Seeking where presence and
absence evoke a time already understood as a flowing of things, an understanding of time therefore comparable to a flux or a current, as if it were composed of instants-contents, of qualities, which themselves flow. Time therefore
analyzed in terms of sensations which "fill" it—even if time, in this analysis,

still claims to be a form, as if form did not repeat the stability, status, or identity of the contents. Sensations or "primary contents" or "hylé" that are interpreted as "quiddities," as givens, as elements of knowledge or appearing. Analysis of time that has recourse to the metaphors of a liquid and its movement. But in terms of its particles, the instants pass, flow, but are retained or anticipated in Husserl. They penetrate one another in Bergsonian duration without the category of the *Same*, which still governs these descriptions, truly being *put in question*, not even by its many syntheses with the *Other*, its many co-positings or compositions, so many figures of simultaneity, of presence in the Same, and without the question wherein the Same is put shaking the repose of positivity, that is to say all this Identity. The other always remains an "other Same," an other "identical to itself," an "*alterum idem.*"

All rationality—all meaning—would therefore reside in the relation between terms identical to themselves, in the presence that secures this relation. Any alteration of identity would recover its lost identity and lost meaning; it would do so in the relation inasmuch as the relation is co-presence, in the co-presence that arranges, by means of retention and pro-tention (by means of representation), the instants of presence itself, as if they coincided in instants. This possibility of synchronizing terms—having issued from a temporality confused with the flowing of qualities—is the very ordeal of meaning; it secures for the difference of terms the stability of the instant wherein, beneath the designation, time and the real continue to be co-founded. The identity of the term referring only to itself in its reference to its punctual position is thus secured. The dis-quiet, restlessness of time is put to rest. The possibility of representation is the possibility of co-presence; the possibility of co-presence is the possibility of presence; and the possibility of presence is the possibility of the *term*—beginning or end—and thus the possibility of the very notion of the original and the ultimate, of the term referring only to itself. Rationality of repose—of position, of positivity, that is to say of Being—rationalism of termino-logy.

Can the restlessness of time signify otherwise than in terms of the continuous mobility that suggests interpreting time according to the privileged metaphor of flux? Do the Same and the Other owe their meaning only to the distinction of qualities and quiddities, that is to say to the given and the discernible? Not if the restlessness of time signifies before all terminology (with a rigorously temporal *before*) with a rigorously temporal significance (and if I dare say it, chronologically) a troubling of the Same by the Other who possesses nothing discernible or qualitative. Troubling of a Same who would be indiscernibly identifiable. This is what it would mean to be identified as Me.[3] Beyond or on this side of "A is A," and, precisely in this sense, *to identify oneself inwardly*, to identify oneself without thematizing oneself, without appearing. Not in the guise of a residual quality "called sub-stance that sub-sists," solid and enduring through change. But how to identify oneself without appearing and before assuming a name? How to identify oneself without a world? I will return to this question at the end of this essay. But for now, we see that seeking can signify in myself a relation with what is not absent provisionally, but with what, unqualifiable, could not coincide with anything; that is to say, it can signify what might not form a present with myself or what might not lodge itself in re-presentation. In this sense, no present would have a capacity equal to its measure because it would be wholly other than a term that would let itself be embraced, contained or designated. Wholly other than content, because *infinite*, it would be unassumable. Un-tenable and uncontainable [*in-tenable*], unrepresentable, outside the having of possession, without punctuality that would let it admit designation, outside what can be encompassed by comprehension where the succession of qualitative duration is synchronized by memory and the project—the In-finite nevertheless does not exclude a relation with the seeker. The seeking would be this very relation of non-indifference in the midst of difference, excluding all common measure, even the ultimate: that of simultaneity. Thus, irreversible diachrony: seeking as Desire. Seeking would no longer signify a deficient possession, but, straightaway, a superlative—a beyond possession as relation with the ungraspable, where possession would tear itself apart and invert into obsession. And it would signify, in the identity of the self, a "levitation" upsetting the equilibrium of the self reposing in itself, even that repose of intentional consciousness resting in the equality of noesis and noema. Seeking as questioning—from before every question about the given—an infinite *in* the finite—fission or putting into question of the one who interrogates. But what could be signified by this *in* which undoes the relation that it seems to establish, if the ethics of "responsibility for the other" does not put me into question, an ethics which I cannot evade—as if the putting into question inasmuch as call to my responsibility would confer a new identity? Questioning where the subject-consciousness frees itself from itself. Levitation tearing the identity of me with myself, like an excess which tears me from the inside, disturbing, troubling my position and my rest, my positivity—but doing so by *excess*, by transcendence. Troubling as awakening. This disturbance by the other *puts into question* the identity where the ess*ance* of Being is defined. This disturbance where the question is merely born, overcoming the identity of the term, of the atom, of the monad, however universally understood as first in our western thought; this "fission" of the Same by the un-tenable Other,[4] at the heart of myself devoted to the search, and where the trouble disturbing the heart at rest (the trouble at the heart of repose)—this is still not reduced to any constellation of terms, of autonomous points like fixed stars. There where the trouble at the heart of repose is not reduced to points of identity burning and shining with their recurrence to themselves, suggesting by this repose the eternity that is older than all trouble—this is philosophy at its awakening.

II. The Alternative

The philosophy that has been transmitted to us has already arranged its time and fixed its program.[5] Its seeking finds a *given*, heads for the result. In it the troubled irreducibility of the Other-in-the-Same is calmed. In the reference to the norms of truth, where a thought is judged in the name of adequation to Being, transcendence is denied. The awakening of philosophy is already fixed in a *state* where philosophy asserts itself as philosophy of the truth and of Being. But the original affirmation of Being proposed as *given* always supposes a fundamental repose, that is to say a repose that justifies the concept of conditioning where conditioning is equivalent to the ess*a*nce of Being (only grounded beings are!), conditioning equivalent to rationality and consequently grounding to the point of a concept of supposition. Affirmation that excludes from rationality the trouble-in-the-midst-of-rest, the mortal disturbance of the Same by the Other, of awakening, of the dia-chrony of time. But, in short, refusing them in the name of the rationality of rest, that is to say in the name of nothing other than this very refusal of troubles.

Here we find ourselves between two questions: Is identity exhaustive of meaning and reason? Doesn't the signifier equal, beyond this identity that lays itself to rest in itself, the incessant questioning of the same by the *vigilance* that no wisdom could enclose in the Same? Here we are between two undecidable questions. Does the question acquire an absolute priority over the affirmation? But the notion of absolute priority—that is to say, the dignity of holding the rank of what conditions, a dignity assigned to the principle posited in a proposition—would already arise from the identity of Being and positive knowledge. In the question, as in the seeking beyond the given, the Other disturbs the same an-archically, without giving itself as presence (for without giving itself), without the absolute priority that would be a beginning and in which the Other would arise within a vision, which, in the Other, would see only an other Same affirming itself in the eternity of Being. The anarchy of the question and its rationality do not belong to the plot of knowledge and Being, even if, in philosophy it can be said only in terms of knowledge and by contradicting itself. Even if western philosophy is precisely an effort to lay the question to rest in the response—that is to say, an effort to understand questioning as always bearing on the given,[6] an effort to bring to rest the trouble that is always judged evil, even when one calls it romantic, and an effort to sit the given on a ground—which is equivalent to conferring on it the ess*a*nce of Being.

III. Philosophy and Positivity

The philosophy that is transmitted to us has therefore already decided against the troubled psyche and awakening, where the Other does not find a place within the order of the Same and disturbs it; it has instead chosen in favor of the knowing psyche (necessary on a certain level, but necessary for awakening) and positivity, that is to say the world. The philosophy that is transmitted to us consists, in effect, in making all signification or all rationality go back to the "act" or path taken by Beings inasmuch as they affirm themselves to be Beings.[7] This "act" of Being inasmuch as Being is this very affirmation. An affirmation that resounds in language, but precedes it: affirmation as position of Beings on solid ground. The Being of Beings, the essance of Beings as their positivity, as their "stance" if I can put it thus! In all movement or every empirical stop—repose, stability on the basis of the substance of the earth itself or the world. Singular activity of repose in this affirmation. Exceptional activity of presence—the pure act of the Greek philosophical tradition.

In a philosophy on guard against positivism, the term *positivity* maintains the value of a virtue. Thought and language are bound to positivity. One has to confer a "content" to ideas and signs. They therefore become positive thought and language, the sole forms of thought and language that merit consideration. But this positivity of content is one with the positivity of essance. Content is what rests on solid terrain, on the earth as soil, and which is not a given. "Possessed" without a grasp,[8] the earth secures the identity of the identical without adding anything new, without adding any *other* to presence beneath the firmament of the heavens ("beneath the sun" as Ecclesiastes says), without adding any *other* to the world that has the solidity necessary to put every term at rest in its place. The negation that pretends to exit from Being still holds, in its opposition, a position on the earth where it is based and from which it takes its leave. The foothold that negation finds in the very terrain where its position is posited, whose dust it carries on the soles of its feet—this reference that negation makes to the positive in contradiction, where at first glance the contradictory terms seem to lack the common terrain still granted to contrary terms, is the discovery of Hegel, who would be the great philosopher of a positivity stronger than negativity. The negation that is based in positivity rejoins it in the identity of the identical and the non-identical.

Terrain or earth beneath the firmament of the heavens, "under the sun," world—ground of all grounding. The solidity or positivity of this ground is presupposed beneath all worldliness when the world is described as the unity of practical references in Care, from which things would draw the signifyingness proper to them from Being-in-the-world, from the *dwelling* that, for Heidegger, is not separate from building. But to put it more accurately (and I noted this above), the logical figure of supposition refers to this conditioning. The positivity of the essence of Being is conditioning, and it is not just a metaphor when philosophy says that the justification of all signification is ground, that systems are structured and obey an architectonic rule. Logic refers to the positivity of the world—that is to say, of the earth that confirms itself in the astronomical prolongation of the cosmos and in the circle of the Same which encompasses the circle of the Other according to Plato's *Timaeus*. It is the world of the *Timaeus*—despite all the Copernican novelties—that remains in its solidity the place where all is posited, that remains place, positivity of meaning as essance. It is legitimate to wonder if this world is the metaphor for the logical order or if, in its positivity, the world does not govern logic, if the formal in its pretension to the purity of the void is possible, if all formal ontology does not trace the curves of a material ontology.

IV. The Emphasis of Positivity

In any case—to assert the agreement between the logical order (which appears as determination of thought and as apophansis before being recognized as ontology) and the order of ess*a*nce or positivity, to thus assert the rationality of Being or to refer all rationality to Being and ontology, does not mean that in a subject's *knowing* the positivity of ess*a*nce something like a miraculous concordance between an intrinsic and pre-established law of thought (structure of "spirit") and the architecture of Being would show itself. The *signifyingness* of Being's "act" is not equal to the fact it is mirrored in a psyche that just happens to receive its reflection owing to the good fortune of some empirical encounter, a reflection that adds itself to its ess*a*nce and by this very fact gives it an intelligibility, as if by the good fortune of an encounter a factual state was established as rational necessity. The rationality of ess*a*nce, its signifyingness, stems from the fact that its positivity *shines* in thought and representation, that thought only enriches an already rich positivity. *Esse* itself, by dint of positing itself, arrives at exposition and succeeds in provoking comprehension; *esse* itself is ontological. The solidity of repose is solidified and affirmed [*La fermeté du repos s'affermit et s'affirme*] to such a degree that it shows itself. The singular activity of repose, by virtue of its energy, exceeds itself in and through manifesting itself. Singular exceeding! Not in the form of some causality, but in the form of a *presence to. . . .* Presence to consciousness whose "first leap" (the psyche) is only the repercussion of this exceeding, of this presence in the full light of the noonday sun without any shadows in which to hide (again recalling the phrase from Ecclesiastes: "Beneath the sun . . .") to the point that it is the act of repose or repose in actuality. The psyche of representation, sustained by the hyperbole of the solidifying of presence converting itself into exhibition, exposition and pro-position of its positivity, into *appearing*, lives on as a phantom finding no place in the positive order—turns into *subjectivity*—for the sake of unfolding as in a mirror, in the form of the synthetic activity of transcendental apperception, the "energy" of the presence which sustains it. The ess*a*nce of Being repeats itself in the positivity of thematization, in the positivity of theses and syntheses. Positivity that does not figure among the themes that absorb consciousness—that is to say, among the attributes that it posits. Consciousness remains extraordinary, is held back behind the theme, does not re-ify itself. The very positivity of ess*a*nce, whose emphasis evokes consciousness, escapes the intentions of this consciousness absorbed by the theme. This positivity shows itself only in a secondary operation of consciousness: in reflection. An operation that is unthinkable without the *awakening*, which does not come from the theme wherein consciousness is engulfed. Awakening that thus attests the rationality of a transcendence, but awakening and rationality at once forgotten in the reflection itself, which is also thematizing, and which recalls from the zone held back only the till now hidden horizons of intentionality, those that show themselves to reflection in the form of objects. Awakening that indicates at the heart of subjectivity understood as the emphasis of positivity a beyond positivity—a beyond positivity that, in relation to the intelligibility of the astronomical repose of immanence, could be called dis-aster[9] and that remains forgotten in the adventure of our traditional philosophy, worried as it is about the ground and about repose, about Being "under the sun"—knowledge of the world which succeeds by describing the ess*a*nce or positivity of Beings by their transcendental *constitution*.

During the manifestation of ess*a*nce and thus contemporaneous with ess*a*nce and thus signifyingness of ess*a*nce, consciousness welcomes the exposition of ess*a*nce in the form of quiddity where the conditioning virtue of essence is reflected only as rationality of the ground. Consciousness welcomes exposition with receptivity, the welcome therefore being inverted into thematization. The welcome, I have said, is unfolded as a positioning event, as a thesis positing the given in the form of terms structured as "somethings" clothed in plastic and illuminated forms, as quiddities. But quiddities that manifest and possibly hide like screens—that is their plasticity. They block the gaze that settles on them inasmuch as they offer a spectacle. Plato in his *Gorgias* speaks of the eyes and ears that interpose themselves between me and the other at the same time as they disclose the other, that clothe as much as they strip bare. Phenomenality! Ess*a*nce of the phenomenon in its ambiguity where appearing is ipso facto the possibility of mere appearance. Rationality as an invitation to incessant recoveries, to the identification of the Same in the manifold, to the verification at the basis of the appearing or apparent forms. Seeking *behind* the given! The illusion presupposed in the appearing opens the play—or the struggle—of manifestation and dissimulation, of day and night, and it sets the stage for what in western civilization counts as Spirit: a game of hide-and-seek. Whether we ally ourselves with the day against the night, or whether we denounce as metaphysical every breakthrough to daylight, every seeking of the day hidden by the night or seeking of an *other* day hidden by the first, or whether we welcome the shadows as light—that is to say, consciously—whatever option we adopt, it is always the gravity or the play of the world that continues: positivity as ess*a*nce exposing itself to consciousness by virtue of the emphasis of positivity in the guise of plastic forms requiring a foundation, positivity in its "act of repose" solidifying itself or affirming itself in constitution or transcendental construction. Priority or ultimacy of repose and of positivity—which also bears the idea of the ultimacy of ess*a*nce and the very idea of the ultimate and the original and in which the identical dwells identical, before arousing, by the emphasis of this very dwelling, the identity of a consciousness that founds pure appearing or position on a ground in this very appearing: the inhabiting of a world. This understanding of intelligibility as manifestation, ground, and construction—and, as a result, this understanding of spirituality as an event of knowledge and manifestation—will reveal its reference to the identity of the identical by means of the rational privilege of ground and construction. This privilege shows itself in the ground and in the constitutive activity of consciousness constituting objects such that it approaches the self-grounding of self-consciousness. The immediacy of a nameless singularity that is designated only by pointing, the abstract here which conveys the traces of the abstraction or the tearing that had uprooted it from the totality—that is to say, from thought. It returns to the absolute repose of identity by means of the manifold figures of mediation, recovering its integral manifestation in self-consciousness, in the Idea that grounds every particular and that leaves nothing outside it, has no limits, and is thus infinite. Likewise manifestation and ground are intelligibility in Husserl: the living presence of a sensible *hylé*, material for knowledge and for Being, with which the consciousness of time is constituted by retention and protention, and a world, too, thanks to the operation of the entangled intentions that animate this sensible time—a world whose constitution is equivalent to its appearing and to its ground in the absolute Ego where the philosopher is up to the task of finding the origin of Being. Is it otherwise with Heidegger and the Heideggerians who see manifestation as the wonder of the appearing of a world situated from the outset, localized in a *place*, where houses are built and the metropolis finds its niche, the wonder of a being-*there* that man inhabits poetically, in his habitable ess*a*nce evoked or maintained by art and poetry, against the exile to which he is condemned by objectification and by the knowing that exposes Being as if behind the window of the universal. In the *appearing*, from the outset situated in the *here* of habitation, such as the phenomenology and etymology of Heidegger and the Heideggerians suggest, and in the ontology and aesthetics of my own body in Merleau-Ponty, Michel Henry, and Maldiney (where lines of thought issuing from Maine de Biran find soil in which to take root), man, consciousness, the subject are in accord with Being, with the world; they are onto-logy, and they find in this accord (or in this comprehension) the plot of Being that belongs to them. In and through this Being (objectification or poetry), they themselves enter into the ess*a*nce of Being. Death and finitude are also measured in relation to this ontology. Death determines the intelligibility of finite ess*a*nce, or intervenes in the infinity of self-consciousness as necessary, by its negation of the individual, in the very progression of subjectivity towards the universal.

The identity of the astronomical world and the knowing that is its emphasis[10] and its assurance is affirmed or confirmed everywhere. Wisdom of identity, of immanence; wisdom of the satisfaction of the at-home, wisdom of the *ne quid nimis*. The boredom that preys on it would express only the insane desire not to be oneself, the madness of a voyage conceived as a going outside without transporting oneself there or recovering oneself along the way. But perhaps Baudelaire saw truly when he saw in boredom something other than folly: in "this menagerie of mankind's vice," boredom as "supremely hideous and not of this world, / Though soft-spoken and not the type to cause a scene," boredom that would "willingly make rubble of the earth / And swallow up the world in a yawn," boredom that "dreams of the hangman while smoking his *houka*."[11] While smoking his *houka*—the pastime of the satisfied, seeking intoxication.

V. The "Forbidden" Meaning

Don't we already glimpse an other signifyingness—an other rationality—besides that of the positivity of the ess*a*nce of Being in the awakening that interrupts the absorption of consciousness by its object, be it only for the sake of leading it to reflection and even if, at one and the same time, consciousness is objectified in its however un-natural reflective position. An interruption that makes it lose its poise and its assurance by expelling it from the land of its birth, the land where dwellings are built, and from the theme, the theme where theses are posited. Letting go of or disappointment with things left on their own—that is the *epoche*! Even if the terrain is immediately recovered in the Hegelian idea or the transcendental Ego at the end of the Husserlian *Krisis*, an Ego that itself gives itself its world, a world emitted almost like an ectoplasm. But it is the interruption of the consciousness latched to the earth that counts, this expulsion on the hither side or beyond the world. An expulsion without the positivity of the opposition where ess*a*nce would resume its course, an expulsion in which subjectivity does not posit itself once again (not even as the unity of transcendental apperception), but in which it identifies itself as indiscernible. To bring this essay to an end, can we briefly specify the signifyingness that signifies thus? We asked at the outset of this study how it might be possible to identify without appearing and without assuming a name. Can identification have a meaning without a world?

On condition that the recurrence of this identification submit itself wholly passive to the point of pathos, that is to say to the point of suffering an accusatory assignation that rules out any evasion. To the point of suffering, in other words, the sensing of sentiment and not of sensation—without slipping away toward representation and thereby trumping the urgency of the assignation. On condition that—without true or false name, without face and without mask, *incognito* but under an unrefusable constraint to responsibility for the Other and as if elected for this inalienable responsibility—the "inner" identity of the me signifies the self in the accusative, in the accusative preceding its denomination in the nominative. On condition that the inner identity of the self reduces to this impossibility of resting calm and content, that it be right away ethical disturbance, that time—rather than being a stream of consciousness of contents (that is to say, a stream of the contents of consciousness)—be the conversion or the turning [*la conversion ou la version*] of the *me* toward the *Other*. Turning toward the other who would jealously preserve his difference in this turning, not assimilable to representation. Turning toward the other that, like a yarn with many knots intricately woven together (to be untied by analysis), responds for the Other [*autrui*], my neighbor.[12] An inalienable responsibility whose urgency identifies me as irreplaceable and unique and whose unavoidable obligation stamps me with my identity as myself. Identification that is thus impossible without the Other, but in which the Other is not assimilated to the Same—by his *difference* refusing common ground (that is to say, thematization) and forbidding me, in his election, the room for evasion. Identity of the Me on the basis of the identity of the self, in this turning without anything that is posited *for self*, without anything that nucleates or subsists in substance through some qualitative alteration.[13] Beneath all substantial identity that could be discerned in such a way that it could show itself in a comportment or in introspection, indiscernible identity, inner identity of the Me—my identity as myself—in subversion.

The *always* of time would signify the impossible synthesis of myself and the Other, diachrony—or the diastole of punctuality, diachrony, discontinuity, the impossible co-position on the same terrain—impossibility of composing on the same terrain, in the world. Impossibility as slippage of the ground beneath my feet, the ground where Beings posit themselves and stand together, aging, incessance of difference stemming from the difference that does not yield, diachrony, patience of this impossibility, patience as the length of time for which subjectivity, subject to the passive synthesis of aging, is only the emphasis. Patience that is not reducible to the anamnesis that gathers, represents, and objectifies continuous duration. The notion of the lapse of time, of this irrecuperable and nearly mortal fall, emphasizes, even in the image of the temporal "flux," the powerlessness of memory against the diachrony of time. Difference does not differ [*diffère*] as a logical distinction in already abstract impassability, but as non-in-difference, as desire for the non-absorbable, the non-containable, as desire for the infinite; precisely as patience, patience which would be called (in the categories of modality and against good logic and ontology) *reality of the impossible*, but where the Infinite that puts me in question is something like a "more" in a "less." This difference is time, the length—and languor—of perpetuity, patient desire for the Infinite, distinct from the tendencies that, erotic in this patience, grow impatient and are, to speak truly, impatience itself.

Turning of the Same toward the Other. Turning and not intentionality. The latter is absorbed in its intentional correlate, but more exactly is correlation, "wants" in proportion to itself and is synchronized with the correlate, the graspable, the given, the term to contain, the possibly contained. Even as protention, intentionality maintains this sense of grasping! The turning turns toward . . . but otherwise. Not that it contents itself with less than the grasp and comprehending do. Concerning the Infinite, intentions that comprehend and encompass would be insufficient. Knowing is not the superlative of the Spirit and the understanding. In the non-in-difference of Difference (in the desire for the Infinite), the identical does better than return to itself after passing through the detour of the non-self in order to identify and comprehend itself; it exceeds its capacity for the Infinite that it cannot equal. Seeking, or Desire, signifies this more in the less. This way for me to think beyond the correlate that is thematized, this way to think without equaling the Excessive and hence without returning to myself through the detour of the object, this is me *put into question* or *awakened* by the Other. Put-into-question does not mean that in one way or another I have to interrogate myself about my own nature and quiddity; it means that from the positivity of Being where I ground myself, I return to the *uncondition* supporting what cannot be contained—the difference of the Infinite. To be in question—this is to be unto God.

A plot recognizable concretely in ethics. Uprooted from the concept of an Ego by the question of the Infinite, I am responsible for the Other [*autrui*], my neighbor. Someone starts to speak in the first person.[14] There is no more Ego in his being put into question—neither as substance nor as concept. Beneath the nucleation into substance, behold!, turning [*version*] toward the Infinite (sub-version) the *always* of the question—time—me speaking in the first person, me not able to slip away from my responsibility and remain in myself and for myself—singular against all generalization in the concept of the Ego, a concept which offers replacements for the irreplaceable me, for me not able to quiet the calling that assigns me and devotes me to responsibility, to the *first person*, to the priority of *I* (which is not the priority of a principle) and that devotes me to it even when I slip away.

Notes

1. The original version of this essay was published as "Philosophie et Positivité" in Emmanuel Levinas, *Positivité et transcendance: suivi de Levinas et la phenomenologie*, ed. Jean-Luc Marion (Paris: PUF, 2000), 19–34. Editor's note: For further context on Levinas's understanding of transcendence, see remarks in this Introduction and the fine Preface, "Philosophy Between Totality and Transcendence" by Pierre Hayat to *Emmanuel Levinas, Alterity and Transcendence* trans. Michael B. Smith (New York: Columbia University Press, 1999, originally *Alterité et transcendance,* Fata Morgana, 1995), ix–xxiv. He writes, "Transcendence cannot . . . be felt otherwise than as a subjectivity in crisis, that finds itself facing the other, whom it can neither contain nor take up, and who nonetheless puts it in question." (xiv).
2. Fragments collected in *L'écriture du désastre*, Gallimard, 1980 [English translation as *The Writing of the Disaster* (Lincoln: University of Nebraska Press, 1986), 1].
3. "Me" translates Levinas's *Moi*—trans.
4. I am using "Other" to translate *Autre* and "other" to translate *autre*. This differs from many English renderings of Levinas where "Other" translates *autrui*, the personal other. Levinas uses the term *autrui* only rarely in this essay, particularly in its final section. There I have followed the standard practice of rendering it as "Other" and indicated in square brackets that this renders *autrui* not *Autre*—trans.
5. No doubt in the orientation taken by Western philosophy, we affirm the priority of identity, of the affirmation of repose, and of priority itself, that is to say of the *principle*. The disturbance of the Same by the Other must here be reduced to the disturbance of one identity by another identity, a disturbance therefore traced back to the order of a system to which the identities all belong, one that reigns between the monads, and one where the variety of

their attributes flows from the relations that all of these monads maintain with all the others (or each with the others in particular constellations), all these variations remaining inside the identity of the totality at rest, in its astronomical order, its immanence.

6. One can nevertheless wonder if the question that effaces itself before the given, the solvable question, does not set out from questioning as Trouble-of-the-Other-in-the-Same and in this way frees consciousness of its identity and thus opens it to the *project* necessary for a response.

7. Throughout this essay I am following the standard practice of using "Being" to translate the French *être* (an infinitive) while reserving "being" for the French *étant* (a participle). Late in Levinas's career, when this essay was written, Levinas does not accept the standard French practice of rendering Heidegger's distinction between *Sein* and *Das Seiende* with the French *être* and *étant*. Instead he expresses a similar (perhaps not equivalent!) distinction as a distinction between *être* and *êtres*. I have rendered the ungrammatical and philosophically novel latter term with an equally improper "Beings" (an infinitive in the plural!). Whether Levinas' way of putting things here translates Heidegger or recasts the problem Heidegger approached should be a question for scholars.—trans.

8. Which the Bible perhaps expresses by saying that the earth belongs to nobody nor to God.

9. See Maurice Blanchot, "Discours sur la patience," in *Le Nouveau Commerce*, 30–31, 21ff. [English translation in *The Writing of the Disaster* (Lincoln: University of Nebraska Press, 1986)].

10. The notion of emphasis which I used in this study would call for an investigation of its own. Its use perhaps connects with the *via eminentiae* of scholastic philosophy. The passage from one idea to another and the disclosure—or more exactly epiphany—of the new idea is produced by hyperbolic tension with the one that suggests it. The search for the ground, even the transcendental condition of possibility, already supposes the rationality of the positive. In the present work, we sought by emphasis the intelligibility of positivity itself and the intelligibility of founding thought.

11. Charles Baudelaire, "Au lecteur" in *Les Fleurs du mal* [English translation in *Charles Baudelaire: The Flowers of Evil*, Marthiel and Jackson Matthews, eds. (New Directions Publishing, 1989 [translation modified])].

12. Cf. My article "God and Philosophy" in *Of God Who Comes to Mind* (Stanford, Calif.: Stanford University press, 1998).

13. In the *Logique de Port-Royal*, III, 20, 267, Nicole writes about "wise men who as much as they can avoid exposing to the eyes of others the advantages they have": "M. Pascal, who knew as much Rhetoric as anyone ever knew, carried this rule to the point of claiming that a gentleman should avoid naming himself and even using the words *I* and *me*, and he often said, on this subject, that Christian piety annihilates the human self and human civility hides and suppresses it."

14. Cf. my *Otherwise than Being* (Dordrecht, Netherlands: Kluwer Academic Publishers, 1991).

4
From the Other to the Individual

BY JEAN-LUC MARION
TRANSLATED BY ROBYN HORNER

I. Emerging from Anonymity

"Being is evil, not because finite, but because unlimited"[1]—this extraordinary declaration certainly fixes the quite dissimulated center of a seminal text (it dates from 1946/7), in any case an essential one, because it accomplishes, for the same reason as the inspired article "Is ontology fundamental?" of 1951, one of the irrevocable decisions starting from which Levinas became what he was—the greatest of French philosophers since Bergson and also the first phenomenologist who had seriously tried to liberate himself from his origin, that is to say from Heidegger.

But how are we to justify the violence of this formula and to protect it from the misinterpretation of a gnostic reading (I am evidently thinking of Simone Weil)? The first response goes without saying, which states that " . . . relation with the Other is . . . not ontology."[2] For, I must insist, Levinas's point of departure comes under the heading of ontology, although by way of transgression: "The analyses that we are going to undertake will not be anthropological, but ontological."[3] But this assertion itself remains to be justified. It has in fact been so justified since 1946, by the formula of "the anonymity of existing."[4] It can be understood in reference to the most traditional definition of being in metaphysics, from Duns Scotus, Suarez, and Malebranche to Hegel and Nietzsche, as the universal concept, abstract and empty, the first, falling to the understanding, indeed even to the imagination, in this way suggesting another formula: " . . . the anonymous existing of being in general."[5] Certainly we could be astonished here to see "existing" substituted for the "being" of "anonymous being,"[6] since this modification had precisely for its purpose, with Heidegger who had inaugurated it, the destruction of the metaphysical concept of indeterminate being, universal and thus anonymous. But this displacement finds in its turn a reason in the reproach made to Heidegger of not having known or been able to think the true and last existent that existence

I wish to acknowledge the generous assistance of Véronique Lyttle, who unlocked some of the difficulties of the French, as well as that of Kevin Hart and Michael Fagenblat, who provided very helpful comments as well as proofreading the text.—Translator would have to furnish—the Other, " . . . the being *par excellence*."[7] For the ontic exemplarity is no longer due to an ontological privilege of *Dasein* as for Heidegger, but, with Levinas, to the ethical privilege of the Other. In effect, even in existence taken in the radically new sense conferred upon it by *Sein und Zeit*, and perhaps especially in this sense, existing is " . . . never attached to an *object which is*, and it is for this reason that we are calling it anonymous" or, what is equivalent, it is only a matter of " . . . an existing which, by itself, would remain fundamentally anonymous."[8] There is indeed existence, but it comes back " . . . to the *there is*, to impersonal existence," to " . . . the anonymous *there is*," and it is " . . . in anonymous existing [that] an existence arises."[9] In other words, the reason that ontology can no longer claim itself unconditionally radical is because it implies radical anonymity—being, existence, or the *there is*, it does not matter—such that it forbids access to the existent or, more exactly, to the Other in his or her own right: " . . . for me, *there is* is the phenomenon of impersonal being."[10] The anonymity of being henceforth offends the name of the Other.* If "being is evil," it owes this in effect not to its finitude (which Heidegger certainly never concluded), but to its limitless anonymity, to its endless prohibition of the naming of the Other as such. Levinas's task can thus be formulated very clearly: ethics will only become first philosophy in the place and the position of ontology if it definitively transgresses the anonymity of ontology and names the existent as such, that is to say, first as the Other.

II. Interrupting solipsism—suffering and death

The difficulty of this program would appear all the more because it divides itself, since it is necessary, before even claiming to name the existent no longer to leave anonymous the one who must be able to name the existent the *I* who speaks of the existent and who thinks. Now, according to the order of anonymous being and of the terror of the *there is*, the *I* can only first hypostasize itself: " . . . fixed to itself," it " . . . is swamped in itself."[11] Under these metaphors (which sound a little too Sartrian) one must recognize the necessity, for any *ego* deployed in the horizon of being (metaphysical or phenomenological), of turning toward substantiality or, what is equivalent, even if it is difficult to accept, to transcendentality. For the Cartesian solipsism of the *substantia cogitans finita* does not disappear with intentionality, but on the contrary: "The intentionality of consciousness allows the distinction of the me from things but does not make solipsism disappear, since its element—light—renders us masters of the exterior world, but is incapable of uncovering for us there an equal. The objectivity of rational knowledge takes away nothing from the solitary character of reason."[12] In order to transgress the anonymity of the other existent therefore, it is first necessary that I liberate myself from my rational universality; for since solipsism attests inevitably to this anonymity, it is necessary to cast off, together, the one and the other.

Levinas envisages this liberation at the price of several displacements of the hypostasis and of solipsism, all radical. (a) First by suffering, which " . . . merges with the impossibility of being detached from the instant of existence, [. . . the] impossibility of retreat," in such a way that I discover myself " . . . in the impossibility of fleeing existence"—in short, existing, until then anonymous because universal, in suffering comes down to an " . . . event where the existent [mine, *I*] has managed to accomplish all its solitude."[13] In suffering, existing loses its objectivity and its indifference to persons—it becomes mine, insubstitutable, unavoidable, thus individuating. (b) Nevertheless, this individuation of the *I* remains imperfect, or rather, its perfection is only accomplished in its being suppressed, since suffering abolishes me in death, where, far from being individualized, " . . . the existing of the existent is alienated."[14] Death, precisely because it never remains to the end a power-to-be-for death, does not assure the individuation of the *I*, but forbids it. (c) It is thus necessary to pass to another instancy, where the uncontrollable mystery that happens to the *I* neither crushes it nor suppresses it, but remains accessible to it as such a mystery. We must name this instancy the other: " . . . the relation with the other is a relation with a Mystery"; but—this is the decisive step—the other only appears authentically and is only phenomenalized as the Other: "The other 'assumed'—is the Other."[15]

We take up the argument once again: being is equal to "evil" because its universal anonymity forbids individuation, and thus forbids access to the Other. This access implies, moreover, as much my own individuation as his or hers. Thus the individuation of the *I* is sketched in suffering, but cannot be taken up in the death that nevertheless achieves it. It is thus necessary to pass directly to the "face to face without intermediary"[16] with the Other.

III. The Other as Femininity

Nevertheless, one thereby enters into an exemplary hermeneutic circle: the Other alone challenges the anonymity of existing, but the Other only becomes accessible to an *I* which itself is already torn from this anonymity by the test of this same Other. In short, the Other would produce non-anonymity, which, nevertheless, alone renders it accessible. A similar circle is marked explicitly, moreover, in two formulae. (a) First in the paradox according to which "The relation to the Other, is the absence of the other," or " . . . this absence of the other is precisely its presence as other." Is it there a matter of a simple reprise, eventually reversed, of the result of the *Fifth Cartesian Meditation*? Or is it already the beginning of the concept of distance, as the enigmatic sentence suggests—"Distance which is also proximity"?[17] Would it not be instead a question of a difficulty that is not yet resolved, or even yet scarcely confronted—that of the mode of individuation demanded by the test of the Other? (b) A second formula, precisely that which led for the first time to positing that the " . . . other 'assumed'—is the Other," proceeds actually with a surprising caution, even a deliberate ambiguity: "This situation where the event happens to a subject who does not assume it, who has no power in its regard [that is, as in the case of suffering and death], but where, nevertheless, *in a certain way* it is in front of the subject [that is, contrary to death], is the relation with the Other, the face-to-face with the Other, the meeting of a face which, *at the same time gives and conceals* the Other. The other 'assumed'—is the Other."[18] Why the conditional[19] and this *"certain way"*? Why and how does the face-to-face, which gives, *at the same time* conceal?

That it is not here a matter of words, but of the very accomplishment of individuation (as much of the *I* as of the Other), thus of going beyond the anonymity and the 'evil' of being, is what the analyses of *eros* and of paternity suggest. The precise function of these analyses is to establish this individuation starting from the face-to-face. Both analyses are governed by the admirable but perfect ambiguity that "The Other, insofar as Other, is not only an *alter ego;* the Other is that which I myself am not."[20] (a) Consider the case of *eros*. Its privilege comes from that which in him, first, " . . . the contrariety which allows its terms [that is, of the asymmetrical relation, the Other] to remain absolutely other, is the *feminine*"; or rather: " . . . alterity is accomplished in the feminine."[21] The surprise comes here first from the choice of one of the two sexes—why the feminine, and not the masculine, as if the point of view of the *I* should, of itself, be implicitly inscribed in the masculine? The surprise then comes from the very neutrality of the feminine, privileged instead of the woman, or more exactly instead of this or that woman, by definition presumed, when she incarnates the Other, unique and unsubstitutable. Even further, *eros* reinforces this neutrality to the point of reestablishing an essential anonymity, even more menacing than that of existing, either because that which " . . . we call *femininity*" does not designate transcendence, but " . . . the equivocation of [the] fragility and this weight of non-significance, heavier than the weight of the formless real,"[22] or because it puts one in relation "Not with a being who is not there, but with the very dimension of alterity."[23] We can thus understand this return to anonymity: *eros* puts me in relation not with a particular woman (or man), but with the possibility of the child, the child not yet actual, therefore with pure alterity—but precisely the alterity of no real named, or in short, phenomenalized Other. *Eros* does not surmount the anonymity of existing, it accomplishes it in displacing anonymity from existing to alterity, and redoubles it in leaving anonymous not only the child who does not yet appear, but the woman who already allows it. (b) Consider next the case of paternity or fecundity (we will not insist on their implicit assimilation), which is defined with a remarkable formula: "I do not *have* my child; I *am* in some way my child." Let us consider the ambiguity of this *some way*. Because it links father and child—and even ontologically, since one gives up there the "impossible dissolution of the hypostasis"[24] that I remain insofar as father—fecundity can by definition *neither* individualize the father, nor the child, any more than it names the mother. Paternity thus dissolves the proper name of the son (or daughter) in the anonymity that would already prevail over *eros*. But if anonymity still remains here, simply transposed from being to the alterity of the Other, then will not the "evil" of being, or at least its horizon, remain unassailed and vanquishing? Would not the effort to individualize one such Other, to privilege ethics over ontology, fail?

IV. The face appears as no other person

We have followed up to this point the itinerary of the lectures on *Time and the Other* and been detained by their aporias. It remains to be determined if the master-work, *Totality and Infinity*, which formalizes fifteen years later these inaugural concepts, can dissolve or at least attenuate these difficulties. It is immediately obvious: the centre of gravity of the analysis of the Other is displaced from the still indeterminate existent to the paradigmatic phenomenon of the face. A question arises: for what reasons does a final projection "beyond the face" (section IV) still come after the description of the "face and of exteriority" (section III)? "Beyond": the authority of this adverb of place in the texts of Levinas does not allow us to underestimate the strangeness and the importance of such a surpassing of the face itself.

Let us first consider the evidence of the displacement: the face, or rather "the epiphany of the face,"[25] brings into glory a new phenomenon; its privilege is due to the fact that no *Sinngebung* constitutes it and no signification precedes it, but that on the contrary it " . . . signifies itself," " . . . signifies by itself" in an " . . . exceptional presentation of itself by itself."[26] The face only refers to itself; it is born without antecedent, with neither cause, nor intentionality— other than that which it exercises on me. This is what Levinas understands by its nudity: "One such nudity is the face. . . . The face is turned towards me— and this is its very nudity."[27] Turning itself towards me, it takes the initiative in its phenomenalization, my intentionality is thus stripped for the first time of it. In short, "The Other—absolutely other—paralyzes possession, which it contests by its epiphany in the face"[28]; one could just as well have said that it contests the constitution and the intentionality that I exercise, thus the signification that intentionality aims at. Moreover, how could the face allow itself to be constituted, that is to say admit a meaning and a noetic-noematic couple, even when it has as its distinctive feature to reveal the infinite—" . . . the infinite or face . . . "[29]— and when the infinite is characterized precisely by the excess of the noema over the noesis, or in other words deploys the paradox of a saturated phenomenon? It is thus necessary to conclude that " . . . the face-to-face remains an ultimate situation," with the same radicality as that of Husserl suggesting that " . . . absolute givenness* is an ultimate [term]—*absolute Gegebenheit ist ein Letzes.*"[30] Levinas will never change this basic fact: the face appears as no other phenomenon succeeds in appearing. Let us say that it appears as no one.

Nevertheless, the relationship between the "ultimate" face-to-face and givenness—itself also ultimate—indicates a first difficulty. It is not due to the finding that " . . . expression does not consist in *giving* us the interiority of the Other. The Other who expresses himself does in fact not *give* himself . . ."[31]— because there it is only a matter of recognizing, with Husserl, this essential law that the Other never belongs to a presence, but only to an appresentation. Were the Other to give himself in the sense of presenting himself, he would disappear as such; he must always inhabit distance. The difficulty is not here due to what presence does not give, but instead due to what it gives well and truly: "Transcendence is not a vision of the Other—but an original givenness."[32] We can understand it in this way: donation gives itself thus in conformity with transcendence, thus does *not* give the Other to be seen. In fact, "The Other *does not appear* only in his face . . ."; one would even be able to say that he does not appear at all in revealing himself as a face, since the face " . . . is not reduced in representation." How does the face reveal itself, and what does it reveal exactly, if it does not give the Other to be seen? The question, explains Levinas, is not to be asked in that way. For the Other does not reveal himself to be seen, but to be heard: "To hear the misery which cries for justice does not consist in representing an image to oneself, but in establishing oneself as responsible."[33] The face reveals exactly because it phenomenalizes that which is *never* seen. Nevertheless, this rule, posited by Heidegger (one has recourse to phenomenology precisely only for that which does not show itself directly and the majority of the time), no longer applies here to the phenomenon of being, but it phenomenalizes, or more exactly makes heard "You will not kill."[34] In the commandment not to kill I test, even if I transgress it, the resistance and the nakedness of the counter-intentionality exercised by the Other, in the Other's pure self-signification. The face appears as a person, since, even if I kill it, I still hear it. It is no longer the privilege of the *ego* to affirm itself in its very disappearance, but henceforth the privilege of the Other—we have thus certainly passed from a first philosophy to another, from ontology (or from the doctrine of science), to ethics. A Copernican revolution.

V. The face appears as no one

Now, this unquestionable fact indicates nevertheless an aporia of the face—the only one perhaps—because it marks that which masks the face: its individuated identity. If one actually asks it according to ethics " . . . the question which examines quiddity . . . " (or in other words if one asks *who* is this Other in *this* face) it would be necessary to respond that the " . . . face is not a modality of quiddity, . . . but the correlative of that which is prior to any question." Without doubt—because we have to admit that the face escapes quiddity understood firstly and for the most part in ontology as a *what*, taken in " . . . a system of relations," for example according to social functions. Of course the Other does not identify himself by a role, by a persona or by administrative data, not even by his names, all of which are improper.[35] It remains no less a necessity, even and especially in ethics, if one claims to have access to a face, to accede to *his* face, thus to identify him as such, to particularize the face, to individuate it. The same text recognizes, moreover, the legitimacy of this second demand, such that it builds on the first: "To the question *who?* responds the unqualifiable presence of a being who *presents himself* without referring to anything and, *nevertheless, distinguishes himself from all other beings.*" But precisely how does this Other distinguish himself from all other Others, if he refers to no other than to a self that nevertheless he never allows to be seen? No indication can specify it, except that here the " . . . respondent [that is, this other] and that responded to [that is, his face as such] coincide." The other thus does not say *which* Other it is, but only the fact that he reveals himself as and in a face. Consequently, if an individuation is accomplished, it seems that it is not that of *this* other, but mine, since " . . . in accosting the Other, . . . I am present *to myself.*"[36] In positing the question of individuation, the privilege is thus passed once again from the Other to the *ego:* I am, myself, individualized by the call of the face,[37] but this face itself remains the face of no-one. Solipsism is reestablished, simply displaced from knowledge to ethics.

Accordingly, the face appears as no one: it must be understood henceforth no longer only as superlative phenomenality, but as its anonymity; it appears as "no-one," as no individual, as no particular person, in short, it neither appears in person nor as a person. With the Other, no-one yet appears. Confirmatory arguments are not lacking. I will mention the principal ones. (a) The fact that "Thou shalt not kill" is valued universally as a matter of principle, thus for every other Other, without distinction between persons. If it first privileges the poor and the stranger, the widow and the orphan, it does not thereby exclude the others, the powerful and the familial, but admits no exception, even to the extreme. In all these cases, even the poor, the stranger, the widow, and the orphan remain as yet indistinct, without name, without individuality; they must be respected and served insofar as they are such, that is, precisely not inasmuch as they are this person or that person. It is a matter of anonymous or even unknown recipients—who must remain so in order that the prohibition can function. (b) The face also suffers from another anonymity, no longer by way of universality, but by way of duplicity, for it can withdraw in its very opening, deceive. In effect, the " . . . face, all straightforwardness and frankness, dissimulates in its feminine epiphany, allusions, insinuations," it can even " . . . leave its status as person," founder in its "impersonal neutrality," or even in the "animality" of " . . . a young animal."[38] Certainly, here again, we could equally muse on a masculine epiphany—that of Don Juan, for example—who plays a similar game of dissimulation. But the essential is elsewhere. The face does not speak of the one of whom it is the epiphany and cannot say it: the look of an innocent can repulse more than that of a criminal; the face of an executioner can charm more than the disfigured face of his victim; openness is never so apparent than in the face of a liar, who cannot lie effectively apart from this condition. The face suppresses and masks individuality, even if, or even because, it reveals the infinity of its anonymous transcendence. According to a universal rule, no face shows its situation and its ethical bearing. Phenomenologically, the banality of evil finds its place in the anonymity of the face itself. (c) Certainly *Totality and Infinity* does not dodge the question of individuation, but enshrines on the contrary a powerful thesis: "Separation is the very act of individuation."[39] Nevertheless, this thesis does not satisfy the difficulty. This is first because it only here concerns the *ego*, which is individualized in fact by its separation from interiority following the test of the infinite, which, paradoxically, implants it in itself alone.[40] And it is next because it is a matter of an implicit quotation of Aristotle: " . . . entelechy separates."[41] Now, Aristotle can himself arrive at the individuation of every being, thus eventually of Socrates or of the "musician" (according to the established misunderstanding), because the "act" separates here as essence, which it accomplishes and delimits in itself. But how could an "act" separate, and thus individuate, without recourse to essence? How can individuation occur without the act of an essence being bound to the ethical regime, precisely beyond essence and all ontology? The separation of the finite by the infinite thus does not permit individuation, except, in the best of cases, that of the *ego*. But it is a matter of the individuation of the Other. It is therefore lacking.

The Other thus appears as no one—that we will undoubtedly understand in the sense that Ulysses would like to assign to the term: he does not appear as any individuated person, playing only the character *(persona)* of any possible Other. It is also necessary to read this formula literally : "The epiphany of the face as face opens *humanity*."[42] The face opens onto the humanity of the other man, but not onto this particular otherness of this particular Other. Or else, " . . . in the concrete world, the face is abstract."[43] So the face is not the meaning of persons, it is not the face of anyone.[*]

Certainly, one could legitimately claim " . . . to have broken with the philosophy of the Neuter,"[44] if neutrality limits itself to the Same, ontological or logical, which obscures the Other in general. But we have not yet finished with the Neuter, if we discover it still and always triumphant in the anonymity of a face, which certainly reveals humanity, forbids it to murder, or even reveals the original donation of transcendence, but is never *the one* whom I could love more than myself. For it would be necessary, in order to arrive at that point, to individualize that one more than I could individualize myself.

VI. Individuation and the "ambiguity" of love

Beyond its own proper difficulty, this result attests to a graver aporia: if the Other cannot be individualized, if the face does not show anyone in particular, but " . . . opens humanity," if it thus remains anonymous, or even neutral, does it not *itself* compromise the flight of the existent beyond existence, the passage out of the "horror of the *there is*," and thus the transcendence of being by ethics? Would the establishment of ethics as first philosophy not thus require more than this Other reduced to " . . . that which I myself am not"?[45] Would the tearing away of the primacy of the horizon of being—this "evil"—not demand more than the ethical determination of the Other, namely to accede in fact and by right to the individuation of his ipseity?

The aporia of individuation would not have been able to block a thinker such as Levinas, if it had not already prevented others. It seems it can scarcely be doubted that *Totality and Infinity* returns to Kant's situation, or even adopts its lexicon. "The fact that, existing for the Other, I exist otherwise than in existing for myself—is morality itself. . . . Transcendence as such is 'moral consciousness.' Moral consciousness accomplishes metaphysics, if metaphysics consists in transcendence. . . . The being as being is only produced in morality."[46] Now morality, insofar as it exercises itself according to its sole appropriate motive, respect, bears on the universal law, but never on the individual— morality does not favor anyone and is not aimed at anyone in particular: "All respect for a person is only properly respect for the law (the law of honesty, and so on), of which this person is an example." I never respect—in the strict sense, I never see—anyone in particular, but the moral law in the circumstance of one of its undifferentiated agents. And, in order that it be really the law that I respect, I must not examine any individual, I must examine no particular person. "The only respect to which I am by nature obliged is that of the law in general *(revere legem)*, and to follow this law, even relatively to other men, neither in order to revere other men in general *(reverentia versos hominem)*, nor in order to procure something for them, is a universal and unconditioned human duty with regard to the other, which can be demanded of everyone as respect [which is to him] originally owed."[47] The paradox of morality is due not only to that which the moral action cuts through, so to speak, the one or ones that it knots in its intrigue, in order, across and beyond any individual, to relate itself to the law in its absolutely abstract universality, neutral and anonymous; but it goes to the point of considering that the Other, as individualized as he might wish to be, has nothing more or better to expect on my part than this neutral universality itself. It is thus no more fitting to reproach the visitation of the face (Levinas), than respect for the law (Kant) for not reaching the Other in his individuated person, since they have nothing to arrive at—or better, since they must absolutely not privilege anyone. As much as respect for the law, and for the same reasons, the face only remains an epiphany of morality in keeping itself indifferent to any particular person. To pass from the Other to a particular Other, or even to One such Other, would be equal to turning away from the universal imperative—"You shall not kill"—which every face dictates, as also to invalidate the universality characteristic of the moral law–"Act in such a way that the maxim of your will can *always* be valid *at the same time* as a principle of *universal* legislation."

Would passing to a particular Other imply thus—according to the implicit avowal of Levinas himself—a passing beyond the face; for in fact " . . . *Eros* goes beyond the face"?[48] Certainly, especially if one considers that the last section of *Totality and Infinity* tackles "the ambiguity of Love" and that, according to an interview of 1987, love characteristically concerns the unicity of the Other: " . . . to open itself to the unicity of the unique in [the] real, that is to say to the unicity of the Other. That is to say, in the end, to love."[49] But why does love find itself, in 1961, straight off and so often stigmatized by "ambiguity"— as in—" . . . equivocal *par excellence* . . . ," " . . . at the limit of immanence and transcendence"?[50] Because it is necessary to distinguish between, on the one hand, erotic love, " . . . expression which ceases to express itself," where the face " . . . is dulled . . . in its impersonal and inexpressive neutrality" and which ends by " . . . loving itself in love and thus returning to itself"[51]; and, on the other, " . . . the gravity of the love of neighbor—of love without concupiscence . . . ," " . . . responsibility for the Other, or love without concupiscence . . . ."[52] And it is this confusion which makes of love " . . . a term which is a little adulterated," " . . . used and ambiguous . . . ," "prostituted," which one must "mistrust. . . . "[53] There are thus two loves: the one which is achieved in the injunction of the face, ethical, but anonymous; the other, which transgresses the face, but comes back to the self and regresses thus from the ethical to the erotic.

There is scarcely any doubt that this distinction between two instances of love, equally ruinous as far as access to a particular Other, sends us back, once again, to Kant. "Pathological love" (egoistic concupiscence) cannot evidently be applied, as the inclination of fanaticism claims, to God—because it offers no object of the senses." But neither can it describe correctly the relationship to the Other, since one could then no longer understand by what right God commands us to love our neighbor. In these two instances, it is thus necessary to admit a "practical love," which is exercised in fact purely and simply as " . . . the respect for a law which *commands love [das Liebe befiehlt]*."[54] In this way we return to the law and to its universality, giving up the possibility of immediate and identifying access to the Other (or to God). In this way perhaps Levinas only passes beyond the face in order to test there a "beyond of the personal." *Eros*, even when fertile, still only registers " . . . the very ipseity of the me, of the very subjectivity of the subject," far from acceding to a particular Other.[55] The aporia of Levinas would repeat that of Kant.

VII. "This word too beautiful or too pious or too vulgar"

Nevertheless, this does not seem to me to be the final position of Levinas, for two basic reasons. First, because *Otherwise than Being or Beyond Essence* reestablishes a unified meaning of love, in requalifying the definition of philosophy not only as "love of wisdom," but even in recognizing in it " . . . its larger definition: wisdom of love." In effect, if philosophy focuses on " . . . non-indifference *for* the other—. . . ," its love of wisdom bears on love itself, and it can follow: " . . . — philosophy: wisdom of love at the service of love."[56] Such a redoubling of love, here defined as origin and end of wisdom, cannot be underestimated; it implies at the very least a clean break with the Kantian agenda; or better, one can see there a way of returning to a quasi-Platonic determination, since the concept of love is referred—at least for once without any ambiguity—to the beyond of essence, the Good: "The Good grants freedom—he loves me before I have loved him. By this anteriority—love is love." The Good is no longer reduced here to the " . . . end of an erotic need, of a relationship with the Seducer which resembles the Good, to the point of being mistaken for it" (and even Levinas lets himself "be mistaken"); in effect it is a question of the " . . . Good as the Infinite," whose goodness nothing escapes.[57]

Still more remarkable: the determination of such a love by its anteriority not only reappears in 1974—" . . . in love, —unless not to love out of love—, it is necessary to resign oneself to not being loved," but echoes an indication, fleeting, however precise, from 1961: " . . . love . . . designates a movement by which the being searches for that to which it was connected even before having taken the initiative to search . . . is also a predestination, a choice which had never been chosen."[58] Such an example of facticity was able, in 1961, to appear as a renunciation of transcendence; it seems, nevertheless, if one rereads it from the point of view of 1974, to mark a new mode of foundational asymmetry of the relation to the Other: the Other precedes me and gets the better of me, to the extent that even my transcendence is received from the facticity that the Other imposes on me. Such a rereading seems not only possible, but even probable, since the phrase *Otherwise than Being* takes away the major prohibition with which *Totality and Infinity* would stigmatize love—that of being silent, of remaining inexpressive while the face speaks and in this way phenomenalizes ethics. In effect, following another indication of 1974, I can " . . . love *in saying* love to the loved one—sing of love, the possibility of poetry, of art."[59] Not only does love speak—like the face—but it makes possible the most accomplished form of the spoken word—poetry, which tears itself in this way from its ontological determination (Heidegger), in order to take on ethical status.

This sketch of another concept of love, however scattered and secret it remains, alone at least permits us to do justice to the notes, in tentative form, which mark the last interviews of Levinas. In this way in 1982,[60] the Kantian severity of a love which is "commanded" abandons the universal (and thus Kantian morality) in order to ponder the fact that responsibility towards the Other happens to me as an election. In effect, " . . . there is there an election, because this responsibility is inaccessible" and must come to me from the Other (for " . . . the Other resembles God"),[61] thus is imposed on me with the facticity and the asymmetry already recognized in love. There follow two decisive consequences. (a) From now on " . . . love is original," and no more a misleading or derived transcendence; it no longer blurs the face, but waits for it like one who watches for the dawn, since " . . . love tends over justice." Ethics would thus itself have a condition of possibility—love, or even charity— " . . . justice is itself born of charity." Does ethics still remain first philosophy, or does it cede this function to the "wisdom of love at the service of love"? (b) From now on love, such that my very election to ethical responsibility attests it (which no longer thus disqualifies it, but presumes it), also necessarily shares with it the function of individuating me. In effect, " . . . responsibility is an individuation, a principle of individuation." How can we from this point not ask if love also fixes the individuation of the Other, since it fixes mine? It is precisely that which a text from 1985 affirms: "Being subject to the order which orders man—orders me—to respond to the other—that which is perhaps the harsh name [that is, Kantian] of love. Love is not yet that which this prostituted word of our literature and of our hypocrisies expresses, but the very fact of the approach of the unique and, consequently of the absolutely other, piercing that which only *shows* itself, that is to say remains "individual" in a genus. Love, which implies all psychic or subjective order—or disorder—would no longer be the abyss of the arbitrary where the sense of ontology loses itself, but the very indispensable place of the promotion of the *logical* category of *unicity*, beyond the hierarchy of genus, species and individuals, or, if one prefers, beyond the distinction between the universal and the particular."[62] A prodigious return. Not only does love no longer belong to pathology, but even its "severity" from now on englobes all that is "psychical" and "subjective," reunifying what Kant had separated. In such a way it alone allows me to make the proof of unicity—the only authentic "beyond of the face," since it allows me alone to confront this or that particular face, not the universal. For could I be responsible for the universal? Could my responsibility, even limitless, exercise itself on me, if it was not exercising itself against a particular Other, where alone the universal phenomenalizes itself?

In the debate of 1986, which remains famous, I took the chance of predicting to Emmanuel Levinas that he would have in the future to " . . . put ethics in second place, substituting the term 'love'." To this audacity, which was a little abrupt, he responded in these terms: "I am completely in agreement. I would like to add that 'irreversible relation' suggests a relationship with diachrony. What does this relation signify? Or rather, from where does it gain its ground? At what moment? I know that it is not an intentionality, but it has a sense; and the reason why I say this word more easily, this word which is too beautiful or too pious or too vulgar . . . is because it signifies that the relation with the other, is the relation with the unique. I do not speak immediately of the unique one who commands it [God?], I speak of the one who is the 'object' of love: the Other, the unique and thus the individual who is still part of a genus. It is even the only possibility for the unicity of concrete being. It is concrete in love."[63]

The advance of Levinas thus goes further than the common reading allows. In order to reestablish the primacy of the existent over existence (first stage), it is accordingly necessary to first invert the intentionality in assigning it to the Other, who exercises it on my responsibility (second stage—ethical); it is yet necessary to individualize this Other, that is to say to love this Other (third stage—beyond ethics). In effect, the façade becomes a side [*une face*], a face, only if in its worldly visibility the invisibility of the infinite shines through. For on a mask, be it a death-mask or a theatrical mask, the Other shows himself as much (if not more) than a face; and nevertheless he only shows himself as a truly appointing, constraining and interlocuting Other if his surface visibility is weighted with an essential invisibility—Levinas names it the Infinite—which alone affects me as such. The face addresses itself to me, and to me alone, only if it individualizes me and thus individualizes itself. This double concentration, which renders us unsubstitutable, one for the other, is not accomplished in the ethical relation, but in the meeting of love. In other words, " . . . to respond to the Other, is to grapple with the Other as unique—isolated from all multiplicity and outside collective necessities. Now, to grapple with someone as unique in the world, is to love them."[64] And it seems to be at this stage, that the last thought of Levinas has come. That is why, perhaps beyond phenomenology, he still precedes us.[65]

The question, to which Levinas has, willingly or reluctantly, led might be asked in this way: if transcendence does not refer first to the epistemological transcendence of the intentional object outside of the theoretical consciousness (Husserl), if transcendence does not amount either to the ontological transcendence of the self-projecting and self-decided *Dasein* (Heidegger), does it amount only to the ethical, universal and abstract openness to the face of the Other? Or does not finally transcendence make the claim to the unsubstitutable individuality of the Other, which means does it not finally end up with the exigency of love?

Notes

1. *Le temps et l'autre* (1946/7, published in 1948, was strangely only reprinted in 1979 at Montpellier, then in Paris, PUF, 1983, quoted according to the 1991 edition, 29) [*Time and the Other and Additional Essays*, trans. Richard A. Cohen (Pittsburgh: Duquesne University Press, 1987) 51]. It is necessary to understand it in the light of this other remark: "It is not the finitude of being, which constitutes the essence of time, as Heidegger thinks, but its infinity" (*Totalité et l'infini, Essai sur l'extériorité*, The Hague, 1961, 260) [*Totality and Infinity*, 284] See the phrase "To be without being a murderer," proposed as a paradox by *Difficile Liberté. Essais sur le judaïsme*, Paris, 1961, 135 [*Difficult Freedom. Essays on Judaism*, trans. Seán Hand (Baltimore: Johns Hopkins University Press, 1990) 100].

   [The translation of the terms *autrui* and *autre*, as they are used by Emmanuel Levinas, poses a number of difficulties. I will follow the convention of Alphonso Lingis by rendering *autrui* as "Other" and *autre* as "other." Unfortunately this does not allow for the distinction that Levinas sometimes suggests by his use of *Autre*, but has the advantage of maintaining the personal sense of otherness in distinction from the impersonal. See Lingis's note in Emmanuel Levinas, *Totality and Infinity: an Essay on Exteriority* (Pittsburgh: Duquesne University Press, 1969), 24–25n. See also in contrast Seán Hand, ed., *The Levinas Reader* (Oxford: Blackwell, 1989), vi.—Trans.]

2. "L'ontologie est-elle fondamentale?" *Revue de Métaphysique et de Morale*, 1951/1, reprinted in *Entre nous. Essais sur le penser-à-l'autre*, Paris, 1991, 20 ["Is Ontology Fundamental?," *Basic*

Philosophical Writings, ed. Adriaan T. Peperzak, Simon Critchley and Robert Bernasconi (Bloomington: Indiana University Press, 1996), 2–10, 7; *Entre Nous: On Thinking-of-the-Other*, trans. Michael B. Smith and Barbara Harshav (New York: Columbia University Press, 1998), 7.]

3. *Le temps et l'autre*, 17 [*Time and the Other*, 39]. This confirms the opening of "L'ontologie est-elle fondamentale?"—and its conclusion: " . . . there are the themes which follow from this first contestation of the primacy of ontology" (Loc.cit., 13 and 24 [*Time and the Other*, 35 and 44]. On this question, see G. Petitdemange, "L'un et l'autre. La querelle de l'ontologie: Heidegger-Levinas," in J. Rolland (ed.), *Emmanuel Levinas*, "Cahiers de la nuit surveillée," Lagasse, 1984; J. Taminiaux, "La première république à l'ontologie fondamentale", in M. Abensour and C. Chalier (eds.), *Emmanuel Levinas*, L'Herne, Paris, 1991; finally, C. Chalier, "Ontologie et mal" and J. Greisch, "Ethique et ontologie. Quelques considérations hypocrites", in J. Greisch and J. Rolland (eds.), *L'éthique comme philosophie première*, "Cahier de la nuit surveillée", Paris, 1993.

4. *Le temps et l'autre*, 26, 44 and 47. [*Time and the Other*, 47, 62, 65]

5. *Le temps et l'autre*, 78 [*Time and the Other*, 86].

6. *Le temps et l'autre*, 31 [*Time and the Other*, 52].

7. *Entre nous*, 23 [English version, 10]. Which should be taken as radically as possible: the Other "The being would then not be justiciable to the 'comprehension of being' or ontology. . . . The being, *par excellence*, is man": man does not take the place of God in the function of being *par excellence*, but the being, in as much as it is, in as much as being, exemplifies itself otherwise uniquely, at least primarily, in man, " . . . simply the *being*" (*Totalité et infini*, 92 [*Totality and Infinity*, 119]. See: "In the face, the being *par excellence* presents itself" (*Totalité et infini*, 239 [*Totality and Infinity*, 262]).

8. *Le temps et l'autre*, 27 (where the term *object* seems particularly inappropriate) and 31 [*Time and the Other*, 48 and 52]. [In the first quotation, Marion has used *accordé* (granted) where Levinas has used *accroché* (which I have, along with Richard A. Cohen, translated "attached")—Trans.

9. *Le temps et l'autre*, 27, 65 and 38 [*Time and the Other*, 48, 77, 57] See: "The pure nothing of Heideggerian anxiety does not constitute the *there is*. Horror of being opposed to the anxiety of the nothing; fear of being and not at all for being; being prey to, being delivered over to something which is not a "something," and "horror of being . . . " (*De l'existence à l'existant*, Paris, 1947, 102 and 103) [*Existence and Existents*, trans. Alphonso Lingis (The Hague: Martinus Nijhoff, 1978), 62, 63n]. In the same way: " . . . the anonymous *there is*, horror, trembling and dizziness, perturbation of the I that does not coincide with itself . . . "; or again: "The absolute indetermination of the *there is*—of an existing without existents . . . " (*Totalité et infini*, 117, then 257; See 165) [*Totality and Infinity*, 143, borrowing from Lingis' translation, then 281. See 190].

10. *Ethique et infini*. Dialogues avec Philippe Nemo, Paris, 1982, cited from 1986, 37 [*Ethics and Infinity*, Conversations with Philippe Nemo, trans. Richard A. Cohen (Pittsburgh: Duquesne University Press, 1985), 48].

* Marion's text reads "L'anonymat de l'être, l'anonymat d'être . . . ," a distinction which is difficult to render in English—Trans.

11. *Le temps et l'autre*, 38 and 46 [*Time and the Other*, 57, 63. The former reference, which in context reads *"le définitif même du je rivé à soi-même"* is translated by Richard A. Cohen as "the very finality of the *I* riveted to itself."—Trans.]

12. *Le temps et l'autre*, 48 [*Time and the Other*, 65].

13. *Le temps et l'autre*, 55, 66 and 71 [*Time and the Other*, 69, 78 and 80].

14. *Le temps et l'autre*, 63 [*Time and the Other*, 75]. Or: "How can the existent exist as mortal and nevertheless persevere in its 'personality,' maintain its conquest over the anonymous *there is*, its subject's mastery, its conquest of subjectivity?" (*Le temps et l'autre*, 65) [*Time and the Other*, 77].

15. *Le temps et l'autre*, 63 and 67 [*Time and the Other*, 75, 79]. Or: "How can one give a definition of the subject which resides in some manner in its passivity? . . . it is the relation with the Other." (p.73) [*Time and the Other*, 81–82]. See: "The *other insofar as other is the Other*," and: " . . . the alterity of the other, here, does not result from its identity, but constitutes it: the other is the Other" (*Totalité et infini*, 42–43 and 229) [*Totality and Infinity*, 71 and 251].

16. *Le temps et l'autre*, 89 [*Time and the Other*, 94].

17. *Le temps et l'autre*, 83, 89 and 10 [*Time and the Other*, 90, 94, 32]. See " . . . distance preserves, moreover, the most unavoidable proximity to that which we can no longer idolize"

(*L'idole et la distance*, Paris, 1977, 96) [*The Idol and Distance: Five Studies*, trans. Thomas A. Carlson (New York: Fordham University Press, 2001), 76].

18. *Le temps et l'autre*, 67 (emphasis added) [*Time and the Other*, 78–79].

19. That one finds elsewhere: "The situation of the face-to-face would be the very accomplishment of time." (*Le temps et l'autre*, 69) [*Time and the Other*, 79].

20. *Le temps et l'autre*, 75 [*Time and the Other*, 83].

21. *Le temps et l'autre*, 77 and 81 [*Time and the Other*, 85, 88] (with, it is true, a questioning without response on this point: " . . . and it would have to be seen in what sense this can be said of masculinity or of virility, that is to say of the difference between the sexes in general," 14 [*Time and the Other*, 36]. The same assumption can be seen in *Totalité et infini*: "The welcoming of the face . . . is produced, *in an original manner*, in the gentleness of the feminine face . . . ." (p.124, emphasis added [*Totality and Infinity*, 150, borrowing from Lingis's translation of *douceur*]). Or: "the feminine is described [that is, in *Time and the Other*] as the *of itself other*, as the origin of the very concept of alterity" (*Ethique et infini*, 58) [*Ethics and Infinity*, 66, borrowing from Cohen's translation of "le *de soi autre*"].

22. *Totalité et infini*, 234 [*Totality and Infinity*, 257]. See: "The equivocal constitutes the epiphany of the feminine." (*Totalité et infini*, 241) [*Totality and Infinity*, 264. Marion has *l'épitaph* where Levinas has *l'épiphanie*.].

23. *Le temps et l'autre*, 81 (emphasis added) [*Time and the Other*, 88]. *Totalité et infini* will define it still more negatively.

24. *Le temps et l'autre*, 86 [*Time and the Other*, 91]. See: "My child is a stranger (Isaiah 49:14ff.), but who is not only me, because he *is* me" *Totalité et infini*, 245, and 254 and 255ff.) [*Totality and Infinity*, 267, 277, 278].

25. *Totalité et infini*, 170 and 188 [*Totality and Infinity*, 194 and 199].

26. *Totalité et infini*, 113, 239 and 177 [*Totality and Infinity*, 140, 261, 202].

27. *Totalité et infini*, 47 [*Totality and Infinity*, 74–75].

28. *Totalité et infini*, 145 [*Totality and Infinity*, 171].

29. *Totalité et infini*, 182 [*Totality and Infinity*, 207]. " . . . the idea of the infinite—revealing itself in the face" (*Totalité et infini*, 125) [*Totality and Infinity*, 151]; consequently, one can say that the "immeasurableness [that is, of the infinite], measured by Desire, is the face" (*Totalité et infini*, 33) [*Totality and Infinity*, 62]; the face does not show a noema measured by a noesis, but an infinite noema in a finite noesis; this tension or compression even implies from now on going beyond a phenomenology of manifestation to a phenomenology of revelation. Others, such as M. Henry, have followed the same path.

*   Marion's translation of the German *Gegebenheit* with the French *donation* opens up a difficulty when translating into English, where *Gegebenheit* is often rendered "giveness" rather than "donation." Elsewhere I will keep the ambiguity of the French "*donation*" by using its English counterpart.

30. Respectively *Totalité et infini*, 53 [*Totality and Infinity*, 81] and Husserl, *L'idée de la phénoménologie*, Hua.II, 61, tr.fr., 8 (modified) [Edmund Husserl, *The Idea of Phenomenology*, trans. William P. Alston and George Nakhnikian (The Hague: Martinus Nijhoff, 1964), 49].

31. *Totalité et infini*, 176, see also 276 [*Totality and Infinity*, 202, 297].

32. *Totalité et infini*, 149 [*Totality and Infinity*, 174].

33. *Totalité et infini*, 190 [*Totality and Infinity*, 215]. See: "I do not know if one can speak of a 'phenomenology' of the face, since phenomenology describes that which appears," for " . . . the face is not 'seen' . . . ," on the contrary, the " . . . face speaks. It speaks insofar as it is the face that renders possible and begins all discourse. I have resisted . . . the notion of vision to describe the authentic relation with the Other; it is discourse and, more exactly, response or responsibility, which is this authentic relation" (*Ethique et infini*, 79, 81 and 82) [*Ethics and Infinity*, 85, 86 and 87–88]. And even there where he maintains that " . . . the *phenomenon* which is the appearance of the Other, is also *the face* . . . ," it is in order to underline that it is not seen, so much as it comes towards me as a "visitation," since "the face speaks." (*Humanisme et l'autre homme*, Montpellier, 1972, 47ff.) ["Meaning and Sense," *Basic Philosophical Writings*, ed. Adriaan T. Peperzak, Simon Critchley and Robert Bernasconi (Bloomington: Indiana University Press, 1996), 34–64, 53ff.].

34. *Totalité et infini*, 172 and 281 [*Totality and Infinity*, 199 and 303]. See *Entre Nous*, 20 [English trans. 9–11] ["Is Ontology Fundamental?," 9–10], *Ethique et infini*, 83, etc. [*Ethics and Infinity*, 88ff.].

35. See my remarks in "La voix sans nom. Hommage à partir de Levinas," *Emmanuel Levinas. Visage et Sinaï*, Collège International de Philosophie, Paris, 1998.

36. *Totalité et infini*, 152ff. (emphasis added) [*Totality and Infinity*, 177].

37. In the sense in which I uncover it in *Etant donné. Essai d'une phénoménologie de la donation*, Paris, 1997, §26 and 28; *Being Given: Studies in Saturated Phenomena*, trans. Jeffrey L. Kosky (Stanford: Stanford University Press, 2002).

38. *Totalité et infini*, 242 and 241 [*Totality and Infinity*, 264 and 263].

39. *Totalité et infini*, 276 [*Totality and Infinity*, 299].

40. Curiously the question of individuation (and of ipseity) is treated most often, for that matter well done, there where it does not pose a difficulty (for the *ego* that I am) and less than for the *ipse* of the Other. See recently R. Calin, "La voix du soi. Ipséité et langage chez Levinas," *Alter*, n. 5, Paris, 1997. [For *là où elle en pose pas* I am reading *là où elle ne pose pas*—Trans.]

41. *Metaphysique*, Z, 13, 1039a7.

42. *Totalité et infini*, 189 (emphasis added) [*Totality and Infinity*, 213].

43. *Humanisme de l'autre homme*, 48 ["Meaning and Sense," 53.]

*   For "ne pas acception," I am reading "n'est pas acception"—Trans.

44. *Totalité et infini*, 274 [*Totality and Infinity*, 298].

45. *Totalité et infini*, 75.

46. *Totalité et infini*, 229ff. [*Totality and Infinity*, 261ff.]. See: " . . . the encounter with the face— that is to say the moral conscience" ("L'ontologie est-elle fondamentale?," *Entre Nous*, 23 [English trans. 11), a text which indeed " . . . accepts this ethical resonance of the word [that is, religion] and all its Kantian echoes" (20/8) ["Is Ontology Fundamental?" 10, 8].

47. Kant, respectively *Fondements de la métaphysique des mœurs*, I, Ak.A. IV, 402 (tr.fr. "Pléiade," t.2, 261) [*Groundwork of the Metaphysics of Morals*, trans. and ed. Mary Gregor (Cambridge, U.K.: Cambridge University Press, 1998) 14n, then *Métaphysique des mœurs*, §44, note, Ak.A. VI, p.468 (tr.fr. t3, p.765) [*The Metaphysics of Morals*, trans. and ed. Mary Gregor (Cambridge: Cambridge University Press, 1996) 213: "The only reverence to which I am bound by nature is reverence for the law as such (*revere legem*); and to revere the law, but not to revere other human beings in general (*reverentia adversus hominum*) or to perform some acts of reverence for them, is a human being's universal and unconditional duty toward others, which each of them can require as the respect originally owed others (*obserantia debita*)."].

48. *Totalité et infini*, 242 [*Totality and Infinity*, 264]. Which explicitates the title, itself quite strange, of the last section, "Au-delà du visage," 227 ["Beyond the Face," 249].

49. "De l'utilité des insomnies" (Interview with B. Révillon, 10 juin 1987), in *Les imprévus de l'histoire*, Montpellier, 1994, texts collected by P. Hayat), 199.

50. *Totalité et infini*, 233 and 232 [*Totality and Infinity*, 255, 254].

51. *Totalité et infini*, 241 (See the " . . . impersonality of voluptuousness . . . " 243) and 244 [*Totality and Infinity*, 263, 265, 266].

52. Respectively, *De Dieu qui vient à l'idée*, Paris, 1982, 247 (and p.263) [*Of God Who Comes to Mind*, trans. Bettina Bergo (Stanford: Stanford University Press, 1998) 176 (and 163)], "L'autre, utopie et justice" (interview from 1988), *Entre nous*, 259 [English trans. 228]. See: " . . . instinct of '*natural* goodwill' or love" (*Autrement qu'être ou au-delà de l'essence*, The Hague, 1974, 142) [*Otherwise than Being or Beyond Essence*, trans. Alphonso Lingis (The Hague: Martinus Nijhoff, 1981) 112].

53. Respectively *La mort et le temps*, Paris, 1991, 121, *Entre nous*, 126 [English trans. 104], *Ethique et infini*, 42 [*Ethics and Infinity*, 52].

54. *Critique de la raison pratique*, Ak.A. V. 83 (tr. fr., t.2, 709ff.) [*Critique of Practical Reason*, trans. Lewis White Beck (Chicago: University of Chicago Press, 1949) 190ff.]. On this relationship, see the helpful notes of P. David, "Le nom de la finitude. De Levinas à Kant," in *Emmanuel Levinas*, op.cit., Paris, 1984.

55. *Totalité et infini*, 242 and 254 [*Totality and Infinity*, 264 and 277].

56. *Autrement qu'être*, 37 and 207 [*Otherwise than Being*, 29 and 162].

57. *Autrement qu'être*, 13, note 7 [*Otherwise than Being*, 187, note 8].

58. *Autrement qu'être*, 153 [*Otherwise than Being*, 120] and *Totalité et infini*, 232 [*Totality and Infinity*, 254].

59. *Autrement qu'être*, 185 (emphasis added) [*Otherwise than Being*, 199n10]. As with page 13 [11], it is here a matter of a note: love earns its rehabilitation by dove-steps—the event of it is only greater, no doubt.

60. "Philosophie, Justice et Amour" (Interview with R. Fornet and A. Gomez), in *Entre Nous,* 125ff. [English trans. 103ff.].
61. *Totalité et infini,* 269 [*Totality and Infinity,* 293].
62. "Diachronie et représentation" (conference in honor of P. Ricœur), in *Entre nous,* 193ff. [English trans. 159ff.] [see also "Diachrony and Representation," in *Time and the Other and Additional Essays,* 97–120, 116—Cohen's translation is evidently from a 1982 version of the essay].
63. *Autrement que savoir* (debate at the Centre Sèvres, June 3, 1986), Paris, 1988, 75. He was specifying, in the section that I have omitted, " . . . it is perhaps under your influence, or thanks to your courage"; there was some generosity there, but also an anticipated response to J.-F. Lyotard and to his " . . . keeping guard . . . against the transcription of your idea of alterity in terms of love" (79).
64. "La vocation de l'autre," Interview with E. Hirsch, in *Racismes. L'autre et son visage,* Paris, 1988, 95.
65. For further discussion, see Marion, *De Surcroit,* Paris: PUF, 2001), trans. as *In Excess, Studies of Saturated Phenomenen,* (New York: Fordham University Press, 2002), in particular chapter 4, "The Icon or the Endless Hermeneutic"; and *Le phenomene erotique,* (Paris: Grasset, 2003).

5

The Betrayal of Transcendence

BY ROBYN HORNER

In an essay on the thought of Emmanuel Levinas that appears elsewhere in this collection ("From the Other to the Individual"), Jean-Luc Marion argues for an experience of transcendence that is at once resistant to rational calculation and yet able to be thought. He articulates three stages on the way to naming this experience. The first of these involves the recognition that transcendence cannot be thought according to the terms of an economy. So, with Levinas, Marion rejects the ultimacy of being, proposing that the order of being can be transgressed. In this instance it is transgressed by the other person, the Other who "is" *otherwise than being*. Transcendence resists economic recuperation. That is not to suggest, however, that with this formula transcendence can simply be opposed to the economy, for that would economize it all the more. This is why Plato's "good beyond being," which is often put to work in Levinas's writing, is better expressed as being's "otherwise." The metaphysical danger to which we are exposed in attempting to think transcendence is the duplication of one economy with another, higher one to which it corresponds. To adopt more of a Derridean inflection, transcendence inhabits the economy instead in the mode of interruption; transcendence is always transcendence-in-immanence. This is clarified in the least theological way by a thinking of textual excess. *Différance* is a good example of where the withdrawal to transcendence does not mean an escape by an infinite term to a place outside the text, but the constant undoing of the text by its own infinitude. Let us be clear that to attempt to speak of transcendence, therefore, is not necessarily to propose the existence of a hidden order beyond the borders of the text, but to allow for a kind of immanent excess. Economic terms restrict that excess even as they are simultaneously made possible by it. But having recognized the resistance of transcendence to economy, we arrive at the real dilemma signaled by Marion: how to experience transcendence *as such*, when it cannot be reduced to the economic categories that define "experience" as theoretical, represented to a self-conscious consciousness.

The second of Marion's stages moves to overcome that difficulty, at least in part. What he will claim is that transcendence is experienced as a pressure, a "call" that is recognized only in the response that one is compelled to make to it. This, he observes, is what Levinas proposes as the ethical priority that precedes all economic determination. But a new problem emerges at this stage, one that is observed in the impossibility of recognizing a specific caller *as such* or even of acknowledging that the call is made specifically to *me*. In Levinas's thinking of the face—the face being what I have described elsewhere as a "valve" opening onto transcendence—there can be no individuation, for an empirical face would reduce transcendence to an object.[1] So, at least, runs the argument of Jacques Derrida, and it seems that Marion in some way agrees, for he goes on to propose a third stage that would allow for individuation while resisting both rationalist and empiricist recuperations of transcendence. In this stage, individuation of both transcendent Other and self is made possible through a movement of love. It becomes possible to love *this* Other who, nevertheless, does not betray transcendence even in specificity, where the weight of transcendence is experienced as loving, and where the response to that weight is a loving that prompts the emergence of a self who can love. Put more simply, Marion argues that love begets love, and in so doing, enables the emergence both of beloved and lover without diminishing the infinitude of either. What must be asked here is whether or not such a specification in this way is possible. And to answer that question adequately demands an investigation of Marion's methodology as it is worked out in his other texts.

Marion's indebtedness to Levinas is already apparent, but in many respects his work will turn upon moments that remain only half thought in Levinas. Their respective readings of the potential of phenomenology come back to one such moment: the recognition that more is given to consciousness than consciousness can contain. For Levinas, this alerts us to the need to move beyond phenomenology, whereas for Marion, the ability to open onto this excess marks the point of phenomenology's greatest success. The difference between the two thinkers hinges, in other words, upon the capacity of phenomenology to deal with the question of transcendence. Ironically, it is with the suspension of the question of transcendence that phenomenology begins. Springing as it does from a kind of failure in philosophy, Husserlian phenomenology is designed to offer a way out of an impasse. With Husserl, we suspend our questions about the transcendence of objects in making the phenomenological reduction, to consider what gives itself simply as it is given to intuition. There is an attractiveness about this position. No longer realist or strictly idealist, phenomenology seems to avoid the traps of both. The constitutive powers of the subject are admitted, but they are, in a sense, demoted in favour of noematic self-manifestation. Or are they? So many of those thinkers who begin with the possibilities of phenomenology as they are explored by Husserl end by finding there, too, a type of failure. It is a failure that largely revolves around two metaphysical poles: subjectivity and presence. In suspending the problem of the transcendence of objects (the question of whether or not they "exist" apart from their noematic representation in consciousness) Husserl develops a method that relies, in the end, on a self-present subject who is able to make transcendence present to itself. What appears to draw us closer to whatever manifests itself in fact places a limit on what can appear, although it will become evident that the use of the word "appear" is itself problematic. This is something of the criticism of Husserl made by Martin Heidegger, and it is taken further, in devastating fashion, by Derrida in his *Introduction to Edmund Husserl's 'Origin of Geometry,'* where phenomenology is the wolf of metaphysics in sheep's clothing.[2]

Seeking to rehabilitate Husserl, Marion argues that phenomenology contains the possibility of referring to the impossible without limiting it to the dimensions of the self-present subject. Phenomenology, for Marion, need not be characterized as a continuation of metaphysics, but can be understood instead as a radical thought of transcendence. This is suggested most strongly in two arguments. Marion insists that the I, seen to be phenomenologically constitutive, does not present itself but is only signaled in the phenomenological reduction. It is so excepted both from the realm of "what is" and from what it "means to be," although evidently it is not bereft of all meaning. Since the I precedes objectivity, it also precedes the ontology that makes objectivity possible: it "is" an exception to Being.[3] Marion explains: "The anteriority of the I with regard to every object and of subjectivity with regard to objectivity designates a deviation on this side of ontology: phenomenology occupies this deviation; it presents itself thus in the strictest sense as the instance of that which has not yet to be in order to exercise itself." Ontology only has a conditional legitimacy: it is subject to the I that makes the reduction. The reduction not only puts in parenthesis ontology as such, but also the whole question of Being.[4] But the I itself is attested to only in making the reduction, and if the reducing I is excluded from Being, where is it located? Heidegger would say that Husserl fails because he leaves the Being of the I undetermined. Marion suggests instead that: " . . . the I, thus the phenomenological reduction with it, *is not*."[5] In spite of Heidegger's critique, Husserl actually makes a leap outside the horizon of Being. In other words, Husserl takes phenomenology further than Heidegger—beyond the question of Being: " . . . the *ultimate* possibility of phenomenology would not consist more in the question of Being than it exhausts itself in the objectivity of the constituted object: beyond the one and also the other, a last possibility could still open up for it—that of posing the I as transcendent to the reduced objectivity, but also to the Being of the being, to place it, by virtue of the reduction taken to its ultimate consequences, outside Being."[6] Husserl does not thematize this possibility, but Marion argues that his use of the reduction pushes us towards it.[7] The transcendence of the I signifies in the making of the reduction, but does not have to be thought according to Being. " . . . [T]he I can offer itself through other transcendences, or even offer itself to other transcendences which the reduction, ceaselessly radicalized, like a new apophantics, will free up for it."[8] So runs the first argument.

The other main argument that Marion employs to disengage phenomenology from metaphysics is again related to the I, but this time it is related not to its exception from Being but to its constitutional weakness. According to this argument, there are certain phenomena that, in giving themselves to consciousness, exceed the capacity of consciousness to contain them, such as death, the idea of the infinite, or the Other. Such phenomena are therefore not constituted by consciousness but put consciousness in question.[9] Stripping consciousness of its ability to master and understand, these phenomena reduce consciousness to the role of witness. In *Réduction et Donation*, consciousness is so put in question by "the call" that transgresses the call of Being, and by the face of the Other, which similarly resists ontological determination.[10] But perhaps in response to criticism that "the call" (or "claim") as it is outlined in that text can be linked with a "Caller," and that the "Caller" might come to be identified with God, Marion shifts in *Étant donné* to the placing in question of consciousness by what he calls "saturated phenomena," thinking anticipated by Marion's early understanding of the icon as referring beyond itself, to excess.[11]

The criticism that Marion's phenomenology is a closet theology comes from a number of sources, and has recently been renewed in highly polemical fashion by Dominique Janicaud.[12] Derrida suggests as much with a reference he makes to *Reduction and Givenness* in *Given Time: 1. Counterfeit Money*.[13] It is vigorously argued by Marion that his text makes no theological assertions, and it is true that the possibility of such an identification rests on a suspicious reading of a very small section of the text. "The Call of the Father" is discussed in relation to Heidegger, and is followed by a discussion of Levinas and the possibility of a Jewish call.[14] Marion himself points out: " . . . Who or what claims the *interloqué*? To evoke here God, the other, self-affection, and all the figures of difference allows one only to name the difficulty, not to resolve it. . . ."[15] In other words, Marion here recognizes the impossibility of determining the source of the call, and hence a theological reading, while always a possibility, remains only such. The difficulty is compounded, however, when *Reduction and Givenness* is placed in the context of Marion's other texts. His earlier reading of Heidegger in *God Without Being*, for example, suggests a much more positive identification of the caller. And to the extent that such a reading might be revoked in *Réduction et donation*, at least from a phenomenological perspective, it might equally be argued that this work reopens the question. This is suggested in Marion's passing comment later that "[t]o my knowledge, this locution [phenomenon of revelation] does not occur in *Reduction and Givenness*, but a lucid reader cannot help but guess that the question of revelation governs this work quite essentially."[16] Elsewhere, in relation to subjectivity, we read: "Grace gives the *myself* to *itself* before the *I* even notices itself. My grace precedes me."[17] Hence the theological connection seems to be reasserted. Or again, in *Étant donné*, revelation is used as the superlative example of saturation.

We arrive here at a difficulty that requires careful consideration. Marion's work cannot simply be dismissed on the basis that it opens onto theological concerns, for such a move would take on the tones of the ideology it presumes to reject. At the same time, it is fair to ask whether or not phenomenology can validly open onto those same concerns. Janicaud insists that phenomenology is methodologically atheistic: if he is correct, Marion's work is excluded on the grounds that phenomenology is compromised. Derrida argues that phenomenology fails: if he is correct, Marion's work is excluded on the grounds that it does not recognize that failure and uses theology as a guarantee of truth.[18] One of the questions that is relevant to both sources of criticism is the extent to which Marion argues for the possibility rather than the necessity of revelation. And once again, we return to the problem of thinking transcendence *as such*. In a particular sense, it does not matter whether we are referring to theological transcendence or the transcendence of the other person, since the problem of identification is the same.

Marion maintains that phenomenology opens onto transcendence. Since the basic tenet of phenomenology is that it be without presupposition in terms of what can be given to consciousness, he claims that the phenomena consciousness receives might not only be limited to those that are met with the fullness of intuition. Consciousness might be given, in other words, phenomena that are invisible or excessive. I have sketched two of his arguments in support of this claim: the first, that the I, in making and yet being excepted from the reduction, exceeds consciousness and still has a meaning; the second, that there are other phenomena that are given otherwise than according to theoretical experience. In terms of his examination of Levinas in "From the Other to the Individual," Marion attempts to deal with the problem of how that givenness might be recognized without its simultaneous betrayal. The remaining part of this essay will be informed by four questions: is it possible for phenomenology to contextualize an experience of excess, and if so, to what kinds of phenomena might it be open, how might they be recognized, and do they demand a kind of theological authorization?

In *Étant donné*, Marion identifies two limits on the capacity of phenomenology to open onto excess.[19] One of these is the apparent domination of the constituting subject, the other, the need for that subject to constitute experience against a horizon of intelligibility. We have already seen that Marion unsettles the mastery of the subject by putting it in question with the performance of the reduction. The I that is signaled phenomenologically is not the subject present to itself but a *me* who in making the reduction still escapes close examination. A question remains, however, about how that signaling functions, if it is not according to the measure of comprehension. Surely, if it is to signal at all, it must signal in a context or against a horizon. Husserl speaks of the horizon as the background from which things are extracted as particular objects of consciousness.[20] Expressing this in more Kantian terms, a horizon is a condition of possibility for knowing anything at all, since the horizon forms the frame for knowledge of individual things. And thinking horizon as context leads us to Heidegger's usage, where it is less a question of the horizon being something which moves, expands, or changes (in a factical or existential sense), than something which is the always and already given existential limit within which *Dasein* works.[21] In each of these cases, the horizon is a border that includes or allows for particular possibilities, that fences an economy of thought and action.

As Marion's work progresses we see a shift in the way he uses the concept of the horizon. While in his early work he tries to think otherwise than according to the horizon of being, he still maintains the need for a horizon. In *The Idol and Distance*, evidently a theological work, he speaks of the horizon of the Father. By the time of *God Without Being*, he speaks of the horizon of the call, an emphasis that is continued more broadly in *Reduction and Givenness*. But in *Étant donné*, givenness has become its own horizon. In this work, Marion asks whether or not there are some phenomena that go beyond their horizons.[22] Yet he still claims that it is not about dispensing with a horizon altogether, since there can be no manifestation without a horizon, but about using horizon in another mode, freeing it from its anterior delimitations so that it does not forbid the appearance of an absolute phenomenon. He imagines three examples. In the first example, the phenomenon fits within the horizon but at the same time pushes it open, working against it (bedazzlement). In the second example, the phenomenon goes beyond the limits of the horizon. It is seen according to different horizons that are in fact opposed, so that it remains undefined. The third example is rare: in this case, there is no horizon and no combination of horizons that can contain the phenomenon.[23] While Marion has asserted the need for the maintenance of a horizon, it is evident from these examples that he is envisaging the possibility of a phenomenon that shatters all horizons. This possibility is fully appreciated by the time of "On the Gift," where Marion observes: "I said to Levinas some years ago that in fact the last step for a real phenomenology would be to give up the concept of horizon. Levinas answered me immediately: 'Without horizon there is no phenomenology.' And I boldly assume he was wrong."[24]

Having reached a point where he is prepared to give up the need for a horizon, Marion still maintains that it is possible to speak of phenomena. Returning to the question about how the I signifies, then, we would have to say both that it signifies as excessiveness and that it is simultaneously recognized as the I in spite of that excessiveness. If this is not achieved according to the measure of a horizon, since the horizon is shattered, then there must be some other mechanism that allows for recognition. It seems to me that this is a hermeneutical mechanism: the excessive phenomenon can nevertheless be named because the marks it traces in experience can be read decisively in a particular way.[25] The importance of Marion's recent work on subjectivity, including and especially the article on Levinas in this volume, is that it emphasizes the *responding* subject. In other words, the subject signifies in its act of responding, or in this case, making the reduction. It is not presented as *what it is* so much as signaled in its withdrawal from the scope of the reducing consciousness. But is it, in this signaling, given absolutely as a phenomenon, or does it require a further act of interpretation to become known as such? This is the nub of the problem. If we were doing Husserlian phenomenology, we would expect the givenness to be absolute and self-evident. As Derrida observes, phenomenology is about *seeing*, it is photology, it is seeing something *as* something.[26] And here we are given the clue: phenomenology is inevitably hermeneutics. In admitting that the reduction does not deliver the I in presence to consciousness, we also have to admit that its excessiveness can only be contextualized by an act of interpretation. In other words, it takes a kind of faith to link the I (or better, *me*) that eludes the reduction with the *ego* that is the object of self-conscious reflection. This is not to deny the reasonableness of taking an interpretative stance, but to recognize the elements of risk and ambiguity that a "phenomenology" now entails, to recognize that phenomenology thus leads beyond phenomenology.

The argument that phenomenology is a de facto hermeneutics can be further put to the test by examining other phenomena whose primary effect could, from the point of view of intentionality, be considered overwhelming excess. In particular, I am interested in returning to the question of the Other.[27] Marion's consideration of this question can be situated in the contexts of his writing on love, and on the icon, as well as on the saturated phenomenon. If a sense of the theological is already apparent, that is because Marion's thinking of the Other takes place where there is no limit to transcendence, which is reminiscent of Levinas, even if their respective theological interests might be quite different.[28] In the following examination, the questions of relevance will not be whether or not Marion's theological concerns are legitimate as such, but whether or not his thinking of the Other is possible, and the extent to which it concerns the actuality rather than the possibility of revelation.

The theme of idol versus icon is recurrent in Marion's texts, which is hardly surprising given his evident interest both in art and in religion. The idol is characterized, not as the personification of its god, but as the image by means of which the worshipper is referred only to the human experience of divinity.[29] The icon, in contrast, is characterized as that which works as a kind of negative theophany.[30] While the idol is about preserving the proximity of the divine, the icon manifests distance. Concepts, too, can function idolatrously or iconically. Therefore Marion is able to understand the Nietzschean "death of God" in terms of the death only of an idolatrous concept of God.[31] Yet words can also refer, he maintains, to the unspeakable. Where theology has been practiced as onto-theology, the conceptual idols of metaphysics are rightly condemned. But where theology preserves "distance," where it allows for the divine to overflow what is merely human, it goes beyond idolatry.[32]

Marion's understanding of how idols and icons function is deepened in *God Without Being*. Here he perceives that the difference between them lies in

their "manner of being for beings," rather than in their being two classes of beings. Frequently the same object can function as idol or icon: it is a question of
veneration. An object is venerated when it is seen as a sign of the divine; artistic works are so venerated when "they no longer restrict their visibility to
themselves . . . but, as such and thus remaining absolutely immanent in themselves, . . . they signal indissolubly toward another, still undetermined term."[33]
Where an idol "depends on the gaze it satisfies," the icon "does not result from
a vision but provokes one."[34] The idol stops the gaze, reflecting to the idolater
the limits of her or his aim.[35] The icon allows instead the visible to be saturated
by the invisible, without being reduced to the visible. Invisibility is represented
in the visible insofar as the visible constantly refers to what is other than itself.
In a complex movement, infinity is made visible in the icon, as that divine intention which envisages the human and which overflows the capacity of the
human gaze, and which is then reflected as glory by the human face.[36]

There are two important features of the icon that have been pointed out
thus far. One is the way in which the visible refers to the invisible; the other is
the way in which the invisible envisages the human in the icon. These features
are equally evident in the description of the relationship with a human Other.
In the essay, "L'intentionalité de l'amour," Marion notes that the look of the
other does away with the horizon of the visible. The invisible regard of the
other puts me in question. Here it is the face, or more particularly the eyes, that
open onto transcendence.[37] In *La croisée du visible* (1991) and in the case of a
lover, " . . . that which someone wants to see does not coincide with that which
the face gives to be seen to every other regard. . . ."[38] It is the weight of the
other's regard that is glimpsed. "I do not see the visible face of the other, object
still reducible to an image . . . but the invisible regard which swells up from the
obscure pupils of the other; in short, I see the other of the visible face."[39] In
love, therefore, I am no longer bound to the image.[40] These are the emphases
brought out in "From the Other to the Individual."

At one point in *La croisée* Marion undertakes an examination of Christ as
icon, as the superlative example of visibility referring to invisibility:

> Christ offers an icon to the regard only in manifesting a face, that is to say a look,
> itself invisible. It is therefore a matter, in the first place, of a crossing of regards, as
> it is for lovers; I look, with my invisible look, an invisible look which envisages
> me; in the icon, in effect, it is not so much me who sees a spectacle as much as an
> other regard which sustains mine, confronts it, and eventually, overwhelms it. But
> Christ does not only offer to my regard to see and to be seen by his [regard]; if he
> demands from me a love, it is not a love for him, but for his Father. . . . But since
> the Father remains invisible, how am I able to see the Father in seeing Christ?
> Would not Christ constitute only what can be seen of the Father in the place of
> the Father, that which holds visibly the place of the invisibility of the Father?[41]

Christ is the visible image of the invisible as invisible, as that which regards,
which meets the regard of the one who prays before it, which weighs upon that

regard. The image functions iconically where the visible renounces itself, and it is this kenosis which characterizes Christ's ministry and which means that he is able to manifest the glory of the Father. In losing his human figure, Christ becomes the figure of the divine will. With a quasi-Levinasian touch, Marion adds: "In the gestures of his body accomplishing not his will, but the will of God, the Christ indicates, not his face, but the trace of God."[42] In Christ, then, we see not God's face *as* the face of Christ, but the trace of God passing *in* the face of Christ.

A potential criticism of Marion's work on the icon is that it places the gaze of the infinite within the same frame as the observer. John Milbank undertakes an extensive analysis of the crossing of regards, which, he maintains, can only be supported by the prior projection of an I.[43] The evidence is readily available in Marion's work. For example, he maintains that the other is like me in that each of us is characterized by an intentional "aim." Further, he speaks of my experience of the regard of the other as a "weight," but as a weight that is only recognized *after* I become aware of my obligation to the other. And further again, he seems to set up a structure whereby the other regard is only "activated" in response to my first regarding. Marion's "reverse intentionality" may be part of iconic theology, but it cannot be sustained phenomenologically without the (metaphysical) presumption that the Other is in some way like the Same, and, therefore, without the loss of the otherness of the Other.[44]

What can save Marion's iconography? His own insistence that " . . . the excess of intuition cannot be described in terms of [a] metaphysics of presence, precisely because intuition by excess does not live under the regard as a permanent object, but resists all comprehension or seizure . . . " is testimony to the fact that what gives itself in the icon is not to be simply understood.[45] Marion's work on the icon is an attempt to deal with the possibility of an experience of transcendence without at once prompting its betrayal. We saw earlier, in relation to the exception of the I from the realm of being, that the recognition of transcendence demands a hermeneutic. The experience of the Other similarly demands a risking rather than a seizing of identification. This impinges upon the theological imperative of Marion's work: if the icon, or the face of Christ, refers unconditionally to a transcendent term, then that term has become part of the economy. To avoid this betrayal, but also to avoid the charge that he is imposing belief on theory, Marion's theological reading of the icon must be destabilized by an element of undecidability. The theological reading can be possible but not essential. And if this is the case, then all we are given in the icon, as in the face of the lover, is indefinable excess. The face of Christ may refer us to God, or may refer us to otherness, or to an infinite number of Others. In spite of the problems that "the face" as a phenomenon poses for Levinas, this would be a very Levinasian, and, I might add, a very scriptural solution.[46] There would be no knowing whether or not God had passed in the face of Christ, only a believing that this had been so, made concrete in a movement of the will, that is, in a response of love. Love would indeed witness to love, but not without risk.

In the final essay of *La croisée du visible*, Marion addresses questions raised in the iconoclast controversy. These are, in fact, questions upon which we have been meditating, and Marion sums up the difficulty well where he observes:

> But every spectacle only accedes to its visibility in submitting itself to the conditions of possibility of objects of visual experience, that is to say an intuition, intelligible or sensible; in one and the other case, the intuition is measured according to the dimensions of the mind receiving them and thus is defined by finitude. Phenomenology is in agreement on this observation with critical philosophy: no phenomenon can enter into the visibility of a spectacle, unless it is first submitted to the conditions of this very visibility: givenness to a finite mind. Consequently, the most elementary piety will hold itself to this inevitable dilemma: either the Holy keeps itself as such, but refuses in this case [the entry into] any visible spectacle—and the holiness of God remains with neither image nor face; or the image which delivers the holy to the visible only abandons itself to it as a victim to the outrage of the hangmen—and the image, bereft of any holiness, accomplishes an obscene blasphemy. Either the invisible, or imposture.[47]

Marion subsequently examines the Cross as the measure for all icons, turning this abandonment, this blasphemy, into the condition for the manifestation of holiness. The Cross only gives a figure of Christ under the paradox which hides his glory: in fact, the Cross gives nothing to see, but is a scandal. What is more, those who view the Cross interpret it differently.[48] The type of the Cross thus only carries the mark of the Holy where the Holy abandons itself fully to rejection and injury, repeating the rejection of Christ. And the Cross at once manifests holiness and protects it, by constantly referring away from itself.[49] Now it would be overstating the case to say that Marion holds to a line of complete undecidability with regard to the functioning of the Cross as an icon. But the way that the Cross carries with it the possibility of a mis-referral, that is, carries its own marks of betrayal, is suggestive of the kind of *différantial* play which alone can keep us from the betrayal of transcendence.

I turn now to the second of Marion's strategies for thinking excessive phenomena: the "saturated phenomenon." His essay from 1992, "Le phénomène saturé," marks an early exploration of this idea; in *Étant donné* we find a more complete exposition.[50] In both these texts, we find Marion cautious in linking phenomenology and religion, since he recognizes that what can be objectively defined may lose its religious specificity, while what is religiously defined may lose its objectivity. Importantly, his reading is that the religious phenomenon is impossible, or marks the point at which phenomenality is no longer possible.[51] Nevertheless, this view of the impossibility of the religious phenomenon rests on the assumption that a phenomenon is that which is possible. Marion prefers to ask about the terms of possibility, and to think about the religious phenomenon as a "privileged indication of the possibility of phenomenality."[52] This leads to a lengthy conversation with Kant, for whom possibility means that which accords with the formal conditions of experience. For Kant, possibility depends on phenomenality: not on the phenomenal object as such, but on its power to be known. Like Leibniz, Kant ties this power of knowability to the principle of sufficient reason.[53] In contrast, Husserlian phenomenology opposes the Kantian definition of phenomenality with a "principle of principles" which admits of phenomena without condition.[54] However, this principle is problematic where it seems to limit phenomena to the constituting intuition.[55] According to this principle, and as we have already seen, phenomena can therefore only appear according to a horizon.[56] It is these factors that seem to exclude the possibility of an "absolute" phenomenon.[57] So Marion asks whether or not it is possible to envisage a phenomenon that is unconditioned; it is here that he perceives an opening for the thinking of religious phenomena.

The impossibility of unconditioned and irreducible phenomena is related to the determination of the phenomenon as given in a weakness of intuition. So Marion asks about the possibility of phenomena which are instead saturated in intuition: " . . . why not respond with the possibility of a phenomenon where intuition would give *more, indeed immeasurably more*, than the intention would ever have aimed at, or could have foreseen?"[58] Kant takes up the possibility of an intuition for which an adequate concept cannot be found when he speaks of aesthetic experience.[59] Where there is an excess of intuition, there is an excess of givenness.[60] " . . . [I]ntuition no longer exposes itself in the concept, but saturates it and renders it overexposed—invisible, not by default, but by an excess of light."[61] How could such a phenomenon be described? Marion sketches an answer using the Kantian categories of quantity, quality, relation, and modality—except that the saturated phenomenon relates negatively to these categories since it will exceed them: not an object, the saturated phenomenon prefigures the possibility of a phenomenon in general.[62]

The saturated phenomenon exceeds the category of quantity because it defies the ability of intuition to apply successive syntheses to it. It cannot be aimed at, is thus unforeseeable, and cannot be measured according to what has preceded it. It exceeds the category of quality because it defies the ability of intuition to bear it: it is blinding, giving reality without limitation or negation, an excess, glory, joy, an overflow.[63] The saturated phenomenon is absolute according to the category of relation because it defies the ability of intuition to bring it back to any analogy with experience. Marion asserts that not all phenomena have to respect the unity of experience, giving as an example the event. "Event, or non-foreseeable phenomenon (from the past), not exhaustively comprehensible (from the present), not reproducible (from the future), in short absolute, unique, happening."[64] The saturated phenomenon goes beyond any horizon.[65] And it exceeds the final category of modality because it is irregardable. Where Kant's use of modality relates to the accordance of objects of experience with the power to know, which inevitably relates to a transcendental I, Marion argues that with a saturated phenomenon, the I cannot constitute the object but is in fact constituted by it. This is the imposition of a "counter-experience" on experience.[66] "Confronted with the saturated phenomenon, the *I* cannot not see it, but it cannot look at it like an object, either." What does the I see? It sees no-thing, no objectifiable given, but is simply dazzled by brilliance, by a paradox.[67] The paradox suspends the relation of the phenomenon to the I and inverts it, so that the I is constituted by the phenomenon as a *me*, a witness.[68] Importantly, Marion stresses that this constituting givenness does not necessarily have theological implications. It is also of interest that Marion here refers to the "trace" of the saturated phenomenon, which is far more suggestive of undecidability.[69] With his description of the saturated phenomenon, Marion goes beyond both Husserl and Kant. Yet he maintains that the possibility of a giving without reserve is very Husserlian. The saturated phenomenon is a possibility that goes beyond the very conditions of possibility, the possibility of the impossible.[70] It is readily exemplified in the Cartesian Idea of the Infinite, Kant's sublime, and Husserl's internal time-consciousness.[71]

Saturated phenomena are paradoxical insofar as they cannot be anticipated by an intention while being given to intuition. Marion observes four types of paradoxical phenomena, according to the saturation and subversion of each of the four Kantian determinations of quantity; quality; relation, and modality.[72] The historical event saturates the category of quantity.[73] The idol potentially saturates the category of quality.[74] Flesh saturates the category of relation.[75] And the icon saturates the category of modality.[76] The icon offers nothing to see, but itself "regards": the I simply becomes a witness of the givenness. It is in this context that Marion raises the possibility of the saturated phenomenon of the Other, who always precedes me.[77] Now, it is evident that with his discussion of the icon, Marion has moved deliberately to include the possibility of religious phenomena. It is at this point that the debate with Janicaud and Derrida again becomes very real, and also that echoes of Marion's previous work start to become dominant. The point that Marion initially wishes to illustrate is that in spite of the fact that the four phenomena named are similar by virtue of their saturation, they vary in degrees of givenness. He then wishes to address the question of how far saturation can extend, a question that he frames in terms of two conditions: phenomenality and possibility.[78] Once again pointing out his reservations in linking phenomenology with theology, he argues that the phenomenon that could best achieve these conditions would be the phenomenon of revelation.[79] This is primarily because a phenomenon of revelation would give itself as each of the types of saturated phenomenon listed, effectively becoming a fifth "super" type, the paradox of paradoxes: " . . . it saturates phenomenality to the second degree, by saturation of saturation."[80] At the same time, the phenomenon of revelation would always remain just a possibility, which could be described without the assertion that it had occurred. In fact, that assertion would lie beyond the bounds of phenomenology. A phenomenon of revelation would define itself as the possibility of impossibility, where impossibility would not destroy possibility (which is the case of death), but where possibility would allow for impossibility.[81] Marion therefore describes his task as considering the possibility of revelation, refraining from the judgment about it that would rest in the realm of revealed theology. So, he underlines in response to Janicaud, phenomenology and theology must remain completely separate disciplines.[82] Nevertheless, he uses the manifestation of Jesus Christ as a paradigm of revelatory phenomena according to the four modes that he has previously outlined.

With regard to quantity, Christ is an un-anticipatable phenomenon. Marion explores this with regard both to the incarnation and to texts referring to the *parousia*, both of which meet the conditions of the event.[83] In relation to quality, the intuition that saturates Christ as phenomenon goes beyond what the phenomenological regard can bear. What cannot be borne is the recognition of Christ as such: exemplified in texts such as the transfiguration, and Jesus's command not to touch him after the resurrection, which meet the conditions of the idol.[84] From the point of view of relation, Christ appears as an absolute phenomenon because he saturates every horizon. He is not of this world, a point which is reflected in the need for a plurality of titles for Christ, since no single title is adequate. This is a saturation of the flesh.[85] And concerning modality, Marion maintains that Christ constitutes the one who adores him, rather than the other way around. Christ in this way operates iconically. Here we are given examples of Jesus's inversion of values, particularly in the story of the rich young man. From this story Marion observes two essential traits. One concerns the constituting regard of Jesus, which is given differently to each person. His election of the person does not objectify or reify them, but witnesses his love for them. The other trait concerns the redoubling of saturation. Obedience to the commandments, for the rich young man, is a first saturation, and the giving of everything to the poor a second type. Taken together, coming before the regard of Christ means not only doing good in obedience to the law but loving the poor.[86] This redoubled saturation meets the conditions of the icon. Superlative saturation. In Christ, Marion asserts, we have the saturated phenomenon par excellence. The phenomenon of revelation gives itself without reserve and without conditions. It is not subject to the need for evidence, for conceptualization, or for the opening of *Ereignis*.

The idea of the saturated phenomenon has great potential, for it allows for experience which is not reducible to the realm of theoretical intentionality, a touch of transcendence which does not imply its betrayal. The experience of the saturated phenomenon is experience without an object. Since the saturated phenomenon only signifies as a trace, it can only be interpreted undecidably, which protects it both from idolatry and from lapsing into the mode of the metaphysical. What relationship does the saturated phenomenon bear to experience, that means it can be perceived at all? The answer has to be that it bears no relationship: the saturated phenomenon is absolute. If it can be experienced, it can only be experienced as an interruption, an excess, an overflow, without any context whatsoever. Only the complete suspension of the horizon will suffice to sustain such a thought of otherness. The relationless relation which is the theme of my questioning is clearly impossible, unless the impossibility is thought by way of the unthinkable, or in Marion's terms, in a "saturation" which can do nothing but disorient. Perhaps such disorientation is akin to Blanchot's *dés-astre*, "being separated from the star."[87] Saturation as the impossibility of knowing, as submission to the impossibility of constructing any starlit horizon, seems to offer the best possibility for Marion's phenomenology.

What about the role of the *ego*? Marion recognizes that the constituting subject poses a problem where the encountered phenomenon is reduced to being a projection of the I. He refers to the transcendental I as a "screen" for lived experiences, seeking to withdraw it from any major causal or constitutional role. The transcendental function of the I can never be denied, but it seems to me that where the given totally defies comprehension, the I really has been reduced to its most basic role as witness rather than actor. This is what Marion means when he speaks about the I being constituted by the saturated phenomenon rather than being its constitutor. To accept that the I becomes mere witness means accepting an I who is destitute. This I or me who is (was) affected, is so (was so) almost prior to my being myself. In that being affected, I am (I was) not yet I, am (was) not yet the one who can analyze or identify. If there is to be an interruption to the horizon of my economy, it will only be (have been) in an experience which can have no object. And it will only be after, always and already after, that I can try to imagine what being affected means.

With his discussion of "counter-experience," Marion runs close to repeating his "counter-intentionality" argument. There is a difference, however, and that is that where he stays with the undecidability that disables the capacity of the I even to contextualize the phenomenon in relation to itself, he preserves the integrity of the alterity that imposes (or reveals) itself. In *Étant donné*, Marion emphasizes "counter-intentionality" less, except where he speaks about Jesus, and then in terms of the experience of the disciples rather than exclusively in terms of the icon. "Counter-anything" nevertheless suggests a way of speaking of otherness in terms of the same, and this drives the point home that it is extremely difficult not to think of interruption as what happens—even chaotically—framed by a context. With respect to the counter-intentionality of Jesus, it is very interesting that Marion turns to the figure of Jesus sketched in the Gospels, even as he wants to say that Jesus functions iconically. For in fact what he describes are incidents where, in his actions, Jesus cannot be understood: a trace removes us from constituting to witnessing, but witnessing we know not what. The exhortation to give every possession to the poor saturates intuition because it is impossible (who can give everything away and yet live?). And perhaps the "constituting regard" of Jesus saturates the intuition because in it there is a call that is not anything and which cannot be explained (who can respond to such a call?). Marion speaks of Jesus as the most perfect example of a saturated phenomenon. One way of interpreting Marion, however, would be to say not so much that Jesus (a person in space and time, or even the figure of an icon) is an example of a saturated phenomenon—since if he is considered in any way as a "counter-regard" then he has been to some extent constituted by an I—but that he occasions saturated phenomena where in his actions or in his attitude he opens upon the impossible. All that anyone has, all that the disciples had, are or were these marks of withdrawal which make no sense at all, which trace in a witness love or desire or fear or perhaps all three.

What has motivated this discussion is the problem of referring to transcendence. How can we think what cannot be thought? How can what utterly transcends thought enter thought without being betrayed, manna turned to refuse in the keeping? Marion suggests that phenomenology offers to us the possibility of thinking transcendence, because only phenomenology, he argues, begins without presupposition. Only phenomenology waits patiently for whatever gives itself to give. But as it has been pointed out, phenomenology is not entirely without its presuppositions. For all that the reduction does away with every precondition, it cannot ultimately do without a horizon and a constituting I, because it must reduce to what can be known. And where Marion maintains that it does do without these conditions, the phenomenology he practices has gone beyond phenomenology. In his figure of saturation, we have the perfect example of the positive failure of phenomenology. I say "positive," because that it fails is not in every respect a failure. Instead, the failure of phenomenology opens onto the greatest possibilities. But what exactly are these possibilities? Does the failure of phenomenology open onto theology? As far as I can judge, there is no better opening than this one. Theology can only begin in the failure of thought.[88] But at the same time, the theology that emerges from this opening cannot rest secure in dogma. If God were to give Godself in saturation, then how could that saturation be understood? Quite simply, words like "understood" would cease to have any meaning in the present. And failing in the present, we would be referred endlessly to traces of an immemorial past. Any "experience" of saturation would leave us only with the task of interpretation, an interpretation which could never be once and for all. Like worry beads in the pocket, the traces of saturation would remain only to be unceasingly turned over. That is not to deny that interpretation frequently occurs within the context of communities, and that there is a role for religious tradition in interpretation. But it is also to say that no interpretation will ever exhaust the event, and that any attempt to close meaning will betray what is affirmed in faith as revelation. The hardening of dogma betrays transcendence. Here I go well beyond what Marion has to say, although I pursue what seem to me to be the implicit conclusions of his thought of saturation.

I began this article by reflecting on the possibility of recognizing transcendence through a moment of love. I conclude by observing that such a movement can have no reason, that its signification must, for its own sake, rest on a hermeneutics of risk. With Marion, we can affirm that not all experience can be reduced to the dimensions of the knowing subject, that experience can exceed "experience," as it were. Derrida's name for this moment is aporia, that of Marion: icon, or saturated phenomenon. In neither are we given any more than sheer excess. A thought of transcendence is therefore possible, but only as the impossible, as that which will not yield a content or a determination but which, nevertheless, affects us. This is not, therefore, to insist on a theological truth, but simply to come up against the limits of knowing.

Notes

1. See my *Rethinking God as Gift: Marion, Derrida, and the Limits of Phenomenology* (New York: Fordham University Press, 2001), 66. This text was published subsequent to the initial draft of this article and expands on what is presented here.
2. Jacques Derrida, *Edmund Husserl's 'Origin of Geometry': An Introduction*, trans. John P. Leavey Jr. (Lincoln: University of Nebraska Press, 1989).
3. Jean-Luc Marion, *Réduction et Donation* (Paris: PUF, 1989), 235 [hereafter Marion, *RED*]. *Reduction and Givenness*, trans. Thomas A. Carlson (Evanston: Northwestern University Press, 1998), 157–158 [hereafter Marion, *RAG*]. All translations are mine unless otherwise indicated.
4. Marion, *RED*, 236; *RAG*, 158.
5. Marion, *RED*, 240; *RAG*, 161.
6. Marion, *RED*, 241. *RAG*, 161–162.
7. Marion, *RED*, 245–246. *RAG*, 164–165.
8. Marion, *RED*, 246–247; translation taken from *RAG*, 165.
9. And, in fact, saturated phenomena are simply at the higher end of all phenomena that, for Marion, are *self*-manifesting.
10. Marion, *RED*, 294–295; *RAG*, 196–197. These themes are also developed in Jean-Luc Marion, "Le sujet en dernier appel," *Revue de Metaphysique et de Morale* 96 (1991): 77–95; "The Final Appeal of the Subject," trans. Simon Critchley, in Simon Critchley and Peter Dews, *Deconstructive Subjectivities* (Albany, N.Y.: SUNY, 1996), 85–104.
11. Jean-Luc Marion, *Étant donné* (Paris: PUF, 1997) [hereafter Marion, *ED*]; *Being Given*, trans. Jeffrey L. Kosky (Stanford: Stanford University Press, 2002) [hereafter Marion, *BG*].
12. Dominique Janicaud, *Le tournant théologique de la phénoménologie française* (Combas, France: Éditions de l'éclat, 1991); *La phénoménologie éclatée* (Paris: L'éclat, 1998). The first of these texts has now been translated in Dominique Janicaud, Jean-François Courtine, Michel Henry, Jean-Luc Marion, and Paul Ricoeur, *Phenomenology and the 'Theological Turn': The French Debate* (New York: Fordham University Press, 2001).
13. Jacques Derrida, *Given Time: 1. Counterfeit Money*, trans. Peggy Kamuf (Chicago: University of Chicago Press, 1991), 50–52n.
14. *RED*, 298ff.; *RAG*, 196ff.
15. *RED*, 302; *RAG*, 202. Translation from *RAG*.
16. Jean-Luc Marion, "Réponses à quelques questions," *Revue de Métaphysique et de Morale* 96.1 (Janvier-Mars 1991): 65–76, 73 (my translation).
17. Jean-Luc Marion, "Le sujet en dernier appel," 95; "The Final Appeal of the Subject," 104.
18. For a more comprehensive examination of this dilemma, see my *Rethinking God as Gift*. See also Thomas A. Carlson's introduction to Jean-Luc Marion *The Idol and Distance: Five Studies*, trans. Thomas A. Carlson (New York: Fordham University Press, 2001) xi–xxxi. The translation will hereafter be referred to as Marion, *IDFS*.
19. Marion, *ED*, 259ff.; *BG*, 185ff.
20. See Edmund Husserl, *Ideas: General Introduction to Pure Phenomenology*, vol. 1, trans. W.R. Boyce Gibson (London: Allen and Unwin, 1972), for example at §27.

21. See the note by Heidegger's translators in *Being and Time*, trans. John Macquarrie and Edward Robinson (Oxford: Blackwell, 1962), 1n.
22. Marion, *ED*, 292; *BG*, 209.
23. Marion, *ED*, 293–296; *BG*, 209–212.
24. Jean-Luc Marion in "On the Gift: A Discussion between Jacques Derrida and Jean-Luc Marion, Moderated by Richard Kearney," *God, the Gift and Postmodernism*, ed. John D. Caputo and Michael J. Scanlon (Bloomington: Indiana University Press, 1999), 66.
25. And this is, in fact, suggested by Marion in the comment: "If, by contrast, its specificity is recognized, the bedazzlement it provokes would become phenomenologically acceptable, indeed desirable, and the passage from one horizon to another would become a rational task for the hermeneutic." Marion, *ED*, 296; *BG*, 211.
26. Jacques Derrida, *The Gift of Death*, trans. David Willis (Stanford: Stanford University Press, 1995) 98ff.
27. Elsewhere I do not capitalize Other when referring to Marion's usage. I am following the Levinasian convention here to be consistent with my translation of "From the Other to the Individual."
28. See, for example, "From the Other to the Individual": "In the debate of 1986, which remains famous, I took the chance of predicting to Emmanuel Levinas that he would have in the future to '. . . put ethics in second place, substituting the term "love".' To this audacity, which was a little abrupt, he responded in these terms: 'I am completely in agreement. I would like to add that "irreversible relation" suggests a relationship with diachrony. What does this relation signify? Or rather, from where does it gain its ground? At what moment? I know that it is not an intentionality, but it has a sense; and the reason why I say this word more easily, this word which is too beautiful or too pious or too vulgar . . . is because it signifies that the relation with the other, is the relation with the unique. I do not speak immediately of the unique one who commands [God?], I speak of the one who is the "object" of love: the Other, the unique, and thus the individual who is still part of a genus. It is even the only possibility for the unicity of concrete being. It is concrete in love.'"
29. Marion, *L'idole et la distance* (Paris: Grasset, 1977), 19–22 [hereafter Marion, *ID*]. See also *IDFS*, 7.
30. Marion, *ID*, 23–24; *IDFS*, 25. Where Paul names Christ the "icon of the invisible God," Marion explains, God the Father does not lose invisibility so much as become visible in transcendence.
31. Marion, *IS*, 15–16, 45ff. This is affirmed once again in *GWB* chapter two.
32. Marion, *ID*, 24–42; *IDFS*, 9–26.
33. Marion, *GWB*, 8.
34. Marion, *GWB*, 10, 17.
35. " . . . it represents nothing, but presents a certain low-water mark of the divine; it resembles what the human gaze has experienced of the divine." Marion, *GWB*, 14.
36. Marion, *GWB*, 17–29.
37. Jean-Luc Marion, "L'intentionalité de l'amour," *Prolegomènes à la charité*, 2ᵉ ed. (Paris: Editions de la Différence, 1986), 89–120; "The Intentionality of Love," *Prolegomena to Charity*, trans. Stephen Lewis (New York: Fordham, 2002), 71–101.
38. Jean-Luc Marion, *La croisée du visible* (1991; Paris: PUF, 1996), 101 [hereafter Marion, *CV*].
39. Marion, *CV*, 102. This is a very useful reading of Levinas on the face.
40. Marion, *CV*, 102.
41. Marion, *CV*, 103
42. Marion, *CV*, 110.
43. John Milbank, *The Word Made Strange* (Oxford: Blackwell, 1997), 38.
44. Milbank in effect prefers to admit a kind of metaphysics of objectivity, which seems strange in the light of his objection. See his discussion of the gift, "Can a Gift be Given?" in *Rethinking Metaphysics*, ed. L. Gregory Jones and Stephen E. Fowl (Oxford: Blackwell, 1995), 119–161, 130ff. Marion, on the other hand, maintains that the regard is invisible and so non-objectified.
45. Jean-Luc Marion, in private correspondence to Robyn Horner, June 14, 1999.
46. cf. Mt.25:40.
47. Marion, *CV*, 119–120.
48. Marion, *CV*, 127–129.
49. Marion, *CV*, 130ff.

50. Since the writing of this text, which was essentially completed early in 2001, the third book in Marion's phenomenological trilogy has been released: *De Surcroît: Etudes des phénomènes saturés* (Paris: Presses Universitaires de France, 2001), which has subsequently been translated as *In Excess: Studies of Saturated Phenomena*, trans. Robyn Horner and Vincent Berraud (New York: Fordham University Press, 2002).

51. Marion, *PS*, 79–80.

52. Marion, *PS*, 80. See also *ED*, 251ff.; *BG*, 179ff.

53. Marion, *PS*, 80–83; *ED*, 253–257; *BG*, 180–184.

54. Marion, *PS*, 83–84. Marion quotes what elsewhere he has listed as the third principle of phenomenology. See also *ED*, 257–258; *BG*, 184–185.

55. Marion, *PS*, 84–86; *ED*, 262–264; *BG*, 187–189.

56. Marion, *PS*, 86–88; *ED*, 259–262.; *BG*, 185–187.

57. Marion, *PS*, 88.

58. Marion, *PS*, 103; *ED*, 275–277. Marion's footnote on page 276 of *ED* (*BG*, 362n.37) is also instructive.

59. Marion, *PS*, 103; *ED*, 278; *BG*, 198.

60. Marion, *PS*, 104.

61. Marion, *PS*, 105.

62. Marion, *PS*, 105–121; *ED*, 280–305; *BG*, 199–219.

63. Marion observes, incidentally, that holiness blinds us to the One we cannot see without dying. *PS*, 110.

64. Marion, *PS*, 113.

65. Marion, *PS*, 116–118; *ED*, 289ff.; *BG*, 206ff.

66. Marion, *PS*, 119–121. For his discussion of modality in *ED*, see pp.296ff.; *BG*, 212ff.

67. Marion, *PS*, 121.

68. Marion, *PS*, 121. Marion elsewhere names this "me" "the interlocuted," or in *ED*, "*l'adonne*," "the gifted one" (this can also be read as "the devoted one" or "the one given over"). It is possible to hear religious resonances here.

69. Marion, *PS*, 122.

70. Marion, *PS*, 123–125; *ED*, 303–305; *BG*, 216–219.

71. Marion, *PS*, 124–125; *ED*, 305–309; *BG*, 219–221. While he considers it in the context of other authors, Graham Ward's analysis of the sublime and its theological implications is very pertinent here. "With Lyotard's (and Cixous's) examination of the 'present' or the 'event' we are brought again to the theology of the gift and the economy of mediated immediacy. The moment itself, for Lyotard, is without content. It is an encounter with nothingness . . . consequent upon a certain personal ascesis. . . . Karl Barth consistently emphasized that revelation was a mediated immediacy in which the hidden face of God was revealed." Graham Ward, *Theology and Contemporary Critical Theory* (Basingstoke, U.K.: Macmillan, 1996), 129.

72. Marion, *ED*, 314–317; *BG*, 225–228.

73. An historical event is something that cannot be limited to an instant, a place, or an empirical individual. He gives the example of Waterloo, where no one actually "saw" this battle as such. Its possible horizons are infinite in number. Marion, *ED*, 318–319; *BG*, 228–229.

74. The idol stops the gaze (and returns it to the viewer like a mirror). Marion gives the example of the painting, which gives itself without concept. Nevertheless, the idol is different from other saturated phenomena, because it provokes solipsism. Marion, *ED*, 319–321; *BG*, 229–31.

75. As we find in Levinas, Maurice Merleau-Ponty, and Michel Henry, flesh, or bodiliness, cannot be reduced to consciousness. Marion speaks of auto-affection, and the absolute experiences of agony, suffering, grief, desire, and orgasm such that they saturate the horizon. He further specifies bodily experience in two ways: first, it is unlike the idol but like the historical event, in that it isn't really about seeing; and second, it is unlike the historical event but like the idol, in that it provokes and demands solipsism. Further, it is my affections that make me identical to myself, which give me myself. Marion, *ED*, 321–323; *BG*, 231–232.

76. The icon contains within it the characteristics of the three preceding phenomena: it encompasses many horizons, it demands revisitation, and it dislodges the transcendental I. Marion, *ED*, 323–325; *BG*, 232–233.

77. Marion, *ED*, 323–324; *BG*, 232–233.

78. Marion, *ED*, 326–328; *BG*, 234–236.

79. In *PS*, Marion defines revelation phenomenologically as " . . . *une apparition purement de soi et à partir de soi . . .*", 127. Note the ambiguity with references to "revelation" and "Revelation"; in *Being Given* revelation is mentioned at 5, 235, 236, 241, 242, 243, 244, 245, 246, and 367n90, and Revelation at 4, 5, 141, 234, 242, 243, 246, and 367n90. This is an important point, along with the further redefinition of revelation in *In Excess*. My discussion here should be read in conjunction with the later article, "Aporia or Excess? Two Strategies for Thinking r/Revelation," to appear in *Other Testaments: Derrida and Religion*, ed. Kevin Hart and Yvonne Sherwood (London: Routledge, 2004).
80. Marion, *ED*, 327; *BG*, 235.
81. Marion, *ED*, 327–328; *BG*, 235–236.
82. Marion, *ED*, 329n; *BG*, 367n90.
83. Marion, *ED*, 328–331; *BG*, 236–237.
84. Marion, *ED*, 331–332; *BG*, 237–238. In his awareness that recognition of Christ as such cannot be borne, Marion seems to be in accord with the view that recognition comes only after the event, that is, immemorially. Elsewhere Marion describes the idol as that which reflects the gaze of the idolater.
85. Marion, *ED*, 332–334; *BG*, 238–240.
86. Marion, *ED*, 334–335; *BG*, 240–241.
87. Maurice Blanchot, *The Writing of the Disaster*, trans. Ann Smock (Lincoln: University of Nebraska Press, 1995), 2.
88. That is not to say, nevertheless, that it involves an absence of reason, or better, reasonableness, but this is another question.

6
Othello and the Horizon of Justice[1]

BY REGINA SCHWARTZ

I. Transcendent Justice

Among many other philosophers of religion, Levinas understands the content of the religions of the book to be not faith in an unseeable divinity or unforeseeable end, but acts of justice in daily life. "The realm of religion is neither belief, nor dogmatics, but event, passion, and intense activity."[2] These acts open onto eternity in a completely ethical understanding of transcendence. "Ethics is not simply the corollary of the religious but is, of itself, the element in which religious transcendence receives its original meaning."[3] For all of its association with transcendence, justice is also markedly immanent, for this justice assumes shape in the world, in social relations, in the intersubjective relation. "The dimension of the divine opens forth from the human face . . . It is our relations with men . . . that give theological concepts their only signification."[4] This is not an easy romanticism; to the contrary, the commitment to this understanding of justice is informed by a deep sense of the terrors of history. Levinas tells the story of Leon Blum who wrote in his prison camp that he could not accept that the judgment of his historical present, the triumph of Nazism, could prevail in the end: "A man in prison continues to believe in an unrevealed future and invites one to work in the present for the most distant things, of which the present is an irrefutable negation."[5] But we must not understand this "unrevealed future" as the entry of God into the world: "One only comes into relation with what is other, infinite and transcendent when we interact with another human being in their specificity."[6] Social justice is also transcendent in the sense that no experience gives rise to the idea of justice or confirms it: the good do not prosper for their goodness and evil is not defeated insofar as it is evil. Rather, the world shows itself to us so often as a battlefield of warring self-interests that the Hobbesian imaginary that presupposes this endless conflict has given rise to the various forms of contractual theory that have dominated liberal political theory ever since. Nonetheless, this craving for the simplest (and most difficult to achieve), notion of justice is at the core of religious sensibility.[7] This justice that is beyond economic, retributive, and absolute delimitations, whose only guarantor is transcendence, can be only registered paradoxically as utterly immanent, in human acts of goodness. Not a justice that controls a primordial war for scarce goods, this justice is figured as generous, an ever-flowing abundance: "But let justice roll down like waters, and righteousness like an ever-flowing stream" (Amos 5:21–24).

In the Hebrew Bible, justice breaks into immanence as revelation itself, the Law is the gift of justice. Because elsewhere the gap between justice and the law is so wide—in Christian theology which sees the Pharisaic law as inhibiting the realization of justice, in philosophy where from Plato on, law is formal and justice is substantive, in political theory, which includes those who endorse "procedural justice" for they have abandoned substantive justice, this biblical vision, when the law IS justice is arguably radical. In his work on justice, Derrida elaborates an aporia: the instability of the "distinction between justice and law, between justice (infinite, incalculable, rebellious to rule and foreign to symmetry, heterogeneous and heterotropic) on the one hand, and, on the other, the exercise of justice as law, legitimacy or legality, a stabilizable, statutory, and calculable apparatus [dispositif], a system of regulated and coded prescriptions."[8] He adds, "Everything would be simple if this distinction between justice and law were a true distinction, an opposition the functioning of which was logically regulated and masterable. But it turns out that law claims to exercise itself in the name of justice and that justice demands for itself that it be established in the name of a law that must be put to work (constituted and applied) by force "enforced."[9] But the biblical case defies the usual logic that would separate justice from law, the oft-noted importance of reserving a possibility of a justice that would exceed the law, contradict it, or even be indifferent to it. For here the justice so often believed to be beyond the law is also the justice of the law.[10]

In Deuteronomy, after Moses recounts the scene of the giving of the Law, he offers a powerful summary of the Law, one that affirms Levinas' insight that there is no prescriptive law in Judaism, indeed, that the only positive law is justice itself. What does this Law amount to? The Law requires fidelity to this law, to the Giver of this law, and issues prohibitions against false truths. Without this law, there can be no justice. Next, it forbids abusing others: do not murder another, do not steal from him, and do not slander him—that is kill him with words. Moses continues, ". . . Circumcise your heart then and be obstinate no longer, for your God is never partial, cannot be bribed [his justice will not be overridden to serve some group's self-interest]. It is he who sees justice done for the orphan and the widow, who loves the stranger and gives him food and clothing. Love the stranger then, for you were strangers in the land of Egypt" (Deut 10:12–20, emphasis added).

No circumcision of the mere flesh—no markers of identity—will suffice: the heart must be circumcised. Justice is not an external allegiance, but an interiorized commitment. Jeremiah presses on this demand: "See, the days are coming—it is Yahweh who speaks—when I am going to punish all who are circumcised only in the flesh . . ." (Jer 9:25–26). Paul, then, does not innovate, does not add good news to Judaism when he says "To be a Jew is not just to look like a Jew, and circumcision is more than a physical operation. The real Jew is the one who is inwardly a Jew, and the real circumcision is in the heart— something not of the letter but of the spirit" (Romans 2:28–29). This much was already firmly part of the understanding of the revealed justice: "Circumcise yourself for Yahweh; off with the foreskin of your hearts (men of Judah and inhabitants of Jerusalem) lest my wrath should leap out like a fire . . . in return for the wickedness of your deeds." (Jer, 4:4). As Paul understood, "It is not listening to the Law but keeping it that will make people holy in the sight of God" (Rom. 2:13).

The biblical case is radical in another sense, in its understanding of authority: the force of the law is executed, in this narrative, on those who are in the very process of receiving it, but have not yet. Still, they are accountable to the law. In this sense, even before it is offered and hence can be accepted or violated, it is utterly impossible to reject. The law can be broken; but it cannot be refused. The entry of justice alters the social sphere conclusively. Like Alain Badiou's truth-event, it breaks disruptively, unpredictably, into the given in all of its irreducible, incommunicable singularity, beyond all conventional understanding, "An eventual fidelity is a real break (both thought and practiced) in the specific order within which the event took place. Break because what enables the truth-process—the event—meant nothing according to the prevailing language and established knowledge of the situation."[11] Once it is given, there is no way to be outside of this (divine) justice. To follow another option is to make a golden calf, to worship an idol, to live unjustly. The command that signals the radical entry of the law and justice to the social order is not incidental: the prohibition against idols is given pride of place. This God cannot be ontologized to bolster a substantial identity; this God cannot be hijacked to authorize the purposes of a community. In this scheme, if the biblical name for justice is revelation, then the biblical name for injustice is idolatry.

Fidelity to this revelation proves to be difficult: the first response, according to the narrative, is enthusiastic, "all the people said with one voice, 'All that he has spoken we will do, we will obey.'" (Ex 24:3, 7). Levinas points out that "the term here that evokes obedience ['we will do'] is anterior to that which expresses understanding ['we will listen'], and in the eyes of the Talmudic scholars is taken to be the supreme merit, the wisdom of an angel . . . This obedience cannot be reduced to a categorical imperative in which a universality is suddenly able to direct a will. It is an obedience, rather, which can be traced back to the love of one's neighbor . . . a love that is obeyed. . . ."[12] The only thing close to a "positive law" offered in the revelation, as it is recounted in Ex. 34, is "do not boil a kid in its mother's milk." Do not deal death with what gives life. Surely here, condensed in that magnificent metaphor, is that difficult concept: "a love to be obeyed."

But subsequently, when the Israelites betray the event of the revelation, it is in every sense Badiou enumerates: disavowal, as if nothing had happened, false imitation of the event, and an ontologization of the event, reducing it to a new positive order of being. They doubt the validity of the event, murmuring, "is God with us or not?"; they reduce their emancipation to the material god of a substantial people: "having made themselves a calf of molten metal and worshipped it, they said 'Here is your God, Israel, who brought you up from the land of Egypt!'" But when Moses demands fidelity to the Revelation of justice, only that fidelity—not substantialist identity—will suffice: "whoever is for the Lord," he says, "come to me . . . kill one his brother, another his friend, and another his companion." Belonging offers no exemption.

Ever since Hobbes, contemporary political theory has taken refuge in the notion that it is law—and not justice—that offers a true universal. Substantive justice is particular, contingent, culturally specific. And because one culture's notion of justice is so different from that of another culture, their differences can only be adjudicated through law. Only law, in the sense of procedures, offers a formal universal. Stuart Hampshire has recently offered a very clear expression of this: "Justice and fairness in substantial matters, as in the distribution of goods or in the payment of penalties for a crime, will always vary with varying moral outlooks and with varying conceptions of the good. Because there will always be conflicts between conceptions of the good . . . , there is everywhere a well-recognized need for procedures of confliction resolution . . . This is the place of a common rationality of method."[13] Hobbes unmasks that the embrace of the universalism of procedure is grounded, not just in conflicting notions of the good, but more fundamentally, in the state of endless war over scarce goods, with the contract the constraining effort to impose peace on this warring state of nature, but of course Hobbes understands that because the contract is artificial and fragile, it ultimately requires the enforcement of totalitarianism: "it is no wonder if there be somewhat else required (besides covenant) to make their agreement constant and lasting; which is a common power, to keep them in awe, and to direct their actions to the common benefit. The only way to erect such a common power . . . is to confer all their power and strength on one man, or upon one assembly of men, that may reduce all of their wills, by plurality of voices, to one will . . . And he that carrieth this person, is called SOVEREIGN, and is said to have sovereign power, and every one besides, his SUBJECT."[14] Once justice is emptied; the reign of law becomes a reign of terror. Can we so confidently distinguish this totalitarianism from the monotheism offered in Exodus? Perhaps not confidently, but our task, it seems to me, is to understand the relation between these monotheisms: the instrumental one of particular identity and the universal one of justice. Are they two sides of the same coin? Must they necessarily go hand in hand? Is one, the monotheism of justice, only a mystification produced by the other—of exclusive identity? Is the "unjust" only the name given to the abhorred infidel? Or is there another dynamic at work here that the biblical narrative captures, a constant threat of a relapse from fidelity to transcendent justice to the graven images, the idols of identity and procedure.

To do the work of making the distinction between universal procedure and substantive justice, between "strict" justice—economic, retributive—and transcendent justice, requires more effort, for the temptations of a formal universal are obviously great and the risks that attend a justice of substance even greater—after all, whose justice? Why this version of justice? Levinas offers a radical corrective to the procedural justice embraced by so much political theory. "Justice cannot be reduced to the order it institutes or restores, nor to a system whose rationality commands, without difference, men and gods, revealing itself in human legislation like the structures of space in the theorems of geometricians, a justice that a Montesquieu calls the 'logos of Jupiter', recuperating religion within this metaphor, but effacing precisely transcendence. In the justice of the Rabbis, difference [between man and God] retains its meaning. Ethics is not simply the corollary of the religious but is, of itself, the element in which religious transcendence receives its original meaning."[15] But while Levinas is eager to substitute procedural justice with transcendent justice, it is only to understand this transcendence as radically immanent. This is why the law is most radically realized when it is interiorized, as in the stirring vision of Jeremiah where the covenant is written on the heart:

> "The time is coming," declares the Lord, "when I will make a new covenant with the house of Israel and with the house of Judah. It will not be like the covenant I made with their forefathers when I took them by the hand to lead them out of Egypt, because they broke my covenant . . . This is the covenant I will make with the house of Israel after that time," declares the Lord, "I will put my law in their minds and write it on their hearts. I will be their God, and they will be my people. No longer will a man teach his neighbor or a man his brother, saying, 'Know the Lord', because they will all know me, from the least of them to the greatest." (Jer 31:31)

When the preoccupation with identity and possession "I will be your God if you will be my people" is replaced with interiorized justice, "Then I will be their God and they will be my people," the vision seems to move, albeit subtly and tentatively, from a conditional threat of terror to an unconditional promise, from the idols of identity that exclude to the law's demand for universal justice.

Rejecting the universals of procedural or formal justice, Levinas offers his most succinct enunciation when he says, "Justice itself is born of charity. They can seem alien when they are presented as successive stages; in reality, they are inseparable and simultaneous . . ."[16] As such, justice must hold institutions of justice to account, and as they are answerable to justice, so justice is answerable to love: "Love must always watch over justice." Here the affinity with negative theology becomes apparent: interiorization of justice, emphasis on charity and love, transcendence made immanent. Levinas distrusts mysticism, but my own sense is that this is because he, like many, was reducing mysticism to the ecstatic experience of complete combining, rather than heeding the rigors of the negative theology that eschews nomination, predication, and substantiation. In my work on the sacramental and the secular during the early modern period, I have observed that when a concept of community is not infused with the mystical, it descends quickly into substantialism. When, for instance, the mystical character of transubstantiation was compromised during the Reformation, what was left, to be inherited by the state, was the "substantiation" without the "trans," which took the form of nationalism, called upon to take the place of the eucharistic community, the body of Christ. The command against graven images is, in the end, a mystical command, a mystical law, a mystical and interiored justice. Its God cannot be named, cannot be possessed, delimited, and so cannot be instrumentalized as either belonging or not belonging to the group, and so subjecting them and their brothers to the curse of Cain.[17]

And yet, because so much of humankind is unjust, the just will suffer. In his commentary, "Loving the Torah more than God," Levinas engages an anonymous text that offers itself as a document written during the final hours of the Warsaw Ghetto resistance by one "Yossel, son of Yossel."[18] Doubts flow from his agony: "What can this suffering of the innocents mean? Is it not proof of a world without God, where only man measures Good and Evil?" But these "murmurings" take a very different turn from the generation lost in the wilderness. Instead of betraying the revelation in the midst of this horror, "Yossel, son of Yossel experiences the certainly of God with a new force, beneath an empty sky." Levinas reads the empty sky as the opportunity for a full conscience: "if he is so alone, it is in order to take upon his shoulders the whole of God's responsibilities." An absent God becomes most immanent internally: "this God Who hides His face and abandons the just man to a justice that has no sense of triumph, this distant God, comes from within," from the intimacy of one's conscience.[19] Empty sky, full conscience. In Derrida's own version of this interiorized justice, this transcendence made immanent, he notes the paradox that "the inaccessible transcendence of the law [loi], before which and prior to which man stands fast, only appears infinitely transcendent and thus theological to the extent that, nearest to him, it depends only on him, on the performative act by which he institutes it: . . . The law is transcendent and theological, and so always to come, always promised, because it is immanent, finite, and thus already past."[20]

One can infer that Jesus understood the revelation of Law as justice when he asserted: "Do not imagine that I have come to abolish the Law or the Prophets. I have come not to abolish but to complete them." While Paul can, on occasion, reduce the transcendent justice of the ancient Israelites to mere legalism, to Pharisaism, Jesus typically embraces the demand of justice differently, not only insisting that it must be fulfilled, but also seeing his own death as part of that process. Is his death economic, a vengeful retribution, an exaction of strict justice by the father? Anselm's theory of atonement in Cur Deus Homo has been read and undoubtedly misread that way by many Protestant liberal theologians. But nothing can "pay off" the human failure of rejecting God's gift of justice; nothing makes it right. Genesis Rabbah says about the justice of God: When Abraham addressed his plea to God, "Shall not the Judge of all the earth do justly?" The meaning of his words was: If You desire the world to continue there cannot be strict justice; if you insist on strict justice, the world cannot endure (Gen R. xxxix. 6). As an infinite wrong, that failure would call for an infinite restitution, and man is only finite. In this sense, sin, and for that matter, salvation are necessarily outside of any economy. Rather than paying a debt, the theology of the Incarnation suggests that what is needed is for the gift of justice to be given again, and that is done by God becoming man. God took on humanity so that mankind could have access again to the image of God as he was made, a demonstration of how to restore that lost image, how to act justly. This logic is not the same as the imputation to fallen man of the merits of Christ; it depends instead upon the ethical acts of men imitating those of Jesus. This emphasis on the example is what the eastern fathers wanted to preserve against what they perceived as a western overemphasis on the penal understanding of atonement that reduces it to "the status of a simple transaction, enacted more or less entirely on the cross, and intended solely as an appeasement of the Father's wrath against sin . . . with its unrelenting concentration of the language of penal suffering and remissions from debt."[21]

But if western religious thought in contexts as various as Moses and Jesus, Anselm and Levinas struggles to imagine humanity grasping for justice, how is that preoccupation felt in cultural formations that are less explicitly theological? There is something unbearable about Iago's triumph in Shakespeare's Othello, but where does this that injustice is unbearable come from? Where does the impossible expectation that injustice will end, or the corollary belief— that the triumph of evil must mean the world is out of joint and that eventually it will be righted—come from? I would argue that not only does each act of justice open onto eternity, as Levinas argues; furthermore, the human craving for justice that impels each act is transcendent. Where there is a check upon naked self-interest, relentless aggrandizement, sheer grasping of power, it comes—not from some contractual understanding that our will cannot be done without compromise with the other, some balancing of our freedoms as in Hegel's critique—but from some other-worldly desire to make the world a just place, that is, to partner the creation by securing it through acts of justice. In Othello, this craving for justice becomes particularly painful in part because it is brought into relief precisely in the context of the other justices, economic and retributive, strict and absolute, that triumph disastrously over transcendent justice.

II. The Mass and the Theater

On Sundays in early modern England, when plays could not be performed presumably because they would draw their audience from would-be church goers, Shakespeare and his contemporaries could attend church, a service made uniform by the Book of Common Prayer, a service that represented one hundred and fifty years of conflict and compromise, a service whose forms and meanings had racked Christendom, creating a new religion and a new English church out of controversies in which pens flowed and heads rolled. Among other changes, Reformers sought to dispel the opus operatum—that work through which the Church could be the sacramental organ of the salvation offered by Christ—by their doctrine of faith alone. All of the concerns of the Reformation came into sharp focus over the Mass, marking a sea change from the pre-modern to the early modern world: what was at stake in these debates was not only the obvious issue of redemption, but also the relation of matter to spirit, the visible to the invisible, the universal to the particular, the self to the other, language to its referent, and how and where power is vested: the authority of scripture, of the inner Spirit, of the priesthood, of the church, and by extension, of civil government. On one end of the spectrum of the Reformation controversies over the Eucharist was the Reformers' objection to the material ingestion of Christ and their charge that transubstantiation was tantamount to cannibalism: "thy teeth shall not do him violence, neither thy stomach contain his glorious body. By faith he is seen, by faith he is touched, by faith, he is digested."[22] At the other end was the Catholic fear of losing communion with God altogether, of divinity and humanity locked in a tragic separation that left man wallowing in his sin: "in believing in Christ by faith—which is but an apprehension of the understanding—we do no more really eate the body of Christ than doth the hungrye man his dinner when he apprehendeth and desireth it but cannot have it."[23]

The theater made no claims to perform work; the theater was not trying to effect transformations. The theater cannot do anything to other humans, nor can it offer anything to God. But ironically, it was the Reformer's very insistence on the representation of the sacrifice, rather than the recurrence of the event itself, that brought the character of the Mass closer to the theatre—with its representations of events rather than events themselves. In this way, the Elizabethan theater becomes a space where a community recalls, represents, and remembers sacrifice, but does not perform it. And so if, in one sense, the obvious one, the Elizabethan theater competed with the Mass; in another, deeper sense, it replaced it, becoming the first truly Reformed church.[24]

With "sola fides" as its watchword, much of Reformation theology belies a deep distrust of the senses. Faith is "the evidence of things unseen, the substance of things hoped for." This invisible truth is both profoundly immanent—lodged in the inner Spirit—and transcendent—the God beyond the visible. "Lies" are very often defined as sensory illusions. Cranmer complained of the Catholic

Mass: "is not in the ministration of the holy communion an illusion of our sense, if our senses take for bread and wine that whiche is not so indeed?" Reformers accused priests of creating illusions that they wanted to be taken as reality, that is, they accused them of fraud. And even as anti-Catholic propagandists pejoratively referred to the Mass as fraudulent, they inflicted the same charge on the theatre. Anti-theatrical prejudice found common cause with anti-popery, equating ritual with magic, magic with the theatre, and all of them with lies. "In Stage Playes for a boy to put on the attyre, the gesture, the passions of a woman; for a meane person to take upon him the title of a Prince with counterfeit porte, and traine, is by outward signes to shewe themselves otherwise than they are, and so within the compasse of a lye."[25] This pseudo-Platonic equation of lies with the senses and truth with the invisible is fraught with difficulties. A less debased understanding, one less dependent upon crude binary distinctions between the visible and invisible, would issue in very different valuations: the Mass could provide access to truth and the theatre could be a storehouse of truths. Indeed, even Reformers understood the sacraments as the "seal" of faith, and the most common Renaissance theory of drama was that it offered an image of actual life: "the purpose of playing . . . was and is to hold as 'twere a mirror up to nature."[26] If the theatre could not fulfill the religious craving for justice, it could and did express that craving with stunning eloquence. Whether or not it was "the purpose of playing," it was the power of performance.

If by the late Middle Ages the traditional church rites had, for some, begun to lose some of their former power, one reason was that these rites were perceived to be on a collision course with ethics.[27] Whether the strains of Protestantism indebted to Luther stressed that only faith, through Christ's merit, can ground ethics, or with Calvin emphasized the discipline of the Church, or like Zwingli focused on communal responsibility, all inveighed against the perceived "abuses" of clergy and liturgy—not with secular skepticism, but with the fury of moral indignation. The theatre also addressed this felt need for a moral order, differently, but perhaps as effectively as the church. At precisely the time when the theatre was under attack for fostering immorality and that the rituals of Catholicism were under scrutiny for their "falsity and hollowness," the theatre was reaching its apex: the old Senecan version of revenge tragedy flowered into Elizabethan moral tragedy, that is, into a tragedy of injustice. Because it was the work of propaganda to equate ritual with theater and both with lies, we might do well, for all of their affinities, to regard the equation as deeply suspect. Ritual is not "mere theater" in the sense of false, nor for its part, does theater claim the function of a sacrament. When I understand Shakespeare as "religious," then, it is not because his actors satisfied or did not satisfy longings for magic acts, but because he repeatedly addressed the problem, in his way, that the sacrament also addressed in its way: justice.

When sacraments figured among the important resources he called upon from the stage business of life, Shakespeare turned them to an ethical purpose.

For his audience, a spotted handkerchief in Othello would allude not only to a marriage bed, to virginity and fidelity, but also to a spotted altar-cloth, ocular proof of Christ's miraculous gift of his broken and bleeding body in the Eucharist. Such cloths were relics in Catholic Europe, testimonies to the miracle of the bleeding host. Through lenses that empty it of this sacramental significance, the spotted cloth in Othello becomes a heathenish cloth in which magic, not God, was woven. But that reading is incomplete, for the handkerchief also becomes ocular "proof" of a betrayal that never occurred, a piece of false testimony used to indict the innocent wrongfully. So if the reference to the religious ritual has been "emptied out," Shakespeare has re-filled it.[28] If Shakespeare has "given up on religion," as C.L. Barbar depicts him as having done, surely he has not given up on justice. It is the imaginary that has such a deep hold on his plays that they scarcely can make sense without it. How could we understand Lear as suffering? Hamlet as tormented? Macbeth as guilt-ridden? But where some critics speak of disappointed expectations in tones of lament, I celebrate the remarkable expectation itself—precisely where he is discouraged, I locate hope. The very frustration of redemption is the way theatre performs its moral vision. And this craving for redemption is not a sign that religion is "emptied"; this craving is itself religious. Emptied of its sacral significance, sacrifice is meaningless killing, but Shakespeare does not have meaningless deaths in his tragedy. Like the spotted handkerchief, they are not just emptied, but re-filled—with moral outrage—and more.

III. Murder and Sacrifice

Much of the Reformation was spent negotiating two different meanings of death, as murder and as sacrifice. Whether a death is viewed as an act of murder or an act of sacrifice depends entirely on how it is culturally framed, but in both cases, its definition is usually at the service of some idea of economic justice. Death framed as a sacrifice is most often understood as a gift to a deity, as appeasing his ire for our wrongdoing: "sacrifice" compensates, pays back, recompenses. When the gift offered is pure, chaste, unadulterated, without sin, it compensates for the impure, tainted, adulterated, sinful nature of man. Divine justice is understood to be satisfied by this retribution: "Die he or justice must," as Milton's God puts it in Paradise Lost. Sacrifice is also substitutive and metonymic: the individual dies for the community, on behalf of the community, as Christ dies for mankind. Murder is framed very differently: far from satisfying the demands of justice, murder violates them, and its object is not heroically embracing or stoically accepting destruction; it is an unwilling victim. In murder, the emphasis shifts away from the community to the individual whose death does not satisfy collective justice, but whose murder threatens collective peace. Hence, a different retributive justice comes into play: not the substitutive redemption offered by sacrifice, but the collective apparatus of the law. In that system, murder does not satisfy justice; it cries out for satisfaction.

During the Reformation, as reinterpretations of the ritual of the Eucharist occurred, the relation between sacrifice and murder—and their relation to justice—was also revisited. When Reformers altered participating in the material godhead through transubstantiation to representing God, merit was conferred on undeserving man by Christ's sacrifice "as if" the communicant were also sacrificed; that is, merit was imputed to man for something he did not endure and for a gift he did not give. In the process, the satisfaction of justice and gift of mercy were radically redefined. Retribution was further inflected by two important changes in the theological climate. First, in the eucharistic controversies over sacrifice, agency came to fore: priests were accused of presuming to act as sacrificer, offering Christ at the altar. For its part, Catholicism never claimed that the priest was the sacred executioner, only that he was the means through which Christ repeated his sacrifice of himself, but Reformers, eager to reduce the power of the priesthood, claimed that the agency of the priest was, at best, irrelevant, at worst, idolatrous, for man could not offer God—only God could offer himself. For Luther, the church and its priesthood had no agency in the economy of grace. "Once the Mass has been overthrown, I say we'll have overthrown the whole of Popedom." And so he insisted that the Lord's Supper was only a promise and a testament. "God does not deal, nor has he dealt with man in any way other any than by the word of his promise. So too we can never have dealing with God in any other way than by faith in that word of promise." Distinguishing the Catholic Mass from the Reformed Holy Supper, Calvin explained that, "here is as much difference between this sacrifice and the sacrament as there is between giving and receiving. And such is the most miserable ungratefulness of man that where he ought to have recognized and given thanks for the abundance of God's bounty, he makes God in this his debtor!"[29]

Thomas Cranmer opens his "Defence of the True and Catholic Doctrine of the Sacrament" (1550) with a preface in which he takes pains to distinguish the reformed (that is, original and true) understanding of the Eucharist from the (he thinks) misguided direction it had taken in Rome:

> Our Saviour Christ Jesus according to the will of his eternal Father . . . made a sacrifice and oblation of his own body upon the cross, which was a full redemption, satisfaction, and propitiation, for the sins of the whole world . . . [H]e hath ordained a perpetual memory of his said sacrifice, daily to be used in the Church to his perpetual laud and praise . . . But the Romish Antichrist, to deface this great benefit of Christ, hath taught that his sacrifice upon the cross is not sufficient hereunto, without another sacrifice devised by him, and made by the priest, or else without indulgences, beads, pardons, pilgrimages, and such other pelfry, to supply Christ's imperfection: and that Christian people cannot apply to themselves the benefits of Christ's passion, but that the same is in the distribution of the Bishop of Rome . . .

His concluding response to this assessment is not subtle: "O heinous blasphemy . . . O wicked abomination . . . O pride intolerable . . . For he that taketh upon him to supply that thing, which he pretendeth to be unperfect in Christ, must needs make himself above Christ, and so very Antichrist."[30] Only God could perform a sacrifice. Men perform a murder. To underscore the point, Cranmer returns to what he deems this greatest of offenses at the beginning of Book V of his Defence: it is not transubstantiation nor is it a failure to embrace double predestination, it is presuming to repeat the sacrifice. "The greatest blasphemy and injury that can be against Christ, and yet universally used through the popish kingdom, is this, that the priests make their Mass a sacrifice propitiary, to remit the sins as well of themselves as of other, both quick and dead, to whom they apply the same."[31] Cranmer claimed that the doctrines of the Defence were reflected in the 1549 Book of Common Prayer and we can discern that even as it went through its contested emendations and revisions over the language of the real presence, this much—that the sacrifice occurred once and is now only commemorated in the Lord's Supper—remained unchanged: there are no offertory prayers; the Secret Prayers, offering-prayers that refer to the munus, oblatio, sacrificium, hostia, and mysterium have been eliminated. This distinction between divine and priestly agency was reflected in the careful wording of the Book of Common Prayer (1559): "And although we be unworthy through our manifold sins to offer unto thee any Sacrifice: yet we beseech thee to accept this our bounden duty and service, not weighing our merits but pardoning our offences..Amen."[32] Reading the sacramental logic unsympathetically produced a contradiction unknown to the Roman church: if the act is repeated, then the original must be incomplete, and conversely, if the original were complete, any repetition becomes superfluous.

This harsh emphasis on remembrance alone was somewhat softened, as became evident in the sacred treatment of the wine and bread. John Jewel's understanding of the Eucharist was close to Cranmer's with the exception of his regard for the elements; the bread and the wine needed to be set aside, consecrated, in order to fulfill their sacramental function: "We affirm that bread and wine are holy and heavenly mysteries of the body and blood of Christ, and that by them Christ himself, being the true bread of eternal life, is so presently given unto us that by faith we verily receive his body and blood" (emphasis added).[33] Richard Hooker's "real receptionist" understanding of the Eucharist enunciated in his Ecclesiastical Polity kept the sacramental emphasis on participation: "The fruit of the Eucharist is the participation in the body and blood of Christ."[34] "This bread hath in it more than the substance which our eyes behold, this cup hallowed with solemn benediction availeth ... what these elements are in themselves it skilleth not, it is enough that to me which take them they are the body and blood of Christ."[35] After the accession of James I (provoking the Millenary Petition, and the Hampton Court Conference which ultimately issued in the King James Bible and the Canons of 1604), church doctrine inched closer to asserting the vital importance of the bread and wine—almost, but not quite as an offering of sacrifice—reflected in the felt need to legislate, without precedent, the consecration not only of the bread and wine, but if that supply is supplemented, even the added bread and wine must be consecrated (canon 21). For all of the Reformers' rhetoric against the "grievous error" of making an offering, by 1604, they had rejected it in doctrine far more definitively than in ritual. Nonetheless, that same year, the stage could offer a clearer—more or less satisfying?—sacrifice, of Desdemona, whose name includes the daimon of sacrifice.

Reformers were not only disturbed by the problem of agency in sacrifice; they were also clearly uncomfortable with its materiality, preferring to speak of spiritual eating and drinking instead of the literal body and blood of God: "Take and eat this, in remembrance that Christ died for thee, and feed on him in thy heart by faith, with thanksgiving."[36] When they denied the material body in the Mass, to substitute a seal of the promise of faith, they were implicitly putting the meaning of death— as sacrifice—at risk. Foreseeing the problem, Calvin was careful to claim that the sacrament's meaning depends wholly on the body of God having been sacrificed: "It must be carefully noted that the most conspicuous, indeed almost the whole power of the sacrament resides in these words, 'which is given for you,' . . . 'which is shed for you.' For otherwise is would be of no avail that the body and blood of the Lord should be administered, had they not once for all been sacrificed for our redemption and salvation" (emphasis added, Inst. IV, 17,3).[37] His anxiety is palpable. For with the sacrifice remembered rather than repeated, how can justice be effectively satisfied, the debt paid? What is remembered is the suffering of Christ—but is this a murder victim or a sacrificial victim? The economy of retribution is unsettled and unsettling.

Surely something profound was lost when Reformers gave up the sacrifice of the Eucharist, or, to be more precise, turned it into a commemoration of a sacrifice rather than a reenactment, a commemoration of a moment in the distant past rather than a sacrifice that occurs at the very moment when the communicant ingests the host, a moment when suffering is redeemed, a mysterious moment when our depravity is absolved. Gabriel Biel was one of the most widely read authorities on the Mass at the time of the Reformation—seven editions of his Exposition of the Sacred Canon of the Mass were printed between 1488 and 1547; even Luther said it was the best Catholics possessed on the subject—and he summarizes well what was at stake in the loss of the Mass.

> In this sacrifice there is the commemoration of and calling on that unique and perfect sacrifice by which heaven was opened, grace is given, through which alone our works can be meritorious, through which alone all the sin of men are remitted, and heavenly glory, lost by our sin, is restored . . . (Lectio LVII, lit. D)[38]

During most of Christian history, that work of redemption can occur during the Mass because the sacrifice of Christ was both then and now, because ritual temporality is not simply or strictly linear. Although Christ was offered but once in the natural appearance of his flesh, nevertheless he is offered daily on the altar, veiled under the appearances of bread and wine. This offering of him does not, of course, entail any suffering, for Christ is not wounded, does not suffer and die each day [this distinction came to be known as the bloody and unbloody sacrifices of the Lord.] But this consecration and reception of the Eucharist is called a sacrifice and an oblation for these two reasons: "first, because it represents that true sacrifice and holy immolation made once upon the cross, and is its memorial; secondly, because it is a cause through which similar effects are produced."

How frail "faith" must have felt before the power of rituals, before the sacrifice of the God-man that satisfied justice from the Gospels to Luther. Having dispelled the opus operatum, the Reformers threatened to dispel the sacramental organ of salvation, the means for incarnating Christ within each communicant to enable his redemption. With the English Church's reluctance to offer sacramental deterrence and sacramental remission of sins—that is, sacramental justice—the scene shifted inevitably to the court where evil was fought judicially and, as we have seen, to the theatre where evil was fought imaginatively. If sin was a matter for demonstration, for evidence, as it was for Othello as his madness deepened, it also became a means for evoking moral outrage (tragedy) or envisioning moral order (comedy), and so theatre became its forum. When the Reformers had replaced the Church's transformation with representation and its sacrifice with remembrance, they had left themselves less the power of ritual than (ironically, given its opposition to theatre) the catharsis of spectacle. And while the playwright is no priest, he can represent sacrifice and like his Reformed competitors (the Church had to close the theatres on Sundays to ensure its attendance), through that representation he can invite his audience to receive a grace he cannot give through a faith he cannot confer. Not only because Reformers foregrounded representation were they were unwittingly closer to the theatre they so severely critiqued, but also because they too evinced the moral outrage—the craving for justice rather than its satisfaction—that became the deep structure of the Reformed ritual.

IV. Othello and Justice

I discern a crisis over the distinction between sacrifice and murder in Othello, and will glean allusions to the sacrifice of the Eucharist from the play, not to assert that Shakespeare is more or less Catholic or Protestant, nor to establish his position on the controversy that raged in his day over the Eucharist, but to demonstrate that Othello is a play that evokes longing for justice, longing, that is, for some antidote to the rhetoric of devils and hell that fill the stage, some redressing of the fiendish rituals of murderous vows, blasphemous oaths, and monstrous births of plots engendered by hell and night, invocations of whores and sorcerers, and the triumph of a deadly design that unravels as relentlessly as a providential one—but is so antithetical to providence that is springs from one who inverts the divine name, turning the tetragrammaton of Exodus 3, "I am who I am," into "I am not what I am," thereby setting sin loose upon the world. In a play where the tempter embraces divinity as surely as Milton's Satan does: "divinity of hell . . . So I will turn her virtue into pitch, and out of her own goodness make the net that shall enmesh them all"; "If then his Providence/Out of our evil seek to bring forth good,/Our labor must be to pervert that end,/And out of good still to find means of evil" Paradise Lost I: 162–165—it seems especially terrible that the other shoe does not fall, that infernal ends are not frustrated to bring good out of evil. Desdemona has precisely that intention. When Emilia has just described to her a world in which wrongdoing issues in wrongdoing—"the ills we do their ills instruct us so"—Desdemona objects, "God me such usage send, Not to pick bad from bad, but by bad mend!" Mend, amend, make amends, redemption: Desdemona has articulated her intent to turn evil to good with stunning emphasis at the end of Act IV but that is just before, disturbingly enough, we see evil triumph and Desdemona undone.

Shakespeare challenges us to re-think these differences between a sacrifice and a murder, and further, to re-think their relation to justice. In his tragedies, acts of violence seem to hint toward redemption, but it is not clear that Desdemona's death redeems. Can we see her death as a sacrifice? A remission of sins? A benefit to others? A satisfaction of the demands of retributive justice? Othello himself wants to stage it that way. The murderous Othello stages his "sacrifice" of Desdemona like a priest at the altar and before he kills her, delivers the injunction to confess derived from the communion service: "If you bethink yourself of any crime, Unreconciled as yet to heaven and grace, Solicit for it straight." He tries to stage a ritual death. It is marked by prayers:

Oth. I would not kill thy unprepared spirit, No, heaven forfend, I would not kill thy soul.
Des. Talk you of killing?
Oth. Ay, I do.
Des. Then Lord have mercy on me.
Oth. Amen, with all my heart!

And, in the role of priest, he would extract her confession:

Oth. Therefore confess thee freely of thy sin
    For to deny each article with oath
    Cannot remove, nor shake the strong conceit
    That I do groan withal: thou art to die.
Des. Then Lord have mercy on me.
Oth. I say, Amen.

But this is a perverse priest, for the final prayer that would assure Desdemona's redemption is silenced by Othello:

Des. Kill me tomorrow, let me live to-night . . .

> But half an hour, but while I say one prayer.
> *Oth.* Tis too late.

Othello's carefully orchestrated sacrifice quickly turns into a vengeful murder, as even he admits.

> *Oth.* O perjur'd woman, thou dost stone thy heart
> And makest me call what I intend to do
> A murder, which I had thought a sacrifice.

He has come to her as a divine executor of justice: "vengeance is mine," saith the Lord; "it is the cause" says Othello, bearing the terrible mission of strict justice and retribution: "else she'll betray more men." The performative confusion of Desdemona crying out to the Lord and Emilia crying "My Lord" seems to lure Othello himself into ontological confusion about his divine mission: "I that am cruel, am yet merciful," he pronounces like an Old Testament deity who punishes the hardened heart, but also like the New Testament father who demands the life of his Son. But wait: he is murdering all the while, stifling Desdemona's breath even as he invokes mercy. Is this sacrifice or murder? If sacrifice, it should redeem and indeed Othello alludes to the eclipse and earthquake that marked Christ's death. But none happen. He expects to see cloven hooves on the devil Iago—but has to admit it is only a myth. And so his pretensions to being the divine judge soon collapse and he assumes another role: the betrayer of divinity. No longer God the Father demanding retribution for sin, Othello becomes the Judas who betrays his master. Amidst his confused assertions of justice, Othello virtually confesses that he has sold her:

> nay, had she been true,
> If heaven would make me such another world
> Of one entire and perfect chrysolite,
> I'd not have sold her for it.

Like Judas, Othello brought false evidence against the blessed one, and like Judas, he kissed before he killed.

> Now the traitor had arranged a signal with them: "The one I kiss" he had said, "he is the man." So when the Traitor came we went straight up to Jesus and said, Rabbi, and kissed him and then he turned him over to his death. The chief priests and the whole Sanhedron were looking for evidence against Jesus on which they might pass the death-sentence. But they could not find any. Several, indeed, brought false evidence against him. But the evidence was conflicting. (Mark 14)

False evidence violates justice and the law but Othello's court of justice does not hesitate to admit it.

In the communion service in the Book of Common Prayer, after the recital of the Lord's prayer, it calls for the rehearsal of the ten commandments, with the communicant praying that each of the sins he has committed be forgiven and that grace help him ward off transgression in the future. It is little wonder that this play incites hunger for some vision of redemption, for in it, each of the commandments is broken. The name of the Lord is used in vain repeatedly; "s'blood" (Christ's blood) is the first word out of Iago's cursing mouth; and "zounds" (Christ's wounds) and "by the mass" are blasphemous invocations of the sacrifice. The sabbath day is not kept holy—it sees a brawl; a father is not honored—his daughter flees him in the night and disobeys him; what belongs to the neighbor is coveted—Iago covets Cassio's position; false witness is made—Iago uses the handkerchief; and murder is committed: all of the "thou shalt nots" are violated. The only command of the decalogue that is conspicuously not broken is adultery, and it becomes, in this perverse covenant with a God who-is-not-what-he-is, the provocation of wrath. Othello succumbs to a perversion of the violence of monotheism: "For I am a jealous God, you shall have none but me."[39]

With this old covenant broken, we may well long for a new one, one written on the heart, like that of the prophets, not like the one broken when Israel disobeyed the law, but a Logos incarnated. And the breaking of the old law given in blood may well demand a new gift given in blood, a sacrifice, like that of Jesus. These allusions hover tantalizingly around Desdemona who does her part in tempting us into seeing her own death as a sacrifice. She calls out in her moment of death, "O Lord Lord Lord" as Christ had "Eli Eli." And she withstands her version of the temptation offered to Christ in the wilderness, the gift of all the kingdoms of the world: "all this dominion will I give to you and the glory that goes with it." Just as Jesus need only do homage to Satan to gain the whole world, so in Emilia's test, Desdemona could have the whole world for one infelicity.

> *Des.* Wouldst thou do such a deed, for all the world?
> *Emil.* Why, would not you?
> *Des.* No, by this heavenly light!
> *Emil.* Nor I neither, by this heavenly light. I might do it as well in the dark.
> *Des.* Wouldst thou do such a thing for all the world?
> *Emil.* The world is a huge thing, it is a great price, For a small vice.
> *Des.* Good troth, I think thou wouldst not.
> *Emil.* By my troth, I think I should, and undo't when I had done it; marry, I would not do such a thing for a joint-ring; nor for measures of lawn, nor for gowns, or petticoats, nor caps, nor any such exhibition; but for the whole world? Why, who would not make her husband a cuckold, to make him a monarch? I should venture purgatory for it.
> *Des.* Beshrew me, if I would so such a wrong for the whole world.

The communion service begins with the recitation of the Lord's Prayer, eeking out its Eucharistic significance: "give us this day our daily bread and forgive us our trespasses as we forgive those who trespass against us. And lead us not into temptation and deliver us from evil." Desdemona is not led to temptation, and her dying words suggest that she forgives Othello's trespass: "Commend me to my kind Lord, O farewell!" But is she delivered from evil or to evil? She is the soul of purity who kneels and prays before her murder. Her prayer is drawn from the general confession of the communion service of the Book of Common Prayer: "We [ac]knowledge and bewail our manifold sinnes and wickedness, which we from time to time most grievously have committed, by thoughts, word, and deeds, against thy divine majestie."

> *Des.* Here I kneel: If e'er my will did trespass 'gainst his love
> Either in discourse of thought or actual deed, comfort forswear me.

How can Desdemona's death be figured as a redemptive sacrifice when Othello so resembles a perverse priest or even a sorcerer at a black mass? At the opening of the play, he is arraigned and tried in what is virtually a witch-trial scene, "I therefore apprehend and do attach thee, For an abuser of the world, a practiser of arts inhibited and out of warrant," one whose foul charms, drugs or minerals, have bound her in his chains of magic. But his acquittal by the Venetian Senate in this scene does not put an end to the suggestion of dark arts in this play. He calls Desdemona to the same court, demanding ocular proof of her fidelity—the spotted handkerchief he had given to her: but "ocular proof" was the technical term in witch trials for the mark on the body of the witch, the "witch's teat," as it was so misogynistically called. To demand ocular proof is to demand evidence of sorcery. From at least one of the perspectives that reigns in the play, that of Iago, she is indicted for she has had sexual congress with the devil. According to Trevor-Roper's account of witchcraft beliefs, the devil himself presided at the sorcerer's mass as a big black bearded man, or as a stinking goat or occasionally as a great toad, and an infernal Eucharist took place at the witch's sabbath where the blood of the devil is drunk instead of the blood of God. In that context, Cassio drinks a cup that holds the devil in it at an infernal marriage celebration: "O thou invisible spirit of wine, if thou has at no name to be known by, let us call thee devil!." This seems compatible with a Reformer's version of the Mass the work of the devil, a black mass, in their rejection of transubstantiation for the invisible spirit. Cassio will even invoke transubstantiation, not upwards, of man into god, but downward, of man into beast. "I remember a mass of things," he laments with remorse—and we can be sure the pun on mass was not lost to the audience— "but none distinctly, a quarrel but nothing wherefore. O God, that men should put an enemy in their mouths, to steal away their brains; that we should with joy, revel, pleasure, and applause, transform ourselves into beasts! . . . To be now a sensible man, by and by a fool, and presently a beast! Every unordinate cup is unblessed and the ingredience is the devil." This is the Eucharist from hell.

By means of all these perversions and inversions—all the while calling to mind doctrinal Christian solutions even as they are withheld—Shakespeare is teasing us over and over with the possibility of redemption: an aborted Mass ministered by a demented priest, a communion cup turned into a vessel of drunken disorderliness and bestiality, a prayer ("Lord, have mercy on me") that is really a plea for life from the hands of a murderer, a vow that is really a curse, a sacrifice that is really a murder, a death that does not make the earth quake or the sun stand still, a light that, once put out, will not rekindle. Shakespeare even assigns the most explicit articulation in the play of that yearning for salvation to a drunk: "there are souls that are saved and should that are not, may my soul be saved," slurs Cassio. Again, Shakespeare is only teasing us with the idea of redemption, for Cassio's high but drunken talk of salvation reduces to ludicrous pettiness,

> *Cassio.* For mine own part, no offense to the general, nor any man of quality, I hope to be saved.
> *Iago.* And so do I Lieutenant.
> *Cassio.* Ay, but by your leave, not before me; the lieutenant is to be saved before the ancient.

This tease about the idea of redemption is sustained from the beginning of the play to the end: an "old black ram"—it was a ram caught in the thicket that substituted for the sacrifice of Isaac, the typological prefiguration of the sacrifice of Christ—"tupping your white Ewe," the Lamb of God. But is there a sacrifice? Othello takes by the "throat the circumcised dog"—circumcision, the mark of the old covenant, "and smote him thus"—with the sign of the new covenant? That is, is Othello's suicide a sacrifice? Does it offer, in his self-murder of the self-defined infidel/idolater, a restoration of justice, one confirmed by the legal restitution of order? Or rather, are we left aching for justice in the face of the triumph of evil? I would argue that this unmet craving for justice, so carefully incited and sustained throughout the play, gives the tragedy a transcendent dimension, pointing beyond the terrors of economic justice, strict justice or retribution to another vision of human possibility.

Othello has long been read as a sustained rumination on alterity, but not in the transcendent sense understood by Levinas.[40] Nonetheless, in the course of the play, what unfolds relentlessly are the consequences of the travesties against Levinasian alterity and the transcendent justice that responds to the other. Unable to welcome her alterity, Othello enfolds Desdemona into the pre-given identity of a shared being, a racist and nationalistic identity, and condemns himself to such being in the process. But, as Levinas so well understood, "Implied in the ontological subordination of alterity is the view that the other must be surmounted, enveloped, dominated."[41] Hence, as the logic of this reduction unfolds, we also witness Othello regard Desdemona is as an object to be possessed, whose freedom and power he imagines he must subjugate in order for his own to prosper. But, unhappy warrior that he is, he engages the logic of the state, when "the work of justice" must exceed the "work of the state." We want Othello to love and honor Desdemona, not terrorize her with possession.

Levinas does not only take pains to separate freedom from justice, seeing the kind of weighing of freedoms that dominates political theory as entirely missing the deeper justice of responsibility. He also separates truth from justice: "Society does not proceed from the contemplation of the true; truth is made possible by relation with the Other our master. Truth is bound up with the social relation, which is justice."[42] Othello's obsession with truth becomes ludicrous as it plays into Iago's hands as easily as his need to possess. Twisted into the suggestions Iago plants and the evidence he invents, truth is critiqued roundly by its larger failure to suffice as a substitute for justice.

There is another terrible consequence of the failure of recognizing alterity. When Desdemona has no singular otherness, she is subsumed under the universality of the law, a law that fails to save her as surely as truth had, instead entrapping her in a wrongful conviction and him in the role of executioner: "it is the cause." But as Exodus so dramatically attests with the breaking of the tablets before the disobedient Israelites, there can be no law—or only a broken one—without justice. "Justice does not include me in the equilibrium of its universality; justice summons me to go beyond the straight line of justice, and henceforth nothing can mark the end of this march; behind the straight line of the law the land of goodness extends infinite and unexplored, necessitating all the resources of a singular presence."[43] The consequences of Othello's failure to undertake this march to the land of goodness, to live under the horizon of transcendent justice unfold, then, with dire predictability. This is why the play is so profound to contrast jealously to justice: jealously is the inevitable frustration of the effort "to surmount, envelop and dominate" the other. This failure, this frustration, in turn gives rise to a craving for some other justice: not of being or of truth or of law, but for Othello to embrace Desdemona's transcendent alterity, not conquer her ontological one.

All of this is certainly not to say that Othello is merely a religious allegory; of course it plumbs the depths of all-too-human passions (as do powerful religious myths, for that matter). Nor would I want to suggest, despite the frequent dating of the play to 1604, the very year Convocation was assembled to further emend the Prayer Book in a period fraught with controversy over the Eucharist, that the play became Shakespeare's covert expression of what had been censured on the stage—his stand on the religious controversy. The evidence is conflicting: on the one hand, a deranged Othello imagines himself a priest at a sacrifice as he performs a murder; on the other, an innocent victim, falsely accused but faithful to the last, cries out to the Lord at her death by a deranged killer, invoking prayers that did precede the Anglican communion service but do not save or redeem her. These do not add up tidily either to an argument that Shakespeare is critiquing or that he is embracing the doctrine of the sacrifice of the Mass. Rather, in a play preoccupied with the problem of evil and the problem of justice, I discern Shakespeare needing to invoke the Mass—not only the Catholic Mass, but also its infernal parody—because it addressed the problem of justice forcefully.[44]

In turning from the Mass to the theatre, replacing the sacrifice, the re-enactment of Christ's offering of his body and blood to make amends for Adam's sin with the representation of a murder, what has Shakespeare done? Are we to understand this as a debasement of a mystery, a secularizing impoverishment of transcendence on the order of turning the holiness of the sacramental cup into Iago's sneering remark about Desdemona: "the wine she drinks is made of grapes"? Is the flowering of the early modern theatre consequently a part of an inexorable process of secularization that begins in the period? Is that what we are seeing at work in Othello? In part. But I am arguing for a more nuanced case, that the craving for justice this play incites is transcendent—a more "horizontal" transcendence, perhaps, than "vertical." Othello has raised the specter of the drama of redemption only to resist it, has held forth the justice of economy to expose its failures, and thereby to point to a more difficult justice in "the land of goodness."

When the Reformed communion offers, at most, a memory of a past and a promise of a future event, but no redemption in the present, then the longing for redemption is left as just that: longing—in memory and in hope, memory of the revelation and hope for the eschaton. But when the wine only signifies blood and does not become the blood, communion also risks the slippery slope toward disillusionment: "the wine she drinks is made of grapes." But if there is no wine that is blood—not even Desdemona's—then there are no redeemers, indeed, no humanity, and this is the matter for tragedy and for tears, after all, and not only for religious ritual. That the theatre should flower during the chill of Protestantism's heyday is no mystery. With bodies strewn all over the stage, the theatre became the first truly protestant church, where a community convened and remembered sacrifice—without the operatum of the Church—and where each individual was challenged privately to try to distinguish sacrifice from murder—the question for faith and to crave for justice no longer satisfied by the sacrament. Othello's distorted oath, "My life upon her faith" hauntingly suggests theatre's distinct performative symbiosis of sacrifice and faith in a world that craves for both, for either, for anything but "what you know you know" as an answer to why our demi-devils ensnare our souls.

Notes

1. The first foray of this essay was presented at the Shakespeare Association of America (1999), later versions at the American Academy of Religion (2002), Notre Dame University Department of English (2003), and the University of Chicago Divinity School (2003). I would like to thank those audiences for their helpful insights.
2. Emmanuel Levinas, "Franz Rosensweig, une ensee juive moderne, *Nine Talmudic Readings*, 74.
3. Levinas, *Beyond the Verse: Talmudic Readings and Lectures,* trans. Gary D. Mole. (London: Athlone Press, 1994), 107.
4. Levinas, *Totality and Infinity: An Essay on Exteriority,* trans. Alphonso Lingis (Pittsburgh: Duquesne University Press, 1969, 78–79.
5. Levinas, *Humanisme de l'autre homme.* Montpelier: Fata Morgana, 1972.
6. Levinas, *Nine Talmudic Readings,* trans. Annette Aronowicz. (Bloomington: Indiana University Press,1990), 43–44.

7.   Of course, eastern religions are also preoccupied with justice, but that preoccupation takes a different form from the one elaborated in the religions of the Book.

8.   Jacques Derrida, "Force of Law" in Derrida, *Acts of Religion*, ed. Gil Anidjar (New York: Routledge, 2002), 250. I have extended my discussion in "The Revelation of the Law" in *Other Testaments: Derrida and Religion*, ed. Kevin Hart and Yvonne Sherwood (Routledge, 2004).

9.   Ibid., 250–251.

10.   I should add that when one grasps this fully, the caricatures of Judaism as governed by pharisaic legalism become ludicrous. See my "Revelation and Revolution," in *Theology and the Political*, ed. Creston Davis, (Durham: Duke University Press, 2004).

11.   Alain Badiou, *Ethics: An Essay on the Understanding of Evil*, trans. Peter Hallward (London Verso, 2001), 42–44.

12.   Emmanual Levinas, "Revelation in the Jewish Tradition" in *Beyond the Verse: Talmudic Readings and Lectures,*146.

13.   Stuart Hampshire, *Justice is Conflict* (Princeton: Princeton University Press, 2000), 4–5.

14.   Hobbes, *Leviathan*, ed. J.C.A. Gaskin (Oxford, Oxford University Press, 1996, first published 1651), 113–115.

15.   Levinas, "On the Jewish Reading of Scriptures," in *Beyond the Verse*, 107.

16.   Levinas, *Entre Nous: Thinking-of-the-Other*, trans. Michael B. Smith and Barbara Harshav (New York: Columbia, 1998), 107.

17.   Schwartz, *The Curse of Cain: The Violent Legacy of Monotheism* (Chicago: University of Chicago Press, 1997). If I have been suspicious about the adequacy of narratives about God, then, it is not only because such narratives tend to be projections of human possession, human competition, and human violence but also because of the idolatry of any such description. To speak of representation as idolatry is not new: it is several thousand years old. But to speak of the idol, not as a visual representation, a statue, a painting, but a verbal one, seems to still be somewhat controversial. And yet it is our narrative idolatries that hold us in their grip and hence deserve critique. I have labored to show that the substantialist identities associated with Judaism—whether a community of land, of blood, of shared history, of state, do not delimit Judaism, not even in its founding text, the Hebrew Bible—I should say especially not there.

18.   "Loving the Torah more than God," *Difficult Freedom: Essays on Judaism*, trans. Sean Hand (Baltimore: Johns Hopkins, 1990), 145.

19.   See Hart's discussion in this volume of Blanchot's empty sky in the context of Augustine.

20.   Derrida, *Acts of Religion*, 270.

21.   D. Bentley Hart, "A Gift Exceeding Every Debt: An Eastern Orthodox Appreciation of Anselm's Cur Deus Homo," *Pro Ecclesia* Vol VII. No 3, 333–349, 334.

22.   Edwin Sandys (Archbishop of York), *Sermons*, The Parker Society, 88, 89. Sandys also cites Augustine: "Why preparest thou thy teeth? Believe, and thou hast eaten." In John Ev. Tract. I.4 xxv.12

23.   Matthew Kellison's attack on Calvinism in *A Survey of the New Religion, detecting many grosse absurdities which it implieth* (Douay, 1605), Bk IV, p. 230 (first ed. Printed at Douay in 1603).

24.   English Reformation poets lived on the brink of this new world and most embrace, predictably, the Calvinist doctrine of the spiritual—not material—presence of Christ in the eucharist. But this leaves them with a persistent nostalgia for that material presence, a nostalgia that reaches just shy of the heresy of transubstantiation. Alongside the explicit theological discourse of the period, the poetry, prose and theatre of the period took up these questions. Despite inveighing against the doctrine of transubstantiation in his prose, John Milton describes a whole universe as incessantly and naturally "transubstantiating" into God in his verse: furthermore, his angel eats not "seemingly, nor in mist, the common gloss of theologians" but "with keen dispatch of real hunger, and concoctive heat to transubstantiate" matter into spirit. George Herbert, at the beginning of *The Temple*, composes a visual altar—not a communion table, but an altar—built out of the stones or words of his lyric; this word picture of an altar also forms a capital "I"—he and the sacrifice become one, and in another lyric, he imagines communion as literally ingesting the Bible. For John Donne, the miracle of the Eucharist is the miracle of genuinely combining with the other, soul and body. For him, the longing set in motion by the promise of communion with God is repeated in the longing for consummation with a lover, and he punned endlessly on consume and consummate, communion and common i.e., promiscuous. I have come to understand

these writers as hungry for the mysteries wrought by the sacrament —as their Catholic detractors would have it, condemned to apprehend and desire a dinner that they could not have, but in their work, I have also come to see them concocting their own spiritual food. See Schwartz, *When God Left the World: The Sacramental and the Secular in English Reformation Culture*, 2005.

25. Stephen Gosson, *Plays confuted in five actions* (1582) facsimile ed. (New York: Johnson Reprint Corp., 1972, sigs C5, G6-G7

26. This derives Donatus on comedy where it is attributed to Cicero ('commoediam esse Cicero ait imitationem vitae, speculum consuetudinis, imaginem veritatis').

27. Miri Rubin, *Corpus Christi: The Eucharist in Late Medieval Culture*. (New York: Cambridge University Press, 1991).

28. An accumulating body of criticism has also been willing to think synoptically and more fruitfully about religious ritual and the theatre, sensitive, not only to the ritual origins of drama in ancient Greek religions and the miracle and morality plays of medieval Catholicism, but also to the complex relation between the Elizabethan stage and the English Reformation. Two poles have emerged in these speculations: stressing either that theatre is virtually a religious ritual— "for Shakespeare, the carnal spectacles of the theatre are better than demystifying: they are sacramental" (Jeffrey Knapp, "Preachers and Players in Shakespeare's England" Representations No. 44 [Autumn 1993], 29–59])—or that ritual is mere theatre—"theatrical seduction . . . is the essence of the church." (A Declaration of Egregious Popish Impostures, where Harsnett identifies exorcism with the theatre, quoted in Stephen Greenblatt, *Shakespearean Negotiations* [Berkeley: University of California Press, 1988], 112.) Knapp continues: "Following those Protestants who instead treated the petty materiality of the wafer as proof that the eucharist represented Christ, Henry V suggests that the carnal spectacles of the theater sacramentally highlight, rather than obscure, the operations of the spirit precisely because those spectacles are so conspicuously inadequate to the tales of *Non nobis* and *Te Deum* (4.8.121) they represent. ( )33. In a similar vein, Stephen Greenblatt spoke perceptively of the "emptying out" of ritual as the enabling condition of the "craving" set in motion by theatre for effective ritual. Greenblatt, *Shakespearean Negotiations*, 126–27. Louis Montrose writes of a transfer of the functions of rites of passage from ritual to the theatre. Historians concur: "If the opportunity for popular participation in public rituals was . . . largely removed, that especial meaning which sacred ceremonies and popular rites had periodically conferred on the citizens' tangible environment also fell victim to the new 'secular' order." (Charles Phythian-Adams, "Ceremony and the citizen: The communal year at Coventry 1450–1550," in *Crisis and Order in English Towns 1500–1700* ed. P. Clark and P. Slack [London: Routledge and Kegan Paul, 1972]).

29. John Calvin, Institution of the Christian Religion (1536 Edition) (New York: John Knox Press, 1975), 160.

30. *The Work of Thomas Cranmer*, (Appleford, UK: Courtenay Press, 1964), Vol II. 55- 56.

31. Ibid., 215.

32. Marion J. Hatchett, *The Eucharistic Liturgies of Historic Prayer Books: Historic Rites Arranged for Contemporary Celebration* (St. Luke's Journal of Theology, 1984), 36.

33. John Jewel, *An Apology of the Church of England*, ed. J. E. Booty, New York, 1963, 33.

34. Richard Hooker, *Ecclesiastical Polity*, (London: Everyman, 1907), Book V, chapter lvii, section 6, 322–323.

35. Ibid., chapter lxvii, section 12, 330–331.

36. Ibid., 35.

37. Calvin joined in with vehemence against the Catholic mass attacking the "mass-Doctors" who purport to be the agent of grace instead of Christ: While they have fashioned themselves a god after the decision of their own lust, they have forsaken the living God. Indeed they have worshipped the gifts instead of the giver. In this there is a double transgression: for both the honor taken from God has been transferred to the creature [cf. Romans 1:25], and he himself also has been dishonored in the defilement and the profanation of his gift, when his holy sacrament is made a hateful idol. (148 Institutes).

38. Gabriel Biel, Expositio sacri canonis missae (c. 1488) Brescia edit. 1576.

39. See Schwartz, *The Curse of Cain*.

40. These studies include fine ruminations on race and gender, on what Levinas would understand as ontological designations rather than genuine alterity, among them: Arthur Little, "'An essence that's not seen': The Primal Scene of Racism in Othello," *Shakespeare Quarterly*

44, no. 3 (Fall 1993): 304–24; Jonathan Crewe, "Out of the Matrix: Shakespeare's Race-Writing," *Yale Journal of Criticism* 8, no. 2 (1995): 13–29; Karen Newman, "'And wash the Ethiop white': Feminiity and the Monstrous in Othello," in *Shakespeare Reproduced: The Text in History and Ideology*, ed. Jean E. Howard and Marion F. O'Connor (New York, 1987); Patricia Parker, "Fantasies of 'Race' and 'Gender': Africa, Othello, and Bringing to Light," in Margo Hendricks and Patricia Parker, *Women, "Race" and Writing in the Early Modern Period* (London, 1994); Parker, Newman and Emily Bartels, "Making More of the Moor: Aaron, Othello, and Renaissance Refashionings of Race," *Shakespeare Quarterly* 41, no 4 (Winter 1990), Ania Loomba, *Gender, Race, Renaissance Drama* (Manchester, UK, 1989), among others.

41. Levinas, *Totality and Infinity*, 89.
42. Ibid., 72.
43. Ibid., 245.
44. This inadequacy was felt by the radical Reformers themselves, figures like Menno who needed to solve the problem through a God-man whose heavenly, rather than earthly flesh, offered man the chance to be perfected through communion with that flesh.

7

Unlikely Shadows: Transcendence in Image and Immanence

BY THOMAS A. CARLSON

Is the memory thin and bitter and does it shame you with its fundamental untruth—all nuance and wishful silhouette? Or does the power of transcendence linger . . . something holy that throbs on the hot horizon, the vision you crave . . . ?

—Don DeLillo, *Underworld*

In the radiant light of those countless screens whose images saturate our culture, one might read anew Martin Heidegger's assertion that "the fundamental event of the modern age is the conquest of the world as picture."[1] The photographic, cinematic, tele-visual and computer-generated "worlds" of image that surround and absorb us might seem, at first glance, to confirm such an assertion rather straightforwardly—insofar as they might constitute so many mirrors of the self-assertive human subject whose immanence would ground and define them.[2] A second look, however, might indicate the contrary: the boundless proliferation of image in today's technological and electronic culture might be understood not to mirror any stable or self-identical subject back to itself but rather endlessly to unsettle and provoke the subject, who thus never quite finds itself in any image, a subject always lacking while always seeking, in image after image, "the total thing."[3] From this perspective, the image-world today, a light world of spectacle and speed, might imply not simply the immanence and self-grounding of a self-certain subject, but rather a wounding of that subject and an opening toward something other. That "something other" would best be glimpsed, I believe, if today's image-world were thought in terms of a "negative" cosmology, according to which it is not the human subject who founds or frames, comprehends or conquers the world as picture, or as mirror, but rather the infinitely various and ever-shifting image-world that precedes, exceeds, and unsettles the subject born into it. If the modern "world-picture" opens with a self-positing of the autonomous human subject, it might close with the endless displacement or disappearance of that subject within the all-consuming light of image and immanence—and in that displacement or disappearance we might look for a shadow of transcendence.

Both in his seminal 1938 lecture "Age of the World Picture" and in his major but only posthumously published book of the same period, *Contributions to Philosophy (From Enowning)*,[4] Heidegger speaks of a distinctively modern "conquest of the world as picture" (*die Eroberung der Welt als Bild*), a domination of "world-pictures" (*Weltbildern*) or of "worldview" (*Weltanschauung*) that would mark "a *consequence* of modern metaphysics" (B 27; BG 38) and "the completion of the basic metaphysical position of man" (B 311). Reaching this metaphysical position, man effectively assumes the role of onto-theology's God by positing himself as the ground and measure of being: "I," as thinking subject, will count as truly being, or allow to appear as real, only that which I can re-present to myself as an object of thought. The subject here produces the world as represented object in such a way that beings themselves find a new "highest cause": "These beings, once made by a creator god, then became of human making, insofar as beings are taken in and controlled by their object-ness" (B 77). Bringing metaphysics to its completion through its replacement of God by man, the age of the world as picture is an age of the human as productive, re-presenting subject who sets all beings before himself so as thus to make or to validate, to arrange and control them. In and through this "un-conditioned domination of representing and producing" (B 311), which finds its highest philosophic expression in idealism's absolute subjectivity, the human subject becomes the "relational center" of all that is (WP 128), the *sub-jectum*, who, "as relational midpoint of all putting-before-oneself [*alles Vor-sich-stellens*], decides on beingness and what can belong to it, as well as on the essential forms and stages of representedness" (B 301; BG 427). From this metaphysical position, as Heidegger famously insists, man establishes the distinctively modern relationship to being and "brings into play his unlimited power for calculating, planning, and molding all things" (WP, 135).

According to this influential analysis of modernity's calculative thinking, the modern subject's attempt to produce the world as picture, to capture and control the world in a frame determined solely by the human subject, is bound intimately with that subject's "will to certainty" (B 141) and its related struggle to master the world as object. As Heidegger elaborates in *Contributions to Philosophy*, this struggle yields the relentless and boundless "machination" (*Machenschaft*) that would characterize a modern science and technology whose probing and productive powers, grounded in a "total lack of question-ing" (B 76), eclipse any thought of the "inaccessible" or "impossible." "Every-thing 'is made' or 'can be made'," according to the one who does not question, "if one only musters the 'will' for it" (B 76)—but such a will, and hence this domination in modern culture of *making* by means of *representation*, would presuppose the reduction or restriction of being to the sphere of that which can actually be represented. "For this will, which makes everything, has already subscribed to machination, that interpretation of beings as re-presentable and re-presented. In one respect re-presentable means 'accessible to intention and calculation'; in another respect it means 'advanceable through pro-duction and execution.' But . . . all of this means that beings as such are representable and that only the representable *is*" (B 76). This restriction of being to the sphere of that which can be represented, a restriction bound intimately with the priority assumed by the "I" in modern metaphysics, remains itself, in prin-ciple, without limit, for that which might seem to elude representation—its intention and calculation, and hence all related forms of production and exe-cution—has always already been framed by its logic. Much as in the "disen-chanted" world analyzed by Max Weber, where nothing in principle eludes rational comprehension and its calculative-instrumental power,[5] so here any apparent limit to representational thinking marks only a "not yet": "For machination, what apparently offers resistance and a limit to machination is only the material for further elaboration and the impulse for progress and an occasion for extension and enlargement" (B 76).

Such limitless extension and enlargement of machination—within which the "impossible" and the "inaccessible" never appear, since they are always al-ready reduced to the simply not-yet realized or reached—give rise to what Heidegger names the "the gigantic" (*das Riesenhafte, das Riesige*): "grounded upon the decidedness and invariability of 'calculation' and . . . rooted in a pro-longation of subjective re-presentation unto the whole of beings" (B 310–11), the gigantic "shows the magnitude of the self-certain *subjectum* which builds everything on its own representing and producing" (B 311). Paradoxically, as "the gigantic" grows, the world itself shrinks, for the self-assertion of this self-certain subject who grounds the gigantic operates especially in and through those forms of modern science and technology that yield a "steerability" and "control" allowing for the transgression of spatial and temporal limitation—making the distant near, the remote accessible, and the foreign familiar at an ever accelerating pace.

This transgression of spatial and temporal limitation is most notable—though at the same time ever more disguised—in our technologies of transportation and communication, which serve as signs of the conquest of the world as picture even as they hide that conquest from us: "The gigantic presses forward in a form that actually makes it seem to disappear—in the annihilation of great distances by the airplane, in the setting before us of foreign and remote worlds in their everyday-ness, which is produced at random through radio by the flick of the hand (*Hand-griff*)" (WP, 135). When the foreign and the remote become the everyday, when earthly distance can be traversed in hours by machine, when image or voice[6] can be transmitted at the speed of light by means of ever-extending electronic pros-theses, the world is made smaller not only quantitatively but also metaphysically: "The 'world' becomes smaller and smaller, not only in the quantitative but also in the metaphysical sense: a being as a being, i.e., as object, is in the end so dissolved into controllability that the being-character of a being disappears, as it were, and the abandonment of beings by being is completed" (B 348).

108 • Thomas A. Carlson

Now, just as the growth of the gigantic means for Heidegger a diminution of the world, both quantitative and qualitative, so the self-assertion of subjectivity, which first grounds the gigantic, yields a "hollowing-out (*eine Aushölung*) of man" (B 348; BG 495). When everything is "trapped in planned steerability and exactitude of a secure execution and an 'exhaustive' control" (B 286), an emptiness and desolation of man come into force and give birth to the modern mania for "lived-experience," itself implicitly intended—but never adequate—to "compensate" for such emptiness and desolation, for the "growing 'artificiality' of life" (B43). In order to gain a sense today of such desolation and of its aggravation by the very "lived-experience" meant to compensate for it, one need only think of "reality television" and of its subjection of all human "experience" whatever to the demands of image production and consumption, demands aimed at staging or screening "real life" in such a way as to make it universally and immediately accessible—thus effecting the kind of leveling and abstraction that already troubles Heidegger's guide on these (and other) matters, Søren Kierkegaard, who laments that in our "age of advertisement and publicity" "nothing ever happens but there is immediate publicity everywhere."[7]

In this direction, where the machinations of mass culture and its media might be seen to bring about the hollowing and desolation of man, a leveling and diminution of the human world, Heidegger's analyses resonate significantly also with those of Walter Benjamin on the "decay of the aura" in the "age of mechanical reproduction," a decay that results for Benjamin from the erasure of distance and the leveling of uniqueness—especially and primarily that of the work of art, whose originally sacred status is undone when the work is abstracted from the context of cult and tradition. Replacing the unique and original work with an endless series of copies without original, the technologies of reproduction would give rise to a mass culture characterized by its eclipse of the sacred and reduction of the human to the abstraction of statistical existence.[8] If the reduction of humanity *en masse* to a statistical form of existence, as noted in Benjamin, finds an analogue in the desolation of man as analyzed by Heidegger,[9] so likewise the decay of the aura from Benjamin's analysis would resonate with what Heidegger terms the loss or flight of the gods (*Entgötterung, Flucht der Götter*).

Along with science and technology, along with the movement of art into aesthetics and the conception of human activity as culture, one must see as an essential phenomenon of the modern age a "loss of the gods" (*Entgötterung*)—in bringing about which, Heidegger wants to note, "Christendom has the greatest share" (WP 116, 117). On Heidegger's view, the modern age, beginning philosophically with Descartes and culminating most notably with German idealism (while persisting in Nietzsche), remains faithful to Christian metaphysics—even if inverting that metaphysics—when it conceives truth in terms of the certainty achieved by a human subject no longer reliant on revelation:

> Hence liberation *from* the revelational certainty of salvation had to be intrinsi-
> cally a freeing *to* a certainty [*Gewissheit*] in which man makes secure for himself
> the true as the known of his own knowing [*Wissens*]. That was possible only
> through self-liberating man's guaranteeing for himself the certainty of the
> knowable. Such a thing could happen, however, only insofar as man decided, by
> himself and for himself, what, for him, should be "knowable" and what knowing
> and the making secure of the known, i.e., certainty, should mean (WP 148).

If man's "liberation" here implies a loss or absence of the gods, a profound indifference with respect to the question of the god's flight *or* arrival, that loss
constitutes a paradoxical phenomenon, presenting itself all the more in the
measure of its hiddenness—which, as Heidegger points out, is only intensified
by the ongoing activity of the Churches: "When the distress of lack of distress
breaks out, it strikes against the non-appearance [*Ausbleiben*] of the arrival
and flight of the gods. This non-appearance is all the more uncanny the longer
and seemingly persistently Churches and forms of worship are still maintained, without having the strength to ground an originary truth" (B 168; BG
237, translation modified).[10] Concealed in and through its very presence, the
loss of the gods repeats the logic of modern man's own distress, which, like
Kierkegaardian despair, is deepest when it goes unnoticed: lack of distress is
the utmost distress, Heidegger insists, and "the lack of distress is greatest where
self-certainty has become unsurpassable, where everything is held to be calculable and, above all, where it is decided, without a preceding question, who we
are and what we are to do" (B 87).

If the age of the world picture sustains a culture saturated with image, the
very question of transcendence might there appear, like the loss of the gods and
the distress of man in Heidegger, only through an eclipse or negation, an absence
or non-appearance so thorough that it goes unseen. From this perspective, the
saturation of today's culture with image, the unsettling or dissolution of any stable distinction or distance between image and reality, can seem to involve an immanence so pure that such immanence itself goes unidentified. The immanence
of image, itself invisible because all-present and all-consuming, would seem to
leave nothing outside or beyond—just as it would seem to elucidate and thus
erase or undo every interior secret, every recess of mystery. As Don DeLillo puts
it in the epilogue to his novel *Underworld*, expressing an unease with our totalizing communicational and informational systems, "you touch a button and all
the things concealed from you for centuries come flying into the remotest room.
It's an epidemic of seeing. No conceivable recess goes unscanned."[11] To catch this
epidemic, or to be caught by it and held in it, might be to face a presence so total
that it would, as DeLillo's *Valparaiso* suggests, threaten death—and "in the best
possible sense. In the sense that nothing is left unsaid. Nothing is left unseen."[12]

The world consumed by such an epidemic—where all can seem to be revealed and made available to the hold of a machination that would control

even death—might seem indeed to realize an absolute immanence that leaves nothing of transcendence. And if the tone here grows apocalyptic, surely one of the more powerful theological voices to hear would be that of Thomas J. J. Altizer, who for some forty years now would say Yes and Amen to the "apocalyptic totality" of modernity, where a "total presence" erases every gap of transcendence, fills the space of any longing for a beyond—a presence in which Christianity's transcendent God and the individual human subject formed in that God's image would alike find their death or dissolution, according to a radical kenosis that realizes the very grace of Christ by rendering that grace "all in all" and so un-nameable as such.

If the language and imagination of modernity actualize a total presence that allows no beyond, Altizer insists, that presence is spoken—indirectly—in the most profound anonymity of God, itself answering a new anonymity of the human. The human subject who, beginning with St. Paul, became "the center of a uniquely Western consciousness and society,"[13] the subject who is formed as a unique and inward "I" only in relation to the irreducible otherness of its God, meets, upon the death of that God, "an apocalyptic ending, an ending which is the ending of the world or horizon of every center or subject, as an anonymous consciousness is now becoming all in all" (GA 176). Just as Heidegger ties the machinations of the gigantic to a loss of gods and desolation of man, so Altizer finds in modern mass society the embodiment of God's death and the correlative emergence of a new, anonymous form of humanity. Insofar as that mass society presupposes "a radically new and ever more total technology" (GA 176), one that seems to transgress spatial or temporal limitation, it erases those distinctions that might once have oriented and defined the human subject and its world. Indeed, Altizer argues, with the disappearance of horizon and of center, the naming of world itself proves impossible, cosmos slips into chaos, and we enter an everyday realm in which "there is no longer a real distinction between the without and the within, or the exterior and the interior, or macrocosm and microcosm" (GA 177), "no real distinction between the public and private, or society and the individual, or the unconscious and consciousness" (GA 177). In short, the death of God in our modern "chaosmos" gives way to the clamorous anonymity of a humanity named perfectly in the "Here Comes Everybody"[14] of *Finnegans Wake*—or indeed already, and christologically, in the epic voice of *Ulysses*, which realizes for Altizer "an anonymous consciousness and society, and an anonymous Christ. Now every name and voice is a universal name and voice, a universality which is interior and exterior at once, and so much so that now there is no real distinction between either cosmos and consciousness or Christ and the world" (GA 179).

In his emphasis on the anonymity of mass humanity, Altizer's theological position recalls the analyses of Heidegger according to which the anonymous crowd in its various guises—the "publicness" of the "they-self," the "masses," the "giant-thing called man"—threatens to level the human subject who has

freed itself from revelational truth. "Certainly the modern age has, as a consequence of the liberation of man, introduced subjectivism and individualism,"
Heidegger notes, "[b]ut it remains just as certain that no age before this one
has produced a comparable objectivism and that in no age before this has the
non-individual, in the form of the collective, come to acceptance as valid" (WP
128). The effacement of the individual in the collective proves to be the paradoxical consequence of a metaphysics in which the subject asserts itself in the
definition of being as object. Such objectivism and anonymity are bound intimately to the gigantic and its machinations, exercised through technology's
planetary reach, where "uniformity becomes the surest instrument of total,
i.e., technological, rule over the earth. The modern freedom of subjectivity
vanishes totally in the objectivity commensurate with it" (WP 152–153). Insisting that the "uniqueness of our world is inseparable from a dissolution or
erasure of all interior consciousness," Altizer echoes deeply this Heideggerian
analysis of modernity's mass humanity: "There is now, "Altizer writes, far more
objective knowledge and objective actuality than ever before, but a subjective
interiority has never been so precarious, just as a genuinely human future has
never been so totally in question"[15] (CJ 203–204). Just as in Heidegger the
non-appearance of gods and hollowing-out of man go hand in hand, so in Altizer what might count as a "negative" theology is answered by a "negative" anthropology, for "just as a purely anonymous vision is impossible apart from
the loss or dissolution of an interior and immanent center, so likewise is it impossible apart from the loss or reversal of a transcendent ground or center."[16]

If the death of Christianity's transcendent God implies a dissolution of the
discrete, inwardly constituted subject, such a dissolution and death transpire
for Altizer in a modern culture that is also an electronic culture. Here, noise
and silence prove indistinguishable, and "a truly and uniquely individual voice
is unspeakable" (GA 180), insofar as language is increasingly subjected to "an
abstract and electronic modulation, a modulation that is the very silence of
speech itself" (GA 178). If the electronic modulation of language yields a silence of speech itself, insofar as it absorbs and dissolves the uniqueness of any
individual voice, that silence, which is the same as noise, speaks the anonymity
of a new "electronic humanity" (CJ 187) whose "depth is indistinguishable
from its surface or mask" (CJ 187) and whose "actual name is everyone and no
one at once, an everyone who can only be no one" (CJ 187). If Altizer here
again resonates significantly with Heidegger, we might note not only the clear
ties between these two but also their shared source in Kierkegaard, who in *The
Present Age* laments a culture in which "our talk becomes like the public, a pure
abstraction. There is no longer any one who knows how to talk, and instead,
objective thought produces an atmosphere, an abstract sound, which makes
human speech superfluous, just as machinery makes man superfluous."[17] For
Heidegger and Altizer alike, in this both heirs to Kierkegaard, the age of the
machine, and even more the age of electronics, is the age of the anonymous

mass—what Kierkegaard had already named the "public," the offspring of mass media: "Made up of individuals at the moment when they are nothing, a public is a kind of gigantic something, an abstract and deserted void which is everything and nothing."[18] Nothing because everything, no one because everyone, the public stages a coincidence of opposites where silence and noise, anonymity and polyonymy, reach a point of indiscretion. As modulated electronically and subjected to an increasingly total technology, that coincidence of opposites plays itself out also in terms of incalculable spatial and temporal displacements.

Indeed, if Altizer's "total presence" is spoken in the noisy silence or polyonymous anonymity of an electronic and technological humanity, it would imply also a "simultaneity in which time itself is a wholly abstract or simulated time, and most abstract to the extent that it is simultaneous. So likewise are we being overwhelmed by a ubiquity of space, a space that is omnidirectional, without any actual direction or perspective. Thereby center as center has truly disappeared, just as circumference as circumference has disappeared" (CJ 196). Just as the electronic modulation of language would silence the uniqueness of voice, absorbing it in the abstract universality of a polyonymous anonymity, so according to the electronic simultaneity and ubiquity signaled here, any discrete place (spatial or temporal) would be endlessly displaced. In these directions, one might be inclined to hear the echo or to glimpse a shadow of that mystical God whose center is everywhere and circumference nowhere, the God who assumes all names and none. However, just as Altizer wants to distinguish between the silence of our electronically modulated voice and "an original or integral silence" (GA 178), so he wants to insist that "with the modern realization of the death of God," the ubiquity and simultaneity that we know today, wholly abstract and simulated, are decisively not those of mystical tradition.

In drawing such distinctions, Altizer stands in agreement with other thinkers of the various post-ages (above all, the post-Heideggerian and poststructuralist) for whom the presence of the God or gods can be seen today only as an absence, their givenness given only as loss or abandon. In this direction, Jean-Luc Nancy would be exemplary, when, in his short work on the topic of "divine places,"[19] he evokes an immediate presence or excessive "denuding" that finally constitutes an absence or desertion. By the light of such immediate presence, which, like DeLillo's epidemic of seeing, leaves no recess unscanned, "space is everywhere open, there is no place to receive either the mystery or the splendor of a god. We are allowed to see the unlimited opening of this space, our time is allowed to know—with a knowing more acute than any science and more lucid, more luminous than any consciousness [*conscience*]—how we are delivered to this gaping and naked face. It reveals to us only ourselves, *neither men nor gods*—and that also is a joy" (LD 48). This ubiquitous opening or uncontained luminosity, which would undo both the secret and the splendid—

this pure exposure or nakedness of space, this utter dissolution of any interior place that might be cut off or hidden in its specificity—resembles almost perfectly the total presence of Altizer,[20] and like Altizer's total presence, this immediacy undoes both the god and the human: "we are denuded of discourse and of *cogito*" (LD 50) in face of that presence "which one will not call god" (LD 50); indeed, "one will not say that it is divine: one will not say it—one will let it lay out the places of its reserve and of its generosity" (LD 50). What—and where—are these places? For Nancy, "these places laid out everywhere open up and orient new spaces: these are no longer temples, but rather the opening or the spacing of the temples themselves, a dis-location with no more reserve or sacred enclosure" (LD 50). In place of the defining limits and interiority of the temple (from *templum*, a space cut off), Nancy envisions a space of pure exposure that amounts to a space of utter dis-location, dis-placement, or desertion: "the temples are deserted, and our experience of the divine is the experience of desertion" (LD 47).

When every conceivable recess is opened to luminosity and scanned by vision—to the point that the immediate presence of pure exposure undoes the distinction and self-identity both of the human and of the god—then we would have reached that desert in which a radical polyonymy and a radical anonymity might indeed go hand in hand. The god (or the human) who is everywhere and nowhere, everybody and nobody, is the god (or the human) who carries all names because it is nameless.

Now, just as Altizer wants to insist that there is "obviously" "an overwhelming and uncrossable distance between an unknowability which is a mark or sign of the transcendence of God and an unknowability which is simply and only unknowability" (TP 26), and just as he will argue that "we can sense the truth of this judgment by noting the distinction between a negative attribute of God, or a negative naming of God, and the absence of all naming whatsoever" (TP 26), so Nancy will assert that "on the subject of God, what is most decisive today is undoubtedly this: he is not unnameable in the metaphysical sense of the Being that is inaccessible to all names, of the Being that transcends all names, and thus the name of Being itself, according to a steady tradition that is the very tradition of onto-theology. . . . God is not unnameable in this sense, for in this sense unnameability results from an excess over names and language, whereas the unnameability of the god to whom I address myself (if I can do so) results from a lack of name. God is unnameable, today, in that his name, or his names, are lacking" (LD 10).

Confident that one can distinguish securely between the excess of an unnameable God and the simple lack of any name for God, Nancy and Altizer alike share a more widespread perspective that would distinguish the transcendence of God over language and image in traditional contexts from the lack or emptiness of language and imagination surrounding God in modern and contemporary culture.[21] Such confidence, however, becomes worthy of question to the degree that such distinctions between excess and lack can prove themselves difficult to maintain—as much in the "classic" apophatic traditions as in the contemporary context. One might question the security and scope of an insistence like Altizer's that "in a situation in which images of God no longer appear to be even potentially possible for us, all such mystical language [i.e., that of eclipse, cloud, night, etc.] breaks down. Or breaks down in terms of its original language world, a world in which God is not wholly anonymous, or is anonymous only in that penultimate and purgatorial state which is directed to the dissolution or erasure of all dark or fallen images of God" (TP 28). A closer analysis of language and image in the mystical contexts themselves, I believe, indicates that the anonymity of God is often not, as Altizer suggests, penultimate, but indeed ultimate and irreducible—because endlessly redoubled. Such analysis, then, might allow us to trouble any straightforward contention that "there is a clear and radical distinction between an unknowability which is the consequence of the presence of a transcendent or mysterious identity and an unknowability which is the consequence of the absence of all identity whatsoever" (TP 26).

To move in this direction, one would need to address the understanding of language and image in the mystical writer most decisive for the Western traditions: the enigmatic Eastern monk Dionysius the Areopagite (ca. 500), whose writings in the European Middle Ages were perhaps second only to the Bible in authority and whose thinking thus shaped decisively both medieval approaches to theological language and the theological aesthetics of light that pervade medieval spirituality and culture.

Much as in Altizer's dialectic of everyone and no one, of the named and the nameless, so can one find in Dionysius and subsequent mystical traditions a dialectic of transcendence and immanence according to which God is at once everywhere and nowhere, named infinitely and infinitely nameless, illuminating all and beyond all in luminous darkness. As taken up by thinkers and traditions appearing throughout the Middle Ages and beyond (from John Scotus Eriugena through Meister Eckhart to Nicholas of Cusa), this dialectic seeks to indicate that God is distinct through his indistinction, different through his indifference, absent through his presence—in short, transcendent through his radical immanence. As the most famous Dionysian, Meister Eckhart, puts it, "God is inside all things in that he is existence and thus every being feeds on him. He is also on the outside because he is above all and thus outside all. Therefore, all things feed on him, because he is totally within; they hunger for him, because he is totally without."[22] Or, as an earlier passage from the twelfth-century Dionysian Richard of St. Victor puts it rather beautifully, and highlighting the concept of place (*locus*):

> If He is in every place, nothing is more present.
> If He is outside every place, nothing is more absent.
> Is anything more absent by his greater presence to all,
> and anything more present by his greater absence to
> all, than the One who is not one kind of being or
> another as the being of all?
> But if nothing is more present than the most absent One,
> if nothing is more absent than the most present One,
> is anything more marvelous, anything more
> incomprehensible?[23]

These passages from Eckhart and Richard, echoes of which one could find in countless other mystical writers, from John Scotus Eriugena before them to Nicholas of Cusa after them, signal a type of dialectic that resonates significantly with Altizer's own apocalyptic totality even as it draws its logic and inspiration from the classic Dionysian framework.

In that framework, God is immanent to all as "cause" (*aitia*) of all and can therefore be named or imagined (kataphatically) according to the name and image of every being, and at the same time, *as* immanent to *all*, that God is unlike any single being (which, as finite, is definitively *not all*) and thus transcends all so as to stand (apophatically) beyond every name and image. "And so it is that as Cause of all and as transcending all, he is rightly nameless and yet has the names of everything that is."[24] The God who is both "all in all" and "nothing in anything" is the endlessly named and imagined God whom language and image never reach or capture because his presence amounts to an absence, the God who generates an endless oscillation between the kataphatic and apophatic modes of theology in such a way that negation reaches God just as little as affirmation—which is indicated by the irreducibly third, mystical mode of theology: "Since it is the Cause of all beings, we should posit and ascribe to it all the affirmations we make in regard to beings, and, more appropriately, we should negate all these affirmations, since it surpasses all being. Now we should not conclude that the negations are simply the opposite of the affirmations, but rather that the cause of all is considerably prior to this, beyond privations, beyond every denial, beyond every assertion" (MT 1000B). In sum, the dialectic of immanence and transcendence is answered in Dionysian language by a ceaseless play between polyonymy and anonymity, and that play remains ceaseless to the degree that immanence and transcendence realize one another, one slipping dialectically into the other. The logic of this linguistic operation applies equally to the play of image within the theological aesthetics of Dionysian tradition—an aesthetics that is tied inextricably to Dionysius's cosmological vision.

Indeed, the Dionysian conception of theological language and representation is shaped decisively by Dionysius's fundamentally cosmological orientation, where the cosmological is approached in terms of the aesthetic, and where the aesthetic concerns primarily the dynamic of divine light.[25] The Dionysian dialectic of transcendence and immanence is a dialectic of the divine light in and through the cosmos—according to the movements of procession, return, and remaining (the divine *prohodos*, *epistrophe*, and *mone*, to which answer the kataphatic, apophatic, and mystical modes of theological language). Within this Dionysian cosmology, the revelation and concealment of the divine that generate the basic forms of theological language do so in and through the fundamentally theophanic—and theocryptic—dynamic of the cosmos as a whole. The Dionysian cosmos is a theophanic-theocryptic light show, a "vast field of light" that makes visible the invisible as such; it is a play of light that shows the darkness, a play of image that signals the unimaginable. To understand this cosmological light-aesthetic, one must see the Dionysian cosmos in its essentially hierarchical—and christological—character, which alone, then, would permit an understanding of the Dionysian image.

Dionysius articulates his cosmos in terms of legal, ecclesial, and celestial hierarchies—in short, ordered totalities of interrelation—through which the divine light pours itself out into creation, and through which, correspondingly, that creation moves longingly back toward the divine. The hierarchical cosmos is relational through and through, and to the degree that Jesus "is the source and the being underlying all hierarchy" (EH 372A), or to the degree that "every hierarchy ends in Jesus" (EH 505B), one must interpret cosmic relationality in its christological character, which Dionysius elucidates most fully in his famous third letter:

> What comes into view, contrary to hope, from previous obscurity, is described as "sudden." As for the Love of Christ for humanity, the Word of God, I believe, uses this term to hint that the transcendenthas put aside its own hiddenness and has revealed itself to us by becoming a human being. But he is hidden even after this revelation, or, if I may speak in a more divine fashion, is hidden even amid the revelation. For this mystery of Jesus remains hidden and can be drawn out by no word or mind. What is to be said of it remains unsayable, what is to be understood of it remains unknowable (Letter Three, 1069B).

As the source, being, and end of all hierarchy, the incarnate God—the Light of the Father who is himself the source of all light (CH 121A)—determines the essential character of hierarchy and thus of the cosmos as a whole: the hierarchical cosmos is at bottom a revelation, beyond expectation, of the hidden as hidden. Unveiling mystery as mystery, the cosmic play of light, which finds its logic in the play of incarnation, is a duplicitous movement of revelation and concealment, affirmation and negation—and that duplicity is echoed or outlined in all language and imagination surrounding the divine. Language and image proliferate without end in Dionysius to the degree that they capture the mystery only through their failure.[26] The theological image proliferates exactly where it cannot contain that which it "reveals"; the image "shows" most powerfully on the edge of its disappearance, and thus its undoing is essential to its functioning. Dionysius therefore defines that function in terms of a "dissimilar similarity" or an "unlikely likeness" whose anagogic force is indispensable to the transcendence of souls.

Images can function anagogically—they can effect what Hans Urs von Balthasar calls an aesthetic transcendence—only to the degree that they reveal in a concealing manner, for the "divine ray can enlighten us only by being upliftingly concealed in a variety of sacred veils . . ." (CH 121B–121C). This operation of dissimilar similarity in Dionysius—essential to the dialectic of immanence and transcendence, revelation and concealment—both structures the cosmos as a whole and answers to the constitution of the human subject. As von Balthasar indicates, it is "the greatness and tragedy of man . . . to be immersed in the aesthetics of the world of images and at the same time to have irresistibly to dissolve all images in the light of the unimaginable."[27] Both divisible body and indivisible soul, the human is caught inextricably within the endless, hyper-negative oscillation between the (kataphatic) image and the (apophatic) unimaginable toward which the image would signal. The co-implication here between a negative theology and a negative anthropology is answered, in turn, by a cosmology whose force is likewise negative: "The 'dissimilar similarity' that constitutes every created manifestation of God is both a similarity to be affirmed and a dissimilarity to be denied. Therefore, the universe is both necessary as an image and impossible as a representation of the God for whom there is no adequate representation."[28] The logic of "dissimilar similarity," then, determines the theological, the anthropological, and the cosmological registers in their essential interrelation.

While images function according to both "similarity" and "dissimilarity," Dionysius must finally privilege the negative way insofar as it better respects the unimaginable transcendence of the divine: "Since the way of negation appears to be more suitable to the realm of the divine and since positive affirmations are always unfitting to the hiddenness of the inexpressible, a manifestation through dissimilar shapes is more correctly to be applied to the invisible" (CH 141A). We see here the logic of Dionysius's negative theological method worked out in terms of the image or perceptible symbol whose significance is nothing less than cosmic: just as theological language responds infinitely to the ineffable that it fails to reach, so, in the Dionysian cosmos, image proliferates to the degree that it signals but cannot contain the invisible.

To move now from Dionysius's theological cosmos back toward the contemporary world of immanent image and light, I will take a quick, perhaps unexpected, glance at the intersection of theology and image in Fra Angelico— where, thanks to Georges Didi-Huberman's remarkable study *Fra Angelico: Dissemblance and Figuration*,[29] we can begin to discern an aesthetic logic in Dionysian vision that proves surprisingly helpful today for imagining transcendence in relation to image and immanence today.

Attending to commonly overlooked aspects of Fra Angelico's frescoes at San Marco, Didi-Huberman argues that Fra Angelico's painting seeks primarily to render "the mystery" of the Incarnation, according to which "eternity appears in time, immensity in measurement, the Creator in the creature . . . the unfigurable in the figure, the unnarratable in discourse, the inexplicable in speech, the uncircumscribable in place, the invisible in vision" (Saint Bernardino of Siena, quoted in FA, 35). The paradox involved here is at least double, insofar as the paradox of the incarnation, where the invisible enters visibility, must itself become visible anew in Fra Angelico's painting itself. To imagine such paradox visually, Didi-Huberman argues, Fra Angelico turns to the practice of a "figuration" whose meaning and function are—exactly contrary to what we might expect of "figurative" painting—not to depict or to designate through mimetic representation but rather to hide or obscure through a displacing "dissemblance":

> For as late as the fifteenth century, "figures" signified the reverse of what we understand by the term today. Today, everyone understands that to figure a thing means to represent the visible aspect of that thing. For Fra Angelico and the religious thinkers of his entourage, however, it meant rather to take one's distance from the aspect, to *displace* it, to take a detour away from resemblance and designation: in short, to enter into the paradoxical realm of equivocation and dissemblance (FA, 3).

Didi-Huberman argues that the logic of figuration in Fra Angelico, which derives directly from the theological vision of Dionysius's "dissimilar similarities," is a logic not of re-presentation but of relation, not of depiction but of displacement and dreamlike association.[30] At bottom, it is a poetic logic whose meaning and function are modeled on the biblical exegesis so fundamental to medieval religious life—an exegesis that opened "the inexhaustible possibility of creating an infinite world of relations, of networks where every particle of sacred text entered into an always unique and totally new correspondence with another particle, freeing meaning to an ever greater extent and, with meaning, freeing faith and the imaginary, by making them swirl endlessly around this central kernel—the kernel of the mystery, this impossible divine *scientia*, the kernel of the Incarnation" (FA 6).

Reading the operation of spiritual exegesis according to the logic of displacement and association, Didi-Huberman is able to locate in that operation an ever growing and ever moving network of relations that generate a meaning that itself is never fixed because it turns around a mystery that cannot be contained, the mystery of invisibility made visible:

> Beyond knowledge, therefore, beyond concepts and opinions, exegesis invented relations among things, words, and biblical images that had no relation in the natural order, in the logical order, or in the order of visible resemblances. Hence it drew the natural order toward the mystery, the logical order toward equivoca-

tion, and the visible order toward dissemblance. That is why exegesis was a *poet-ics* more than a method . . . the producer of enigmas, since its object remained at heart the mystery (FA 6).

Such a poetics, Didi-Huberman goes on to argue, can find an apt medium in painting "because its material, color, seemed just the thing for spontaneously playing the game of displacement and of interlacing, the game of equivocal meanings and the subversion of aspect. That is why, finally, religious painting, 'figurative' as it was, was destined to borrow the path that Dionysius the Areopagite had proposed as a means of constituting the image *between* body and mystery: the paradoxical path of *dissemblant similitudes* . . . " (FA, 6).

In Fra Angelico's "violent" whites and blotches of red, in his Proustian "patches" and Pollock-like splatter, Didi-Huberman sees uses of color whose intensity and variety disrupt straightforward depiction or narration and open the painting to allusion and association—to a movement of displacement that always points "beyond." The theological movement of transcendence through negation—which comes to the Western traditions primarily through Diony-sius, in whom the logic of such negation is christological—thus assumes body in the matter of painting:

> Our hypothesis is therefore that the multicolored zones of Fra Angelico's paint-ings function less as iconic signs than as operators of a *conversion of the gaze*: confronted with these colored zones, we do not discern a great deal; if there is meaning, it is veiled, plurivocal, and not to be found in any manual of iconogra-phy. These zones are acts of negation of the common notion of figure; they in-troduce the mystery, "the unfigurable in the figure." They are at once patches of colored matter projected onto a wall, and patches of negative theology (FA 56).

Seeing in the patch of painting a patch of "negative theology," Didi-Huber-man is able to understand such painting, indeed, within the double move-ment of kataphasis and apophasis. In a central example, by taking into view the usually overlooked panels of (non-figurative) color beneath San Marco's (figurative) Madonna of the Shadows, he indicates that "we need to see the upper part of Angelico's fresco as the semblance, the *it is that* . . . and the lower part as a kind of retraction, an extreme modalization, a colored blur-ring that says *no it is not like that* . . . " (FA 56). Like Dionysian theology, which oscillates without end between kataphasis and apophasis, between image and the unimaginable, so such painting oscillates between the position of sem-blant figure and its removal or undoing in the dissemblant blur and intensity of color.[31]

In that "between," the meaning of the mystery appears as it withdraws and withdraws as it appears—in perfect consistency with the Dionysian under-standing of incarnation; this generation of meaning, strictly ceaseless (because the mystery is bottomless), is made possible, Didi-Huberman argues, through a valorization of visuality—which goes beyond fixed story or narrative and frees visual signifiers to generate a meaning that is never fixed. Fra Angelico paints according to the poetic logic of exegesis in such a way that figures do not simply depict identifiable things but rather form relations and connections that lead one onward—infinitely—according to a self-transcending movement of anagogic desire or eschatological expectation.[32] The dissemblant semblance operates between dis-figuration and pre-figuration, in the inter-space where open-ended meaning arises against the horizon of a promise always past and still to come.

The theological aesthetic operative in Fra Angelico can force the subject of vision to move ever beyond—to transcend the present and its presence—insofar as that aesthetic thus disturbs the "economy of representation" (FA 87). Through such a disturbance, the theological aesthetic undoes any certainty or fixity of meaning by enacting the escape of the referent ad infinitum. In this manner, the dissemblant semblance that Fra Angelico paints repeats the logic of Dionysius's entire cosmological vision—a cosmological vision, I would emphasize, that would resist or unsettle the modern world-picture that finds its unshakeable ground in the representing subject:

> In the last analysis, the entire extension of the visible world could be encompassed, subsumed under the category of dissemblant symbolism, on the condition that the world be conceived *negatively*: for every symbol is dissemblant inasmuch as it is a part of an order of reality inferior to what it signifies. This is, then, a very dialectical way of glorifying the visible world—its anagogical vocation—even as the baseness or humbleness of its ontological status is affirmed. This operation allows us both to preserve the *mystery's* transcendence and to put constantly into play the immanence of the *visuality* of figures (FA 54).

While it may seem strange to think the unsettling of the modern world-picture today by looking to the "negative" cosmology of such a pre-modern Dionysian vision, whose ontology can seem so foreign to the modern and contemporary worlds, such a move might nevertheless be justified to the degree that today's image-world could in fact be thought, at least analogically, in terms of just such a "negative" cosmology—where every symbol proves dissemblant and every image fails to figure God, where, in short, the overwhelming immanence of visuality ever signals, without reaching, the invisible. Like the totality of the Dionysian mystical cosmos, wherein souls desire and signal toward but never find or figure the cosmic "cause," so the all-consuming image-world today might contain a subject who cannot comprehend the totality of that very world—a subject who for that reason is ever on the move, from image to image, desire to desire, through relation and connection, association and displacement, without end.

Such a displacement of the subject within today's all-consuming image-world might be registered at several different levels, most of which would concern the various forms of disjunction between individual experience and the incomprehensible totalities that we imagine to determine the "place" of such experience. As Jacques Derrida has put it, gesturing explicitly toward "the transcendence of tele-technology," "because one increasingly *uses* artifacts and prostheses of which one is totally ignorant, in a growing disproportion between knowledge and know-how, the space of such technical experience tends to become more animistic, magical, mystical."[33] In the space of such disproportion, where experience sees the re-emergence of a certain mystery, image would proliferate without end—and it would do so according to the logic that Fredric Jameson has well elucidated in his analyses of postmodern culture: the irreducible play of "figuration" in the deeply superficial world of late capitalism (or of the "tele-technology" inextricably related thereto) signals "some sense that these new and enormous global realities are inaccessible to any individual subject or consciousness . . . which is to say that those fundamental realities are somehow ultimately unrepresentable or, to use the Althusserian phrase, are something like an absent cause, one that can never emerge into the presence of perception."[34] The individual caught in the grip of today's incomprehensible technological and economic totalities consumes—and is consumed by—an endless stream of image that remains endless, precisely, because the causality of those totalities can never be brought fully to consciousness or representation.

In light of just this disjunction between the individual and the global, know-how and knowledge, in light of this endless figuration that signals an ever absent cause, we might fruitfully situate Didi-Huberman's insight that "if the network of figures is infinite" in a rendering of Dionysian vision like Fra Angelico's, "it is because the image—God's image—is always beyond, like an inaccessible object" (FA 89). From this perspective, the absent cause of Jameson's global totalities, or the mystical space opened by Derrida's "delocalizing tele-technoscience,"[35] might resemble or evoke sufficiently the absent cause and mystical unknowing of Dionysian cosmology to suggest that a shadow of the latter's transcendence may well appear somewhere in the former.

In what figures of totality might we seek such a shadow today? The figures of global totality are, at present, inescapably technological figures, and among such figures I would highlight two. We might, of course, think automatically of the World Wide Web or the Internet, the image of an electronic and telematic light-system in which iconic interconnection approaches incomprehensible complexity and unthinkable totality—altering, perhaps unimaginably, our conception of time and space. But we might think also of the thermonuclear bomb, the image of an unthinkably total potential whose actualization would bind us globally, instantaneously, in an unknowable fusion of invisible light and heat. These two figures of a purely human and rational self-assertion, two figures, one might assume, of a pure immanence, might signal also, equally, the utter displacement or dislocation of the self-grounding, modern subject—and in that displacement, I believe, we might glimpse a shadow of transcendence.

Such a shadow appears brilliantly in DeLillo's *Underworld*, whose concluding pages imagine the intersection or fusion of just these two totalizing technologies by recounting the experience of one Sister Alma Edgar, a dying bride of Christ, who, entering the net, faces the kind of pure exposure or unthinkable openness that we see (or don't see) in Altizer's total presence, Nancy's desertion, or Derrida's tele-technological delocalization: "She is not naked exactly but she is open—exposed to every connection you can make on the world wide web," and she discovers that "there is no space or time out here, or in here, or wherever she is. There are only connections. Everything is connected. All human knowledge gathered and linked, hyperlinked, this site leading to that, this fact referenced to that, a keystroke, a mouse-click, a password—world without end, amen" (U 824–25). Caught up in the hyper-links of the web, which always point relationally "beyond," the dying bride of Christ finds a total interconnection that gives a ubiquity and simultaneity that seem to transform space and time to the point of their undoing. And like the endlessly interconnected and irreducibly referential cosmos of Dionysian vision, which both shows and hides all, or like the figures of Didi-Huberman's Fra Angelico, which constitute an infinite system of relation, connection, allusion, and association, all swirling round an unimaginable mystery, so here the logic of the net draws the bride of Christ onward, leading her, through endless displacement, into a totality that approaches the mystical. And so she can wonder, as one might of the mystical God and cosmos, "Is cyberspace a thing within the world or is it the other way around? Which contains the other, and how can you tell for sure?" (U 826). A believer, Sister Alma Edgar is, of course, well aware that "she is in cyberspace, not heaven" (U 825)—but her awareness is uneasy, for "she feels the grip of systems. This is why she's so uneasy. There is a presence here, a thing implied, something vast and bright . . . it's a glow, a lustrous rushing force that seems to flow from a billion distant net nodes" (U 825).

Caught, incomprehensibly, in that rushing force and glow, in that presence vast and bright, implied and thus elusive, DeLillo's bride of Christ approaches, through this first technological figure of totality, a second: the thermonuclear bomb. The two figures intersect—or better contain one another—in a way that might signal the bottomless complexity and interconnection of the technological and economic, scientific and military, industrial and political totalities that give us something like a computer-bomb: "When you decide on a whim to visit the H-bomb page, she begins to understand. Everything in your computer, the plastic, silicon and mylar, every logical operation and processing function, the memory, the hardware, the software, the ones and zeroes, the triads inside the pixels that form the on-screen image—it all culminates here" (U 825). It "all" culminates "here"—all knowledge and power appear here, the atomic and the cosmic intersect here—on the screen whose bottomless light

gives endless image, a screen where technological totality, the logical consequence of "the gigantic" and its "planetary imperialism of technologically organized man," is given as blinding vision:

> First a dawnlight, a great aurora glory massing on the color monitor. Every ther-
> monuclear bomb ever tested, all the data gathered from each shot, code name,
> yield, test site, Eniwetok, Lop Nor, Novaya Zemlya, the foreignness, the otherness
> of remote populations implied in the place names, Mururoa, Kazakhstan,
> Siberia, and the wreathwork of extraordinary detail, firing systems and delivery
> systems, equations and graphs and schematic cross sections, shot after shot,
> summoned at a click, a hit, Bravo, Romeo, Greenhouse dog—and Sister is basi-
> cally in it.
>
> She sees the flash, the thermal pulse. . . . She stands in the flash and feels the
> power. She sees the spray plume. She sees the fireball climbing, the superheated
> sphere of burning gas that can blind a person with its beauty, its dripping christ-
> blood colors, solar golds and reds. She sees the shock wave and hears the high
> winds and feels the power of false faith, the faith of paranoia, then the mush-
> room cloud spreads around her, the pulverized mass of radioactive debris, eight
> miles high, ten miles, twenty, with skirted stem and platinum cap.
>
> The jewels roll out of her eyes and she sees God (U 826).

Here on the screen where all becomes connection and connection becomes
all—where every image, hyper-linked, points beyond itself within an unthinkable totality, where inside is out and outside in, where the mere click of a hand
gives "shot after shot, bomb after bomb," where the bomb itself takes name after
name and calls up place after place, signaling all the places of unthinkable displacement—here the figure of total disaster or ultimate fusion, dripping in
christblood colors, becomes an image of blinding beauty, like that of the God
whom no one can see without dying, the very God who blinds with his holiness.
"No, wait, sorry. It is a Soviet bomb she sees, the largest yield in history . . .
preserved in the computer that helped build it . . . " (U 826). The dying Bride
of Christ, the believer, comes to her senses, of course, for she knows false faith
and she sees that this blinding beauty dripping in christblood colors, this
"end" in which "everything is connected," is not God. Of course: it is surely not
likely that the believer would find on such a screen, in such a vision of total immanence and human self-assertion, any shadow of transcendence. A total
light, after all, would leave no shadow.
And yet—like the God whose purest light is unimaginable darkness, whose
immanence is transcendence, these images of totality can seem to signal that
which would comprehend the human subject more than the subject would
comprehend it. While born of human self-assertion, while issuing from pure
immanence, technological totality can nevertheless seem, at its very height of
power and in its most absolute actuality, to absorb, escape, and undo us—with
nothing beyond. And at such height, or in such absolution—in the always displaced place of purest fusion, could we really say whether we face a presence or

an absence, an immanence or transcendence? Could shadows of transcendence appear where there are no shadows? It all seems wholly unlikely.

Notes

1. Martin Heidegger, "The Age of the World Picture," in *The Question Concerning Technology and Other Essays*, trans. William Lovitt (New York: Harper and Row, 1977), 134. Hereafter cited parenthetically as WP. The original German, "Die Zeit des Weltbildes," is found in *Holzwege* (Frankfurt am Main: Vittorio Klostermann, 1950); when cited, the German page number, indicated by "G," will follow the English.

2. This seems to me the position of Jean-Luc Marion in *La Croisée du visible* (Paris: Presses Universitaires de France, 1996; first edition, 1991), which takes the image of the "audiovisual epoch" to be grounded in the idolatrous gaze of a monadic subject who brings modern metaphysics and its nihilism to their summit.

3. I take this to be Mark C. Taylor's contention in *Hiding* (Chicago: University of Chicago Press, 1998), whose arguments I contrast with those of Marion in my article "Consuming Desire's Deferral: A Theological Shadow in the Culture of Image," in *Parallax*, vol. 5, no. 1, 1999. "The total thing" is Don DeLillo's phrase, from his exploration of today's technovoyeuristic culture in *Valparaiso: A Play* (New York: Touchstone, 1999), 96.

4. Heidegger wrote his *Beiträge zur Philosophie (vom Ereignis)* between 1936 and 1938, but the work was not published until 1989; the English translation, *Contributions to Philosophy (From Enowning)*, trans. Parvis Emad and Kenneth Maly (Bloomington: Indiana University Press, 1999), will be cited here parenthetically as B; when the original German edition is cited, the German page number will follow the English as BG. *Beiträge zur Philosophie (vom Ereignis)* appears as Band 65 of Heidegger's *Gesamtausgabe* (Frankfurt am Main: Vittorio Klostermann, 1989).

5. See especially Weber's classic "Science as a Vocation," in H. H. Gerth and C. Wright Mills, eds., *From Max Weber: Essays in Sociology* (New York: Oxford University Press, 1946), 139.

6. One might note that the conquest of the world as picture extends its reach even over voice—exercising its logic not only in and through the literal image and its technologies but also, already, in and through a medium such as radio.

7. Søren Kierkegaard, *The Present Age*, trans. Alexander Dru (New York: Harper & Row, 1962), 35.

8. See Walter Benjamin, "The Work of Art in the Age of Mechanical Reproduction," in Hannah Arendt, ed., *Illuminations* (New York: Schocken Books, 1968).

9. One might note here Heidegger's contention that in the "outbreak of massiveness," the masses in society "mount up only because numbers and the calculable already count as what is equally accessible to everyone. What is common to the *many* and to *all* is what the 'many' know as what towers over them" (B 85).

10. See also *Contributions to Philosophy*, 97: "The essential mark of 'nihilism' is not whether churches and monasteries are destroyed and people are murdered, or whether this does *not* happen and 'Christianity' can go its ways; or rather, what is crucial is whether one knows and wants to know that precisely this tolerating of Christianity and Christianity itself—the general talk of 'providence' and 'the Lord God,' however sincere these individuals may be—are merely pretexts and perplexities in *that* domain which one does not want to acknowledge and to allow to count as the domain of decision about be-ing or not-be-ing. The most disastrous nihilism consists in passing oneself off as protector of Christianity and even claiming for oneself the most Christian Christianity on the basis of social accomplishments. The dangerousness in this nihilism consists in its being completely hidden...."

11. Don DeLillo, *Underworld* (New York: Scribner, 1997), 812.

12. DeLillo, *Valparaiso*, 104.

13. Thomas J. J. Altizer, *Genesis and Apocalypse: A Theological Voyage Toward Authentic Christianity* (Louisville, Ky.: Westminster/John Knox Press, 1990), 180. Hereafter cited parenthetically as GA.

14. "Chaosmos" is the apt term used by Umberto Eco to frame his brilliant study of Joyce, *The Aesthetics of Chaosmos: The Middle Ages of James Joyce*, trans. Ellen Esrock (Cambridge, Mass.: Harvard University Press, 1982).

15. Thomas J. J. Altizer, *The Contemporary Jesus* (Albany: State University of New York Press, 1997), 203–204. Hereafter cited parenthetically as CJ.

16. Thomas J. J. Altizer, *Total Presence: The Language of Jesus and the Language of Today* (New York: Seabury Press, 1980), 35–36. Hereafter cited parenthetically as TP.

17. *The Present Age*, 77.

18. *The Present Age*, 63.

`19. *Des Lieux divins* (Mauvezin: Editions Trans-Euro-Repress, 1987). Hereafter cited parenthetically as LD.

20. And in many ways also Marion's "saturated phenomenon." On this latter comparison, see my *Indiscretion: Finitude and the Naming of God* (Chicago: University of Chicago Press, 1999), chapter 6.

21. A perspective, one might note, that would bring together figures otherwise as different as Marion and Taylor, for example.

22. Meister Eckhart, *Comm. Ecc.* § 54, in *Meister Eckhart: Teacher and Preacher*, ed. Bernard McGinn (New York: Paulist Press, 1986), 179. For a discussion of Eckhart's main approaches to this dialectic (in terms of dissimilarity and similarity, distinction and indistinction, opposition and non-opposition), see Vladimir Lossky, *Théologie négative et connaissance de Dieu chez Maître Eckhart* (Paris: Vrin, 1973), 254–275.

23. Richard of St. Victor, *The Mystical Ark* 4.17 (PL 196: 157 CD), quoted in Bernard McGinn, *The Growth of Mysticism* (New York: Crossroad: 1994), 421. For McGinn's very helpful discussion see 395–410.

24. Pseudo-Dionysius, *Divine Names*, 596C, in *The Complete Works of Pseudo-Dionysius*, trans. Colm Luibheid (New York: Paulist Press, 1987). The works of Pseudo-Dionysius will henceforth be cited parenthetically as follows: DN = *Divine Names*; MT = *Mystical Theology*; EH = *Ecclesiastical Hierarchy*; and CH = *Celestial Hierarchy*.

25. McGinn highlights this cosmological orientation in Dionysius and, drawing on Hans Urs von Balthasar, relates the cosmological to the aesthetic. See especially *The Foundations of Mysticism* (New York: Crossroad, 1991), 161.

26. The irreducible openness of this double play would be essential to understanding how the same Dionysian *corpus* could be invoked as a definitive authority for *both* sides in the eighth-century Iconoclasm debates—the seeming paradox noted, for example, in Moshe Barasch's account *Icon: Studies in the History of an Idea* (New York: New York University Press, 1995), 159.

27. Hans Urs von Balthasar, *Glory of the Lord: A Theological Aesthetics*, vol. II, trans. A. Louth, F. McDonagh, and B. McNeil (New York: Crossroad, 1984), 179.

28. Bernard McGinn, *The Foundations of Mysticism*, 174.

29. Georges Didi-Huberman, *Fra Angelico: Dissemblance and Figuration*, trans. Jane Marie Todd (Chicago: University of Chicago Press, 1995). Hereafter cited parenthetically as FA. I have at times slightly altered the translation.

30. Bruno Latour develops a similar and very productive analysis of religious representation in the context of discussions treating art and science as well. See "How to be Iconophilic in Art, Science, and Religion?" in Caroline Jones and Peter Galison, eds., *Picturing Science Producing Art* (New York: Routledge, 1998) and "What is Iconoclash? Or is There a World Beyond the Image Wars?" in Bruno Latour and Peter Weibel, eds., *Iconoclash: Beyond the Image Wars in Science, Religion, and Art* (Cambridge, Mass.: MIT Press, 2002).

31. Both Marion and Taylor, it is worth noting, develop similar approaches to the self-effacing image, or the disfiguring figure. See Marion, op. cit., and Taylor, *Disfiguring: Art, Architecture, Religion* (Chicago: University of Chicago Press, 1992).

32. For a classic study of this interplay between exegesis and expectant desire in the life and spirituality of the monastery, see Jean Leclercq's *The Love of Learning and the Desire for God: A Study of Monastic Culture* (New York: Fordham University Press, 1982).

33. Jacques Derrida, "Faith and Knowledge: the Two Sources of 'Religion' at the Limits of Reason Alone," in Derrida and G. Vattimo, eds., *Religion* (Stanford: Stanford University Press, 1998), 2 and 56.

34. Fredric Jameson, *Postmodernism, or, the Cultural Logic of Late Capitalism* (Durham, N.C.: Duke University Press, 1991), 411.

35. Derrida, op. cit., 56.

8

Transcendence and Representation

GRAHAM WARD

Despite modernity's turn towards immanent values and immanent economies, giving rise to the politics of liberalism and the evolutionarism of Darwin,
an appeal was made to that which transcended all immanence. It is the argument of this essay that modernity's transcendence took two, symmetrical
forms: absolute presence (announced in the aesthetics of the sublime) and
profound absence (a meaninglessness aesthetically embodied in the kitsch).
These two forms of transcendence were inseparable from modernity's twofold construal of mimesis or representation in which, on the one hand, beyond
or outside the sign lay direct and pure contact with the immediacy of the object being signified or, on the other, beyond and outside the sign lay direct and
pure contact with the meaninglessness of the contingent flux.

Modernity's dualism with regard to transcendence and representation is
evident in George Steiner's 1967 volume, *Language and Silence*. There is no
essay in the volume with that title, but there are several essays devoted to various forms of association between language and silence, essays which testify to
varieties of silence. In "Retreat from the Word," for example, Steiner treats the
crisis in literacy in the middle years of the twentieth century. It is a crisis in
which language and reality have become divorced; where in a world in which
mathematics map the profundities of what is real, the world of words has
shrunk. In the "retreat from the authority and range of verbal language"[1] we
are heading towards a tawdry banality, a silence of the Muses, a silence into
which civilization will slide and perish. In "Night Words" he treats this increasing banality with respect to the "new pornographers"[2] who parade the vital
privacies of sexual experience, taking away the words that were spoken in the
night to shout them from the rooftops.

In the commercialization of sex, Steiner observes the kenosis of the Word
(capital letter), the impoverishment of Logos itself. And in a selection of six essays, organized under the heading "Language out of Darkness," Steiner treats
what I believe is the root of the traumatizing autism, out of sheer fear of which
Steiner writes: the death-camps and the ethnic cleansing of Nazi Germany.
Again a silence issues: "The language will no longer grow and freshen. It will no
longer perform . . . its two principal functions: the conveyance of humane order

which we call law, and the communication of the quick of the human spirit we call grace."[3] So, among those writers who remained in Germany (when so many others left), Gottfried Benn "withdrew first into obscurity of style, then into silence."[4] And on the very eve of barbarism Schoenberg has Moses cry: "O word, thou word that I lack." German is no longer a language in which to write creatively. First Adorno's famous aphorism "There is no poetry after Auschwitz," and then the suicidal silences of Paul Celan, Sylvia Plath, and Primo Levi appear as refrains through this volume and Steiner's later ones. The silence distends from German to English, from Italian to French as Steiner charts the slide from *Bildung* to bathos, from the catharsis of tragedy to the babbling of the absurd.

It is the election of silence by those most able to articulate that disturbs him most. He explores this election in another essay in the volume, "Silence and the Poet" with respect to Hölderlin and Mallarmé, and in doing so invokes seemingly less nihilistic silences. "Seemingly," because Steiner is aware that Hölderlin's "quiet madness" may be read as "a negation of his poetry" or "the word's surpassing of itself, for its realization not in another medium but in that which is its echoing antithesis and defining negation, silence."[5] Hölderlin's silence is either the descent into Babel or the consummation of the word. Steiner inquires further into the silence of the sublime, the frozen silences of the magic mountain. At eighteen, Rimbaud published *Une Saison en enfer,* then put away his pen and embarked on a short-lived career selling arms in Sudan. He had achieved the perfect. There was nothing more that could be said. As Steiner points out, "In much modern poetry silence represents the claims of the ideal."[6] Words dissolve into the purer notation of music; leaving the verbal behind is a positive spiritual act, cognizant of transcendence, trembling on the neon edge of immediate relation. Steiner writes: "[I]t is decisively the fact that language does have frontiers, that it borders on three other modes of statement—light, music, and silence—that gives proof of a transcendent presence in the fabric of the world. It is just because we can go no further, because speech so marvelously fails us, that we experience the certitude of a divine meaning surpassing and enfolding ours. What lies behind man's word is eloquent of God."[7]

Silence, in Steiner's work, is more ambivalent than the rich densities of meaning in words themselves. But two dominant modes are evident: the silent bankruptcy of language, as rhetoric veils the void, and the silent horizons of the transcendent. Beyond language is either nihilistic despair or divine plenitude. Either way the final condition of words is to become unhinged from the world, taking on a rhetorical density that aims at seduction rather than education. Words are unhinged also from any relation to the divine, for "the categories of God are not parallel or commensurate to those of man."[8] Mathematics and music become both threat and promise. On the one hand, they threaten literacy and "so far, in history, [language] has been the vessel of human grace and the prime carrier of civilization," on the other, music and mathematics "are 'languages' other than languages. Purer, perhaps."[9]

In this essay I wish to revisit this topic of representation and its transcendence, language and silence, and submit Steiner's deliberations to a genealogical critique. For what does Steiner presuppose, and leave unquestioned, about the nature and operation of language in order to produce his various relationships between words and silence, words and the Word? And whence come these presuppositions? For our understandings of the nature and operation of language (and therefore the relationship between language and silence, language and the divine) are culturally and temporally specific. As comparative linguistics from Humboldt, Sapir, Whorf, and the more contemporary examinations of the relationship between translation and colonialism have come to see, different languages encode different symbolic world-views—different construals of time, space, objects, subjects, and their connectedness. Furthermore, theories about the nature and operation of language change; the act and function of naming are conceived differently in other historical epochs. The relationship between words and the world in the work of Gregory of Nyssa, John Locke, John McDowell, and Jacques Derrida differ considerably. And within any cultural evaluation of a language, attention can be given to one part of speech over another, transforming the way the operation of language is understood. An understanding of language as dominated by the role of the verb, rather than the noun, the preposition, or the conjunction, expresses and produces a world-view quite different from the construal of language dominated by nomenclature. With respect to the language of mysticism Frederick J. Streng has pointed out that "different assumptions about the function of language contribute to different interpretations of the soteriological significance found in different sorts of mystical awareness."[10] He observes, concerning the assertions of certain mystics, that "the key function of such claims is to release the individual from attachment to the assumption that words have a one-to-one correspondence with separate entities in either ideal or physical experience."[11] If Steiner represents (and sums up) a prevalent position on the relationship between language and silence—a position which he views as developing from the seventeenth century and reaping its first fruits in the nineteenth-century avant-garde and the twentieth-century crisis of representation—then a genealogical account of this position would unlock other possibilities for the nature and operation of language. From these possibilities we can begin to construct new filiations between language and silence. In doing this we will advocate the need for what Derrida terms "quasi-transcendence" and offer a theological account of representation, modeled in the Christian understanding of incarnation.

On the Sublime and the Kitsch

Steiner's construal of language and silence is caught between two faces of modernity, both of which have a theological past: the kitsch and the sublime.

These two aesthetic categories have a structural relationship to other binaries that structure the modern world-view: body/mind, secular/sacred, immanent/transcendent, particular/universal, public/private, subjective/objective, female/male. We will examine the category of the sublime first.

The experience of the sublime is an encounter with the ineffable, the silence of the unpresentable. It is the entry into the white margins beyond words as in Keats's final line of his sonnet "On First Looking into Chapman's Homer": Cortez straddling the Atlantic and Pacific, gazing out upon immeasurable distances "silent on a peak in Darien." The sublime marks the limit, end, and rupture of the rational order; it remains what Kant termed *unerklärlich*. Jean-François Lyotard, reworking the Kantian sublime, suggests "There are no sublime objects, but only sublime feelings."[12]

Objects dissolve into the immediacy of experience. The feeling is one of grasping the present, one of universal validity, of unlimited freedom. Nothing can prepare for its coming, it arrives as a surprising event which suspends consciousness. I have written about this elsewhere and do not intend to rehearse that analysis.[13] Furthermore, John Milbank has also delineated how the sublime functions as modernity's transcendent and leads directly to the neo-Romantic pursuit by certain post-structural thinkers of aporia, rupture, the impossible, the unpresentable, and the irrational.[14] What is important here is to bring out certain emphases with respect to language and silence. These emphases are: a) the centrality of feeling or experience which displaces consciousness, knowledge, and reason; b) the aspiration towards an immediacy beyond, better than, and determinative of mediation—that is, presence beyond and outside representation; c) the perceiving subject and the objective spectacle which overwhelms both seeing and subjectivity; d) a dislocational event that suspends and denigrates a certain conception of time and space (as both measurable and regular); e) the incommensurate orders of immanence and transcendence which tend towards the hypostasis of difference and alterity; f) the foregrounding of the arbitrary—both in terms of the rupturing, unpredictable event and the relation between language (representation) and the world as present to itself outside language.

These emphases have a theological past. In fact, the development of the sublime from Burke to Philippe Lacoue Labarthe is the rendering into secular aesthetics of erstwhile theological concerns. These concerns were most prominently evident in new existential understandings of revelation—legitimating early Protestant biblicalism—and the development of what Michel de Certeau has termed "the science of mystics."[15]

For Certeau, the cry of the mystic (or the possessed) in the sixteenth and seventeenth centuries was the tearing apart of the social symbolic in an attempt to find another tongue, a more authentic tongue, with which to speak. This tongue would allow the voice of the other to be heard. This ecstatic cry ruptures the routine and quotidian, incising across the surface of the world a testimony to the ineffable distinctiveness of the God beyond being.

Revelation links an ecstatic non-knowing, an abyssal silence, with words. The violence and violation of the mystic event is subsequently rehearsed in what Certeau terms a "manner of speaking" (suggesting a connection between the verbal excesses of mysticism and the visual excesses of Mannerism). While the mystic operates as translator of an ultimate alterity, difference is produced by torturing the everyday use of language. The manner of speaking is likened to circumcision, the cutting away at the flesh of words in order to make manifest the spiritual. Words are shattered and semantic units split. Commenting upon Diego de Jesus's Introduction to the *Obras espirituales* of John of the Cross, Certeau writes about the "process of fabrication" in which "mystic phrases" were constructed: "It was characterized both by a *shift of subject* within the meaning space circumscribed with words and by a *technical manipulation* of these words in order to mark the new way in which they were being used. In short, it was a practice of detachment. It denatured language: it distanced it from the function that strove after an imitation of things. It undid the coherence of signification, insinuating into each semantic unit wily and 'senseless' shifts of interplay."[16] And so the adjective "mystic" deflects attention from the noun it qualifies, from that which the noun represents. And in doing that the signified is erased in favor of the signifier. This is the paradoxical structure of the mystical manner of speaking: the transportation beyond language (which is the content of what is spoken) in fact opacifies the sign, giving weight to its materiality. In pointing towards an outside, to that which exceeds language, it "produces nothing more in language than the effects relative to what is not in language."[7] What remains paramount is the primacy of experience itself: the experience of transcendence translates into the affectivity of rhetoric, the pyrotechnic spectacle of the verbal. The staging of the transcendent imitates the excesses of ecstasy. This new attention to the surfaces of language turns words away from the act of communication and towards a certain commodification—the elaborate productions of spectacle. Such that what we can begin to recognize emerging here is the obverse side of the sublime—the kitsch.

Certeau provides a genealogy for this mystic science and, in part, this genealogy too is theological. Following Henri de Lubac (and in agreement with Congar, Balthasar, and, more recently, Eric Alliez, John Milbank, and Catherine Pickstock), Ockhamist linguistics is very clearly to blame.[8] Nominalism deontologized words. It fostered a metaphysics of linguistic atomism which was subsequently encouraged by the breakup of Latin as a *lingua franca* and the development of vernacular languages. It established the founding dualisms of modernity: epistemology/ontology, word/thing. The dominant role of the verb in Medieval Latin—which was related to Christology for Christ was God's verb—was dethroned in favour of the noun. God is now encountered on the far side of language. I will not rehearse here what has now become so much an intellectual commonplace that the ground is well prepared for revisionist studies of Scotus and Ockham. What is interesting is the way Certeau relates this displacement of the ontological and the increasing questions about whether and how language refers, to a shift in ecclesial practice and politics towards "strategies of the visible."

He notes, again following in the footsteps of de Lubac: "After the middle of the twelfth century, the expression [*corpus mysticum*] no longer designated the Eucharist, as it had previously, but the Church."[19] The Church, as the social body of Christ, begins to make its hidden *(mysticus)* sacramental body visible. In this move to the specular—the origin of which Certeau locates at the Third Lateran Council (1179), and so prior to the work of Ockham (making the nominalist deontologizing of language a product of an earlier theological shift)—the Eucharist "constituted a focal point at which mystical reality became identified with visible meaning. . . . Moreover, it consolidated clerical power. . . . In this instance the sign was the presence it designated. . . . This Eucharistic 'body' was the 'sacrament' of the institution, the visible instituting of what the institution was meant to become."[20] The Eucharist is the first in a developing line of objects fully present to themselves. Eucharistic presence prepares the ground for empiricism. The Eucharist announces a univocity of being which is the basic presupposition of the natural sciences. But simultaneously, and paradoxically, it also produces equivocity. For the Church's "strategies of the visible"—which included professionalizing the clergy and drawing the secrets of secular life into its confessional and juridical spaces—"transformed the very practice of knowledge and signs,"[21] setting up a disassociation between the mystical and the visible, presence and representation. The paradox again: the desire and move towards greater transparency produces an increasing opacity. It is a paradox that will endlessly push apart communion and communication and install a gap, an absence, a lack. The simplicity and purity yearned for generates representational excess; mystical science requires lexical excess.

The kitsch now announces itself, and announces itself first in an *ecclesia* developing its theatricality and spectacle. The kitsch arises in a culture of excess. Unlike the sublime, the kitsch proclaims that the other side of language is not transcendental meaningfulness, but meaninglessness. The sign is not a sign of anything but simply the fabrication of a surface. Hence, Steiner's ambivalent "silence"—the silence eloquent of God and the silence of futility, banality, an atheological account of *nihil:* the silence of full presence and the silence of unredeemable absence; the silence of plenitude and the silence of the void. The German dramatist Wedekind wrote, in 1917, that "Kitsch is the contemporary form of the Gothic, Rococo, Baroque."[22] What comes to be a dominant cultural form, a pseudo-art, in the late nineteenth and twentieth centuries because of techniques for mass production and professional marketing, has its roots in the metaphysics and cultural forms of former epochs. Kitsch is the exaltation of ornamentation for its own sake, of superficiality, of ephemerality. Like camp, it flaunts the glitter and the glamour of its surfaces. It is eclectic and vulgar. Tocqueville, on his first visit to New York, observed how what he first saw as marble temples and palaces along the shoreline turned out, on closer inspection, to be "whitewashed brick . . . [and] columns of painted wood."[23] More recently, Jean Baudrillard has commented on Las Vegas that its buildings are straight from film sets; they aspire to the weightlessness and insubstantiality of theatrical scenery, backed as they are by the desert at the foot of the Sangre de Cristo Mountains. Kitsch announces that though the sign is bankrupt, such emptiness can be entertaining, diverting the gaze away from the meaninglessness, the desert, itself. The kitsch is unashamed idolatry. For Baudrillard simulacrum now embraces its own condition as commodity. It creates an ethos that fosters the contemporary production and promotion of cyberspaces and virtual realities, soft ontologies (Vattimo) and hyperrealisms (Eco). For Baudrillard (and Fredric Jameson) it typifies late capitalism—where alienation of the producer from production and the commodification of the consumer product over both are self-consciously extolled as cultural values. In a world-view which proclaims that pleasures are evanescent and to be seized as they present themselves, the kitsch offers instant and easy enjoyments that are temporary and faddish. It shares borders with decadence and hedonism, but, more significant for the ideas being examined here, it glories in aesthetic inadequacy! It signals the failure of the aesthetic to express, substituting spectacle and parading suggestions of wealth and exaggeration. It is the art form of the haughty, the brash, and the confident.

Wedekind perceptively recognizes the Rococo and Baroque as the predecessors of kitsch. Certeau would add Mannerism also: "The *Meniera,* an elaboration of language upon itself, the subtle and sumptuous effects of which illustrated indefinite capacities, was exalted. This expressionism was made up of artefacts that exorcised the referential and set in movement a space shattered into contrasting fragments. In paintings, the passions depicted portray mainly a passion of forms and colors subjected to the delicious tortures of an art."[24] What Certeau does not do is explore the association between the turn of the Church towards strategies of visibility and the multiplication of "artefacts that exorcised the referential" which characterised Counter-Reformation culture. It is the Church which first fosters the ethos of the kitsch and hence, even today, it is the gory presentations of the sacred heart, the Lourdes water in plastic bottles with blue celluloid caps of the Virgin, and fat yellow candles burning before plaster saints which most clearly typifies the celebration of the superficial.[25] Kitsch draws close to bathos: the most profound suddenly conceived as expensive vulgarity: high art as depictions of a can of Campbell's soup; the barley-sugar twists and tasselled marble drapes of the ornate baldacchino by Bernini in St. Peter's.

The Baroque announces the secularization of perception and visibility out of which the modern engagement with the spectacle that Guy Debord so dramatically portrays emerges. "The spectacle is the nightmare of imprisoned modern society with ultimately expresses nothing more than its desire to sleep."[26] The spectacle, not religion, is the contemporary opiate of the people, and the Baroque, with its exaggerated attention to surfaces, first gave it expression.[27] It was the triumph of that rendering of the invisible visible which Certeau describes as occurring at the end of the thirteenth century; the invisible concerned the divine (the gasps of ecstasy on Bernini's Teresa and the blessed Ludovico Albertoni), the infinite darknesses of Copernicus's universe (as felt and feared by Pascal in *Pensées*) and the passions of the soul (in Rembrandt's depiction of Bathesheba or Jan Six). The secularization of the visible is coupled with a new appeal to the immediate. John Rupert Martin speaks of the "sense of presence imparted by the greatest portraits of the seventeenth century. . . . Here is no barrier between the subject and the observer."[28] This attention to the presence of things leads to their commodification, their glorification. We are on the road to the market fetishism that marks advanced consumerism and the kitsch. The Baroque announces a certain "in your face" triumphalism, with its voluptuous forms, its expressive energies, and its monumentality. The multifigured scenes (many of them Scriptural or based on the lives of the saints) of Carracci and Rubens bespeak what Stephen Calloway terms a culture of enthusiasm for excess. Calloway reminds us, in a way that directly associates the Baroque with the kitsch, that "baroque" was a derogatory term for the "extravagant and whimsical, grotesque, and even coarse and vulgar."[29] There is self-conscious theatricality here, a passionate rhetoric of gestures[30], and an erotic candor all brought to the depthless surface of the work itself. Christine Buci-Glucksmann speaks of the Baroque "erotics of nothing." In the derangement of appearances, the enchantment of illusion, the overembodied universe of the Baroque "this 'nothing of being' changes into an infinity of ecstatic delight . . . a plethora of forms."[31] She continues: "As it becomes impossible to determine finitude and appearances in relation to any identity reference, any essence or substance, we are left with an infinite regress towards a point that is always slipping away, a pure otherness of figure. . . . The baroque signifier proliferates beyond everything signified, placing language in excess of corporeality . . . , baroque reason brings into play the *infinite materiality* of images and bodies."[32] We are close here to Baudrillard's simulacra, to the glorification of surface, the exaltation of the superficial, the surrender to the first devouring look and the ephemeral which is characteristic of the kitsch. Illusion conscious of itself, conscious of its own staging, seeks only to be sensational, not meaningful, spectacular not significant. On the other side of the *trompe l'oeil* visions of eternity lies caricature, "born at the same moment as Baroque art itself,"[33] after Annibale Carracci.

That the Church continued its commitment to such visibility is evident in the decoration of chapels and monuments, the number of votive pictures, paintings from Scripture, baldacchins, altarpieces, statues of saints, the designing of churches, and the patronage of Popes. Italy was the first center for Baroque sensibility, particularly between the pontificates of Sixtus V (1585–90) and Paul V (1604–21). "Having renounced the dreams of temporal hegemony that had haunted some of the Renaissance pontiffs, the new popes transferred the will to power to a spiritual empire, whose grandeur must now be reflected by Rome."[34] Artists were encouraged "to elaborate that 'oratorical' style which was natural to the programme of apologetics and propaganda allotted by the Council of Trent to religious art."[35]

Baroque sensibility displayed a theatrical exercise of secular power, papal power then a sovereign power. The Council of Trent and the publication of Loyola's *Spiritual Exercises* are viewed as two of the foremost influences on the development of the Baroque. But in giving herself over to the triumph of the visible, to the phantasmagoria of worldly goods, the Church sublates any theology of the sign to an aesthetics, and any theology of time to the serial stuttering of the present.

Mimesis in modernity moves between these two poles—the sublime and the kitsch—both of which de-create by insisting upon the inadequacy of signification in signifying. The sublime and the kitsch are mirror reflections of each other, each producing depthlessness, each denigrating the body as such and materiality as such. For both require the disintegration (and proclaim the fundamental illusion) of time and space. That which lies beyond can be either theistically or atheistically interpreted; it can either be plenitude or void. As Steven Katz observes: "Though two or more experiences are said to be 'ineffable,' the term 'ineffable' can logically fit many disjunctive and incomparable experiences. That is to say, an atheist can feel a sense of dread at the absurdity of the cosmos which he labels ineffable, while the theist can experience God in a way that he also insists is ineffable."[36] The relationship that binds and yet polarizes the sublime and the kitsch is the same relationship that binds and yet polarizes theism and atheism. The paradoxical ambivalence of Steiner's observations on the relationship of language to silence shares this same logic. His position is a rehearsal of an implicitly gnostic understanding of language which has dominated Western European culture for centuries, and which Christianity helped to disseminate. But the subsequent emphasis upon the poverty of language issues from viewing signification as descriptive: the signs name that which lies outside the signs and they have established themselves as names through social convention. Katz points to how both the theist and the atheist "label."

To some extent, the move from modernity to postmodernity has only accelerated the development of such an understanding. The attention given by certain post-structuralist thinkers to what Ricoeur terms "the aporetics of discourse," to hiatuses of one sort or another, to ontological ruptures and epistemological breaks, to broken middles and what Foucault calls "eventalization" are all in line with mimesis in modernity. Significantly, Certeau himself, although aware of the theological genealogy of contemporary accounts of signification and aware of alternative theological accounts in the tradition, continues the same gnostic trajectory. At the end of *The Mystic Fable*, he rejects the frank espousal of nihilism evident in Labadie—who embraces darkness, loss, and journeying, like Cain, into endless exile. Labadie "no longer has anything to 'say' but the 'lie' of an image," he tells us. "Labadie has led us to the edge of a shore where there is nothing, formally, but the relation between defiance and loss. That 'excess' marks a boundary. We must return to the 'finite' place, the body, which *mystics* or the mystic 'infinitizes,' and let Labadie pass by."[37] Certeau rejects the way that his fellow countryman, Baudrillard, welcomes. But, despite the rejection and the insistence on a return to the body and the finite—return to a doctrine of creation—he repeatedly wishes to explore "*la rupture instauratrice.*" Furthermore, in two works which cover the period of his most prolific production "*Comme une goutte d'eau dans la mer*" written in 1973 and "*Extase blanche*" written in 1983, he appeals to the transcendentalism of the sublime, he repeats the journey towards erasure. The only difference between Labadie's journey and Certeau's is the employment of daylight rather than darkness. Certeau enters that "daylight forever" that is still being rehearsed today:

> Here is what the final bedazzlement would be: an absorption of objects and subjects in the act of seeing. No violence, only the unfolding of presence. Neither the fold nor hole. Nothing hidden and thus nothing visible. A light without limits, without difference; neuter, in a sense, and continuous. It is only possible to speak of it in relation to our cherished activities, which are utterly annihilated there. There is no more reading which signs no longer are removed from and deprived of what they indicate. There is no more interpretation if no secret sustains and summons it. There are no more words if no absence founds the waiting that they articulate. Our works are gently engulfed in this silent ecstasy. Without disaster and without noise, simply having become futile, our world . . . ends.[38]

This is, as the sublime and the kitsch are, the apotheosis of spectacle producing, affirming, and operating within the parameters of the same dualisms (with their unequal valorizations): presence/absence, language/silence, mediation/immediacy, inside the created world order/beyond in the divine order, here/there, immanence/transcendence, experience/representation of experience, object/word. The self and the subject-object relations engulfed are all products of Cartesianism.

Return to Allegory and the Mystical Sense
Not all poststructualists follow Certeau's trajectory. Some adamantly critique these dualisms which stake out the metaphysical boundaries of modernity (and

postmodernity) and present ways of rethinking the nature and operation of language in a way which attempts to rewrite the relationship between language and silence. In particular, we will look at the quite different programs of Jacques Derrida and Michel Serres with respect to their appreciation of allegory.

The work of both thinkers issues from Saussure's challenge to correspondence theories of language. As I have argued elsewhere, Saussure's thinking develops within a broadly Kantian framework.[39] His concern lies not with the relationship between word and the world it may or may not hook up to. His concern is not then with demonstrating or denigrating any correspondence view of language. His attention is drawn to the synchronic rather than the diachronic axis, to a system of differentials within any speech act rather than to discourse (or linguistic performance). As such he is concerned with the signifier/signified relationship (how names signify), not with the *economy* of the signifier (the movement of the signifier with respect to any textual field). It is the *economy* of the signifier which Derrida thinks through in his construals of *différance*, dissemination, and supplementarity. This post-structural move turns its attention towards time, what Paul de Man, in developing his understanding of allegory, called "the rhetorics of time."[40] The rhetorics of time critiques movements beyond language and putative engagements with ontologies of either presence or absence inferred to lie ultimately on the other side of words. For Derrida, encounters with presence and absence necessitate illegitimate transcendental moves towards atemporality. His poststructural emphasis upon the rhetorics of time forestalls and questions the possibility of such a move. To the freeze-framing attention to names/labels is added an attention to verbs, to economies, to practices, to teleologies and eschatologies. Derrida's examination of the "middle-voice" with respect to *différance* illustrates this.

All discourse is haunted, for Derrida, by this other scene: the scene of iteration, *différance*, dissemination and supplementarity that constitutes deconstruction. It is in this sense all discourse, for Derrida, performs the allegory of *différance*. For allegory is always a negotiation with what is other. Deconstruction is this negotiation: for what is said in allegorical discourse is always inhabited by another sense, another meaning. Saying one thing in terms of another is frequently how allegory is defined. Saying is always deconstructive because it operates in terms of semantic slippage and deferral. So the discourse of negative theology also performs this function. Both allegory and negative theology are self-consciously deconstructive; they are discourses in which the mimetic economy is conscious of itself. As discourses they perform the kenosis of meaning that *différance* announces. Their near-neighbor in this is irony. But in allegory and negative theology, the shifting of sense is semantically constructive—although in different ways. In negative theology one sense is subverted in order to facilitate a higher sense, it serves and supports the possibility of this higher sense. In negative theology this hierarchy of senses, effecting a semantic displacement, is fundamental and theologically informed. In allegory one sense folds into another sense without displacement. The boundaries of where one sense becomes another are impossible to locate because simultaneous senses occupy the same discursive space without priority. Irony is closer to the discourse of negative theology in that it subverts and establishes a hierarchy of sense. But here the subversion is semantically destructive: one sense is undermined by another. The displacement here is violent; whereas in the discourse of negative theology the displacement is "natural" because in accord with a theological ordinance.

What is important to recognize in these distinctions is that difference in allegorical discourse is not made substantive or structural; the "other" sense (and which is the "other sense" is precisely put into question in allegorical discourse) is never separated off and made distinct. The other or different sense has no existence independent of the saying itself. We cannot pass beyond the saying. There is no beyond. The other lives within, is known only within, the familiar. Difference in allegory does not announce a metaphysical or theological apartheid—which is what a hierarchically arranged dualism announces. Difference, the other sense, is intrinsic to and makes possible the significance of any more obvious sense. The movement of sense continually shifts—one coming into focus here, another there. Both subjects and predicates are brought into the wider discursive play of the narrative, performing and producing a temporality encoded in the verbs.[41] The reader is a pilgrim in a tropological land, walking as through a dream where the seeming substantiality of this or that, of here or there, can at any moment become something, or be suggestive of something, else. "How easy is a bush supposed a bear." Allegory is translocational, transpositional, transfigurative, transcorporeal: allegory makes possible the statement "This is my body."

We are coming closer now to the rub of the matter. Negative theology is what Certeau termed "a manner of speaking." Irony and allegory—and *différance*—announce ways of viewing the world or, in theological-speak, doctrines of creation. All three are practices—that is, involvement in speaking about God negatively, in being ironic or allegorical, produces certain subjectivities. But allegory and irony, like deconstruction, "is inseparable from a general questioning of *tekhnē*,"[42] not just a questioning of technical reasoning. Irony points to dislocations, calling into account the world as *commedia*. It unweaves the safety and seductions of synecdoche—the part as the whole—suggesting an ambiguous world-view in which tragedy and serendipitous chance are all too possible. Allegory performs not only the suspension of proper names, but the suspension of the material itself. It dissolves the line between name and thing and any assumption that the world is a static state upon the basis of which knowledge of things through the transparency of words is believable.

In allegory the act of naming escapes, because the names are excessive to a metaphysical essentialism which establishes the law of identification. It em-

phasizes that we see "as." It announces that we read continually, we have to because we see "as." We read the world; a world in which phenomena are time
bound and so never the same from one moment to the next. Creation, in allegory, is a work that is still proceeding; and inseparable from that proceeding is
the meaning of and in the world, which is also ongoing and incomplete. The
deferral of meaning in *différance* allows us to witness transferential relations
between phenomena given in time. Derrida asks, "Is there a proper story for
this thing [deconstruction]? I think it consists only of transference, and a
thinking through of transference, in all the sense that this word acquires in
more than one language, and first of all that of the transference between language."[43] Allegory, like deconstruction, is the performance of transference.
Situated within an allegorical reading—and reading is always itself transferential and a situating of ourselves with respect to that transferential process—
we perform transference. Not that we are transferred from here to
there—which appears to be the logic of the mystical discourse in the seventeenth century (if Certeau is right). For to be transferred from here to there
would again require the law of identification—that I already possess certain
knowledge of who I am, where I am and where there "is." In allegory I am
given over to the process of transference where the other continually arrives
and translates the sense. And in translating the sense I am myself translated,
losing the stabilities of being able to identify, losing the meaningfulness of ascent or descent, inside or outside.

Allegory, like *différance,* installs the quasi-transcendent. This quasi-transcendent refuses the dualism of immanence and transcendence, forestalling
the dualisms of absence and presence, mediation and immediacy, phenomenal
and noumenal, body and spirit. Luce Irigaray, herself attempting to sublate
these dualisms, speaks oxymoronically of a "sensible transcendent," practicing
the linguistic hysteria of the mystics *(mysteria,* she will call it).[44] But elsewhere
she will employ the metaphor of incarnation to make the same point. It is, ultimately, to an inquiry into the nature of incarnationalism that our rethinking
of the relationship between language and silence will conduct us, as we will
see. Derrida will speak of a certain kenosis—without apparently realizing that
kenosis can only be understood theologically in terms of Christ. "God" "is" the
name of this bottomless collapse, of this endless desertification of language.
But the trace of this negative operation is inscribed *in* and *on* and *as* the *event*
(what *comes* what there is and which is always singular, what finds in this kenosis the most decisive condition for its coming or its upsurging)."[45]

Derrida is examining here the apophatic writings of Angelus Silesius. His
language, miming Silesius's, is freighted with negativity: "bottomless collapse,"
"endless desertification." In fact, for those wanting to take up Derrida's work as
a therapeutic tool for examining theological discourse, Derrida's explicit writings on negative theology may not be the most productive place for investigation. For he absorbs and mimes the negativity in a way which needs to be

counterbalanced by his accounts of deconstruction as the "promise" and the "yes, yes." Derrida's discourse on and within negative theology can too easily be dismissed as nihilistic if attention is only paid to the constantive statements that can be extracted from this work. Respect for the very brio of the discourse—its abrasiveness, its elusiveness, the rhetorics of its polyphonic performance—is necessary. For example, there is a staging of at least two voices in his essay "*Sauf le nom*" (since the voices are not named, only several pronominal interjections of "I" located, the voices cannot be numbered). One voice corrects, sometimes questions, sometimes develops the thought of the voice preceding it. So that where statements suggest a passing "over to the other edge"[46] into a total alterity, other statements insist "that the outside would come thus already from the outside."[47] That is, there is no pure outside. The outside is already operating within. And in the movement to absolute surrender there is a recognition that "everything would remain intact . . . after the passage of a *via negativa*."[48] So, while rehearsing Silesius's "bottomless collapse," what Derrida points to in this essay is the way the "collapse" never comes. The edge of the absolutely external is never crossed. So that we never fully make that passage into the desert. We never have access to the abyss as such. Language can never complete the kenotic process. The desertification is a form of playing within God, not a movement over the edge into that which is wholly other. "Negative theology then can only present itself as one of the most playful forms of the creature's participation in this divine play."[49] The other in *différance* is quasi-transcendental and that is why it is inscribed "in and on and as" to the event of writing, finding in the surrender of fixed and stable reference "the most decisive condition for its coming and its upsurging." What Derrida's thinking draws us towards here is a thinking about language in terms of creation and participation. He does not use the metaphor of incarnation, but the economy of discourse transgresses construals of inside and outside, immanent and transcendent, in a way analogous to the Christian understanding of the incarnate Word and the God who is not simply *for us,* but also *with us* and working *through us.* Conceived in this way, kenosis becomes the allegory of deconstruction while deconstruction becomes the allegory of all signifying economies. We are picking up here the theological provenance of allegory, a provenance older than the theological genealogy traced behind Steiner's language and silence polarity. We can read again, and in a different way, the relationship between language and silence.

Before examining the importance of this theological genealogy, with the assistance of the work of Michel Serres, let me just draw out two sets of consequences of this thinking: first with respect to how it counters the construal of language and silence as represented in Steiner's work; secondly with respect to the theological implications of rejecting Steiner's model for the relationship between language and silence.

For Steiner, as we saw, it is axiomatic that language is inadequate. But Derrida's work calls this into question. For whence can one announce that the words employed are inadequate? For who can calibrate the degrees of adequacy and inadequacy? Inadequate to what? The logic of linguistic adequation is concomitant with a correspondence theory of language—where the words are *equal* to that to which they refer. It is a requirement of such thinking that the subject position of the I, from which the identities and essences of both word and things can be assessed, is self-transparent. Adequation is an evaluative term implying judgment and requiring knowledge of the true state of things. It has to come from a position outside the linguistic matrix. It demands a view from nowhere. As Aquinas realized, only God understands the world literally. Derrida's account of *différance* construes language not as simply denotative—accounting for what is there—but as connotative also, and participating in a dynamic unfolding.

Secondly, for Steiner, it is axiomatic that silence lies on the other side of language. Derrida will also call this into question. As there is no pure outside, and therefore no experience of the outside as such, there is no transcending of language into the silences and daylight beyond words. Derrida emphasizes that there is aporia—ambiguity or metaphoricity which prevents language from strictly being denotational, and so prevents language from being the transparent medium for identities and identification. This aporia remains irreducible. But he stresses that it is "Aporia, rather than antimony . . . insofar as it is neither an 'apparent or illusory' antimony, nor a dialectizable contradiction in the Hegelian or Marxist sense, nor even a 'transcendental illusion in a dialectic of the Kantian type,' but instead an interminable experience."[50] He goes on to say that there is no experience of aporia as such: *"the aporia can never simply be endured as such. The ultimate aporia is the impossibility of the aporia as such. The reservoir of this statement seems to me incalculable."*[51] It is in this sense that one has to understand Derrida's infamous statement *"il n'y a pas de hors texte."* We have to rethink, then, the relationship between language and silence in a way that recognizes silence as integral to communication; silence *as* a form of communication.

For Derrida, as there is always a rhetoric of aporia, there will also be a rhetoric of silence. Silence becomes analogous to the blank margins of a page, the space beneath the vaulting of a cathedral, or a musical interval. The margin frames and focuses the text. The empty spaces here establish a certain tension between the arrangement of the letters, the words and the syntax into an encrypted communication and the empty margins that create a space for the cessation of intellection. It is a space for/of breathing. A blank page as such sets up no tension within the reading process, but another rhythm with respect to the context in which the blank page opens. The margins, therefore, articulate, possibly at a somatic level, a certain rest, a certain Sabbath, a space for the activities of prayer and mediation. They articulate through this rhythm and in this rhythm. And every poet knows how to take advantage of this rhythm and make it part of the poem through enjambment, line length, and the spatial dy-namics of the typesetting. The margins are not silent as such. The silence is ar-chitectured and integral to the speaking or the phrasing. Think of the interval between the first and second opening phrases of Beethoven's Fifth Symphony. The hiatus is in continuity with, and therefore part of, the larger musical com-position. This is not a silence, an emptiness beyond communication. Even the sublime moment in Keats's sonnet "On First Looking into Chapman's Homer" is architectured. On this account of language and silence there are no gaps or ruptures or top-down revelations as such. With respect to the discourse of negative theology, there are not then "fissures opened by our language" that are not simultaneously bound and constructed by that language. To accept the in-dependent existence of the fissures as such is to become blind to one's own use of metaphor. There is aporia and there is the constant negotiation of aporia through supplementation. There is quasi-transcendence.

What are the implications for this for a theological account of the relationship between language and silence? Derrida is no theologian, and when he employs theological vocabulary (like kenosis, like the Word) he does not think it through with any theological sophistication. We will return to this. Hence the Word is re-lated to logocentrism (the full, realized presence of meaning) and the transcen-dental signifier that stabilizes and gives identity to all things. Derrida shows little understanding of the relationship of the Word to the Triune Godhead and cre-ation. He shows little understanding of "presence" as it is understood theologi-cally. He reads presence as modernity reads presence—as immediate, direct truth, as self-authenticating meaning, as the full realization in this moment of time (the now) of identity. Derrida does not understand presence as grace. He does not un-derstand the mediatorial operation of the Word and the Spirit within creation, a creation which is not finished, and a Word which is not yet complete. The pres-ence of God in grace is not the violence of the moment—but the unfolding of the divine maintenance and sustenance of the world. Taking the incarnation seri-ously is not being translated out of the world into immediate contact with God; it is recognizing the movement of God in what has been gifted for us in the world. Incarnation cannot admit the inadequacy of mediation and representation; for it is itself implicated in a divinely sanctioned mediation and representation. To ac-cept the antimony of language and silence theologically would implicate us in gnosticism. The contemporary desire for the "daylight forever" like Certeau's de-sire for "white ecstasy" is gnostic.

But Christian theological anthropology begins with human beings *made in the image* of and, as such, the creators and purveyors of image-making. Christ as the incarnation of the Word of God is a quasi-transcendental as such. Der-rida writes about what "takes place, what comes to pass with the aporia"[52] of *différance*: "the absolute *arrivant* does not yet have a name or an identity. It is not an invader or an occupier, nor is it a colonizer, even if it can also become one. . . . Since the *arrivant* does not have an identity yet, its place of arrival is also de-identified: one does not yet know or one no longer knows which is the country, the place, the nation, the family, the language, and the home in general that welcomes the absolute *arrivant*. . . . It even exceeds the order of any *determinable* promise . . . because . . . the absolute *arrivant* makes possible everything to which I have just said it cannot be reduced, starting with the humanity of man."[53] It is not simply that Christ is *différance* or Christ names *différance* or Christ and the operation of the Spirit inform the economy of *différance*. But if we wish to read the relationship between language and silence theologically after Derrida then we have to begin by acknowledging that Christ is neither a proper name that we know how to employ (and what we mean by employing it) nor an identity we can delineate and turn into a template. Aquinas again: "God is not known to us in His nature, but is made known to us from His operations or effects. . . . This name God is an appellative name, and not a proper name."[54]

Without denigrating the function of naming, and yet avoiding the errors of nominalism, *différance* names an operation, a quasi-transcendental allegory that continually draws Derrida back to a theological discourse. But it is a discourse always framed by the metaphysics of presence/absence; by an agenda established by modernity that Derrida wishes to deconstruct. Theologically, discourse is never examined in terms of its own logic. This is where we need to return to the theological genealogy of Derrida's construal of allegory and recognize why only a theological account of allegory can move us beyond the problematics (and the gnosticisms) of modernity. We can do this with respect to the contemporary angelology of Michel Serres.

Serres, like Irigaray, recognizes the contemporary retrieval of the Medieval. "Is it not true that in this age of sophisticated technical apparatus we still frequently turn to the Middle Ages in search of our images and secrets?" Irigaray asks.[55] Serres informs Bruno Latour that "we are living today (and even more so in the United States than in Europe) closer to the Middle Ages than to the salons of the Age of Enlightenment."[56] Serres's book, *Angels: A Modern Myth*, most fully details the connections between the late twentieth century's semiotic turn, advanced communications and the incarnationalism of the Middle Ages. This constellation of connections is framed by a reflection on angels as not only message-bearers but the incarnation of the tidings that they bear. The evil angels are the angels who draw attention to themselves above and beyond the giving of the message; the good angels are given over to/as the communication.

> Today the City is a chattering, language-filled, puritan, message-bearing, advertisement-laden thing . . . the power, the capacity, the speed and the shortcomings of angels haunt this City.

> Throughout the whole world, all the networks are crying out about the hunger, are screaming a thirst for incarnation, in a situation where the body is horribly lacking. But at last, the Good News, the Messiah, the message, is flesh, immanent, which saves itself, in and out of itself.[57]

Creation is conceived by Serres as message-bearing, as doxological, so that psalms rise up from the shores and the rocks.[58] Everything exists in complex intercommunication, a profound relationality. What all these messages suggest is a reign of angels announcing a new birth, "the birth of the Messiah, who makes flesh divine and incarnates love."[59] We live in, and inseparable from, this continual interchange, this universal mediation that God opens up and establishes. Commenting on the Annunciation, Serres writes: "It is God, covering the scene with his bright shadow. Beneath the appearance and the image of an interaction between two people, it all takes place as if God was face to face with God: in potency on the angel's side; in act and end of meaning in the woman's womb. Our physical eyes of flesh see Mary and Gabriel, but faith contemplates, in spirit, the apparition facing the incarnation."[60] This double seeing—by faith and by our "physical eyes"—is fundamental to the re-enchanted world Serres is portraying. This is the focus of his allegorical vision in which the world is "fluid, fluent, even fluctuating, [and] is becoming increasingly volatile."[61] Interpretation is intrinsic to living in such a world; it is fostered and fosters the ongoing transformation through communication. (Hermes is the forerunner of the angels.[62]) In such a world it is not only creation which speaks (for example, the conveying of messages by waves) but mechanical and technological objects are almost endowed with the same qualities as human beings, for they change things, they transform relationships: "To consider them as objects derives from the basic contempt that we still have for human labor."[63] With Serres labor becomes laboring, as in the creative bringing to birth of an incarnate love in and through the interdependence and intercommunication of all things.

Although unlike Derrida in emphatically announcing a Messianic telos to world history (lending a soteriology and eschatology to a project concerning our contemporary network society), Serres, like Derrida, defines a quasi-transcendence. Incarnation is the coming to be, the fleshing, of this quasi-transcendence. His angelology invokes a system of immanent meaning: "So are angels still pantheist? Certainly they are, because by the fact that they pass everywhere and occupy all space, they enable divinity to be seen at all points."[64] And in a world where all physical forces are also spiritual, where all things express intelligence[65], a neopaganism is all too possible. And yet Serres confuses the lines between immanence and transcendence, for all is informed by, because all things mediate, a Word which forever exceeds the system of intercommunication itself. "When we go sunbathing . . .

who can say whether we are immersing our bodies in the sun itself, of which the light is part, or whether our bodies are being exposed to intermediary rays issuing from the mass of the sun and coming across through space to reach us? The infinite distancing of a transcendent God necessitates the existence of angels or radiating transmitters; whereas immanence can do without them."[66] So the final hymn of the volume is to the All High. For, as Serres explains, glory must finally be accorded to God alone if there is to be peace on earth. For such a glory is forever out of our reach and so uncommodifiable.[67]

Now evidently, for the Christian theologian, despite Serres's attention to the incarnate Word, the transcendent God, and the divine energia that opens up this space of mediation and interpretation, his work cries out for a doctrine of the Trinity. But Serres's thinking points to, and begins to sketch, the theological framework that Derrida alludes to and plays with, but cannot elaborate. In doing so Serres retrieves the Medieval world picture that Certeau describes as prevalent before the metaphysics and linguistics of nominalism began to dominate; when all things drew their significance from the space within the incarnate Word. For Certeau, explicitly referring to Augustine, this world picture is characterized by an appreciation of *allegoria facti*, in which *"signa naturalia* escaped human codifications of meaning. It was therefore necessary to learn how to 'interpret' them on the basis of an intelligence that ascended to the divine will, then descended towards its inscriptions in the opacity of 'natural' things. They were the province of a 'spiritual' or divine hermeneutics."[68] *Allegoria facti* was founded upon three conditions, what Certeau names *allegoria theologicae* (where all things are understood from God's point of view, the God who spoke all things into being), *allegoria historiae* (where all *in factis* symbolism is inscribed within chronology), and *allegoria infactis* (where analogies exist between things themselves, like water and the Spirit). As Certeau notes: "These three conditions for the *allegoria facti* (which depended on the status of theology, a certain conception of time, and a specific metaphysics) became less and less conceivable in the fourteenth and fifteenth centuries."[69]

Without this theological frame for allegory—without retrieving, for Derrida's *différance*, the theological genealogy of the account of language it circumscribes—the semiosis of meaning installed by allegory, while deconstructing the binarisms of language and silence (the metaphysics of dualism and the theologies of gnosticism), will forever rehearse (and therefore require) them. And then Derrida is doomed, like Sisyphus, to repeat the same deconstructive gestures, endlessly.[70] With this theological frame, we can reaffirm an incarnational world-view. And the quasi-transcendence, which delights in mediation and recognizes silence as integral to the communication of the Word, no longer waits for the daylight forever (as sublime plenitude or kitsch void), but allows creation's daylight and darkness to constitute a rhythm in the redemption being wrought in Christ.

Notes

1. *Language and Silence,* (London: Faber 1967), 40.
2. Ibid., 98.
3. Ibid., 124.
4. Ibid., 128.
5. Ibid., 67.
6. Ibid., 68.
7. Ibid., 58–9.
8. Ibid., 159.
9. Ibid., 132.
10. "Language and Mystical Awareness" in Steven Katz (ed.), *Mysticism and Philosophical Analysis,* (Oxford: Oxford University Press), 141.
11. Ibid., 150.
12. *Lessons on the Analytic of the Sublime,* trans. Elizabeth Rottenberg (Stanford, Calif.: Stanford University Press, 1994), 182.
13. See "The Ontological Scandal" in Grace Jantzen (ed.) special issue of *John Rylands Bulletin on Representation, Gender and Religion,* Volume 80, No. 3 (Autumn 1998), 235–52.
14. "Sublimity: The Modern Transcendent" in Paul Heelas (ed.), *Religion, Modernity and Postmodernity* (Oxford: Blackwell, 1998), 258–84.
15. Michel de Certeau, *The Mystic Fable: Volume One the Sixteenth and Seventeenth Centuries,* trans. Michael B. Smith (Chicago: University of Chicago Press 1992).
16. Ibid., l40-1.
17. Ibid., 144.
18. See here P.T. Geach, "Nominalism" in *Logic Matters* (Oxford: Blackwell, 1972), 289–301, for an earlier account of Ockhamist linguistics and the heresy they foster.
19. *The Mystic Fable,* 82.
20. Ibid., 86.
21. Ibid., 89.
22. Quoted in Matei Calinescu, *Five Faces of Modernity* (Bloomington: Indiana University Press, 1977), 225.
23. *Democracy in America,* ed. J.P. Mayer and Max Lerner, trans. George Lawrence (New York, 1966), 61.
24. *The Mystic Fable,* 141.
25. See here Baz Lurhmann's *Romeo and Juliet* where Juliet's deathbed scene takes place on a raised dais in the center of a cathedral, surrounded with thousands of burning candles and approached by an aisle illuminated by a dozen or so large blue neon crosses. Or witness Francis Ford Coppola's *Bram Stoker's Dracula* which portrays scenes of licking the blood from the side of the Count as if he were Christ. In fact, the vampire genre is a kitsch presentation of theological motifs—particularly Christology and the Eucharist.
26. *The Society of the Spectacle,* trans. Donald Nicholson-Smith (New York: Zone Books, 1995), 21.
27. It is important to note that I am not condemning all Baroque art as kitsch. The Baroque is far more nuanced than that. It gave us Rembrandt, Poussin, and La Tour. I am drawing attention to a certain logic of the Baroque, a logic of secularized visibility that helped to produce the world modernity sees, investigates, assumes to be there as the "given" state of things.
28. John Rupert Martin, *Baroque* (London: Allen Lane, 1977), 91.
29. *Baroque, Baroque: The Culture of Excess,* (London: Phaidon, 1994), 7. Calloway goes on to point out how the Baroque emerges in the Romantic period, as the Byronic (ironic and sardonic) side of the sublime (12). The book as a whole treats the twentieth century return to Baroque aesthetics and, in particular, examines "The Great Baroque Revival 1980s & '90s" (182–232), where the postmodern films of Greenaway and Jarman, the *haute couture* of Lacroix and Galliano, and the super realist images of Pierre and Gilles conflate the categories of the sublime, the kitsch, the opulent, the decadent, and the macabre.
30. Martin, 86.
31. Christine Buci-Glucksmann, *Baroque Reason: The Aesthetics of Modernity,* trans. Patrick Camiller (London: Sage, 1994), 130.
32. Ibid., 134–39.
33. Martin, 99.
34. Germain Bazin, *Baroque and Rococo,* trans. J. Griffin (London: Thames and Hudson, 1964), 11.
35. Ibid.

36. "Language, Epistemology and Mysticism" in *Mysticism and Philosophical Analysis*, 48.
37. *The Mystic Fable*, 293.
38. See "White Ecstasy" trans. Frederick Christian Bauerschmidt and Catriona Hanley, in Graham Ward (ed.), *The Postmodern God* (Oxford: Blackwell, 1997), 157.
39. *Barth, Derrida and the Language of Theology* (Cambridge, U.K.: Cambridge University Press, 1995).
40. See *Blindness and Insight: Essays in the Rhetoric of Contemporary Criticism* (London: Methuen, 1983), 116–67.
41. P.T. Geach in both his essay "Nominalism" (op. cit.) and *Reference and Generality: An Examination of Some Medieval and Modern Theories* (Ithaca, N.Y.: Cornell University Press, 1962) emphasizes the adverse effects of the two name theory of nominalism, pointing to how any act of naming is dependent upon the language system requiring both name and verb. Allegory's attention to time and, therefore, the verb, effects a relationality between names. Allegory does not eclipse naming in favor of the verb; rather it suspends reference (that to which the name points).
42. *Memories for Paul de Man,* trans. Cecile Lindsay et. al. (New York: Columbia University Press, 1989), 16.
43. Ibid., 14–5.
44. *Sexes and Genealogies,* trans. Gillian C. Gill (New York: Columbia University Press, 1987), 129.
45. *On the Name,* ed. Thomas Dutoit, trans. David Wood, John P. Leavey, Jr., and Ian McLeod (Stanford, Calif.: Stanford University Press, 1995), 55–6.
46. Ibid., 70
47. Ibid.
48. Ibid., 74.
49. Ibid., 75.
50. *Aporias,* trans. Thomas Dutoit (Stanford, Calif.: Stanford University Press, 1993), 16.
51. Ibid., 78.
52. Ibid., 32.
53. Ibid., 34–5.
54. *Summa Theologiae* Pt.1 Q 13 articles 8 and 9.
55. *Sexes and Genealogies*, 58.
56. *Conversations on Science, Culture and Time,* trans. Roxanne Lapidus (Ann Arbor, Mich.: University of Michigan Press, 1995), 25.
57. *Angels: A Modern Myth,* trans. Francis Cowper (Paris: Flammarion, 1993), 285.
58. Ibid., 267.
59. Ibid., 185.
60. Ibid., 111.
61. Ibid., 44.
62. Ibid., 45.
63. Ibid., 48.
64. Ibid., 91–2.
65. Ibid., 295–6.
66. Ibid., 107.
67. Ibid., 288.
68. *The Mystic Fable*, 92.
69. Ibid., 93.
70. This raises the question of whether the poststructural retrieval of allegory is the continuation and apotheosis of modernity's own investment in allegory? In *Origin of German Tragic Drama* (trans. John Osborne, London: New Left Books, 1977), Benjamin characterized Baroque allegory as fixated on mourning, melancholy, and death: "the allegorization of the physis can only by carried through in all its vigor in respect of the corpse" (218). Derridean allegory continues this characterization. He concludes his essay "Mnemosyne" with an account of allegorical metonymy (which could act as a synonym for *différance*) as "a logic or an a-logic of which we can no longer say that it belongs to mourning in the current sense of the term, but which regulates (sometimes like mourning in the strict sense, but always like mourning in the sense of general possibility) all our relations with the other *as other.* . . . Our 'own' mortality is not dissociated from, but rather conditions this rhetoric of faithful memory. . . ." (*Memories for Paul de Man,* 39).

9

Blanchot's "Primal Scene"

KEVIN HART

(A primal scene?) *You who live later, close to a heart that beats no more, suppose, suppose this: the child—is he seven years old, or eight perhaps?—standing by the window* [la vitre], *drawing the curtain and, through the pane, looking. What he sees: the garden, the wintry trees, the wall of a house. Though he sees, no doubt in a child's way, his play space, he grows weary and slowly looks up toward the ordinary sky, with clouds, grey light—pallid daylight without depth.*

What happens then: the sky, the same *sky, suddenly open, absolutely black and absolutely empty, revealing (as though the pane* [la vitre] *had broken) such an absence that all has since always and forever more been lost therein—so lost that therein is affirmed and dissolved the vertiginous knowledge that nothing is what there is* [que rien est ce qu'il y a], *and first of all nothing beyond. The unexpected aspect of this scene (its interminable feature) is the feeling of happiness that straightway submerges the child, the ravaging joy to which he can bear witness only by tears, an endless flood of tears. He is thought to suffer a childish sorrow; attempts are made to console him. He says nothing. He will live henceforth in the secret. He will weep no more.*[1]

"(Une scène primitive?)" determines and overdetermines a narrative space: between the dead and the living, writer and reader, child and adult, inner and outer, this world and a possible beyond. It tells of a vision, and therefore stages the old difficulty of presenting the unpresentable. This would not be the first time that one of Blanchot's characters has enjoyed or suffered a vision. In *Le Très-Haut* (1948) for example, Henri Sorge has "a kind of revelation": "Until very recently, people were only fragments and they projected their dreams onto the sky. . . . But now man exists. That's what I discovered."[2] Here, though, the vision is a child's; and while it may seem to be negative—to present a disaster, in fact—it is not taken so by the child. It is received as sublime, but not in the Kantian sense: no supersensuous destination is indicated.[3] On the contrary, religious consolation is explicitly denied. Yet the revelation is taken to be overwhelmingly affirmative, yielding "the feeling of happiness," and it forms the basis of a secret that is not so much covert information as a way of living and

---

A longer version of this essay appears as chapter two of Hart's forthcoming *The Dark Gaze: Maurice Blanchot and the Sacred*, University of Chicago Press, 2004. It is printed here with their permission.

dying. (The little boy would perhaps agree with Agathe in Robert Musil's novel *The Man without Qualities* (1951) when she says to Ulrich, "You believe that mysticism is a secret through which we enter another world; but it is only, or even, the secret of living differently in our world."⁴) Blanchot's story about that little boy turns on a window. If what the text describes inclines us to regard it as "mystical" or "religious," albeit in a sense that would need to be clarified, the title makes us pause and sends us on a detour via psychoanalysis, with no guarantee of ever returning to those words. For the expression "primal scene" inevitably points us to Sigmund Freud's "From the History of an Infantile Neurosis" (1918 [1914]), better known as the Wolf-Man case, which also features a little boy and a window. Before anything else, then, let us look to Freud.

The Wolf-Man case centers on a dream that the patient had when "three, four, or at most five years old": "*I dreamt that it was night and that I was lying in bed. . . . Suddenly the window opened of its own accord, and I was terrified to see that some white wolves were sitting on the big walnut tree in front of the window. . . .*"⁵ The Wolf-Man traces his dream back to a story related by his grandfather in which a wolf leaps through a window, surprises a tailor, and has his tail docked. A sense that this is not a fully satisfying basis for the dream leads the Wolf-Man to further interpretation. "He thought that the part of the dream which said that 'suddenly the window opened of its own accord' was not completely explained by its connection with the window at which the tailor was sitting and through which the wolf came into the room. 'It must mean: "My eyes suddenly opened." I was asleep, therefore, and suddenly woke up, and as I woke I saw something: the tree with the wolves.'" This points Freud beyond his provisional conclusions, "*A real occurrence—dating from a very early period—looking—immobility—sexual problems—castration—his father—something terrible.*"⁶ It leads, indeed, to a crucial stage in the analysis, one to which Blanchot alludes in the title, or lead line, of his text. Freud ventures a radical hypothesis about the basis of the Wolf-Man's neurosis: "He had been sleeping in his cot, then, in his parents' bedroom, and woke up, perhaps because of his rising fever, in the afternoon, possibly at five o'clock, the hour which was later marked out by depression. It harmonizes with our assumption that it was a hot summer's day, if we suppose that his parents had retired, half undressed, for an afternoon *siesta*. When he woke up, he witnessed a coitus *a tergo*, three times repeated; he was able to see his mother's genitals as well as his father's organ; and he understood the process as well as its significance."⁷ This is Freud's "primal scene," supposedly witnessed by an infant one and a half years old.

What is called into question when Blanchot adds a question mark to "Une scène primitive"? For Hélène Cixous, who devotes part of a seminar to reading the text, nothing is denied, disclaimed, or disputed; the new punctuation simply serves to underline the nature of the event as limit-experience.⁸ From one angle this explanation is perfectly judicious. No one can say with assurance that he or she has enjoyed or suffered a limit-experience; it is not something that one appropriates, remembers, and turns to knowledge: hence the question mark. But there are other possible interpretations that relate more closely to the words in the title. It could be the status of the scene that is threatened: is it a primal scene, an original fantasy, or a screen memory? Or could it be the psychoanalytic reference itself that is called into doubt or at least suspended? After all, Blanchot observes that in his judgment only those "for whom analysis is a risk, an extreme danger, a daily test" have the right to use a psychoanalytic lexicon, and the addition of parentheses around the title, which almost shelter the text from the psychoanalytic allusion and vice versa, could be taken as a sign of Blanchot's discretion.[9] Or is it perhaps the sexual basis of the primal scene that is at issue? The text speaks of *a*, not *the*, primal scene. Maybe there is for Blanchot a scene whose primal status is not related to parental coitus. "I wish," he says, "for a psychoanalyst to whom a sign would come, from the disaster" (9; 20).

Those words suggest that the best way to find an answer to our questions is to read "(Une scène primitive?)" in its final frame, *L'Écriture du désastre*. There we find that it is immediately preceded by a discussion of Donald W. Winnicott and Serge Leclaire on the early construction of selfhood. For Winnicott, the infant is shaken by agonies before a self is formed, and traces of these disturb the adult in later life, being transformed into acute fears of the loss of self in breakdown or death. "There are moments . . . when a patient needs to be told that the breakdown, a fear of which destroys his life, *has already been*. It is a fact that is carried round hidden away in the unconscious."[10] The patient must remember the primitive trauma, "but it is not possible to remember something that has not yet happened, and this thing of the past has not happened yet because the patient was not there for it to happen to" (92). So the analyst must register those immemorial agonies in the analysand's memory by means of transference, and thereby assure him or her that there is nothing to fear because, in a psychologically effective sense, breakdown or death has already taken place. While he concedes the theraputic effectiveness of this technique, Blanchot objects to the fictive realization of an immemorial past, the linearity this imposes on the subject, and the individualization of that past. Taken together, Winnicott's treatment of the fear of death amounts to an endorsement that death is possible—it has a meaning and a truth—and accordingly it results in a steady refusal to accept death as the impossibility of dying, a notion that Blanchot had explored years earlier in *Thomas l'obscur*.

A preferable report on the situation is offered, Blanchot thinks, by Leclaire in his case study "Pierre-Marie or the Child" (1975). Here Leclaire elaborates on the need to kill the *infans* in oneself. "Psychoanalytic practice is based upon bringing to the fore *the constant work of a power of death—the death of the wonderful (or terrifying) child who, from generation to generation, bears witness to parents' dreams and desires. There can be no life without killing that strange, original image in which everyone's birth is inscribed*."[11] Unlike Winnicott, Leclaire will tolerate no confusion of this "first death" and our "second death," deep rooted though their conjunction is in our psyche. To allow those two deaths to become conflated is to fail to recognize "the most imperative summons of our bondage—to be born again and again to language and desire" and to yield to "the glorification of failure or the making of life into a sacred venture, the cult of despair or the defense of faith" (4). In psychoanalytic terms, the *infans* is a primary narcissistic representation whose task in each of us is to accomplish the work of death; and we can live and speak, Leclaire argues, only on the condition that it is forever consigned to death. Because the representation is primary it cannot become conscious, and the silent child can never be killed openly. Moreover, the child can never be destroyed once and for all, since it perpetuates itself with each murderous attack. Already dead, the *infans* is still condemned to suffer an interminable dying, like the Hunter Gracchus in Kafka's story. This "impossible, necessary death" functions as a primal scene for Blanchot, but plainly not in the classical Freudian sense, as the question mark indicates.

Let us circle back to "(Une scène primitive?)" with this renewed understanding of its title or lead line. We need to clarify what kind of text it is, whether it reports on a moment of transcendence (however negative or peculiar) or transgression, and whether we have the right to call it "mystical" or "religious" with appropriate qualifications. Cixous takes the text to be autobiographical, and even if one is skeptical about that word, especially with such a reserved man who, after all, writes of the young boy in the third person, it is easy enough to find other passages in Blanchot's writing that sit with this interpretation, not least of all a remark in *Le Pas au-delà* (1972) that the "'Self' [*"Moi"*]' was "as if fissured, since the day when the sky opened upon its void."[12] Of course it is equally easy to find evidence for the view that the text is a tissue of literary allusions. The image of vacant skies is a commonplace for the absence of God, and there are sources other than Freud for the window motif, all of which would be familiar to Blanchot. I am thinking of Hölderlin 'in his madness "declaiming" at the window [*la fenêtre*]," Baudelaire intoning "Je ne vois qu'infini par toutes les fenêtres," Lautrémont's Maldoror speaking to the little boy sitting on a bench in the Tuileries and, as we have seen, Mallarmé in "Les Fenêtres" pondering the alternative "Que la vitre soit l'art, soit la mysticité."[13] Autobiography, fiction or faction: the pressing questions raised by "(Une scène primitive?)" cannot be contained within these tried and tested literary alternatives, as *L'Écriture du désastre* and in fact the whole of Blanchot's œuvre helps to make clear. To a certain extent that body of work offers itself as a long commentary on "(Une scène primitive?)," even as that text seeks to read everything that Blanchot has written.

Those two short paragraphs about a boy by a window also recall another primal scene, this time by someone who has interested Freudians over the years.[14] I have in mind a passage in Book IX of *The Confessions* where St. Augustine reports on a vision—or, more correctly, an audition—he had enjoyed some six months after his baptism.[15] It could with justice be called a primal scene of Christian mysticism.[16] The event took place at Ostia, when he, his family and some friends were resting on their return from Milan to North Africa where they thought they would be able to serve God by living in a contemplative community. In Blanchot's narrative, the little boy looks through a window into a garden, comes to understand "that nothing is what there is," bursts into tears of happiness, which, being misunderstood, bring someone to comfort him, perhaps a mother or a father. The entire passage is spoken by a dead man—or, more accurately, by someone who imagines he is already dead. By contrast, a parent is intimately involved in the episode that St. Augustine evokes, a mother who is soon to die, as the narrator knows, and the entire passage—indeed, the whole of the *Confessions*—is a prayer:

> The day was immanent when she was about to depart this life (the day which you knew and we did not). It came about, as I believe by your providence through your hidden ways, that she and I were standing leaning out of a window [*fenestram*] overlooking a garden. . . . The conversation led us towards the conclusion that the pleasures of the bodily senses, however delightful in the radiant light of this physical world, is seen by comparison with the life of eternity to be not even worth considering. Our minds were lifted up by an ardent affection towards eternal being itself [*idipsum*]. Step by step we climbed beyond all corporeal objects and the heaven itself, where sun, moon, and stars shed light on the earth. We ascended even further by internal [*interius*] reflection and dialogue and wonder at your works, and we entered into our own minds. We moved up beyond them [*transcendimus eas*] so as to attain to the region of inexhaustible abundance where you feed Israel eternally with truth for food. There life is the wisdom by which all creatures come into being, both things which were and which will be. Furthermore, in this wisdom there is no past and future, but only being, since it is eternal. For to exist in the past or in the future is no property of the eternal. And while we talked and panted after it, we touched it in some small degree by a moment of total concentration of the heart. And we sighed and left behind us "the first fruits of the Spirit" (Romans 8:23) bound to that higher world, as we returned to the noise of our human speech where a sentence has both a beginning and an ending.[17]

Then Augustine reflects on what has just happened, and tells us, "even if in not just this way and with exactly these words," how the conversation reached this height. Were one to rid oneself of all images, quiet the soul and the imagination, bracket all language, and keep silent, then, at just that point, God would speak in an unmediated way. "We would hear his word, not through the tongue of the flesh, nor through the voice of an angel, nor through the sound of thunder, nor through the obscurity of a symbolic utterance." There would be no mediation whatever:

> That is how it was when at that moment we extended our reach and in a flash of mental energy attained the eternal wisdom which abides beyond all things. If only it could last, and other visions of a vastly inferior kind could be withdrawn!

Then this alone could ravish [*rapiat*] and absorb and enfold in inward joys [*interiora gaudia*] the person granted the vision. So too eternal life is of the quality of that moment of understanding after which we sighed. (IX. x. 25)

In several ways "(Une scène primitive?)" refigures the audition at Ostia. Where Augustine and Monica touch "eternal being itself," *idipsum*, the boy encounters the "there is," *il y a*, the eternal rustling of nothingness at the heart of being.[18] Neither being nor non-being, the *il y a* is an index of what Blanchot calls the neuter or the Outside: a stagnant void in which time has no direction and possibility has no hold. This is not a non-place like Plato's *khôra* or Kant's noumenal realm; it does not subtend phenomenal reality in an unconditioned manner. Neither is it *tohu va bohu*, the formless waste before Creation imagined in Genesis 1: 2. Nor does Blanchot regard it as an illusion to which we are prey: he will tell us that it is neither subjective nor objective. Without examining the notion closely here, we can point to the horror the *il y a* evokes in Thomas at the beginning of *Thomas l'obscur* where the night neither gives itself to experience nor withdraws so that it cannot be experienced. It fascinates and frightens. Elsewhere Blanchot defines mystical ecstasy, like that enjoyed at Ostia, as "experience of what is not given in experience."[19] This would be the sheer "abundance" to which mother and son testify, not the "nothing" that the boy discovers.[20] Infinitesimally close in how they are described, the experience of God and of the *il y a* are also infinitely distant from each other.

Exactly how the two experiences differ can be charted more closely. Mother and son broach a life beyond this life, the boy by the window has his mortality absolutely confirmed. The Christians ascend beyond all created things and are finally touched by the eternal wisdom "beyond all things," *super omnia*, while the boy appears to be passive throughout his revelation; it is the *sky* that is "suddenly open, absolutely black and absolutely empty." If the sky is empty, though, it cannot be active: mystery does not abide in the heavens but in a way of seeing, as Blanchot long ago explained with respect to Paulhan. So the boy receives the revelation by way of himself, by not quite coinciding with himself; he experiences the event as an image in the moment when the classical distinction between "reality" and "image" breaks down. In both scenes the participants enter a darkness, pass from external scenes to an inner world, yet Augustine and Monica transcend that interiority while the boy lives inside a secret which, as we are later told, "*is not linked to an 'I'*" (137; 208) and is therefore not interior. The episode in Ostia turns on conversation, while the event in France is solitary: however, conversation will become, for the mature Blanchot, that which forbids mystical fusion.[21] For all their differences, the passages conclude on a similar note: mother and son sigh, the little boy cries. Each of the participants is "ravaged" with joy.

All this can be deduced from a comparison of the two narratives when they are held at a little distance from their respective contexts. Once returned to their usual homes, the extent of the refiguring is more fully revealed, as is the complexity of specifying the relations between them. For one thing, just as Augustine reflects on the experience he has evoked, so too Blanchot meditates on his child's vision, directly in passages also called "(Une scène primitive?)" and indirectly in other fragments. At first one might think that Blanchot simply affirms an atheistic vision over and against Augustine's Christian ecstasy. If we examine both passages in their contexts, however, things are a little more complex. Is it so clear in the first place, people have asked, that Augustine reports a *Christian* experience?[22] Of course, the passage quotes from and extensively alludes to scripture, and this testifies to the fact that he interpreted his and Monica's experience in Christian terms.[23] Yet he had already reported a heightened experience of being after having studied the books of the Platonists in Milan in 386, and his Platonism is a medium of the audition at Ostia, one that remains in the *Confessions* even though it was composed some ten years after the event.[24]

As a young man, Augustine was strongly influenced by Cicero's exaltation in the now lost *Hortensius* to study philosophy, and, in doing so, to learn how to transcend mere earthly things and so gain happiness in contemplation. Readers of Plotinus will remember the tractate on beauty, especially the description of the ascent towards the Good in *Enneads* I. 6. 7. At the same time, the episode runs counter to Plotinus who in *Enneads* V. 1. 6 speaks of "leaning in soul towards Him by aspiration, alone towards the alone," something that does not happen when mother and son approach the deity in prayer.[25] To find traces of Platonism in Augustine's description of the audition at Ostia in no way compromises the claim that it was an experience of the God whom Christians adore. The borderlines between Christianity and Platonism were divided and at times unmarked in fourth-century Roman culture.[26] Perhaps it is best to say simply this. An audition was surely enjoyed at Ostia: it was pre-understood in terms of Christianity and for Augustine this Christianity had itself been approached by way of Plotinus's *Enneads*, in part if not whole, and Porphyry's *De regressu animæ*. Augustine's understanding after the fact is equally important: it is possible that the experience confirmed for the son the value of the mother's interpretation of Christianity. No philosopher herself, she nonetheless guided her son in and through her faith to the most intense spiritual moment of his life to date.[27]

Turning to Blanchot, there is reason to be cautious when saying that "(Une scène primitive?)" is atheistic. We are told, in the very book that houses the passage, that atheism does not simply erase God from one's concerns or one's vocabulary. "We carry on about atheism, which has always been a privileged way of talking about God" (92; 145), he says. Indeed: there is the moral privilege claimed by protest atheism, the right to prosecute God for the sheer horror of exposing innocents to evil; and there is the methodological privilege, about which Heidegger speaks so firmly, that requires the philosopher not to invoke the deity precisely in order to philosophize freely about the event of being.[28] Blanchot makes it plain that a line runs between the experience evoked in "(Une scène primitive?)" and events such as Augustine's. "I call disaster," he says, "that which does not have the ultimate for a limit: it bears the ultimate away in the disaster" (28; 49). It needs to be underscored that he calls this loss of the divine a *disaster*: we are detached from all hope of heaven, left with the truth that there is no overarching meaning to life and the cosmos, and while this is to be affirmed, its aspect as a catastrophe for humankind is to be acknowledged. His atheism is neither cold nor triumphalist. In fact it mimics the phrasings of the mystics, dangerously so, as Blanchot is the first to realize. Only once we are safely "well outside of mysticism" are we asked to recognize certain traits that associate the thought of the *il y a* or the neutral with the divine. We are invited to hear "the undemanding, the disastrous demand of the neutral" (74; 120). The neutral is no divinity, of course, and certainly no ineffable Godhead beyond divinity. All the same, Blanchot cannot resist miming a prayer to it: "O neutral, free me from my weariness, lead me to that which, though preoccupying me to the point of occupying everything, does not concern me."[29]

As I have already mentioned, the main evidence for regarding "(Une scène primitive?)" as autobiographical is in *Le Pas au-delà*, not *L'Écriture du désastre*, and it makes those two paragraphs represent a moment when the "'Self' [*Moi*]" was "as if fissured, since the day when the sky opened upon its void" (2; 9). What is striking here is that the import of the vision concerns not the reality of God but the construction of the subject. The child does not experience a sudden loss of self in ecstatic union with the deity but rather realizes that selfhood (and the identity, presence, and unity it assumes as form, ground, or horizon) has been immemorially lost, forever divided from itself. "'I' [*'Je'*] die before being born" (101; 157), we are told some pages after we read the story of the boy. Always and already fissured, the self has never been substantial. On the face of it, Blanchot might be taken to be arguing for a position much like David Hume's, namely that there is no such entity as the self, only a bundle of affects and percepts; and in some respects his view of the self does converge with the Scottish philosopher's.[30] Hume would agree that the self is a "*canonic abbreviation of a rule of identity*," as it is put in *Le Pas au-delà*, though he would not be sympathetic to Blanchot's affirmation of a neutral realm that is irreducible to the phenomenal world.[31] Descriptions of this non-place as "where being ceaselessly perpetuates itself as nothingness" or "that which has never come, which is neither staunched nor spurting forth but coming back—the eternal lapping of return" would strike him as idle metaphysical speculation.[32] Exactly how Blanchot establishes the reality, if the word be allowed, of this strange realm will become more clear as we go on. In *L'Écriture du désastre*, though, it is starkly declared as a revelation, much as Friedrich Nietzsche told us of his sudden insight into the eternal return at Sils-Maria in August 1881.[33] Interestingly, the element of repetition is not given in the revelation itself but in the fragments that foreshadow and reflect on it. At issue in those passages is a way of being in relation "to the most ancient," the Outside, "to what would seem to come from furthest back in time immemorial without having ever been given" (3–4; 11).

If we take all this on credit, as we have to do if we confine ourselves to *L'Écriture du désastre*, we must say that the child's vision is, strictly speaking, not an event but the return of an event that has never actually occurred, that has never found a moment in which to present itself.[34] There can be no talk of a black-and-white contrast between the two events since for Augustine the self is always divided by competing desires, though it seeks unity. "What then am I? What is my nature?" he asks God in the *Confessions*, then says, "It is characterized by diversity, by life of many forms [*varia, multimoda vita*], utterly immeasurable."[35] More differences between the two passages can be drawn out. Augustine and Monica touch the eternal which has no past and no future; the young Blanchot encounters that which cannot lodge in the present but which is "always already past" and "yet to come" (1; 7). The black, empty sky that opens before the boy is not an invisible presence that the day has concealed until now; it is "un ciel antérieur," albeit of a somewhat different kind from that which Mallarmé evoked, and far removed from "la Beauté." It escapes representation. Elsewhere, Blanchot calls it "the *other* night," that eerie interruption of time when absence impinges on consciousness as though it were a mode of presence, that state of chronic insomnia when one is confronted by the impossibility of sleep. "It is not true night, it is night without truth, which does not lie, however—which is not false. It is not our bewilderment when our senses deceive us. It is no mystery, but it cannot be demystified."[36] In other words, "the *other* night" is neutral.

Two important and related things follow from Blanchot's account of the revelation that the child receives. First, the boy does not have what we could call, in all rigor, "an experience"; for how can one experience a return of what never happened? From now on "experience" in this context must be rethought without direct reference to presence and, at the same time, without coding absence as negative. Since this experience is not a "lived event" it is "already nonexperience," Blanchot concedes, before adding that it is "just an excess of experience" (51; 85). This enigma marks all Blanchot's later writing, helps to explain its paradoxical flair and, more than that, its sheer difficulty; it calls for constant vigilance. This encounter with the neutral, neither an experience nor a non-experience, "(falsely) imitates transcendence," Blanchot admits, and then adds, "transcendence . . . always wins out, even if only in a negative form."[37] It is easy to see what he has in mind. Augustine talked of the transcendent God as "Measure without measure" as "Number without number" and as "Weight without weight."[38] And Blanchot finds that the neutral imposes the same syntax on him but with a quite different sense: "death without death," "being *without* being" and "relation without relation."[39] Second, while the child "will live henceforth in the secret" he has no interiority to be sharply distinguished from an exteriority. "(Une scène primitive?)" shows that what Bataille calls an "inner experience" is neither interior nor an experience but rather communication with the Outside. In saying that, it should now be palpable that the question mark in the title also puts at risk both "scene" (there is no representation) and "primal" (the event never took place).[40] Or, as Blanchot would have us say, the event was lived as an image: the child was neither free to choose a response nor able to remain disinterested.[41] The recognition that being is fissured and discloses the *il y a* or the Outside or the neutral is a matter of ontological attunement.

2

Let us begin again, once more with "(Une scène primitive?)," but this time I would like to recall another claim it has on us: its right to be regarded as literature. Now literature in Blanchot's sense of the word denotes a text that has "an underlying deceitfulness in it," which means that it denies what it represents.[42] So if "(Une scène primitive?)" is literature it can scarcely be taken as a belated report of an experience, as one might have been tempted to do on a first reading. More particularly, "(Une scène primitive?)" is an example of what has been known in France as a *récit*. The word can mean simply the act of telling something, and Pierre Corneille (1606–84) was one of the first to use it in that way. He also uses it in a literary sense, as the narration of an event that has come to pass, and this is more relevant to our purposes. It was this meaning of the word that Ramon Fernandez had in mind when in the 1920s he distinguished *roman* and *récit* in an important essay on Honoré de Balzac.

It is instructive to see how Fernandez draws the distinction and, in particular, what he says about the *récit*. "*The novel is the representation of events which take place in time, a representation submitted to the conditions of apparition and development of these events.—The* récit *is the presentation of events which have taken place, and of which the reproduction is regulated by the narrator in conformity with the laws of exposition and persuasion.*"[43] So *Madame Bovary* is a novel, Fernandez says, while *Adolphe* is a *récit*: in the one, the event "*takes place*" while, in the other, it "*has taken place*" (63). In the former, characters are developed in space and time; in the latter, events are "withdrawn from the action of time and from an actual place in space" (64): they are made known, but by "abstract schemes which simplify them" (64). More precisely, the *récit* "*tends to the substitution of an order of conceptual exposition for the order of living production, and of rational proofs for aesthetic proofs*" (65). Not only will one find analyses in a *récit* but also they seem "*to determine and justify the action*" (66). The following passage is worth quoting in full. It will resonate with anyone who has read *Thomas l'obscur*, *L'Arrêt de mort* or any of Blanchot's *récits*:

> A *récit* . . . is in direct relation with the life which it recounts, the painting of living reality, and the success of such painting remains after all its principal objective and the measure of its validity. The narrator has to reascend the slope of his

first conception and to establish a relation of reciprocal justification between his ideas and the concrete representations which form the aesthetic part of the work. But a *récit* will always betray the modalities of its genesis and the intellectual work which has presided at its formation. However much the deceptive pieces of scenery [*les trompe-l'œil*] may be multiplied, the effects varied, and the narrator's emotions be justly and beautifully conveyed [*traduire*], it will be impossible to prevent the thing told from being *terminated* and its representation from having become independent and obeying only the laws of combination of the impersonal mind. (67)

Blanchot performs a remarkable twist on the *récit* as described by Fernandez. He remarks the inability of the text to be terminated by orienting it, insofar as possible, to what he calls "the interminable, the incessant": the neutral Outside to which writing leads us.[44] In figuring the *récit* in this way, he takes it to be not one literary genre among others but the hidden process of literary composition.[45]

For Blanchot, "*récit*" means several things: first, it relates just the one unusual event; second, it does not report an event but creates it in the process of narration; and third, it is a curious movement, "toward a point—one that is not only unknown, ignored, and foreign, but such that it seems, even before and outside of this movement, to have no kind of reality; yet one that is so imperious that it is from that point alone that the narrative draws its attraction [*le récit tire son attrait*], in such a way that it cannot even "begin" before having reached it; but it is only the narrative [*récit*] and the unforeseeable movement of the narrative [*récit*] that provide the space where the point becomes real, powerful, and alluring."[46] It is this point to which Blanchot attends in preference to the transcendent point that Breton extols in the *Second Manifesto*. To get a better fix on it, I turn to Blanchot's remarks on Freud's primal scene in *L'Entretien infini* (1969). The primal scene is rendered there as a "primary 'event'" ["'*événement' premier*"] that is "individual and proper to each history, a scene constituting something important and overwhelming, but also such that the one who experiences it can neither master nor determine it, and with which he has essential relations of insufficiency."[47] From here Blanchot departs from the classical Freudian account.

The primary event is a beginning to the extent that it is singular and unique for each person, yet it cannot function as a beginning because once named it becomes enmeshed in a set of differential relations and is therefore "always ready to open onto a prior scene, and each conflict is not only itself but the beginning again of an older conflict it revives and at whose level it tends to resituate itself" (231; 346). The origin cannot be touched, although the limit can be transgressed. Not only is the primal scene unable to be recalled to consciousness but also it retreats from being named through deferred action. "Every time," Blanchot says, "this experience has been one of a fundamental insufficiency; each of us experiences the self as being insufficient" (231; 346). This conclusion can lead to a thinking of the community, and Blanchot does just that in his *La Communauté inavouable* (1983). Here, though, in *L'Entretien infini*, he follows another path that takes him to the newborn child for whom "everything is exterior, and he himself is scarcely anything but this exterior: the outside, a radical exteriority without unity, a dispersion without anything dispersing."[48]

If we substitute "*récit*" for "self," Blanchot's view of narration becomes more distinct, not because narrative is one of the ways in which psychoanalysis is performed but because each of "*récit*" and "self" strives to find its own kind of primal scene. Freud searches for the event that will connect everything, Blanchot for the point that will inaugurate the artwork and render it interminable, at least in principle; the one isolates a past that was never present to a consciousness, the other a past unpresentable to any consciousness.[49] The movement toward the unknown and unknowable origin must be true of all *récits*, Blanchot thinks, although there will be some narrations that thematize this structural truth. Samuel Beckett's *L'Innommable* (1953) is one of these. "Aesthetic feelings are no longer appropriate here. We may be in the presence not of a book but rather something much more than a book: the pure approach of the impulse from which all books come, of that original point where the work [*l'œuvre*] is lost, which always ruins the work, which restores the endless pointlessness [*désœuvrement*] in it, but with which it must also maintain a relationship that is always beginning again, under the risk of being nothing."[50] The same can be said of his own *récits*. They are errant quests for an inaccessible point outside literature but having no existence before the act of writing, and the approach to which is what makes them literature. In other words, Blanchot's narrations and some of his essays are attempts to uncover a primal scene while indicating that both "primal" and "scene" are themselves to be contested by the movement of discovery. The primal scene withdraws as it attracts.

In *L'Espace littéraire* Blanchot calls this movement of attraction and withdrawal "the original experience [*l'expérience originelle*]" and makes a crucial move in linking it to a "radical reversal [*renversement*]." This reversal has quietly echoed throughout *L'Espace littéraire*, beginning with the essay on Mallarmé: "Writing appears as an extreme situation which presupposes a radical reversal" (38; 37). To write poetry, *le maître* found, is not to find being or the deity but nothingness and the absence of God. Now, though, we are to find a wider sense of "radical reversal" in which even Mallarmé can be placed, albeit in a position of high honor. Let us play back the meditation, "La littérature et l'expérience originelle," near its end when Blanchot is rapidly reviewing his argument in order to forge the link:

> But what is art, and what can we say of literature? The question returns now with a particular violence. If we have art—which is exile from truth, which is the risk of an inoffensive game, which affirms man's belonging to the limitless outside where intimacy is unknown, where he is banished from his capability and from all forms of possibility—how does this come about? How, if he is altogether possibility, can man allow himself anything resembling art? If he has art, does this

not mean that, contrary to his apparently authentic definition—the requirement which is in harmony with the law of the day—he entertains with death a relation which is not that of possibility, which does not lead to mastery or to an understanding or to the progressive achievements of time, but exposes him to a radical reversal? [51]

Earlier in *L'Espace littéraire*, Blanchot identified Hegel, Nietzsche, and Heidegger as philosophers who, for all their many differences, concur in thinking of death by way of the possible.[52] Human being is to be approached, they agree, starting from death. This is not simply the familiar claim that modern philosophy rejects religious transcendence and correspondingly affirms immanence and finitude. Rather, it is suggested that modern thought is a concerted attempt to render death possible: to find in death a meaning and a truth that will orient our understanding of life. Now these three philosophers also make high claims for the importance of art. For Hegel, art has been the sensuous manifestation of *Geist*; and for Heidegger it is what lets the truth of beings come to us. That art is supremely valuable is also Nietzsche's view—art is "'more divine' than truth," he declares—though in no sense does he think that art reveals a higher or more profound truth.[53] "*Honesty* would lead to nausea and suicide," we are told elsewhere. "But now there is a counterforce against our honesty that helps us to avoid such consequences: art as the good will to appearance."[54] In other words, art's value consists in its ability to deceive in the interest of affirming life. It is this sentiment that animates the dramatic sentence of 1888 that Blanchot quotes admiringly, and that he thinks serves to disengage Nietzsche from Hegel and Heidegger: "We possess *art* lest we *perish of the truth*."[55] Unlike Heidegger, Blanchot does not take this aphorism to indicate the main ways in which the will to power holds sway with regard to human beings.[56] Nor does he interpret it to mean that art is merely of use in distracting us from serious philosophizing we might do or from the horrors to which life can lead us. Rather, Blanchot thinks, art takes us to the abyss where truth can find no traction.

Blanchot's gloss on Nietzsche can be grasped only when one sees that for him all artistic creation is a fall, what he called a "disaster" some thirty-five years before the appearance of *L'Écriture du désastre*.[57] As we have seen, literature is a quest for a point, an obscure origin that comes into being only once the journey has commenced and that withdraws when approached. This quest begins as a necessary movement of negativity: an image is formed of a thing (an object, a tableau, a situation), and this image bears the meaning and the truth of the thing. Such is the traditional understanding of the image; the representation is held at a distance from what is being represented. To remain at this level of understanding, however, is to allow the classical image to occlude the relationship of resemblance in being. For, like Levinas, Blanchot insists that an event or a thing resembles itself;[58] it is doubled in its appearing, being both itself and its image. It is this doubling that Blanchot calls the relationship

of resemblance. We cannot grasp it because it has always and already happened, and it does not reassure us with a meaning and a truth as the image,
classically understood, does. Rather than consoling us with the thought that
the real and the image are distinct and stable orders, that we can measure the
truth of an image against the reality it represents, it tells us that the imaginary
is within a thing or, as Blanchot likes to put it, that the distance *between* a thing
and its image is always and already *within* the thing. It is none other than being
that subverts any attempt to compare the real and the imaginary.[59]

Negativity generates ambiguity: on the one hand, an image that is subsequent to the thing; while, on the other hand, a relationship of resemblance that
suggests the imaginary cannot be separated from being. "Yes, at that time,
everything becomes image," Blanchot says of the moment when one discerns
the relationship of resemblance, and the essence of the image is to be entirely
outside, without intimacy, "and yet more inaccessible and more mysterious
than the innermost thought."[60] Fascinated as one is by the dark gaze of the
imaginary at the heart of being, no one can remain before it: the ambiguity between image and the imaginary cannot be resolved. An image gives us a grip
on reality; the imaginary makes us lose that grip. We pass from meaning to
non-meaning, from truth to non-truth. An artwork "makes what disappears in
the object appear": the statue makes us alive to the marble, the poem alerts us
to the words on the page or in the air.[61] The marble does not retreat before its
function, as in a building, nor do the words become transparent, as in a report;
rather, the materials are disconnected from being, they are appearances only,
with no work to do or, if you like, their work *is* nothing other than an idling in
the artwork. To the extent that we can read a poem and make decent sense of it,
the poem answers to the negativity of the concept and the image as usually understood. Yet the poem also opens onto the imaginary where we lose a positive
relation with present being. The first aspect of the work is the realm of the possible: it remains in relation with the world and names it. The second aspect
yields to the impossible: there is no relation with the world as constituted by
consciousness, for the imaginary is always fixed in a past that never occurred
and has no place in which it may abide.[62] Here one encounters the ghostly
image of language, of words without being. It is an anonymous and impersonal abyss, a neutral space, and one is mesmerized by an empty repetition, the
eternal return of what never truly begins and never remains itself.

Art shows us, Blanchot thinks, that human being is linked to the neutral
Outside, the space of impossibility; it does so not by aesthetic or formal effects
but because being is always and already doubled. Because a thing resembles itself, being is riven and perpetuates itself as nothingness in a poem or a sculp-
ture. There is no question then of an aesthetic attitude brought to bear on
being and this generating a neutral realm.[63] Instead, being gives rise to the absence of being as well as its presence. Even so, art can be summoned to judge
those philosophies that construe death as a possibility. Nietzsche helps us to

criticize Hegel and Heidegger, and we must try to read Nietzsche against himself. Where modern philosophers and artists have established a metaphysics, an epistemology or an ethics and then worked out the consequences for art, Blanchot examines the nature of art based on a phenomenological consideration of being and uses the insights gained there to criticize modern thought *en bloc* as a philosophy of possibility. It may be that Hegel magisterially reveals to us that life is in truth the animation of death.[64] And it may be that Heidegger brilliantly establishes that death is "the possibility of the absolute impossibility of *Dasein*."[65] But the sheer fact that we have art suffices, Blanchot thinks, to cast doubt on the confidence with which Hegel orchestrates the dialectic, Nietzsche pronounces on the right time to die, and Heidegger regards the impossible as within a dying man's power, as the last possibility that he can realize. Art involves us in a "radical reversal," a turn that points us to the impossible rather than the possible.

Notice that Blanchot does not simply reject the Hegelian dialectic, Nietzsche's injunction to die at the right time, or Heidegger's claim about *Dasein*'s demise, for there is a clear sense in which death remains linked to possibility. His concern is otherwise: to disclose an aspect of death that opens onto impossibility, and he calls this "dying." The image fascinates us with the absence of being, and because it offers us no end it can be regarded as the very space of dying. Levinas puts it well: "In *dying*, the horizon of the future is given, but the future as a promise of a new present is refused; one is in the interval, forever an interval."[66] Yet the question of how death and dying are related is very far from new. One of the most significant discussions takes place in *The City of God* (completed in 426), which is well known because of St. Augustine's insistence that death is an evil even for the man or woman who dies in the odor of sanctity. What agitates is not death but dying:

> For as there are three times, before death, in death, after death, so there are three states corresponding, living, dying, dead. And it is very hard to define which is before death, nor dead, which is after death, but dying, which is in death. For so long as the soul is in the body, especially if consciousness remain, the man certainly lives; for body and soul constitute the man. And thus, before death, he cannot be said to be in death; but when, on the other hand, the soul has departed, and all bodily sensation is extinct, death is past, and the man is dead. Between these two states the dying condition finds no place; for if a man still lives, death has not arrived; if he has ceased to live, death is past. Never, then, is he dying, that is, comprehended in the state of death [*Numquam ergo moriens, id est in morte, esse conprehenditur*].[67]

Faced with these difficulties, we should submit to common usage and talk of "before death" and "after death," Augustine adds, while conceding that "no words can explain how either the dying are said to live." Certainly the dead cannot be said to be dying, even though they are "in death"; and it is pointed out that the Latin *moritur*, "he is dying," cannot be declined in the perfect tense.

Augustine correctly sees that dying cannot be incorporated into an economy of life and death: for him, the dying die and pass into the next life where they will be judged. Were Augustine not to have been bound to the dogma of immortality, Blanchot would perhaps say, he could have teased out his fundamental insight that dying opens onto a neutral state. Where the saint develops a dualism of life and death, the writer explores the duality of death and dying. *L'Écriture du désastre* may not tell us what we have already heard from *The City of God*, that "two cities have been formed by two loves: the earthly by the love of self, even to the contempt of God; the heavenly by the love of God, even to the contempt of self" (XIV.28), but it does speak of "two languages . . . one dialectical, the other not; one where negativity is the task, the other where the neutral remains apart, cut off both from being and from not-being" (20; 38). And he adds in a rare moment of advice, "In the same way each of us ought both to be a free and speaking subject, and to disappear as passive, patient—the patient [*le patient-passif*] whom dying traverses and who does not show himself" (20; 38).

Blanchot is committed to the possible and the impossible as phased counterparts, not to a dualism of the earthly and the heavenly. Indeed, his second novel *Aminadab* (1942) expressly rejects the metaphor of ascent. The main character, Thomas, has been slowly making his way up to the highest floor of a strange boarding house he entered at the start of the story. On the verge of his goal, meeting the girl whose face he perhaps glimpsed from the street, he comes across a young man who censures his ambition "to reach the heights, to pass from one floor to another, to advance inch by inch" while suffering privation and disease.[68] All this time he has been following the wrong path. Instead of ascending, he should have descended, and in the beautiful caves beneath the earth he would have truly found himself. It is too late, however, and Thomas continues with his quest. A young girl tells him that in the final room, right at the top of the house, night will unfold completely, she will become truly beautiful, and the lamps will be turned so that their inscriptions which he has wanted to read will be facing him. And yet the girl also says that if the night covers Thomas he will not experience it, he will not be able to see her, and the lamps will not be lit to illuminate the inscriptions: "Everything will be covered in darkness." And she goes on: "But in a moment we will be permanently united. I will stretch out my open arms; I will embrace you; I will roll with you through great secrets. We will lose each other and find each other again. There will never be anything to separate us. What a shame you will not be able to witness this good fortune!"[69]

Strangely enough, it is the novel's enigmatic title that illuminates these two meetings. "Aminadab" names several persons in the Hebrew Bible, but the most relevant source is Cant. 6:12, "Or ever I was aware, my soul made me like the chariots of Amminadib," a particularly vexing *crux interpretum*, the details of which need not concern us. In this verse Aminadab (to use the Romance spelling) has been taken to stand for both Christ and Antichrist, and in the reading that is of most interest to us, that of St. John of the Cross, it is plainly the latter.[70] I quote the final stanza of "The Spiritual Canticle" in English translation:

No one looked at her,
Nor did Aminadab appear;
The siege was still;
And the cavalry,
At the sight of the waters, descended.[71]

And here is John of the Cross's commentary on the second line of that stanza:

In Sacred Scripture [Cant. 6: 11], Aminadab, speaking spiritually, symbolizes the devil, the soul's adversary. He endlessly combated and disturbed her with the countless ammunition of his artillery to prevent her entry into this fort and hiding place of interior recollection with the Bridegroom. But in this place where she now dwells, she is so favored, strong, and victorious with the virtues, and with God's embrace, that the devil dares not come, but with immense fear flees and does not venture to appear. Also because of the practice of virtue and the state of perfection, the soul has so conquered and routed him that he no longer appears before her. And thus, Aminadab did not appear with any right to hinder this blessing I am after.[72]

Aminadab does not and cannot appear in the mystic marriage. What we see in the final scenes of Blanchot's novel is not a perfect union of spiritual Bride and Bridegroom but inner experience. It should come as no surprise that Bataille quotes the passage at length in *Le Coupable*.[73]

What if Thomas had chosen the better path, the one commended by the young man, and descended into the cool and beautiful caves beneath the earth? Then he would have encountered Blanchot's Aminadab who guards the way into the underground. A new Orpheus, he would have sought another woman—or is she the one glimpsed from the road?—Eurydice, "the profoundly dark point towards which art, desire, death, and the night all seem to lead."[74] She is not the transcendent point dreamed of by the surrealists but a point beneath the world that attracts and withdraws. She is the object of a vigilant and hopeless quest, yet her passivity exercises a certain power, no less conventional, for she fascinates Orpheus in her impossibility. We shall encounter her again.

3

After observing that the little boy in "(Une scène primitive?)" is spoken of in the third person, that all the assertions in that story are preceded by the incantation "suppose, suppose this," and that the entire passage is framed, from within and without, as autothanatography, the thought nonetheless persists that we must also consider it as a testimony. If "(Une scène primitive?)" is autobiographical, among other things, the event related there would have occurred around the beginning of the First World War. *L'Écriture du désastre*, the collection of fragments in which it figures prominently, broods not only on the "impossible, necessary death" that disperses the "I" but on the unspeakable disaster, the holocaust. It is the holocaust that makes the Second World War the most horrific of all wars, horrific not because of the scale of the conflict, which was already more tragic than could be borne, but because of what passed for so long under its cover. Here "disaster" means not only being cut adrift from a star—from guidance and hope—but also, in a cruel paradox, being given a star to wear in the death camps. One sharp fragment recalls "that young prisoner of Auschwitz":

> (he had suffered the worst, led his family to the crematorium, hanged himself: after being saved at the last moment—how can one say that: *saved?*—he was exempted from contact with dead bodies, but when the SS shot someone, he was obliged to hold the victim's head so that the bullet could be more easily lodged in the neck). When asked how he could bear this, he is supposed to have answered that he "observed the comportment of men before death." I will not believe it. . . . Saved at the last minute [*le dernier instant*], the young man of whom I speak was forced to live that last instant again and each time to live it once more, frustrated every time of his own death and made to exchange it every time for the death of all [*chaque fois frustré de sa mort, l'échangeant contra la mort de tous*]. (82; 130–31)

How this passage offers itself to be read changed significantly in 1994, fourteen years after it was published, with the appearance of *L'Instant de ma mort*.[75] Blanchot's last *récit*, if it is one, tells of a young man, presumably Blanchot himself, who is taken by force from his house ("le Château") by a Nazi lieutenant. He leaves "in an almost priestly [*sacerdotale*] manner," is put before an impromptu firing squad, and then saved at the last moment.[76] The lieutenant is distracted, leaving time for a soldier to say, "'We're not Germans, Russians'. . . . 'Vlassov army'" (5; 4). He makes a sign for the young man to disappear, and he does. "I think he moved away," the narrator says, capturing the dreamlike state of the moment while also associating himself all the more tightly with the character. The young man retains "the feeling of lightness" and eventually finds himself "in a distant forest, named the 'Bois des bruyères' where he remained sheltered by trees he knew well" (5; 4). The *récit* ends with the narrator evoking "the instant of my death henceforth always in abeyance [*l'instant de ma mort désormais toujours en instance*]" (11; 10).

The young prisoner in Auschwitz and the young Blanchot taken from the Château are both placed before firing squads: the one time and again, the other only once. The prisoner relives his death each time he is made to perform his repugnant task; the writer finds that he has survived death and that, from then on, death no longer frightens him. In Auschwitz, the young prisoner exchanges his death for the deaths of others; in the French countryside, the young writer discovers to his horror that he has inadvertently done the same. The young writer has worked with the Resistance; and the man he will become, who will write about that young prisoner, will declare that in the camps "resistance is spiritual."[77] He will meditate endlessly on Auschwitz: not by way of reparation for indirectly supporting a culture of anti-Semitism by contributing to *Combat, Aux Écoutes*, and other journals of the far right—he knows all too well that there can be no atonement: the dead cannot forgive—but by way of keeping the memory of horror alive and testifying that it is irreducible to the order of knowledge. One index of this can be found in a letter of 1989, replying to a query about his involvement in drafting the *Manifeste de 121* (1960) and his public intervention in politics at precisely that time. In his answer Blanchot ignores the request for information and speaks instead about the issue of the day, the hotly debated erection of a Carmelite monastery at Auschwitz. At one point he addresses the murdered directly, "You who are now dead, you who died for us and often because of us (because of our shortcomings), you must not be allowed to die a second time, and silence must not mean that you sink into oblivion."[78] In no sense are the dead of Auschwitz to be represented by way of Eurydice.

"Know what has happened, do not forget," Blanchot says when ending his fragment on the young prisoner in Auschwitz, "and at the same time never will you know" (92). It is with this in mind that I would like to read a few lines of *L'Instant de ma mort*:

> I know—do I know it—that the one at whom the Germans were already aiming, awaiting but the final order, experienced [*éprouva*] then a feeling of extraordinary lightness, a sort of beatitude (nothing happy, however)—sovereign elation? The encounter of death with death?
>
> In his place, I will not try to analyze. He was perhaps suddenly invincible. Dead—immortal. Perhaps ecstasy. Rather the feeling of compassion for suffering humanity, the happiness of not being immortal or eternal. Henceforth, he was bound to death by a surreptitious friendship. (5; 4)

"I know," the narrator tells us, and immediately the statement becomes perplexed. The lack of a question mark at the end of "do I know it" renders the expression ambiguous: it is both a question (do I know it?) and a redoubling of the claim to knowledge (I know it all too well). Yet there is reason to believe the event actually occurred. We can cite a letter from Blanchot to that effect, and we can also turn to *La Folie du jour* (1947): "I was made to stand against the wall like many others. Why? For no reason. The guns did not go off."[79] At the same time there is reason to doubt that the event entered into the order of knowledge. We recall Blanchot's strictures about the possibility of recalling ecstasy: "there is evidence—overpowering evidence—," he says (and he is thinking of Eckhart), "that ecstasy is without object, just as it is without a why, just as it challenges certainty. One can write that word (ecstasy) only by putting it carefully between quotation marks, because nobody can know what it is about, and, above all, whether it took place: going beyond knowledge, implying unknowledge, it refuses to be stated other than though random words that cannot guarantee it."[80] That the event happened is certain, as is the feeling of lightness, although what sort of event it was can never be known with any certainty. "Perhaps ecstasy," is the most that the narrator will risk.

Inevitably, we recall the event that occurred in the earlier war, "(Une scène primitive?)" The later *récit* uses the vocabulary of mysticism more freely than the earlier one, although once again it is impossible to decide firmly what is being affirmed or questioned. It is "a sort of beatitude": does "sort" serve to distance us from the claim that it is beatitude, or does it specify that it is a species of beatitude? It is "sovereign elation": are we to think of the elation of the mystics, or Bataille telling us "Sovereignty is NOTHING," or both?[81] It is "Perhaps ecstasy": does the adverb express reserve with respect to the claim that it is ecstasy, or reinforce that even authentic ecstasies cannot be retained by an individual? "(Une scène primitive?)" tells us that in understanding that "nothing is what there is" the boy is straightaway submerged by "the feeling of happiness," and that this is the scene's "interminable feature," the element that could be discussed endlessly "*in the order of conceptual exposition*" as Fernandez says when describing the nature of the *récit*. In the later scene, however, the narrator explicitly tells us that the young man's feeling has "nothing happy [*rein heureux*]" about it. The anteriority of death, which forms the burden of *L'Écriture du désastre*, takes away the fear of death considered as the breakdown of personal identity and thereby leads to happiness. But the child of "(Une scène primitive?)" is not about to die. Awaiting execution, the young man outside the Château becomes a site where anterior death can collide with empirical death, where the death "within" might touch the death "without." Very quickly, the parenthetical assurance "nothing happy, however" is revised, for we are told the young man feels "the happiness [*le bonheur*] of not being immortal or eternal." In fact the feeling is double: happiness to be mortal and "compassion for suffering humanity," and this complex emotion carries more weight for the narrator than the possibility that his younger self experienced ecstasy ("Rather the feeling of compassion . . ."). Whatever foldings of Christian mysticism occur in the first of the two paragraphs I have quoted are made even more complex by a vocabulary that recalls the Buddha. It is not the first time that Blanchot's language draws near to the language of the great oriental religions.[82]

Let us stay close to the strange experience or non-experience that crosses the young man as he faces the firing squad. It takes hold in two distinct registers: with regard to the self (it is mortal) and with regard to justice (one must show compassion). In the paragraphs that follow it is the latter that is explored, for when the young man who has been hiding in the "Bois des bruyères" returns to the world he discovers that the farms are burning, three sons of local farmers have been slaughtered, but that the Château has only been looted: the young writer has lost a manuscript. "No doubt what then began for the young man was the torment of injustice. No more ecstasy; the feeling that he was only living because, even in the eyes of the Russians, he belonged to a noble class" (7; 6). It is as though Blanchot quietly indicates a basis of his political shift from right-wing monarchism to left-wing radicalism.[83] Saved at the last minute, only because of his class, he has been made to exchange his death for the deaths of the young farmers. The contrast with the young prisoner of Auschwitz is sharp: the young writer has been able to observe only his own comportment before death, and that experience has made death into a friend.

"No more ecstasy," he says: whatever inner experience had been enjoyed has been firmly replaced by a moral outrage directed partly against the invading army, partly against the injustice of class (and hence partly against himself: recall the words he addressed to the dead "you who died for us"). But the temporal pattern that would allow "no more" its scope and strength has long since been disrupted:

> There remained, however, at the moment when the shooting was no longer but to come, the feeling of lightness that I would not know how to translate [*traduire*]: freed from life? the infinite opening up? Neither happiness, nor unhappiness. Nor the absence of fear and perhaps already the step beyond [*le pas au-delà*]. (7–9; 6–7)

The allusion to the intractable difficulty of translating inner experience into a written text recalls the closing passage of Blanchot's review of *L'Expérience intérieure* where we learn that "translation, although never being satisfying, still keeps an essential part of authenticity insofar as it imitates the movement of challenge that it borrows" (41; 52). Here, though, the experience is not represented by way of fragments but is roughly translated into two questions, an evocation of the neutral, and a qualified affirmation of *le pas au-delà*.

To understand what is at risk in that strange expression, I turn to the book to which it lends itself as a title. "The circle of the law is this: there must be a crossing in order for there to be a limit, but only the limit, inasmuch as uncrossable, summons to cross, affirms the desire (the false step [*le faux pas*]) that has always already, through an unforeseeable movement, crossed the line."[84] No transgression without limit, then, and no limit without transgression: the logic is very well known. More arresting is Blanchot's claim that death wears "the face of the law" (24; 38) and that it is dying that is transgressive because, as we saw with Augustine, it is neutral. A later fragment, mostly consisting of a dialogue between two unidentified voices, considers what follows from this transgression. The law says that "it is forbidden to die *in the present*," observes one voice. To which comes the distorted echo: "there is no present for dying." The final exchange is perhaps the most interesting: "Thus a time without present would be 'affirmed,' according to the demand of the return," says the one, and "This is why even transgression does not accomplish itself," adds the other (107–8; 148).

The eternal return, a vision of which was vouchsafed to Nietzsche at Sils-Maria, is not to be grasped as having to live one's life over and over again. Rather, what eternally returns is the Outside, and it does so neutrally, as the ghost of what has never actually taken place. It was Pierre Klossowski who raised this question with regard to Nietzsche, Blanchot thinks, and thereby determined "a change so radical that we are incapable of mastering it, even of undergoing it [*le subir*]."[85] The change imagined here is thinking of time forever and always divided by the neutral, and so yielding a present without presence. Granted, we live in time but every moment opens onto a neutral realm, a time with no arrow, that we cannot master because no dialectic can get a foothold there, and that we cannot undergo because with respect to it there is no "I." Perhaps the "primal scene" can explain much about life, then, but unlike Freud's primal scene it does not reduce life to the realm of the possible. Blanchot's questions—"freed from life? the infinite opening up?"—are hardly rhetorical, yet the freedom and the infinity at issue are scarcely consoling.

Notes

1. Blanchot, *The Writing of the Disaster*, trans. Ann Smock (Lincoln: The University of Nebraska Press, 1986) 72; *ED*, 117. This text was originally published as "Une scène primitive" in *Le Nouveau Commerce* cahier 39–40 (Trimestriel-Printemps, 1978), 43. It begins, however, with the same lead line we find in the later publication, "(Une scène primitive?) ."

2. Blanchot, *The Most High*, trans. and introd. Allan Stoekl (Lincoln: University of Nebraska Press, 1996), 23; *TH*, 29. Pierre Klossowski offers an interesting reading of the novel from a Heideggerian theological perspective in "Sur Maurice Blanchot," *Le Temps Modernes* 40 (1949), 298–314. A shorter version appears in *Un si funeste désir* (Paris: Gallimard, 1963), 161–83.

3. Immanuel Kant, *The Critique of Judgement*, trans. James Creed Meredith (Oxford: Clarendon Press, 1952), §25.

4. Robert Musil, "From the Posthumous Papers," trans. Burton Pike, in *The Man Without Qualities*, 2 vols (New York: Alfred A. Knopf, 1995), II, 1358. See Blanchot's "Musil" in his *The Book to Come*, 134–149; *LV*, 184–206.

5. Angela Richards, ed. *Case Histories*, II, The Pelican Freud Library, 15 vols, trans. James Strachey (Harmondsworth, U.K.: Penguin, 1979), IX, 259.

6. Freud, *Case Histories*, II, 265.

7. Freud, *Case Histories*, II, 268–69.

8. See Hélène Cixous, *Readings: The Poetics of Blanchot, Joyce, Kafka, Kleist, Lispector, and Tsvetayeva*, ed., trans. and introd. Verena Andermatt Conley (Minneapolis: University of Minnesota Press, 1991), ch. 1.

9. Blanchot, *The Writing of the Disaster*, 67; *ED*, 110. It should be recalled that Blanchot studied medicine in the early 1930s, specializing in neurology and psychiatry. Christophe Bident, Maurice Blanchot: Partenaire invisible (Seyssel: Champ Vallon, 1998), 49.

10. Donald W. Winnicott, "Fear of Breakdown," in *Psycho-Analytic Explorations*, ed., C. Winnicott, R. Shepherd and M. Davis (London: Karnac Books, 1989), 90. The paper first appeared, posthumously, in *International Review of Psycho-Analysis* 1: 1–2 (1974), 103–7, and appears to have been written in 1963.

11. Serge Leclaire, *A Child is Being Killed: On Primary Narcissism and the Death Drive*, trans. Marie-Claude Hays (Stanford, Calif.: Stanford University Press, 1998), 2.
12. Blanchot, *The Step Not Beyond*, trans. Lycette Nelson (Albany: State University of New York Press, 1992), 2; *PD*, 9. Christophe Bident phrases the matter carefully when he says that "(Une scène primitive?)" is "donnée comme autobiographique," *Maurice Blanchot*, 17. It should be noted that, in French psychoanalysis, "Moi" also means ego.
13. Blanchot, "Atheism and Writing, Humanism and the Cry," *The Infinite Conversation*, trans. Susan Hanson (Minneapolis: University of Minnesota Press, 1993) 258; *EI*, 386. Baudelaire, "Le Gouffre," *Les Fleurs du mal*, introd. by Claude Pichois (Paris: Gallimard, 1978), 220; Lautréamont, *Maldoror and Poems*, trans. Paul Knight (Harmondsworth, U.K.: Penguin, 1978), 77.
14. See for example, Charles Kligerman, "A Psychoanalytic Study of the *Confessions* of St. Augustine," *Journal of the American Psychoanalytic Association* 5 (1957) and Paul W. Pruyser, "Psychological Examination: Augustine," *Journal for the Scientific Study of Religion* 5 (1966), 284–89.
15. I follow J. J. O'Donnell in his commentary on *Confessions*, IX. 10. 24. See his edition, Augustine, *Confessions*, 3 vols, *III: Commentary on Books 8–13, Indexes* (Oxford: Clarendon Press, 1992), 133.
16. Also see the ascent described in *Confessions*, VII. xvii. 23 but, as Augustine himself says, this occurred when he was "cold, removed from the fire of the Spirit," *Confessions* IX. vii. 15. There has been considerable debate over whether or to what extent the vision at Ostia is mystical. Paul Henry argues that the experience is indeed mystical in his *The Path to Transcendence: From Philosophy to Mysticism in Saint Augustine*, trans. and introd. Francis F. Burch (Pittsburgh, Penn.: The Pickwick Press, 1981). The book appeared in French in 1938. In broad agreement with Henry, George St Hilaire maintains that Augustine and Monica received infused grace and that they therefore had mystical ecstasy, "The Vision at Ostia: Acquired or Infused?," *The Modern Schoolman* 35 (1958), 117–35. John Mourant, however, urges that the experience does not merit being described as "mystical" in his "Ostia Reexamined: A Study in the Concept of Mystical Experience," *International Journal for Philosophy of Religion* 1 (1970), 34–45. Wilma von Jess argues against Mourant in her "Augustine at Ostia: A Disputed Question," *Augustinian Studies* 4 (1973), 159–74, who defends himself in "A Reply to Dr von Jess 'Augustine at Ostia: A Disputed Question'," *Augustinian Studies* 4 (1973), 175–77.
17. St. Augustine, *Confessions*, trans., introd. and notes Henry Chadwick (Oxford: Oxford University Press, 1991), IX. x. 23–24.
18. On *idipsum*, the self-same, understood to be the highest good, which is God, see Augustine, *The Trinity*, III. 2. 8.
19. Blanchot, "A Toute Extrémité ," *La Nouvelle NRF*, 26 (1955), 290–91.
20. It must be stressed that the sense of generosity explored by Guillaume Apollinaire in his lyric "Il y a" is completely foreign to the sense of the expression detailed by Levinas and Blanchot.
21. The rejection of mysticism should be balanced with the fact that Blanchot's model of conversation derives from a Jewish idea of prayer. See *The Dark Gaze*, ch. 7.
22. See, for example, Pierre Courcelle, *Recherches sur les Confessions de Saint-Augustin* (Paris: E. de Boccard, 1950), 222–26.
23. The line separating quotation and allusion in *Confessions* IX. x, as elsewhere in Augustine, is often far from clear. Appeals to Rom. 8:23, Matt. 25:21 and I Cor. 15:51 are made, and allusions are made to Phil. 3:13, John 14:6, Is. 64:4, Ps. 35:10 (36:9) 79:2 (80:1), Ezek. 34:14, and Prov. 8:23–31, among other passages.
24. See Augustine, *Confessions*, VII. x. 16 and VII. xvii. 23.
25. Plotinus, *The Enneads*, trans. Stephen MacKenna, rev. B. S. Page, foreword E. R. Dodds, introd. Paul Henry (London: Faber and Faber, 1962), V. 1. 6.
26. If those lines have been drawn more sharply since, it is still difficult if not impossible to separate Christianity from Philosophy, even in the modern sense of "philosophy." See Karl Barth, *The Göttingen Dogmatics: Instruction in the Christian Religion*, 2 vols projected, ed. Hannelotte Reiffen, trans. Geoffrey W. Bromiley (Grand Rapids, Mich.: William B. Eerdmans, 1991), I, 259.
27. In his commentary on the Ostia passage O'Donnell remind us of Monica's role as *mulier sapiens* at Cassiciacum, and rightly observes, "M. represents an alternative path," Augustine, *Confessions*, III, 123. It should also be noted that the vision at Ostia is part of a short biography of Monica. The emphasis throughout is on the significance of the mother for the son.

28. See Martin Heidegger, *An Introduction to Metaphysics*, trans. Ralph Mannheim (New York: Anchor Books, 1961), 6.
29. Blanchot, *The Infinite Conversation*, xx; *EI*, xxi.
30. See David Hume, "Of Personal Identity," *A Treatise of Human Nature*, ed. L. A. Selby-Bigge (Oxford: Clarendon, 1896), I. 4. vi.
31. Blanchot, *The Step Not Beyond*, 19; *PAD*, 31.
32. Blanchot, "Literature and the Original Experience," *The Space of Literature*, trans. Ann Smock (Lincoln: University of Nebraska Press, 1982) 243; *EL*, 326.
33. Nietzsche's first allusion to the vision is found in *The Gay Science: With a Prelude in Rhymes and an Appendix of Songs*, trans. and commentary Walter Kaufmann (New York: Random House, 1974), §341. The book first appeared in 1882. Also see Nietzsche's account of the idea of eternal recurrence as "the highest formula of affirmation that can possibly be attained" in *Ecce Homo: How One Becomes What One Is*, trans. R. J. Hollingdale, introd. Michael Tanner (1979; rpt. London: Penguin, 1992), 99.
34. Derrida draws attention to Blanchot's notion of an event that occurs but does not happen. See the brief discussion of *survenir* and *arriver* in his "A Witness Forever" in Kevin Hart, ed., *Nowhere without No* (Sydney: Vagabond Press, 2003).
35. Augustine, *Confessions*, X. xvii. 26.
36. Blanchot, "The Outside, the Night," *The Space of Literature*, 164; *EL*, 214.
37. Blanchot, *The Writing of the Disaster*, 65, 91; *ED*, 108, 143. Cf. Blanchot's remarks on the word "God" in *The Step Not Beyond*, 48; *PAD*, 69–70.
38. St. Augustine, *The Literal Meaning of Genesis*, trans. John Hammond Taylor, 2 vols (New York: Paulist Press, 1982), I, iv. 3. 8.
39. Blanchot, "Literature and the Right to Death," trans. Lydia Davis, *The Work of Fire*, trans. Charlotte Mandell (Stanford, CA: Stanford University Press, 1995), 340; *PF*, 327; "The Great Refusal," *The Infinite Conversation*, 47; *EI*, 67; "The Relation of the Third Kind (man without horizon)," *The Infinite Conversation*, 73; *EI*, 104. Also see Derrida, "Pas," *Parages* (Paris: Gallimard, 1986), 90–91.
40. On the non-occurrence of the event, also see "Encountering the Imaginary," *The Book to Come*, trans. Charlotte Mandell (Stanford, CA: Stanford University Press, 2003) 9; *LV*, 18, and "The Fragment Word," *The Infinite Conversation*, 310; *EI*, 455.
41. See Blanchot, "The Two Versions of the Imaginary," *The Space of Literature*, 261; *EL*, 352.
42. Blanchot, "Literature and the Right to Death," *The Work of Fire*, 301; *PF*, 294.
43. Ramon Fernandez, "The Method of Balzac" in *Messages: Literary Essays*, trans. Montgomery Belgion (New York: Harcourt, Brace and Company, 1927), 63. The essay, "La Méthode de Balzac," appeared in *Messages: première série* (Paris: Gallimard, 1926). Rather than use Belgion's word "recital" I have retained the original French "*récit*." Blanchot follows Fernandez's distinction in "The Enigma of the Novel," *Faux Pas*, trans. Charlotte Mandell (Stanford, CA: Stanford University Press, 2001) 190; *FP*, 217.
44. See Blanchot's section, "The Interminable, the Incessant" in "The Essential Solitude," *The Space of Literature*, 26–28; *EL*, 20–23.
45. Certainly Blanchot comes to be uneasy with the designation "*récit*" with regard to several of his own narratives. *La Folie du jour* was first entitled "Un récit" or "Un récit?," depending on whether one reads the cover of *Empédocle* 2, mai 1949, or the title of the text, and then the word was withdrawn. *L'Arrêt de mort* was marked as a *récit* but the 1971 re-edition of the work omitted the word. Similarly, *Le Dernier homme* was first published as a *récit* and then, also in 1971, deprived of its generic designation. No such thing happened with either *Au moment voulu* or *Celui qui ne m'accompaignait pas*.
46. Blanchot, "Encountering the Imaginary," *The Book to Come*, 7; *LV*, 14. Also see Blanchot's comments on the *récit* in his review of Marcel Arland's *Zélie dans le désert: Récit* (Paris: Gallimard, 1944). I would especially like to draw attention to these lines, "Nous croyons à un événement qui s'est passé, et s'il est touchant, nous sommes émus. Mais nous aimons aussi croire ce qui n'a peut-être tout à fait réel, ce qui exprime une expérience sans la reproduire," "Récits," *Journal des Débats* 13–14 juillet 1944, 2. Blanchot had discussed the *récit* earlier that year in "Contes et récits," *Journal des Débats* 3 mars 1942, 3, and he returns to the topic in "Nouvelles et récits," *Journal des Débats* 20 avril 1944, 2–3.
47. Blanchot, "The Speech of Analysis," *The Infinite Conversation*, 231; *EI*, 345.
48. Blanchot, "The Speech of Analysis," 231–32; *EI*, 346.

49. For Blanchot, however, to enter analysis is to begin to hear "what is unceasing and interminable: the eternal going over, and over and over again, whose exigency the patient has encountered but has arrested in fixed forms henceforth inscribed in his body, his conduct, and his language," "The Speech of Analysis," 236; *EI*, 353.

50. Blanchot, "Where Now? Who Now," *The Book to Come*, 213; *LV*, 290–91.

51. Blanchot, "Literature and the Original Experience," *The Space of Literature*, 240–41; *EL*, 322–23.

52. See Blanchot, "The Work and Death's Space," *The Space of Literature*, 96; *EL*, 119. The reflection first appears in a review of Paul-Louis Landsberg, *Essai sur l'experience de la mort suivi de Problème moral du suicide* (Paris: Seuil, 1951) and Camille Schuwer, *La Signification métaphysique du suicide* (Paris: Aubier, 1949), *Critique* 62 (juillet 1952), 921.

53. Friedrich Nietzsche, *The Will to Power*, trans. Walter Kaufmann and R. J. Hollingdale (New York: Random House, 1968), § 853.

54. Nietzsche, *The Gay Science: With a Prelude in Rhymes and an Appendix of Songs*, trans. and commentary by Walter Kaufmann (New York: Vintage Books, 1974), § 107. It must be kept in mind that over the course of his long writing career Nietzsche vacillated on the question of the right relationship of art and truth. In 1873, for instance, we find him in a notebook counting art as one of the three "truest things in his world"—the others are love and religion—and observing that while love penetrates to the core of the suffering individual, art "gives consolation for this suffering by telling stories about another world order and teaching us to disdain this one," *Unpublished Writings from the Period of "Unfashionable Observations,"* trans. and with an afterword (Stanford, Calif.: Stanford University Press, 1999), 192.

55. Nietzsche, *The Will to Power*, § 822. On Heidegger's understanding, "truth," here, means "the 'true world' of the supersensuous, which conceals in itself the danger that life may perish, 'life' in Nietzsche's sense always meaning 'life which is on the ascent'. The supersensuous lures life away from invigorating sensuality, drains life's forces, weakens it," *Nietzsche*, 4 vols, I: *The Will to Power as Art*, trans. David Farrell Krell (San Francisco: Harper and Row, 1979), 75.

56. Heidegger, "The Word of Nietzsche: 'God is Dead,'" *The Question Concerning Technology and Other Essays*, trans. and introd. William Lovitt (New York: Harper and Row, 1977), 93.

57. In "Parler de Blanchot," a discussion among Robert Antelme, Dionys Mascolo, and Maurice Nadeau, Mascolo suggests that "Le première apparition du mot 'désastre' chez Maurice Blanchot se trouve dans un texte anonyme de *Comité* (octobre 68)," Dionys Mascolo, *À la recherche d'un communisme de pensée* (Paris: Fourbis, 1993), 408. However, one hears the word in Blanchot's first essay on Kafka—"Kafka's narratives are among the darkest in literature, the most rooted in absolute disaster"—as early as 1945. See "Reading Kafka," *The Work of Fire*, 10; *PF* 18. And the word can also be heard later but before 1968 ("Yes, we are tied to disaster"), *The Space of Literature*, 244; *EL*, 327.

58. See Emmanuel Levinas, "Reality and its Shadow," *Collected Philosophical Papers*, trans. Alphonso Lingis (The Hague: Martinus Nijhoff, 1987), 5–8; *IH*, 132–36. In his account of the image Blanchot focuses on the cadaver resembling itself: see "The Two Versions of the Imaginary," *The Space of Literature*, 254–63; *EL*, 341–55.

59. It is worth noting the difference between Blanchot's understanding of death and Cocteau's in his *Thomas l'imposteur*, a novel sometimes regarded as partly inspiring *Thomas l'obscur*. When Guillaume Thomas is hit by a bullet he says to himself, "*Je suis perdu si je ne fais pas semblant d'être mort*," and the narrator observes, "Mais en lui, la fiction et la réalité ne formaient qu'un," *Thomas l'imposteur* (Paris: Gallimard, 1923), 174. For Blanchot, death is not the coinciding of image and reality; rather, dying approaches us when we recognize that reality is ontologically insecure.

60. Blanchot, "The Experience of Proust," *The Book to Come*, 14; *LV*, 23.

61. Blanchot, "Literature and the Original Experience," *The Space of Literature*, 223; *EL*, 297.

62. For an intriguing instance of this in Blanchot's narrative writing, see *When the Time Comes*, trans. Lydia Davis (Barrytown, N.Y.: Station Hill Press, 1985), 69–70; *AMV*, 157.

63. Blanchot notes that the question of literature is one that "a secular tradition of aestheticism has concealed, and continues to conceal," "Note," *The Infinite Conversation*, xi; *EI*, vi.

64. On this theme see Kojève's lectures on Hegel and Bataille's response to those lectures: "Hegel, Death and Sacrifice," trans. Jonathan Strauss, *Yale French Studies* 78 (1990), 9–28; *OC*, XII, 326–45.

65. Martin Heidegger, *Being and Time*, trans. John Macquarrie and Edward Robinson (Oxford: Basil Blackwell, 1973), 294.
66. Levinas, "Reality and its Shadow," 11; *IH*, 143.
67. Augustine, *The City of God*, trans. Marcus Dods, introd. Thomas Merton (New York: The Modern Library, 1950), XIII.11.
68. Blanchot, *Aminadab*, trans. and introd. Jeff Fort (Lincoln: University of Nebraska Press, 2002), 185; *Am*, 211.
69. Blanchot, *Aminadab*, 196, 197; *Am*, 224, 225.
70. John of Ford, on the other hand, takes Aminadab to be the bride's name for the Son. See the sixtieth sermon in his *Sermons on the Final Verses of the Song of Songs*, 7 vols (Kalamazoo, Mich.: Cistercian Publications, 1983), IV, 193. Origen's famous commentary on the Canticle, as historically received, contains no comments on Cant. 6: 12.
71. Kieran Kavanagh and Otilio Rodriguez, trans. *The Collected Works of St John of the Cross* (Washington, D.C.: ICS Publications, 1979), 563. Roland E. Murphy indicates the mystic's use of the scriptural reference in his *The Song of Songs: A Commentary on the Book of Canticles or The Song of Songs*, ed. S. Dean McBride, Jr. (Minneapolis: Fortress Press, 1990), 176.
72. Kavanagh and Rodriguez, *The Collected Works of St John of the Cross*, 564.
73. See Bataille, *Guilty*, trans. Bruce Boone, introd. Denis Hollier (Venice, CA: The Lapis Press, 1988) 81–82; *OC*, V, 323–25.
74. Blanchot, "The Work and Death's Space," *The Space of Literature*, 99; *EL*, 225.
75. See Gerald L. Bruns's subtle reading of this passage in his *Maurice Blanchot: The Refusal of Philosophy* (Baltimore: The Johns Hopkins University Press, 1997), 224–25.
76. Blanchot, *The Instant of My Death*, bound with Jacques Derrida, *Demeure*, both trans. Elizabeth Rottenberg (Stanford, CA: Stanford University Press, 2000) 3. Blanchot does not call *L'Instant de ma mort* a *récit*, although it could be argued that it participates in that genre.
77. Blanchot, *The Writing of the Disaster*, 83; *ED*, 132. The statement should be read alongside Blanchot's very early comment, made with Mahatma Ghandhi in mind, "Toute révolution est spirituelle," "Mahatma Ghandhi," *Les Cahiers mensuels*, troisième série no. 7, juillet 1931.
78. Quoted by Bernard-Henri Lévy, *Adventures on the Freedom Road: The French Intellectuals in the Twentieth-Century*, trans. and ed., Richard Veasey (London: The Harvill Press, 1995), 318. It needs to be added that Blanchot condemned the "persécutions barbares contre les juifs" in "Des violences antisémites à l'apophéose du travail," *Le Rempart* 1 mai 1933, 37.
79. Blanchot, *The Madness of the Day*, trans. Lydia Davis, *en face* edition (Barrytown, N.Y.: Station Hill, 1981), 6. That the event is not a literary fiction is underscored by Jacques Derrida when he quotes a letter from Blanchot: "July 20. Fifty years ago, I knew the happiness of nearly being shot to death," Derrida, *Demeure*, 52. Maurice Nadeau reports in his literary memoirs, "Durant la guerre, le révoltent les ignominies, d'Hitler d'abord, de Vichy ensuite, contre les juifs. Il est pris comme otage dans une ville du Midi où il séjourne, il va être fusillé, il échappe à la mort par miracle, dans des circonstances qu'il me décrit mais qu'il appartient à lui seul de révéler," *Grâces leur soient rendus* (Paris: Albin Michel, 1990), 71.
80. Blanchot, *The Unavowable Community*, trans. Pierre Joris (Barrytown, N.Y.: Station Hill Press, 1988), 18–19; *CI*, 36–37.
81. Blanchot quotes Bataille's remark, *The Writing of the Disaster*, 90; *ED*, 142.
82. In this regard see *The Writing of the Disaster*, 50; *ED*, 84. Also see "On Hindu Thought," *Faux Pas*, 33–36; *FP*, 42–46, and "Le Pèlerinage aux sources," *Journal des Débats* 13 janvier 1944, 2–3. I would like to draw attention to an alternate account of this passage by Philippe Lacoue-Labarthe in his essay "The Contestation of Death," trans. Philip Anderson, in Kevin Hart and Geoffrey Hartman, eds., *The Power of Contestation: Perspectives on Maurice Blanchot* (Baltimore: Johns Hopkins University Press, 2004).
83. Leslie Hill proposes a fascinating reading of *Le Très-Haut* as offering "cogent expression" of Blanchot's "political opinions" in the years following World War II. See his *Bataille, Klossowski, Blanchot: Writing at the Limit* (Oxford: Oxford University Press, 2001), 181–206. I quote from 185 n. 8.
84. Blanchot, *The Step Not Beyond*, 24; *PAD*, 38.
85. Blanchot, "On a Change of Epoch: The Exigency of Return," *The Infinite Conversation*, 273; *IE*, 408. Blanchot has in mind Klossowski's *Nietzsche and the Vicious Circle*, trans. Daniel W. Smith (Chicago: University of Chicago Press, 1997), although his own meditation on the eternal lapping of the Outside in *The Space of Literature* is at least of equal importance here.

10
Kafka's Immanence, Kafka's Transcendence

BY MLADEN DOLAR

The question of immanence and transcendence in Kafka easily calls for confusion. To put it quickly, there is a whole line of interpretation which maintained that the predicament of Kafka's universe can best be described in the terms of the transcendence of the law. Indeed it seems that the law is inaccessible to Kafka's "heroes," they can never find out what it says, the law is an ever receding secret, even its very existence is a matter of presumption. Where is the law, what does it command, what does it prohibit?[1] One is always "before the law," outside of its gate, and one of the great paradoxes of this law is that it doesn't prohibit anything, but is itself prohibited, it is based on a prohibition of the prohibition, the prohibition itself is prohibited.[2] One can never get to the locus of prohibition—if one could do that then one would be saved, or so it seems. The transcendence of the law, on this account, epitomizes the unhappy fate of Kafka's subjects, and the only transcendence there is in Kafka's world is the transcendence of this law which seems like an unfathomable, ungraspable deity, a dark god emitting obscure oracular signs, but one can never figure out its location, purpose, logic, or meaning.

Yet this elusiveness of the transcendent law is but a mirage: it is a necessary delusion, a perspectival illusion, for if the law always escapes us this is not because of its transcendence, but because it has no interior. It is always deferred from one instance to another, from one office to the next one, because it is nothing else but this movement of deferral, it coincides with this perpetual motion of evasion. The unfathomable secret behind some closed door, behind some inscrutable façade, is no secret at all, there is no secret outside this metonymical movement, which can be seen as the movement of desire. If the law has no interior, it has no exterior either: one is always already inside the law, there is no outside of law, the law is pure immanence, "the unlimited field of immanence instead of infinite transcendence," to quote Deleuze and Guattari,[3] for this second account has been made justly famous by their book on Kafka, one of the most influential recent interpretations.

So what on the first account appeared as pure transcendence is on the second account seen as pure immanence. On the first account one is always already and irretrievably excluded, on the second account one is always included

175

and there is no transcendence, one is trapped in the immanence of the law which is at the same time the immanence of desire. Does one have to decide between the two, join one camp or the other? Are the two accounts irreconcilable? Although the second reading is no doubt far more useful and effectively dissipates the misunderstandings advanced by the first one, it still perhaps doesn't quite cover what is at stake in Kafka. By promoting the dimension of pure immanence it perhaps eludes, reduces and avoids a paradox. The paradox of an emergence of a transcendence at the very heart of immanence, or rather of the way that immanence always doubles itself and intersects with itself. Or to put it another way: there might be no inside, there might be no outside, but they still intersect.

Let us try to establish a shift, a slightly different third possible position starting from Agamben's account of sovereignty, bearing in mind the point of paradox. The gate of the law is always open, the doorkeeper doesn't prevent the man from the country from entering, yet the man finds it impossible to enter through the open door. The openness itself immobilizes, the subject stands awestruck and paralyzed in front of the open door, in a position of exclusion from the law, but which is exactly the form of his inclusion, since this is the way that the law holds him in sway. Before the law one is always inside the law, there is no place before the law, the very exclusion is inclusion.

The exclusive inclusion or the inclusive exclusion is the way in which Agamben describes the structure of sovereignty: it is the point of exception inscribed in the law itself, the point which can suspend the validity of laws. On the first pages of his book he defines sovereignty, following Carl Schmitt, as a paradox:

> The sovereign is at the same time outside and inside the juridical order. . . . The sovereign, having the legal power to suspend the validity of the law, is legally situated outside the law. This means that the paradox can equally be formulated in this way: "The law is exterior to itself," or rather: "I, the sovereign, who am outside the law, declare that there is no outside of the law."[4]

So sovereignty is structurally based on exception which is included in the law as its own point of exteriority. The sovereign is the one who can suspend the legal order and proclaim the state of emergency where the laws are no longer valid and the exception becomes the rule. At the opposite end of the sovereign we have its inverse figure, the converse point of exception, which is the *homo sacer*: the bare life excluded from the law in such a way that it can be killed with impunity, yet without entering into the realm of the sacrifice. Being outside the law, his bare life exposed to be killed with impunity, the *homo sacer* is exposed to the law as such in its pure validity. The state of emergency is the rule of law in its pure form—precisely the excess of validity over meaning (*Geltung ohne Bedeutung*, to use the expression from Scholem's correspondence with Benjamin in the thirties), the suspension of all laws and therefore the institution of the law as such. One could say: Kafka is the literature of the permanent state of emergency. The subject is at the mercy of the law beyond all laws, without any defense, he can be arbitrarily stripped of all his possessions, including his bare life. The law functions as its own transgression. Kafka's heroes are always *homines sacri*, exposed to the pure validity of the law which manifests itself as its opposite. Kafka has turned *homo sacer* into the central literary figure, thus displaying a certain shift in the functioning of the law which has taken place at the turn of the twentieth century, and inaugurated a new era, with many drastic consequences which will define the century.

Agamben proposes an optimistic reading of the parable "Before the law," precisely at the point where the interpreters merely saw the defeat of the man from the country, for he never succeeded to get into the law, he died outside the gate and, when dying, learned that this gate was reserved only for him. Yet, the last sentence reads: "This gate was made only for you. I am now going to shut it. [*Ich gehe jetzt und schließe ihn.*]" (4) But if the very openness of the law is the pure form of its closure and of its unqualified validity and power, then the man succeeded in a most remarkable feat: he managed to attain the closure. He managed to close the door, to interrupt the reign of pure validity. The closed door is a chance of liberation, it sets the limit to the pure immanence. It is true, he was successful only at the price of his own life, so that the law is interrupted only when he is dead—one reading would be: the law has no power over the dead alone, one doesn't stand a chance while alive. Still, there is a perspective of closure, of invalidating the law if only one persists far enough. Was the man from the country so naïve or so shrewd? On the one hand he was very timid, he let himself be subdued very quickly, he is easily diverted from his initial intention, instantly intimidated. But on the other hand he displayed an incredible stubbornness, persistence, and determination. It is the struggle of exhaustion; it is true that they manage to entirely exhaust him with the open door, yet in the end he is the one who exhausts the law. If one is prepared to persist to the end one can put an end to the validity of the law.

This seems a desperate strategy. But what other strategies are there in this impossible predicament? If there is always some way out of the closure, there seems to be none out of the openness. This is why Kafka is generally misperceived as the depressing author of total closure with no exit, but this is also where the solution of pure immanence doesn't quite offer a good answer. In what follows I will examine three strategies which offer an exit, as it were, and they are all connected with the instance of the voice—precisely as a point of a paradox.

Why the voice? What makes the voice be placed in a structural and privileged position? The law always manifests itself through some partial objects, through a glimpse, a tiny fragment that one unexpectedly witnesses and which in its fragmentation remains a mystery; by morsels; by servants, doorkeepers, maids; by trivia, by trash, the refuse of the law. The massive validity without meaning is epitomized by partial objects, and those are enough for the construction of fantasies, enough to capture desire. And among those there is the voice, the senseless voice of the law: the law constantly makes funny noises, it emits mysterious sounds. The validity of the law can be pinned to a senseless voice.

When the land surveyor K. arrives at the village under the castle he is lodged in an inn and he is eager to clarify the nature of his assignment. He was sent for, he was summoned, and he wants to know why, so he calls the castle, he uses this recent invention, the telephone. But what does he hear on the other side of the line? Just a voice which is some kind of singing, or buzz, or murmur, the voice in general, the voice without qualifications.

> The receiver gave out a buzz of a kind that K. had never before heard on a telephone. It was like the hum of countless children's voices—but yet not a hum, the echo rather of voices singing at an infinite distance—blended by sheer impossibility into one high but resonant sound that vibrated on the ear as if it were trying to penetrate beyond mere hearing.[6]

There is no message, but the voice is enough to stupefy him, he is suddenly paralyzed: "In front of the telephone he was powerless." He is spellbound, mesmerized. This is just one example chosen at random among many.

The intervention of a voice in this place is crucial and necessary. The voice epitomizes at best the validity beyond meaning, it is structurally placed at the point of the exception of the law. For the law is the law only insofar as it is written, that is, given the form which is universally at the disposal of everyone, always accessible and unchangeable—but with Kafka one can never get to the place where it is written to check what it says, the access is always denied, the place of the letter is infinitely eluding. The voice is precisely what cannot be checked, it is ever-changing and fleeting, it is the non-universal par excellence, it is what cannot be universalized. This is why the superego, the reverse side of the law, is always manifested by a voice.[6] And this is the point of Lacan's use of the shofar: this ancient primitive instrument used in the Jewish rituals is the presentification of the supposed voice of the dying primal father which keeps resonating, thus endowing the letter with authority. The letter of the law, in order to acquire authority, has to rely, at a certain point, on the tacitly presupposed voice which makes certain that the letter is not "the dead letter," but exerts power and can be enacted. So the voice is structurally in the same position as sovereignty, which means that it can put into question the validity of the law: the voice stands at the point of exception, the internal exception which threatens to become the rule, where it suddenly displays its profound complicity with the bare life. The emergency is the emergence of the voice in the commanding position, its concealed existence suddenly becomes overwhelming and devastating. The voice is precisely at the unplaceable spot at the same time in the interior and the exterior of the law, and hence a permanent threat of the state of emergency. And with Kafka the exception has become the only rule. The letter of the law is hidden in some inaccessible place and may not exist at all, it is a matter of presumption, and we have only voices in its place.

K. is spellbound by the voice emanating from the castle through the telephone, as the wanderer is spellbound by the song of the Sirens. What is the secret of that irresistible voice? Kafka has an answer in his short story "The Silence of the Sirens," "*Das Schweigen der Sirenen*," written in October 1917 and published in 1931 by Max Brod who has also provided the title. The Sirens are irresistible because they are silent, yet Ulysses nevertheless managed to outwit them. Here we have the first strategy, the first model of escape from the unstoppable force of the law.

"To protect himself from the Sirens Ulysses stopped his ears with wax and had himself bound to the mast of his ship." (430) The first sentence is already one of Kafka's wonderful opening *coups de force*, like the opening paragraph of his novel *Amerika* where we have his hero Karl Roßmann arriving by boat in New York harbor, admiring the Statue of Liberty with her sword rising high in the sun. One almost doesn't notice, but where is the sword of the Statue of Liberty? Here we have Ulysses stopping his ears and tied to the mast, while in the legend it was the oarsmen who had their ears stopped with wax while Ulysses was tied to the mast. There was a division of labor, indeed the very model of the division of labor, if we follow the argument that Adorno and Horkheimer developed in *The Dialectic of the Enlightenment*. There is a sharp division between those who are doomed to be deaf and to work, and those who listen and enjoy, take pleasure in art, but are helplessly tied to the mast. This is the very image of the division between labor and art, and this is the place to start scrutinizing the function of art, in its separation from the economy of work and survival, that is, in its powerlessness. The aesthetic pleasure is always the pleasure in chains, it is thwarted by the limits assigned to it, and this is why Ulysses confronting the Sirens is so exemplary for Adorno and Horkheimer.

Kafka's Ulysses combines both strategies, the aristocratic and the proletarian. He takes double precautions, although all know that this is useless: the song of the Sirens would pierce any wax and the true passion would break any chains. But the Sirens have a weapon far more effective than their voice, which is their silence, that is, the voice at its purest. The silence which is unbearable and irresistible, the ultimate weapon of the law. "And though admittedly such a thing has never happened, still it is conceivable that someone might possibly have escaped from their singing; but from their silence certainly never." (431) One cannot resist silence for the good reason that there is nothing to resist. This is the mechanism of the law at its minimal: it expects nothing of you, it doesn't command, one can always oppose commands and injunctions, but not the silence. The silence is the very form of the validity of the law beyond its meaning, the zero-point of voice, its pure embodiment.

Ulysses is naïve, he childishly trusts his devices, and he sails past the Sirens. The Sirens are not simply silent but they pretend to sing: "He saw their throats rising and falling, their breasts lifting, their eyes filled with tears, their lips half-parted," and he believed they were singing and that he has escaped them and outfoxed them, although their singing was unstoppable. "But Ulysses, if one may so express it, did not hear their silence; he thought they were singing and that he alone did not hear them." (431) If he knew they were silent he would be lost. He imagined that he has escaped their power by his naïve cunning, and in the first account we are led to suppose that it was his naïveté that saved him.

Yet the truth of the story is perhaps not in his naïveté at all: "Perhaps he had really noticed, although here the human understanding is beyond its depths, that the Sirens were silent, and held up to them and to the gods the aforementioned pretence merely as a sort of shield." The shrewd and canny Ulysses, the sly and cunning Ulysses—Homer never fails to accompany his name by one of those epithets. Is his ultimate slyness displayed by putting up an act of naïveté? So in the second account he outwitted them by pretending not to hear that there is really nothing to hear. They were going through the motions of singing and he was going through the motions of not hearing their silence. One could say that his ruse has the structure of the most famous Jewish joke, the paragon among Jewish jokes, in which one Jew says to another at the railway station: "If you say you're going to Krakow, you want me to believe you're going to Lemberg. But I know that in fact you're going to Krakow. So why are you lying to me?"[6] So by extension: "Why are you pretending that you don't hear anything when you really don't hear anything? Why are you pretending not to hear when you know very well there is nothing to hear? You pretend so that I would think you don't hear anything while I know very well that you really don't hear anything." The Jewish joke is Ulysses's triumph, he managed to counter one pretence with another. In the joke the first Jew, the one who simply told the truth about his destination, is the winner, for he managed to transfer the burden of truth and lie to the other one, who could only reply with a hysterical outburst. One is left with the same oscillation as in our story: was the truth-teller so naïve or so shrewd? This is exactly the question which remained in the air with the man from the country dying on the threshold of the law. Ulysses's strategy is not unrelated to the strategy of the man from the country: Ulysses counters pretence by pretence, the man counters deferral by deferral, exhaustion by exhaustion—he manages to exhaust the exhaustion, to bring an end to the deferral, to close the door.

This doesn't work with the Sirens. To be sure, they are defeated: "They no longer had any desire to allure; all they wanted was to hold as long as they could the radiance that fell from Ulysses's great eyes." (431) Are they suddenly seized by the yearning for the one who managed to get away? "If the Sirens had possessed consciousness they would have been annihilated at that moment. But they remained as they had been; all that had happened was that Ulysses had escaped them." (432) They have no consciousness, all their behavior is going through the motions, they are automatons, they are inanimate, they are machines imitating humanity, they are cyborgs, and this is why their defeat cannot have any effect. This one has escaped, but that cannot dismantle the mechanism.

So can one fight the law by turning a deaf ear to it? Can one just pretend not to hear its silence? This is no simple strategy, it defies human understanding, says Kafka; it boggles the mind. It takes supreme cunning, yet it doesn't introduce a closure of the law. Ulysses was an exception, and everybody else is the rule.

Let us now turn to another strategy which has again the voice at its kernel, the voice which can counter the voice, or the silence, of the law. "Josephine the Singer, or the Mouse Folk," "*Josefine die Sängerin oder das Volk der Mäuse*," is actually the last story that Kafka ever wrote, in March 1924, a couple of months before his death. By virtue of it being the last one it necessarily invites us to read it as his testament, his last will, the *point de capiton*, the quilting point, the vantage point which would shed some ultimate light on his work, provide a clue which would illuminate, with finality, all that went before. And it is no doubt bizarre and ironical that this clue, this suture, is provided not only by the voice, but by the tiniest of voices, the minute microscopic squeak,[8] and one is structurally inclined to take this minuscule peep as the red thread that could retroactively enlighten Kafka's obscurity.

There is a vast question of Kafka's multiple uses of the animal kingdom which are so prominent in his work—Deleuze and Guattari dwell upon this at some length. There is, most notoriously, the becoming-animal of Gregor Samsa, which features, among other things, his voice, the incomprehensible chirping sounds which come out of his mouth when he tries to justify himself in front of the chief clerk. "'That was no human voice,' said the chief clerk . . . " (98); it is the signifier reduced to pure senseless voice, reduced to what Deleuze and Guattari call the pure intensity. The general question can be put in the following way: is animality outside the law? The first answer is: by no means. Kafka's animals are never linked to mythology, they are never allegorical or metaphorical. Here is the well-known line by Deleuze and Guattari: "Metamorphosis is the contrary of metaphor,"[9] and Kafka is perhaps the first utterly non-metaphorical author. The animal societies, the mice and the dogs to which we will come in a moment, are organized "just like" human societies,[10] which means that animals are always denaturalized, deterritorialized animals, there is nothing pre-cultural, innocent, or authentic about them. Yet on the other hand they nevertheless represent what Deleuze and Guattari call *la ligne de fuite*, a certain line of flight. The becoming-animal of Gregor Samsa means his escape from the mechanism of his family and his job, the way out from all the symbolic roles that he had assumed, his insecthood being at the same time his liberation. Metamorphosis is an attempted escape, though a failed one. But there is a double edge to this: one can read the becoming-animal on the first level as becoming that which law has made out of subjects, that is, reduced to bare animal life, the lowest kind of animality represented by insects, the crawling disgusting swarm to be decontaminated, the non-sacrificial animality (the insect is the anti-lamb), the bare life of *homo sacer*. The law treats subjects as insects, as the metaphor has it, but Gregor Samsa destroys the metaphor by taking it literally, by literalizing it, and thus the metaphor collapses, the distance of analogy evaporates and the word becomes the thing. But by fully assuming the position of bare life, the reduction to animality, a *ligne de fuite* emerges, not outside of the law but at the bottom of the full assumption of the law. Animality is the internal outside which is endowed with ambivalence precisely at the point of fully realizing the implicit presupposition of the law.

Josephine's voice presents a different problem. It is not a question of metamorphosis, but of the emergence of another kind of voice in the midst of the society governed by the law; a voice which wouldn't be the voice of the law, though it may seem indistinguishable from it. Josephine's voice is endowed with a special power in the midst of this entirely unmusical race of mice. (A parenthesis: what Freud and Kafka curiously have in common, apart from the obvious analogies of their Jewish origins and sharing the same historical moment and the space of Central Europe, is their claim that they are both completely unmusical, that music is the one thing they don't understand at all. Couldn't one say that this absence of musical gift is the best entry into the susceptibility to the voice?)

What is so special about Josephine's voice?

> Among intimates we admit freely to one another that Josephine's singing, as singing, is nothing out of the ordinary. Is it in fact singing at all? . . . Is it not perhaps just piping [whistling, *pfeifen*]? And piping is something we all know about, it is the real artistic accomplishment of our people, or rather no mere accomplishment but a characteristic expression of our life. We all pipe, but of course no one dreams of making out that our piping is an art, we pipe without thinking of it, indeed without noticing it, and there are even many among us who are quite unaware that piping is one of our characteristics. . . . Josephine . . . hardly rises above the level of our usual piping. . . . (361)

Josephine merely pipes, whistles, as all mice do, all the time, even in a less accomplished manner than the others. "Piping is our people's daily speech . . ." (370), that is, the speech minus meaning. Yet her singing is irresistible. This is no ordinary voice, though indistinguishable from others by its positive features. Whenever she starts singing, and she does it in unpredictable places and times, in the middle of the street, anywhere, there is immediately a crowd that gathers and listens, completely enthralled. So this very ordinary piping is suddenly placed on a special spot, all its power stemming from the place it occupies, as in Lacan's definition of sublimation, "to elevate an object to the dignity of the Thing." She may well be convinced herself that her voice is very special, but it is just "to a straw" like any other. This is 1924, ten years after Duchamp displayed his *La roue de bicyclette* (1913), the ordinary bicycle wheel, this art object which mysteriously looks exactly like any bicycle wheel. As Gérard Wajcman put it, Duchamp invented the wheel for the twentieth century.[11] There is an act of a pure *creatio ex nihilo*, or rather *creatio ex nihilo* in reverse: the wheel, the object of mass production, is not created out of nothing, but rather it creates the nothing, the gap that separates it from all other wheels, and which presents the wheel in its pure being-object, deprived of any of its functions, suddenly in its strange sublimity.

Josephine's voice is the extension of the ready-made into music. All it does is to introduce a gap, the imperceptible gap that separates it from all other voices while remaining absolutely the same—"a mere nothing in voice" (367). This can start anywhere, everywhere, at any time, with any kind of object: this is the art of the ready-made, and everything is ready-made for art. It is like the sudden intrusion of transcendence into immanence, but a transcendence which stays in the very midst of immanence and looks exactly the same, the imperceptible difference in the very sameness. Her art is the art of the minimal gap,[11] and this is the hardest nut to crack.

> To crack a nut is truly no feat, so no one would ever dare to collect an audience in order to entertain it with nut-cracking. But if all the same one does do that and succeeds in entertaining the public, then it cannot be a matter of simple nut-cracking. Or it is a matter of nut-cracking, but it turns out that we have overlooked the art of cracking nuts because we were too skilled in it and that this newcomer to it first shows us its real nature, even finding it useful in making his effects to be rather less expert in nut-cracking than most of us. (361–2)

So any voice will do to crack the nuts, provided it can create nothing out of something. Josephine's genius is in having no talent, which makes her all the more the genius. An accomplished trained singer would never have pulled off this feat.

Josephine is the popular artist, the people's artist, so the people take care of her as the father of the child, while she is persuaded that she is the one that takes care of the people; when they are "in a bad way politically or economically, her singing is supposed to save" them and "if it doesn't drive away the evil, at least gives us strength to bear it" (366). Her voice is a collective voice, she sings for all, she is the voice of the people, who otherwise form an anonymous mass. "This piping, which rises up where everyone else is pledged to silence, comes almost like a message from the whole people to each individual." (367) In a reversal, she embodies the collectivity and relegates her listeners to their individuality. There is the opposition between her oneness and the collectivity of people—they are always treated *en masse*, they display the uniformity of their reactions, despite some minor divergences of opinion, and their commonsensical opinion is rendered by the narrator (*Erzählermaus*, as one commentator put it), the bearer of the doxa.[13] They are non-individuals, while she, on the other side of the scale, is the exceptional one, the elevated individuality who stands for, and can awaken, the lost individuality of others.

But in her role of the artist she is also the capricious prima donna, there is the whole comedy of her claims for her rights. She wants to be exempt from work, she requires special privileges, the work allegedly harms her voice, she wants due honor paid for her services, she wants to be granted a place apart. She "does not want mere admiration, she wants to be admired exactly in the way she prescribes" (362). But the people, despite the general esteem, don't want to hear about any of this, they are cold in their judgment; they respect her, but want her to remain one of them. So there is the whole charade of the artist who is not appreciated as she deserves, doesn't get the laurels that she thinks belong to her, the act of the genius not understood by contemporaries. In protest she announces that she will cut down her coloratura, this will teach them a lesson, and maybe she does, only nobody notices it. She keeps coming up with all sorts of whims, she lets herself be begged and only reluctantly gives in. There is the comedy of hurt narcissism, megalomania, the inflated ego, the high mission of the artist's overblown vocation. Then one day she indeed stops singing, firmly believing that there will be a huge scandal, but nobody cares, nobody gives a damn, everybody goes about their business as usual, without noticing a lack. That is, without noticing the lack of the lack, the absence of the gap.

> Curious, how mistaken she is in her calculations, the clever creature, so mistaken that one might fancy she has made no calculations at all but is only being driven on by her destiny, which in our world cannot be anything but a sad one. Of her own accord she abandons her singing, of her own accord she destroys the power she has gained over people's hearts. How could she ever have gained that power, since she knows so little about these hearts of ours? . . . Josephine's road must go downhill. The time will soon come when her last notes sound and die into silence. She is a small episode in the eternal history of our people, and the people will get over the loss of her. . . . Perhaps we shall not miss so very much after all, while Josephine . . . will happily lose herself in the numberless throng of the heroes of our people, and soon, since we are no historians, will rise to the heights of redemption and be forgotten like all her brothers. (376)

Despite her vanity and megalomania, people will easily do without her, she will be forgotten, no traces will be left of her art, this is not a people of historians and archivists, and besides, there is no way one could stack, collect, archivize her art, which consists purely in the gap.

So this is the second strategy, the strategy of art, of the art as the non-exceptional exception, which can arise anywhere, at any moment, which is made of anything, of the ready-made objects, providing it can provide them with a gap, make them make a break. It is the art of the minimal difference. Yet the moment it makes its appearance this difference is bungled by the very gesture which brought it about, the moment this gesture and this difference became instituted, the moment art becomes an institution to which a certain place is allotted and certain limits are drawn. Its power is at the same time its powerlessness, the very status of art veils what is at stake. Hence the whole farce of the egocentric megalomania and the misunderstood genius, the special privileges and so forth which occupy the largest part of the story. Josephine wants the impossible: she wants a place beyond the law, beyond equality—and equality is the essential feature of the mouse-folk, the equality in tininess, in their miniature size (hence her claims to greatness are all the more comical). But at the same time she wants her status of the exception to be legally sanctioned, symbolically recognized, properly glorified. She wants to be, like the sovereign, both inside and outside the law. She wants her uniqueness to be recognized as a special social role, and the moment art does this, it is cooked. The very break it has introduced is reduced to just another social function, the break becomes the institution of the break, its place is circumscribed and as an exception it can fit very well into the rule. That is, into the rule of law. As an artist who wants veneration and recognition she will be forgotten, relegated to the gallery of memory, that is, of oblivion. Her voice which opens the crack in the seamless continuity of the law, is betrayed and destroyed by the very status of art, which reinserts it and closes the gap. At the best it can be a tiny recess:

> Piping is our people's daily speech, only many a one pipes his whole life long and does not know it, where here piping is set free from the fetters of daily life and it sets us free too for a little while. (370)

Just for a little while, but by setting us free it only helps us bear the rest all the better. The miniature size of the mouse is enough to open the gap, but once it is instituted and recognized, its importance shrinks to the size of the mouse, despite its delusions of grandeur. It is the voice tied to the mast, and the oarsmen, although they may hear it in the flash of a brief recess, will continue to be deaf. Thus we end up not with Kafka's version of Ulysses, but are stuck with Ulysses *tout court*, or rather with the Adorno and Horkheimer version. Her sublime voice will finally be *den Mäusen gepfiffen*, as the dictionary has it (and this German expression may well be the origin of the whole story), that is, piped to the mice, piped in vain to someone who cannot understand or appreciate it—not because of some obtuseness of the mass, but because of the nature of art itself. One could say: the art is her mousetrap.

So the second strategy fails, is ruined by its own success, and the transcendence that art promised turned out to be of such a nature that it could easily fit as one part in the division of labor, the disruptive power of the gap turned out to accommodate continuity all too well.

Let us now consider a third option. "Investigations of a Dog," "*Forschungen eines Hundes*," written in 1922 (two years before his death) and published in 1931, the title again being given by Max Brod, is one of the most obscure and bizarre among Kafka's stories—and this is to say something—apart from being one of the longest. Here we have a dog who lives a normal dog's life, like everybody, and who is suddenly awakened from this life by an encounter with seven rather special music-producing dogs.

> . . . out of some place of darkness, to the accompaniment of terrible sounds such as I had never heard before, seven dogs stepped into the light. . . . they brought the sound with them, though I could not recognize how they produced it. . . . At that time I still knew hardly anything of the creative gift for music with which the canine race alone is endowed, it had naturally enough escaped my but slowly developing powers of observation; for though music had surrounded me as a perfectly natural and indispensable element of existence ever since I was a suckling, an element which nothing impelled me to distinguish from the rest of existence . . . ; all the more astonishing, then, indeed devastating, were these seven great musical artists to me. (281)

To start with, the situation is similar to that of Josephine's singing: music is everywhere in dogs' lives, the most run-of-the-mill thing, utterly inconspicuous, and it takes "great musical artists" to single it out, that is, to produce the break. But there is a twist:

> They did not speak, they did not sing, they remained generally silent, almost determinedly silent; but from the empty air they conjured music. Everything was music, the lifting and setting down of their feet, certain turns of the head, their running and their standing still, the positions they took up in relation to one another . . . [their] lying flat on the ground and going through complicated concerted evolutions; . . . . (Ibid.)

Where does the music come from? There is no speaking, no singing, no musical instruments. It just came from nowhere, from the empty air, *ex nihilo*. Music was everywhere in dogs' lives, ready-made, but this one was created out of nothing. We have seen that Josephine's problem was to create a nothing out of something, in *creatio ex nihilo* in reverse, *creatio nullius rei*, but here it's even better: their problem is how to create nothing out of nothing, the gap of nothing which encircles the ready-made object made out of nothing. There we have the great wonder: the ready-made nothing. The ready-made nothing is epitomized by the voice without a discernible source, what Michel Chion called the acousmatic voice.[13] It is the voice as pure resonance.

In one of his (rather rare) reflections about the voice in the (unpublished) seminar on anxiety (June 5, 1963) Lacan argues for his tenet that the object voice has to be divorced from sonority. He curiously makes an excursion into the physiology of the ear, he speaks about the cavity of the ear, its snail-like shape, *le tuyau*, the tube, and goes on to say that its importance is merely topological, it consists in the formation of a void, a cavity, an empty space, of "the most elementary form of a constituted and a constituting emptiness [*le vide*]," like the empty space in the middle of a tube, or of any wind instrument, the space of mere resonance, the volume. But this is but a metaphor, he says, and continues with the following rather mysterious passage:

> If the voice, in our sense, has an importance, then it doesn't reside in it resonating in some spatial void; rather it resides in the fact that the simplest emission . . . resonates in the void which is the void of the Other as such, *ex nihilo*, so to speak. The voice responds to what is said, but it cannot be responsible for it [*La voix répond à ce qui se dit, mais elle ne peut pas en répondre*]. In other words: in order to respond we have to incorporate the voice as the alterity of what is said [*l'altérité de ce qui se dit*].

I will take up just one thread in this difficult passage. If there is an empty space in which the voice resonates, then it is only the void of the Other, the Other as a void. The voice comes back to us through the loop of the Other, and what comes back to us from the Other is the pure alterity of what is said, that is, the voice. This is maybe the original form of the famous formula that the subject always gets back his own message in an inverted form: the message that one gets back in response is the voice. Our speech resonates in the Other and is returned as the voice, something we didn't cater for: the inverted form of our message is its voice which was created from a pure void, *ex nihilo*, as an inaudible echo of the pure resonance, and the non-sonorous resonance endows what is said with alterity. One expects a response from the Other, one addresses it in the hope of a response, but all one gets is the voice. The voice is what is said turned into its alterity, but the responsibility is the subject's own, not the Other's, which means that the subject is responsible not only for what he said, but must at the same time respond for, and respond to, the alterity of his own speech. He said something more than he intended, and this surplus is the voice which is merely produced by being passed through the loop of the Other. This is I suppose at the bottom of the rather striking phenomenon in analysis, the dispossession of one's voice in the presence of the silence of the analyst: whatever one says is immediately countered by its own alterity, by the voice resounding in the resonance of the void of the Other, which comes back to the subject as the answer the moment one spoke. And this resonance dispossesses one's own voice, the resonance of the Other thwarts it, burrows it, makes it sound hollow. The speech is the subject's own, but the voice pertains to the Other, it is created in the loop of its void. This is what one has to learn to respond for, and respond to.[15]

But this is just a digression, made in the wild hope of clarifying one obscurity by another, that of Kafka by that of Lacan, the hope that two combined obscurities might produce some light—*ex nihilo*. If we take up just the slogans of "the resonance of the Other," "the void," "*ex nihilo*," then we see that the seven dogs' voices are coming out of a pure void, they spring up from nothing, a pure resonance without a source. As if the pure alterity had turned into music, the music that pervades anything and everything, as if the voice of this resonance had got hold of all possible points of emission, and not the other way round. The resonance of the voice functions not as an effect but as a cause, a pure *causa sui*, but which in this self-causality encompasses everything. It is as if the pure void of the Other would start to reverberate in itself in the presence of those great musicians, whose art consisted merely in letting the Other resonate for itself.

The hapless young dog is overwhelmed:

> ... the music gradually got the upper hand, literally knocked the breath out of me and swept me far away from those actual little dogs, and quite against my will ... my mind could attend to nothing but this blast of music which seemed to come from all sides, from the heights, from the deeps, from everywhere, surrounding the listener, overwhelming him, crushing him, and over his swooning body still blowing fanfares so near that they seemed far away and almost inaudible. ... the music robbed me of my wits. ... (282)

This experience entirely shatters the young dog's life, it is the start of his quest, his investigations. His interest in all this is not artistic at all, there is no problem of the status of this voice as art, as with Josephine, his interest is an epistemological one. It is the quest for the source, the attempt to gain knowledge about the source of it all. One of Josephine's endeavors was to preserve the dimension of the child in her art, in the midst of that race of mice which is both very childish and prematurely old at the same time, they are like children infused with "weariness and hopelessness" (369), and Josephine's voice was like preserving their childhood against their economy of survival, against the always premature adulthood. But the young dog is at the very opposite end of this: he decides that "there are more important things than childhood" (286). "*Es gibt wichtigere Dinge als die Kindheit*":[16] this is one of Kafka's great sentences, it should be taken as a motto, or indeed as a most serious political slogan. A political slogan in the time of the general infantilization of social life, starting with the infantilization of infants, the time which loves to take the despicable opposite line, namely that we are all children in our hearts and that this is our most precious possession, something we should hold on to. There are more important things than childhood: this should also be seen as the slogan of psychoanalysis, which indeed seems to be all about retrieving childhood, but not in order to keep this precious and unique thing, but to give it up. Psychoanalysis is on the side of the young dog who decides to grow up, to leave behind "the blissful life of a young dog," to start his investigations, turn to research, to pursue a quest.

But his quest takes a strange and unexpected turn. The question "Where does the music come from? Where does the voice come from?" is immediately translated into another question: "Where does the food come from?" The mystery of the incorporeal resonance of the voice is without further ado transformed into the mystery of a very different kind, of the most corporeal kind imaginable. The voice is the resonance from nowhere, it doesn't serve anything (Lacan's definition of enjoyment), but the food is at the opposite end, the most elementary means of survival, the most material and bodily of elements. Indeed, it is the question about a mystery where there doesn't seem to be any mystery. The dog sees a mystery where nobody else sees a mystery, the simplest and the most palpable thing suddenly becomes endowed with the greatest of secrets. A break has happened, from nowhere, and he wants to start his inquiries with the simplest things. In a few sentences, in a few lines, one passes from the enigma of song to the enigma of food—the stroke of Kafka's genius at its best, in a passage which is completely unpredictable and completely logical at the same time. Once one starts asking questions, there is no end to mystery. What is the source of food? The earth? But what enables the earth to provide food? Where does the earth get the food from? Just as the source of the law was an enigma which one could never disclose, so is the source of food an ever elusive enigma. It seems as though food, the pure materiality and immanence, would suddenly point to the transcendence, if only it is pursued far enough.

So the dog goes around asking other dogs, who all seem quite unconcerned by such self-evident trivialities. Nobody would dream of taking seriously such banal inquiries. When he asks them about the source of food, they immediately assume that he must be hungry, so instead of an answer they give him food, they want to nourish him, they want to stuff his mouth with food, they counter his questioning by feeding.

(I cannot resist the temptation to quote some Lacan in the brackets:

> Even when you stuff the mouth—the mouth that opens in the register of the drive—it is not the food that satisfies it. . . . As far as the oral drive is concerned . . . it is obvious that it is not a question of food, nor of the memory of food, nor the echo of food, nor the mother's care. . . . (167–8) . . . the fact that no food will ever satisfy the oral drive, except by circumventing [circling around] the eternally lacking object. (180)[17])

The dog's mouth cannot be stuffed, he is not put off that easily, and he gets so involved in his investigation that he eventually stops eating. The story has many twists and turns that I cannot go into, all of them illuminating and strangely wonderful; I will just jump to the last section.

The way to discover the source of food is to starve. Like "A Hunger Artist," "*Der Hungerkünstler*," the story written in the same year, not the starving artist, which is a common enough phenomenon, but someone who has brought starvation to an art. The starvation was his ready-made, since his secret was that he actually disliked food. It was an art not adequately appreciated, just like Josephine's, and this is why the hunger artist will die of hunger.

But the dog is no artist, this is not the portrait of the artist as a young dog, this dog is a would-be scientist and he is starving on his quest for knowledge, which almost brings him to the same result. But at the point of total exhaustion, when he was already dying (like the man from the country), there is salvation, the salvation at the point of the "exhaustion of exhaustion." He vomits blood, he is so faint that he faints, and when he opens his eyes there is a dog which appears from nowhere, a strange hound standing in front of him.

There is an ambiguity—is this last part a hallucination of the dying dog? Or even more radically, is this the answer to Hamlet's question "But in that sleep of death, what dreams may come"? Is this last section a possible sequel to "Before the Law," the dreams that may come to the man from the country at the point of his death? Is it all a delusion, the glimpse of salvation only at the point of death? A salvation only at the price that it doesn't have any consequence? But Kafka's describing this delusion, his pursuing it to the end, bringing it to the point of science, the birth of science from the spirit of a delusion on the threshold of death: this is all the consequence that is needed, something that affects the here and now, and radically transforms it.

The dying dog tries at first to chase away the apparition of the hound (is it a ghost which intervenes at the end, as opposed to the other one which intervened in the beginning?). The hound was very beautiful and at first it even appears that he is trying to pay court to the starved dog; he is very concerned about the dying dog, he cannot let him be. But all this dialogue is but a haphazard preparation for the event, the emergence of song, the song again coming from nowhere, emerging without anyone's will.

> . . . then I thought I saw something such as no dog before me had ever seen. . . . I thought I saw that the hound was already singing without knowing it, nay, more that the melody separated from him, was floating on the air in accordance with its own laws, and, as though he had no part in it, was moving toward me, toward me alone. . . . the melody, which the hound soon seemed to acknowledge as his, was quite irresistible. It grew stronger; its waxing power seemed to have no limits, and already almost burst my eardrums. But the worst was that it seemed to exist solely for my sake, this voice before whose sublimity the woods fell silent, to exist solely for my sake; who was I, that I could dare to remain here, lying brazenly before it in my pool of blood and filth. (314)

The song again appears from nowhere, it starts from anywhere, from a void, it is separated from its bearer, it is only *post festum* that the bearer steps in, that the hound can assume it, acknowledge it as his. And this song is directed towards the starving dog alone, it is for his ears only, the impersonal call which addresses only him personally, just as the door of the law was meant only for the man from the country. It is like the pure voice of a call, just like the irresistible call of the law, like its irrepressible silence, only this time the very same call as its opposite, the call of salvation.

So this voice from nowhere introduces the second break, the dog suddenly recovers on the threshold of death, the voice gets hold of him and instills new life in him, he who couldn't move cannot but jump up now, resurrected, the born again dog. And he pursues his investigations with redoubled forces, he extends his scientific interest to the canine music. "The science of music, if I am correctly informed, is perhaps still more comprehensive than that of nurture" (314–5). The new science he is trying to establish encompasses both his concerns, the source of food and the source of the voice, it combines them into a single effort. The voice, the music, like the pure transcendence, and the food as the pure immanence of the material world: but they have the common ground, the common source, they are rooted in the same kernel. The science of music is held in higher esteem than the science of nurture, it reaches the sublime, but this is precisely what prevents it from penetrating "deeply into the life of the people," it is "very esoteric and politely excludes the people" (315). It has been erroneously posited as a separate science, different from that of nurture, its power was powerless by being relegated to a separate realm. This was Josephine's unhappy fate, her song was separated from food, the sublime was her mousetrap, just as being immersed in nurture, the survival, was the unhappy fate of all the rest. Just as the science of nurture had to lead through starvation, so the science of music refers to silence, to "*verschwiegenes Hundewesen*," the silent essence of the dog, or the essence kept in silence, the essence that, after the experience of the song, can be discovered in any dog as its true nature. For penetrating this essence, "the real dog nature," the path of nurture was the alternative and simpler way, as it seemed, but it all boils down to the same, what matters is the point of intersection. "A border region between these two sciences, however, had already attracted my attention. I mean the theory of incantation, by which food is called down. [*Es ist die Lehre von dem die Nahrung herabrufenden Gesang.*]" (315, 454 in German) The song can call down, *herabrufen*, the food: the source of food was mistakenly sought in the earth, it should have been searched for in the opposite direction. The voice is the source of food that he has been seeking. There is an overlapping, an intersection between nourishment and voice. One can illustrate it with one of Lacan's favourite devices, the intersection of two circles, the circle of food and the circle of the voice, the music. What do we find at the point where they overlap? What is the mysterious intersection? But this is the best definition of what Lacan called *objet a*. It is the common source of food and music.[18]

Food and voice, both pass through the mouth. Deleuze keeps coming back to that over and over again. There is an alternative: either you eat or you speak, use your voice; one can't do both at the same time. They share the same location, but in mutual exclusion: either incorporation or emission.

> Any language, rich or poor, always implies the deterritorialization of the mouth, the tongue, and the teeth. The original territoriality of the mouth, the tongue, and

> the teeth is food. By being devoted to the articulation of sounds, the mouth, the tongue, and the teeth are deterritorialized. So there is a disjunction between eating and speaking. . . . To speak . . . is to starve. (Deleuze and Guattari, op. cit., 35–6)

By speech mouth is de-naturalized, diverted from its natural function, seized by the signifier (and for our purposes, by the voice which is but the alterity of the signifier). The Freudian name for this deterritorialization is the drive (if nothing else, it has the advantage that one is spared that terrible tongue-twister, but it aims at the same thing). Eating can never be the same once the mouth has been deterritorialized, it is seized by the drive, it turns around this object, it keeps circumventing, circling around this eternally elusive object. The speech, in this de-naturalizing function, is then subjected to the secondary territorialization, as it were; it acquires a second nature, with its anchorage in meaning. Meaning is a reterritorialization of language, its acquisition of a new territoriality, a naturalized substance. (This is what Deleuze and Guattari call the extensive or representational function of speech, as opposed to the pure intensity of the voice, if I undertake a small *forçage* here.) But this operation can never be successful, and the bit that eludes it can be pinned down as the element of the voice, this pure alterity of what is said. This is the common ground it shares with food, that in food which precisely escapes eating, the bone that gets stuck in the throat (one of Lacan's formulas is precisely that *objet a* is the bone that gets stuck in the throat of the signifier).

So the essence of the dog concerns precisely this intersection of food and voice, the two lines of investigation converge, from our biased perspective they meet in the *objet a*. So there would have to be a single science, the dog, on the last page, inaugurates a new science, he is the founding father of a new science. Though by his own admission he is a poor scientist, at least by the standards of the established sciences that went before. He couldn't pass

> even the most elementary scientific examination set by an authority on the subject. . . . the reason for that can be found in my incapacity for scientific investigation, my limited powers of thought, my bad memory, but above all in my inability to keep my scientific aim continuously before my eyes. All this I frankly admit, even with a certain degree of pleasure. For the more profound cause of my scientific incapacity seems to me to be an instinct, and indeed by no means a bad one. . . . It was this instinct that made me—and perhaps for the sake of science itself, but a different science from that of today, an ultimate science [*einer allerletzten Wissenschaft*]—prize freedom higher than everything else. Freedom! Certainly such freedom as is possible today is a wretched business. But nevertheless freedom, nevertheless a possession. (315–6)

This is the last sentence of the story. The last word of it all, *le fin mot* as *le mot de la fin*, is freedom, with an exclamation mark. Are we not victims of a delusion, shouldn't we pinch ourselves, is it possible that Kafka actually utters this word? This is perhaps the only spot where Kafka speaks of freedom in explicit terms, but this doesn't mean at all that there is unfreedom everywhere else in his universe. Quite the opposite, freedom is there at all times, everywhere, it is Kafka's *fin mot*, like the secret word one doesn't dare to utter although it is constantly on one's mind. The freedom that might not look like much, that might actually look wretched, but is there at all points, and once we spot it there is no way of going away from it, it is a possession to hold on to, it is the permanent line of flight, or rather the line of pursuit. And there is the slogan, the program of a new science which would be able to treat it, to take it as its object, to pursue it, the ultimate science, the science of freedom. Kafka lacks the proper word for it, he cannot name it, this is 1922, but he would only have to look around, to examine the ranks of his fellow Jewish Austrian compatriots. Of course, psychoanalysis.

Notes

1. "The problem of our laws": "Our laws are not generally known; they are kept secret by the small group of nobles who rule us. We are convinced that these ancient laws are scrupulously administered; nevertheless it is an extremely painful thing to be ruled by laws that one does not know.... The very existence of these laws, however, is at most a matter of presumption. There is a tradition that they exist and that they are a mystery confided to the nobility, but it is not and cannot be more than a mere tradition sanctioned by age, for the essence of a secret code is that it should remain a mystery.... There is a small party who... try to show that, if any law exists, it can only be this: The Law is whatever the nobles do." (437–8) All quotes from Kafka's stories are from *The Complete Stories*, ed. by N. N. Glatzer, New York: Schocken Books, 1995.
2. Cf. Jacques Derrida, "Préjugés, devant la loi," in J.-F. Lyotard, *La faculté de juger*, Paris: Minuit 1985, 122 and passim.
3. Gilles Deleuze and Félix Guattari, *Kafka. Pour une littérature mineure*. Paris: Minuit 1975, 79.
4. Giorgio Agamben, *Homo sacer*. Paris: Seuil 1997, 23.
5. Franz Kafka, *The Castle*, trans. Will and Edwin Muir (New York: Schocken, 1995), 27.
6. Hence the voice stands at the opposite end of the Kantian categorical imperative, and it is crucial to draw the line between the moral law and the superego. Cf. Alenka Zupancic, *The Ethics of the Real*, London: Verso 2000, 140–167.
7. This is of course one of the grand examples from Freud's book on jokes. *Jokes and their Relation to the Unconscious*, The Pelican Freud Library, 6, Harmondsworth etc. 1976, 161. In the Index of jokes at the end of the volume this joke is laconically referred to as "Truth a lie (Jewish)," and indeed, as I have tried to argue elsewhere, this joke most economically epitomizes the problem that "Jewishness" presented for Western culture: the indistinguishable character of truth and lie, the fact that not only do they look alike but actually coincide, so that "Jewishness" seems to undermine the very ground of the truth-telling capacity of language. This is the very problem with the "Jews": they look exactly like us, just as the lie looks exactly like the truth.
8. The German dictionary offers the following expression: *das trägt eine Maus auf den Schwanz fort*, for a quantity so small that a mouse could carry it on its tail (with all the German ambiguity of the word, tail/penis). There is a rather vulgar expression in Slovene, "the mouse's penis," which means the smallest thing imaginable, one cannot possibly conceive of anything smaller; the mouse's voice is of that order of magnitude. The mouse's penis—a circumlocution for castration? Is Josephine a *castrato*, is this the secret of her voice?
9. Deleuze/Guattari, op. cit., 40. "There is no longer a proper sense and a figurative sense, but a distribution of states along the fan of the word.... What is at stake is not a resemblance between an animal and a human behavior, and even less a play upon words. There is no longer a man or an animal, since each deterritorializes the other.... The animal doesn't speak 'as' a human, but extracts from language the tonalities without meaning...." (Ibid.)
10. On closer inspection both mice and dogs in many respects strangely resemble the Jews and their destiny, as several interpreters have pointed out, but I will not go into this. Cf. "No creatures to my knowledge live in such wide dispersion as we dogs...; we, whose one desire is to stick together... we above all others live so widely separated from one another, en-

gaged in strange vocations that are often incomprehensible even to our canine neighbors, holding firmly to laws that are not those of the dog world, but are actually directed against it." (279–280) But it is the literalization that annihilates the metaphor: to live like a dog, poor as a mouse. To say nothing about *mauscheln*, with all its connotations in German (a word derived from Yiddish for Moses, *Mausche*, and meaning to speak Yiddish, and by extension to speak in an incomprehensible way, and by extension, secret dealings, hidden affairs, deceit).

11. Cf. Gérard Wajcman, *L'objet du siècle*, Paris: Verdier, 2000, for the best comment on Duchamp.

12. I can only add in a footnote that this resonates exactly with Kierkegaard's problem: how to introduce a gap in the continuity as the transcendence in the immanence.

13. Kafka, in the manuscript, crossed out four instances where the narrator spoke in the first person—his is the voice of anonymity and must remain without an "I."

14. Michel Chion, *The Voice in Cinema*, New York: Columbia University Press, 1999. Chion found its supreme cinematic example in the mother's voice in *Psycho*, another voice *ex nihilo*.

15. Bernard Baas (*De la chose à l'objet*, Peeters/Vrin, Leuven, Belgium, 1998) puts it very well: "The voice is never my own voice, but the response is my own response." (205)

16. For the German original I use *Die Erzählungen. Originalfassung*, ed. by Roger Hermes, Frankfurt/M: Fischer 2000, 420.

17. The quotes are, of course, from *The Four Fundamental Concepts of Psychoanalysis*, London: Penguin 1979 (trans. A. Sheridan). Cf. also: "The *objet petit a* is not the origin of the oral drive. It is not introduced as the original food, it is introduced from the fact that no food will ever satisfy the oral drive, except by circumventing [circling around] the eternally lacking object." (180)

18. "If music be the food of love . . . " is another great literary testimony which most economically marks that place, although it immediately obfuscates it with the rhetoric of love.

11
Walt Whitman's Mystic Deliria

BY CHRISTIAN SHEPPARD

At the time of his death, Walt Whitman's brain was removed from his body, deposited in a glass jar, and sent to the American Anthropometric Society for weighing and measuring. Whitman had always been proud of his brain. Even before he was a famous poet, he had had his brain inspected, albeit through scalp and skull, by Manhattan's best phrenologist, who rated the immense-headed young man high for, among other attributes, "Self-Esteem" and "Amativeness"—important attributes for a poet who would espouse self-reliance and the sacredness of sexual love.[1] In the preface to his first edition of *Leaves of Grass*, Whitman boasted that the poet's "brain is the ultimate brain." (9)[2]

Whitman's brain under glass serves as a macabre emblem of the despair that haunted him and his contemporaries. This despair was brought on by Kant's philosophy, a skeptical despair that we do not have direct access to reality. We are trapped within our own skulls, like prisoners in Plato's cave. But while Plato offers philosophers the possibility of turning to face the cave's opening and ascending to the sun to see ultimate reality, Kant offers no such possibility; there is no direct access to reality, ultimate or otherwise. After Kant, experience is always only our own, and reality, no longer signifying things in themselves but mere appearances, must always implicitly be qualified by quotation marks. This understanding, that we are sealed off from reality as if trapped within a glass jar, understandably causes some to despair.

Kant never intended such a crisis. He intended his critical philosophy to allay the anxiety aroused by Hume's radical skepticism. In response to Hume's claim that the mind has no unity but is a mere "bundle of perceptions,"[3] Kant demonstrated the synthetic unity of the mind. But it was a unity sealed off from reality. Here, where Hume and Kant agreed, the crisis ensued: neither allowed reason direct access to reality, neither allowed any access to transcendence.[4] Hume and Kant both professed that we must retreat, reasonably, to "the fertile lowland of experience" and be satisfied with immanent reality.[5] Thus, although their different models of the mind result in different accounts of experience—while Hume saw immanent experience occurring as in a hall of mirrors, Kant demonstrated that immanent experience actually occurs in a well-defined and confined space, a space neatly ruled by reason and hard-wired for freedom, immortality, God and, of course, moral duty—Hume and Kant agreed that our reasoning minds are separated from what, if anything, might be beyond our experience, and that any speculation about the beyond ought to be met with skepticism. Certainly the tones of their skepticisms are different: Hume's is an ironical skepticism buoyed by trust in common sense— good humor based on good faith—while Kant's is a skepticism tempered by Protestant piety. It is this difference in tone that may account for why Kant caused such a crisis of despair where Hume did not. One might go along with or shrug off David Hume—Hume seems in his portraits and his prose to be smiling, albeit knowingly, upon the *status quo*[6]—but one could not so easily shrug off Immanuel Kant and his earnest imperative. Nietzsche perfectly captures the tone of Kant's "reality":

> The real world unattainable, unprovable, unpromisable, but the mere thought of it a consolation, an obligation, an imperative.
>
> (The old sun in the background, but seen through mist and skepticism; the idea become sublime, pale, Nordic, Königsbergian.)[7]

The crisis caused by Kant's critical philosophy touched not only those who had moored their hopes to the powers of human reason. It also affected those who harbored non-fideist hopes for religious faith, that is, for faith buttressed by reason. Although intended "to make room for faith,"[8] the rigor of Kant's response in fact affirmed skepticism to such an extent that faith seemed compelled. Faith became the only option other than an endless skepticism, a skepticism that could drive one to despair, or beyond despair to madness.[9]

To an American reader of Kant, such as Whitman, reality itself suddenly seemed as remote as the God of the Puritans. Whitman expresses this despair clearly in a poem of 1860:

> Of the terrible doubt of appearances,
> Of the uncertainty after all, that we may be deluded,
> That may-be reliance and hope are but speculation after all,
> That may-be identity beyond the grave is a beautiful fable
>   only,
> May-be the things I perceive, the animals, plants, men, hills,
>   shining and flowing waters,
> The skies of day and night, colors, densities, forms, may-be
>   these are (as doubtless they are) only apparitions, and
>   the real something has yet to be known,
> (How often they dart out of themselves as if to confound
>   me and mock me!
> How often I think neither I know, nor any man knows,
>   aught of them,)[10]

Whitman testifies to this despair of mocking doubt again in "Song of Myself": "I know the sea of torment, doubt, despair and unbelief."[11]

Whitman's reception of Kant—and his corresponding despair over Kant's account of experience—is mediated by Emerson. In "Experience," Emerson describes the "temperament" of our minds, after Kant's analysis, as trapping us "in a prison of glass which we cannot see."[12] He deems this "the most unhandsome part of our condition," meaning both that our condition is unattractive and that the conditions of possible experience as analyzed by Kant's critical philosophy do not allow for us actually to grasp reality.[13] Reality eludes us—"it slip[s] through our fingers."[14] Emerson relates this "unhandsome condition" to his grief over the death of his son:

> People grieve and bemoan themselves, but it is not half so bad with them as they say. There are moods in which we court suffering, in the hope that here, at least, we shall find reality, sharp peaks and edges of truth. But it turns out to be scene-painting and counterfeit. The only thing grief has taught me, is to know how shallow it is. That, like all the rest, plays about the surface, and never introduces me into the reality, for contact with which, we would even pay the costly price of sons and lovers. Was it Boscovich who found out that bodies never come in contact? Well, souls never touch their objects. An innavigable sea washes with silent waves between us and the things we aim at and converse with. Grief too will make us idealists. In the death of my son, now more than two years ago, I seem to have lost a beautiful estate,—no more. I cannot get it nearer to me . . . : it does not touch me: some thing which I fancied was part of me, which could not be torn away without tearing me, nor enlarged without enriching me, falls off from me, and leaves no scar. It was caduceus. I grieve that grief can teach me nothing, nor carry me one step into real nature.[15]

Emerson professes that grief can teach him nothing, yet confesses that he grieves. His grief represents for him the unapproachability of reality itself.

Neither Whitman nor Emerson is famous for his expressions of desperation, and while the above-quoted passages are not characteristic, they are crucial to keep in mind if we are to appreciate their better-known, more hopeful visions of the self as ultimately reliable and of reality as something to celebrate. Against the backdrop of Kant-inspired despair, we see how hard-won these most hopeful American visions are, and what looked at first like a cheap American optimism suddenly seems more like an outrageous wager of faith. Whitman opts for Emerson's faith, a faith different than Kant could have imagined or allowed: self-reliance.

Risk is inherent in self-reliance. More than the risk of, say, freezing some winter night in one's under-heated cabin on Walden Pond while conducting an experiment in rugged individualism (not Thoreau's project anyway), self-reliance risks traditional certainties, including moral certainties, in order to allow individuals to be "true to themselves." While Kant claims a categorical imperative, Emerson admits that his faith might be mere "whim," and that what he answers when he answers "his heart" might rather be the call of the devil.[16] To risk being profoundly mistaken in being true to oneself might be personally unfortunate or criminal or even tragic. But to risk, as the ex-minister Emerson preaches, permitting everyone to be mistaken in being true to their selves is to risk cultural relativism, political anarchy, and perhaps, as in Whitman and Emerson's own time, civil war. Stanley Cavell nicely appreciates the risks and rewards of self-reliance:

> To say, "Follow me and you will be saved," you must be sure you are of God. But to say, "Follow in yourself what I follow in mine and you will be saved," you must merely have to be sure you are following yourself. This frightens and cheers me.[17]

Thus self-reliance not only calls for Emerson to be true to himself, but also to respect the truths others hold. Emerson's essays reflect his self-reliant faith, being at once tactful and idiosyncratic, making them easily readable and yet provocatively (or frustratingly) obscure. As Cavell has shown, Emerson's essays are in conversation with themselves and at the same time self-conscious of being overheard and concerned for the selves who overhear.[18] Whitman's work, in turn, implies a reader who must risk her self-understanding in order to understand what she is reading. Questioning the meaning of Leaves of Grass means questioning the religious, social, economic, political, historical, racial, sexual, and aesthetic conventions with which one has previously identified. Whitman imagines a democratic republic of self-reliant readers and adapts Plato's classic attack on poetry, poetic mimesis being a copy of a copy of a copy and thus three removes from the truth, to insist that "conformity goes to the fourth-removed" (43, 396).

What allows Whitman to rely upon himself, even to celebrate himself and others in a social context that he recognizes as avaricious, racist, sexist, homophobic, and aesthetically arid, is his mysticism. In this way, he is again influenced by Emerson. It is mysticism that persuades Emerson to trust himself, when he has ceased to trust religious traditions and institutions. Emerson famously presents his mystic vision in Nature: "I become a transparent eyeball; I am nothing; I see all; the currents of the Universal Being circulate through me; I am part or particle of God."[19] This vision gives Emerson confidence that when he relies on himself he is not, in fact, placing his faith in mere whim or following the devil. Even in the more cautious essay "Experience," Emerson testifies to a vision of something beyond, something that suffices for him to have faith in himself and others, if they will only have faith in themselves:

> And yet is the God the native of these bleak rocks. That need makes in morals the capital virtue of self-trust. We must hold hard to this poverty, however scandalous, and by more vigorous self-recoveries, after the sallies of action, possess our axis more firmly.[20]

Whitman, whose phrenological analysis cryptically read "You are yourself at all times,"[21] readily accepted self-reliance and seconded Emerson's mysticism with even more extraordinary experiences and assertions of his own. Whitman escapes Kant's glass prison of pure reason through his sense of touch. Touch leads his other senses in bringing on a mystical mood. In (the above-quoted) "Of the Terrible Doubt of Appearances," Whitman's doubts "are curiously answered by my lovers, my dear friends,/ When he whom I love travels with me or sits a long while holding me by the hand. . . ."[22] Or in "Song of Myself," where Whitman's doubts are directly related to his mystical vision, he asks, "Is this then a touch . . . quivering me to a new identity?" (53, 618) This new identity will be a mystical identification with the "kosmos." All he can imagine, he imagines, becomes part of his self for him to celebrate. "There is that lot of me," he says, "and all so luscious" (49, 545).

If Emerson is an all-seeing transparent eyeball, Whitman is an all-sensing omnisexual love organ, an uncanny combination of pumping heart, pulsing penis, and kissing, singing tongue. Whitman brings all of these body parts together in "Song of Myself"'s surreally spiritual "transparent summer morning" episode:

> I believe in you my soul . . . the other I am must not abase
>   itself to you,
> And you must not be abased to the other.
> Loafe with me on the grass . . . loose the stop from
>   your throat,
> Not words, not music or rhyme I want . . . not custom or
>   lecture, not even the best,
> Only the lull I like, the hum of your valved voice.
> I mind how we lay in June, such a transparent
>   summer morning;
> You settled your head athwart my hips and gently turned
>   over upon me,
> And parted the shirt from my bosom-bone, and plunged
>   your tongue to my barestript heart,
> And reached till you felt my beard, and reached till you
>   held my feet.
> Swiftly arose and spread around me the peace and joy and
>   knowledge that pass all the art and argument of the
>   earth. . . . (28–29, 73–82)

Whitman characterizes the anatomically odd coupling of his body with his soul as peaceful, joyful, and giving cosmic knowledge. But later, in a section on touch, the scene is repeated and recast in a decidedly different mood:

> On all sides prurient provokers stiffening my limbs,
> Straining the udder of my heart for its withheld drip,
> Behaving licentious toward me, taking no denial,
> Depriving me of my best as for a purpose,
> Unbuttoning my clothes and holding me by the bare waist,
> Deluding my confusion with the calm of the sunlight and
>   pasture fields, (53, 622–27).

Note in this section that, as in his "transparent summer morning" episode, Whitman's waist is bared, his heart is conflated with his genitalia—where earlier his heart was placed halfway between beard and feet, between his hips, here it is placed below "stiffening limbs" and compared to an udder that strains to drip, presumably something white. While in his "transparent summer morning" episode body and soul couple as a prelude to gaining mystical peace and knowledge, this episode, equally sexual and equally part of his mystical vision, represents deliria, a confusion of the mind and the senses. Whitman's mysticism, like Emerson's, accepts the epistemological and ethical risks of self-reliance, and also risks what Whitman calls "mystic deliria."

Whitman likes to call himself a "kosmos" (48, 499). As David Reynolds explains, Whitman pointedly prefers the more "Greek" spelling of the word with a "k" to distinguish his understanding from the modern scientific term "cosmos."[23] What science describes as "cosmos" is merely one aspect of what Whitman celebrates as "kosmos."[24] The modern scientific notion of "cosmos," which twenty-first century Americans still popularly associate with Carl Sagan, mid-nineteenth-century Americans associated with Alexander von Humboldt, whose *Kosmos* (1845), with an uppercase German "K," described all empirical reality, from distant stars to the grass under foot, as held together by inner forces in an equilibrious whole. Whitman combines Humboldt's modern notion of "cosmos" with the ancient idea of "kosmos," as expressed, for example, by Plato's *Timaeus*. According to this idea, humans are not only part of the greater whole, but actual microcosms of the macrocosm, such that one could intuit the kosmic whole by following the Socratic injunction to "know thyself." Knowing oneself means knowing the cosmos and knowing one's place in the cosmic order. (Now that the distinction has been made we can use the usual "c"-spelling to refer to the more fulsome idealist intuition of cosmos.) First, last, and at the center of the cosmic order in Neo-Platonist cosmologies was the demiurge; and in Christian cosmologies, God. In Whitman's cosmology, in contrast, anything and everything can occupy first, last, and center. At the end of his "transparent summer morning episode," Whitman places God in a list that culminates with pokeweed. There is God, there is pokeweed, they exist in equilibrium and are, moreover, somehow equal. "And there is no object so soft but it makes a hub for the wheeled universe" (83, 1269). In an early notebook Whitman defines "kosmos": "noun masculine or feminine, a person who[se] scope of mind, or whose range in a particular science includes all, the whole known universe."[25] By the time of "Song of Myself," Whitman has expanded this notion to identify himself as a cosmos and to observe the order of the cosmos in a leaf of grass.

Whitman's cosmology as vividly expressed in his "transparent summer morning" episode is part of the larger spiritual project of *Leaves of Grass,* a project of spiritual exercise best understood as a mystical itinerary. Spiritual exercises have been part of the practice of philosophy and religion in the West from antiquity to the present. Pierre Hadot explains that by means of spiritual exercise the individual "re-places himself within the perspective of the Whole."[26] Whitman intended the reading of his *Leaves of Grass* to be just such a spiritual exercise. The "Whole" within whose perspective the reader is to re-place herself, Whitman calls "kosmos." Whitman's cosmic perspective is not a view from some sublime or spiritually elevated place above the fray of ordinary life, but rather a mood that colors all views of reality. Whitman understands his cosmic perspective to be a kind of mystical "mood."[27] The early editions of *Leaves of Grass* present a mystical itinerary aimed to bring its reader to such a mystical mood, a mood in which all of experience is seen from a cosmic perspective.

While *Leaves of Grass* records mystical experiences, such as the "transparent summer morning" episode, its ultimate aim is not to present or repeat such experiences for its readers, but rather to inculcate a more pervasive mystical mood. To this end, the record of mystical experiences is only one of Whitman's literary strategies, only one aspect of his mystical itinerary. Another strategy is the presentation of the cosmos as a map. Whitman maps the cosmos with what he calls a "dividing line," an image that recalls Plato's cosmic diagram, the divided line. Whitman also employs parataxis, paradox, and a verse line that combines imagistic concision with a seemingly natural flowing rhythm, whose "natural" artfulness argues for the self-evidence of the cosmic order from design. Whitman does not want to create a particular reader response with such literary strategies, but instead to inspire a general mystical mood that will color all of the reader's responses, whether responding to the book of poems in front of her or looking up from her book to respond to the world at large or to things in particular. Whitman's readers are to come to "cosmic consciousness," to use a phrase of one of Whitman's early admirers and one of the pioneers in the modern study of mysticism, Richard Maurice Bucke.[28] All experience, experience as such, is thus to be colored by a mystical mood.

Whitman's mystical mood has a certain spectrum, at one end of which is peace, joy, and knowledge. At the other end is "mystic deliria."[29] Whitman's mystical itinerary traverses a "sea of torment," not simply the troubled waters of doubt traditionally bridged by reasonable faith, but a storm of madness that qualifies both reason and faith.[30] Faith has two meanings for Whitman. It first means trust: to be true, as to a lover. Whitman is thus true, true to himself, self-reliant, loving himself, and loving others as they love and rely upon themselves. His innovation of Emerson's faith is to associate self-reliance with love. Love, equally spiritual and carnal, holds Whitman's cosmic whole together. He knows "that a kelson of creation is love" (29, 86). Love quiets his doubts, allows him to have faith in himself, in the cosmos, and in himself as cosmos. This is the wager of Whitman's loving self-reliant faith. Thus faith, for Whitman, secondly means a way of passage, as faith traditionally provides a way of passage over "the sea of torment, doubt, despair, and unbelief." Whitman's way of passage, his mystical itinerary revealed through his sense of touch, frees him from Kant's glass prison of mere appearances, even as it requires him in his mystic deliria to hazard madness. And he intends with *Leaves of Grass* to lead his readers through a mystical itinerary to their own passage of faith.

Whitman develops this mystical itinerary from classic Platonic and Neo-Platonic accounts of transcendence. One of philosophy's most famous images of transcendence comes in *Republic* VI when Socrates draws for his audience "the divided line."[31] This divided line, first separating "the visible from the intelligible" and then obscurity from lucidity, divides the world and measures our separation from the ideal, an ideal described in chapter VI as "the good beyond being."[32] The image of the divided line can be read into the *Republic*'s next chapter, dividing us from the realm of the ideas and measuring our separation from the sun beyond the threshold of the cave. The divided line maps the removes of mimesis, of copies and copies of copies from the original idea—charting one of the arguments with which Socrates bans the poets from his city. And the divided line can also be read into the cosmic myth of the *Republic*'s last chapter, the Myth of Er, in which the line that divides is the River Lethe, a taste of whose waters separates us, a river of forgetfulness cutting short our memories, from the hereafter and the divine forms. (Emerson takes up this image in his essay "Experience" to express our separation, after Kant, from things in themselves.)[33] Moreover, the divided line can be read beyond the *Republic* into other dialogues. We, philosophy's ephebes, stand at one end of the line, on one side of the divide: on the other side, at the other end of the line, beckons the Beautiful (*Symposium*) or the One (*Parmenides*). If we read these dialogues as providing more than a mere description of our cosmic situation and the microcosmic situation of our souls, but also as offering an itinerary for spiritual exercise (as indeed philosophy does for Plato and others, including the American transcendentalists), then the divided line can be seen to have a trajectory—upward. The divided line provides an itinerary in multiple senses, as the map of a journey, the journey itself, and the record of that journey.[34] In short, the divided line can be read as an itinerary for the spiritual journey of the philosophic life.

One of the most famous records of such a journey, a description of actually encountering the ideal, comes in the Sixth *Ennead* of Plotinus:

> Here, we put aside all the learning; disciplined to this pitch, established in beauty, the quester holds knowledge still of the ground he rests on, but, suddenly, swept beyond it all by the very crest of the wave of the Intellect surging beneath, he is lifted and sees, never knowing how; the vision floods the eyes with light, but it is not a light showing some other object, the light is itself the vision. No longer is there thing seen and light to show it, no longer Intellect and object of Intellection; this is the very radiance that brought both Intellect and Intellectual object into being for later use and allowed them to occupy the quester's mind.[35]

Here the philosopher is not a detached observer, but (in Stephan McKenna's wonderful translation, giving the impression of the philosopher as a knight in search of the Grail) a "quester." And the quest has come to a point where the divided line seems to have been washed away ("no longer Intellect and object of Intellection"). Also washed away is the quester's knowing control ("suddenly, swept beyond," "never knowing how"). Yet beyond his own control, beyond the possibility of knowledge, beyond his ability to act, the quester receives a vision (Plotinus develops Plato's analogy of the sun from the *Republic*, applying it here to the One), a vision of light that "is itself the vision." This is a vision of mystical union.

Plotinus develops Plato's image in the *Republic* of the divided line and the image in the *Symposium* of ascending from one division to the next. Indeed *Enneads* VI, 7, 36 (quoted above), Pierre Hadot points out, alludes to both dialogues.[36] Hadot also suggests that the image of the rising wave comes from Homer:

> And now two nights, and now two days were past,
> Since wide he wandere'd on the wat'ry waste;
> Heav'd on the surge with intermitting breath,
> And hourly panting in the arms of death.
> The third fair morn now blaz'd upon the main;
> Then glassy smooth lay all the liquid plain,
> The winds were hush'd, the billows scarcely curl'd,
> And dead silence still'd the wat'ry world.
> When lifted on a ridgy wave, he spies
> The land at distance, and with sharpen'd eyes.[37]

Plotinus contrasts his philosophical quester with Homer's wandering Odysseus. While Odysseus fearing death is lifted by a wave to spy the life-saving shore, the philosophical quester, after his own long but focused journey of "learning," is "suddenly" lifted beyond all knowing to be taken up the divided line by a vision of the One.

We should read Whitman's mystical itinerary in light of Plotinus's reading of Plato and Homer, but before we do, we must first understand what Whitman means by reading. For Whitman, reading is a spiritual exercise. Generalizing an earlier Judeo-Christian model of reading that takes the Bible as the Book of God mirrored by the Book of Nature, Whitman sees any book he reads, whether it is a play by Shakespeare or his own *Leaves of Grass*, as a mirror of the book of nature around him. Both books, of "literal" words and of "metaphorical" nature, offer a "mystic cipher" whose meaning waits to be "unfolded."[38] Thus for Whitman, reading a book involves appropriately reading himself and everything around him. In fact, in order not to be overwhelmed by whatever classic work he was reading, Whitman actually sought out equally overwhelming places in nature to sit and read; thus he could keep his equilibrium.[39] "It makes such a difference *where* you read."[40] So, for example, when he read Dante he went out to the woods, presumably to match the dark woods where Dante first finds himself in the *Inferno*. Analogously Whitman offers us his own book as more than mere mimetic verse, but as equipment for spiritual living to help us decipher ourselves and our world, both of which he considers "mystic."

Whitman liked reading the *Iliad* by the seashore,[41] and presumably also the *Odyssey*. Compare Odysseus's fear of death by drowning (quoted above) with Whitman's heroic coupling with the sea in "Song of Myself":

> You sea! I resign myself to you also . . . I guess what you mean,
> I behold from the beach your crooked inviting fingers,
> I believe you refuse to go back without feeling me;
> We must have a turn together . . . I undress . . . hurry me
>   out of sight of the land,
> Cushion me soft . . . rock me in billowy drowse,
> Dash me with amorous wet . . . I can repay you.
> Sea of stretched ground-swells!
> Sea breathing broad and convulsive breaths!
> Sea of the brine of life! Sea of unshovelled and
>   always-ready graves!
> Howler and scooper of storms! Capricious and dainty sea!
> I am integral with you . . . I too am of one phase and of all
>   phases. (45–6, 451–61)

Where Plotinus saw, in implicit contrast to the shipwrecked Odysseus, an emanating wave lift his philosophical quester above mundane reality to experience mystical union with the One, Whitman seeks sexual and mystical union with the ocean itself. For Whitman, mystical union with the cosmos comes through sensuous contact with reality—a touch.

Furthermore, Whitman adapts the Homeric epithet for his own spiritual poetic purposes (thereby adapting a literary device most characteristic of a hypotactical work to his own most paratactical book). While Homer's epithets attach themselves to one character or thing, like the "Dawn with lovely hair" (indeed Whitman presents a similar image at the close of "Song of Myself" when at dusk he "departs as air" and "shakes his white locks at the runaway sun,"(86, 1327) becoming himself the clouds that halo the sunset), Whitman's epithets break free of their referents and connect ideas and images from all parts of his poems—and, he hopes, from all parts of his readers' lives. This is the rhizomic or grass-like structure of *Leaves of Grass*. Whitman's epithets are the visible green "flags" that mark the complex root system of semantic connections implied beneath his poems. They are, as he says, the "flags of his disposition," (29, 92) a disposition, of course, characterized by his mystical mood.

Such an epithet or flag is the word "guess" and its cognates. In the passage quoted above, Whitman claims to have guessed what the sea means. A few pages later, Whitman knots this guess and this (unsaid) meaning with other guesses and meanings:

> Swift wind! Space! My Soul! Now I know it is true what
>   I guessed at;
> What I guessed when I loafed on the grass,
> What I guessed while I lay alone in my bed . . . and again as
>   I walked the beach under the paling stars of the
>   morning. (57, 709–11)

What is it Whitman guessed? The other "guesses" refer to other sections of the poem: the "transparent summer morning" episode; and a section where Whitman describes the morning after "God" came as his "loving bedfellow." After reading these sections, we are left to guess what Whitman guessed. Is he being coy or discrete, or both? We are left to guess for ourselves.

The rhizomic structure of *Leaves of Grass* relies, like the Bible, on parataxis.[42] *Leaves of Grass* calls for a hermeneutic strategy akin to that for Christian readings of the Hebrew Bible. A pre-understanding—the *intellectus spiritualis*—of Christ in history, His death, resurrection, and second coming is required for a believing Christian to interpret the "Old Testament." *Leaves of Grass* does not call for Christian but for a self-reliant figural interpretation. It calls, of course, for a pre-understanding of Walt Whitman as cosmos, but also for an understanding of each self-reliant self as equally cosmic. By interpreting the poem from this cosmic perspective, in such a mystical mood, the reader finds that she is also a cosmos. Thus the paratactical structure of *Leaves of Grass* affirms its implicit faith in self-reliance. But because self-reliance is such a risky faith, where we may in good faith be a cosmos or only be a cosmos on our own deluded whim, Whitman admits that what he asserted earlier in his cosmic vision of "the transparent summer morning," what he presented with such confidence, was, in fact, only a guess, his most hopeful interpretation. Whitman asserts that his guess has been shown true, but he admits that it was just a guess. What is the dividing line between a knowledge that "passes all the art and argument of the earth" and a "guess"?

Whitman's conspicuous reticence at these crucial points in his poem creates suspense, pauses the pace of our reading, and throws us back upon ourselves. Whitman has caused an aporia in the middle of our reading, an aporia analogous to our experience of interpreting ourselves and our surrounding world. This discursive aporia is part of his mystical itinerary, insisting on a kind of reading that is not only spiritual, but real (hermeneutical) exercise. Whitman forces us to ask ourselves, how does guessing relate to mystery, to the mystical, to faith?

> Do you guess I have some intricate purpose?
> Well I have . . . for the April rain has, the mica on the side
>   of a rock has.
>
> Do you take it I would astonish?
> Does the daylight astonish? or the early redstart twittering
>   through the woods?
> Do I astonish more than they? (42–3, 381–85)

What Whitman guesses while walking the beach he later describes as his "liquid, mystic theme."[43] In "Song of Myself" and the early editions of *Leaves of Grass*, this "liquid, mystic theme," while not everywhere explicit, is everywhere an undercurrent, an "*influence*."[44] Whitman develops this "liquid mystic theme" into a map for his mystical itinerary in his essay "Sea-Shore Fancy:"

> The sea-shore—that suggesting, dividing line, contact, junction, the solid marrying the liquid—that curious, lurking something, (as doubtless every objective form finally becomes the subjective spirit,) which means far more than its mere first sight, grand as that is—blending the real and the ideal, and each made portion of the other.[45]

This passage answers Plato's diagram of the divided line with an emblem of the sea-shore as dividing line, a line not once and for all divided, but a line always already dividing. How can we read this always already dividing line? It seems to have two, ambiguously related meanings, each of which can be expressed as an analogy. The first analogy plots the places on Whitman's mystical map. It is a three-part analogy, corresponding to the above-quoted passage's three punctuating dashes: solid is to liquid as objective form is to subjective spirit as real is to ideal—

solid: liquid::
objective form: subjective spirit::
real: ideal.

As solid may liquefy and liquid solidify, the objective inspires the subjective and the subjective informs the objective, the real becomes ideal and the ideal real. If this analogy were drawn according to the traditional neo-Platonic hierarchy—imagine a vertical line ascending to the sun or the One, rather than a horizontal line undulating along the beach—if Whitman's line strictly separated the real from the ideal, then his cosmos might be directly comparable to that of Plotinus. But Whitman paradoxically blends the real and the ideal, as in his poetry he will blend "body and soul," "seen and unseen." His line divides, but also offers "contact" and "junction." It "marries" and "blends." Plotinus's line marks our removes from the ideal as well as the steps of our ascension. Whitman's line wants to be walked along, like a child walking along the seashore, one foot on sand, the other in the water.[46] Whitman's "dividing line" resembles what he elsewhere describes as "the open road,"[47] and maps the mystical itinerary of "Song of Myself" as well as of other mystical poems such as "Crossing Brooklyn Ferry." Both offer a way of journeying closer to the wandering of Odysseus than to the disciplined itinerary of Plotinus's philosophical quester.

There is, however, a second analogy implied by this "Sea-Shore Fancy," and it counters the first. We may easily miss this counter analogy if, allowing ourselves to be swept away too swiftly by the rhythm of the prose and the hopeful prospect of its message, we miss the divided connotations of its terms. This two-part analogy is: solid and liquid is to objective form and subjective spirit as real is to ideal—

solid/liquid: objective form/subjective spirit::
real: ideal.

In other words, form and spirit both only belong to the realm of the ideal. If we can explain this analogy by extending it to say that real is to ideal as phenomena are to noumena, then we can say that Whitman draws his dividing line within our minds, just as Kant draws there his version of Plato's divided line. This counter reading suddenly shadows the entire passage. The suggestion that "doubtless every objective form finally becomes the subjective spirit" recalls Whitman's earlier "terrible doubt of appearances." And the "mere first sight" of the sea-shore, "grand as that is," may not mean "far more" grand, but may actually only be—"grand" as it is—a mere appearance. Without the strong reasoned divisions of a Platonic or Kantian divided line, the analogies of Whitman's dividing line threaten to collapse into a chaos of mere appearance.

By allowing such a crucial ambiguity to shadow his account of the dividing line, Whitman admits the ever-present danger of Kant-inspired despair. At the same time as he admits this danger, however, Whitman transcends it by fiat of faith. In "Sea-Shore Fancy," Whitman tethers his faith to the word "suggesting"—"the suggesting, dividing line." Throughout his boldly paradoxical, subtly allusive, paratactical work, Whitman suggests a mystical understanding of the cosmos and seeks the affirmation of this suggestion in the response of his readers.

But I set out with the intention also of indicating or hinting some point-character-istics which I since see (though I did not then, at least not definitely) were bases and object-urgings toward those "Leaves" from the first. The word I myself put primar-ily for the description of them as they stand at last, is the word Suggestiveness. I round and finish little, if anything; and could not, consistently with my scheme. The reader will always have his or her part to do, just as much as I have had mine. I seek less to state or display any theme or thought, and more to bring you, reader, into the atmosphere of the theme or thought—there to pursue your own flight.[48]

Doubts and ambiguities seem necessary accompaniments to Whitman's sug-gestiveness. For the sake of his own self-reliant faith, Whitman risks mislead-ing himself and his readers into despair. At the same time, he risks deliria.

What would we risk, Whitman asks, "to drink the mystic deliria deeper than any other man"? He answers: "To be lost if it must be so!"[49] These lines are from "One Hour to Madness and Joy." In "Song of Myself," the stakes risked are higher than a mere hour, a measure of time: Whitman stakes con-sciousness itself, space, time, reason, the whole Cartesian ball of wax. He risks deliria. "To be lost" recalls the opening of Emerson's "Experience"—"Where do we find ourselves?"—and his rehearsal there of Kant-inspired despair. Whitman's respect for his readers' self-reliance forces us to ask ourselves: What side of the dividing line are we on? How do we know if we are on the open road or only lost?

Walking the open road would be to move in harmony with an omnific cos-mos always in flux. Being lost, like Odysseus upon the ocean, is the opposite of cosmos; in Platonic terms, it is chaos. If we are lost, our mystical visions are worse than mere appearances, they are delusions. Roberto Calasso traces this fear of a chaos of mere appearances back to Plato:

> More than anyone before him, Plato was seized by a dizzy terror when faced with the proliferation of images. The "boundless ocean of unlikeness" crashed its waves all around him. If we wish to circumscribe the territory of his dispute with Homer, then, then we can call it the territory of appearance, of images, of simu-lacra, of the *eídola*.[50]

Rather than entertain the despair of being denied access to the transcendent, his "terrible doubt of appearances," Whitman explicitly risks chaos with his mystic deliria. No longer despairing, but delirious, Whitman's vision risks a different sort of madness than that inspired by Kant. Not the paranoia of a ver-tiginous skepticism, but the delusion of perfect faith—Whitman boasted that, in addition to having the "ultimate brain," he also had "the greatest of faiths."[51] Emblematic of the madness Whitman risks with mystic deliria is the ultimate fate of his brain, dropped by a careless laboratory assistant, bursting its glass confines, and splattering into an immeasurable mess.[52]

Notes

1. For a concise account of Whitman's relation to phrenology, see David S. Reynolds, *Whitman's America: A Cultural Biography* (New York: Alfred A. Knopf, 1995), 246–51.
2. All parenthetical numbers refer to Walt Whitman, *Leaves of Grass*, Malcolm Cowley ed. (New York: Penguin, 1959), first page numbers, then line numbers.
3. See David Hume, *Treatise of Human Nature*, L. A. Selby-Bigge ed. (Oxford: The Clarendon Press, 1978), 251.
4. "High towers and metaphysically great men resembling them, round both of which there is commonly much wind, are not for me. My place is the fruitful bathos of experience; and the word "transcendental" . . . does not signify something passing beyond all experience but something that indeed precedes it *a priori*, but that is intended simply to make knowledge of experience possible. If these conceptions overstep experience, their employment is termed "transcendent," which must be distinguished from their immanent use, that is, use restricted to experience." Immanuel Kant, *Prolegomena to Any Future Metaphysics*, Lewis White Beck trans. (Upper Saddle River, N.J.: Prentice-Hall, 1997), 122n2.
5. Ernst Cassirer, *Kant's Life and Thought*, James Haden trans. (New Haven, Conn.: Yale University Press, 1981), 92.
6. See, for example, "A Portrait of David Hume," 1754, by Allan Ramsay.
7. Friedrich Nietzsche, "How the 'Real World' Finally Became a Fable: History of an Error," *Twilight of the Idols*, Duncan Lange trans. (New York: Oxford University Press, 1998), 20.
8. Immanuel Kant, *Critique of Pure Reason*, Werner S. Pluher trans. (Indianapolis: Hackett, 1996), B xxx, 31.
9. For an example of such Kant-inspired despair from another periphery of the Romantic movement, consider Heinrich von Kleist's famous "Kant Crisis." See Joachim Maass, *Kleist: A Biography*, Ralph Manheim trans. (New York: Farrar, Strauss, Giroux, 1983), 35–7.
10. Whitman, "Of the Terrible Doubt of Appearances" [1860,1867], *Leaves of Grass, Walt Whitman: Poetry and Prose* (New York: The Library of America, 1982), 274.
11. Whitman, "Song of Myself," *Leaves, Poetry and Prose*, 237.
12. Ralph Waldo Emerson, "Experience," *Emerson: Essays and Lectures* (New York: The Library of America, 1983), 474.
13. See Stanley Cavell, "Introduction: Staying the Course" in *Conditions Handsome and Unhandsome: The Constitution of Emersonian Perfectionism* (Chicago: University of Chicago Press, 1990), 1–32.
14. Emerson, "Experience," 473.
15. Ibid., 472–73. Also, read these lines as an ex-minister's bitter homily on Christ's Passion.
16. Emerson, "Self-Reliance," 262.
17. Stanley Cavell, "An Emerson Mood" in *The Senses of Walden: An Expanded Edition* (Chicago: University of Chicago Press, 1992), 160.
18. Ibid., *passim*.
19. Emerson, *Nature*, 10.
20. Emerson, "Experience," 490.
21. Reynolds, *Whitman's America*, 247.
22. Whitman, "Of the Terrible Doubt of Appearances," *Leaves, Poetry and Prose*, 274–5.
23. Reynolds, *Whitman's America*, 242–45.
24. For a more general discussion of kosmos and cosmos, see Louis Dupré, *Passage to Modernity: An Essay in the Hermeneutics of Nature and Culture* (New Haven: Yale University Press, 1993), 3, 16–23.
25. Reynolds, *Whitman's America*, 247.
26. Pierre Hadot, *Philosophy as a Way of Life*, Michael Chase trans., Arnold Davidson ed. (Oxford: Blackwell, 1995), 82.
27. See Jerome Loving, *Walt Whitman: The Song of Himself* (Berkeley: The University of California Press, 1999), 175.
28. Richard Maurice Bucke, *Cosmic Consciousness* (New York: E.P. Dutton, 1969).
29. The phrase "mystic deliria" appears twice in *Leaves of Grass*. First in the *Calamus* section, the section that celebrates love between men, in the poem "From Pent-up Aching Rivers." Second in the *Children of Adam* section, the section that celebrates love between men and women, in the poem "One Hour to Madness and Joy."
30. Cf. Emerson's "Experience" (quoted above): "An innavigable sea washes with silent waves between us and the things we aim at and converse with."

31. A more literal translation might be the "separated line," but the image has been most commonly known as the divided line. Plato's *Republic* in *Plato: The Collected Dialogues*, Edith Hamilton and Huntington Cairns eds. (Princeton, N.J.: Princeton University Press, 1961), 509d.

32. Picture the divided line, as Plato most likely did after Pythagoras, as the different string lengths on the musical scale of the monochord. See Edward Rothstein, *Emblems of Mind: The Inner Life of Music and Mathematics* (New York: Times Books, 1995), especially 229–242.

33. Emerson, "Experience," 472.

34. Evelyn Underhill recalls this scheme in her famous *Mysticism*. Boethius perhaps offers its most influential expression for the post-classical West in *The Consolation of Philosophy* (Book III, Chapter 9).

35. Plotinus, *The Enneads*, Stephan McKenna trans. (New York: Penguin, 1991), VI, 7, 36, 505.

36. The allusions are to *Republic* (505a2) and *Symposium* (210e3–4). See Pierre Hadot, *Plotinus, or the Simplicity of Vision*, Michael Chase trans. (Chicago: University of Chicago Press, 1993), 62n24.

37. *Homer's Odyssey*, Book V, lines 496–505, spiritedly translated by Alexander Pope, whom Whitman, alas, tastelessly referred to as "a machine – he wrote like a see-saw." See *Intimate with Walt: Selections from Whitman's Conversations with Horace Traubel, 1888–1892*, Gary Schmidgall ed. (Iowa City: University of Iowa Press, 2001, 200.

38. Whitman, "Shakspere-Bacon's Cipher," *Leaves of Grass* (1891–92), *Poetry and Prose*, 633. Also see Alberto Manguel, *A History of Reading* (New York: Viking, 1996), 163–9.

39. One may also read the outrageous expansions of himself as poet in *Leaves of Grass* as an attempt to equal the kosmos he describes with the kosmos he claims himself to be.

40. Whitman, "A Backward Glance O'er Travel'd Roads," *Leaves, Poetry and Prose*, 665. The great Whitman scholar James E. Miller, Jr. used to recommend to his classes that *Leaves of Grass* may be best read standing in the middle of a wide green grassy city-street median (it would have to be a city planned by Olmstead) chanting the poems aloud to passing traffic.

41. Whitman, "A Backward Glance O'er Travel'd Roads," *Leaves, Poetry and Prose*, 665.

42. See Erich Auerbach, *Mimesis: The Representation of Reality in Western Literature*, Willard R. Trask trans. (Princeton: Princeton University Press, 1953), 70–75.

43. Whitman gives this theme its most explicit expression in a poem originally titled "A Word from the Sea" (a poem later and better known as "Out of the Cradle Endlessly Rocking") *Leaves, Poetry and Prose*, 388–394.

44. This liquid mystic theme is represented in *Leaves of Grass* (1855) in "Song of Myself" by [sec. 11]; [sec. 17], 361; [sec. 22], 451–461 (quoted above); [sec. 46], 1228–1230; [sec. 42], 1082–1230, and in "The Sleepers," [sec. 3].

45. Whitman, "Sea-Shore Fancies" in *Specimen Days*, *Poetry and Prose*, 796–97.

46. Whitman develops this motif in "Out of the Cradle Endlessly Rocking." Wallace Stevens picks up this Whitmanian motif in the "The Idea of Order at Key West," and in "Like Decorations in a Nigger Cemetery," describes Whitman walking along the shore.

47. Whitman, "Song of the Open Road," *Leaves, Poetry and Prose*, 297–307.

48. Whitman, "A Backward Glance O'er Travel'd Roads," *Leaves, Poetry and Prose*, 666–67.

49. See "One Hour to Madness and Joy" [1860], *Leaves, Poetry and Prose*, 262–63.

50. Roberto Calasso, "Metamorphic Knowledge" in *ARTES*, volume II (New York: Ecco Press, 1995), 36. Cf. Whitman, "Eidólons," *Leaves of Grass* (1891–92), *Poetry and Prose*, 168–70.

51. " . . . and the least of faiths," Whitman, "Song of Myself" (75, 1093), *Leaves of Grass* (1855) 75. It is the "least of faiths" because it believes in reality as given.

52. See Justin Kaplan, *Whitman: A Life* (New York: Simon and Schuster, 1980), 53.

12
Sublimity: The Modern Transcendent

BY JOHN MILBANK

I

"And God said, Let there be light and there was light" (Genesis 1:3). This sentence has been accorded an equivalent status in the history of modern attempts to relate the Bible to the inheritance of classical rhetoric, as the "I am who I am" of Exodus was given in earlier attempts to coordinate the language of revelation with ontological speculation. It was cited as a supreme example of sublime or elevated utterance by Pseudo-Longinus, an unknown pagan author who probably wrote towards the end of the first century A.D. His treatise *Peri Hypsous* was first translated into a vulgar tongue by Nicolas Boileau in the late seventeenth century, after which the concept of the sublime came to dominate modern aesthetic theory.[1]

It's significance, however, quickly came to exceed the sphere of the aesthetic alone. For in accord with Longinus's solitary pagan citation of the Hebrew Bible, the concept was used to re-articulate the very notion of transcendence as such: which is to say the conception of "divine height," of the most ultimate and primal reality imaginable.

Without a grasp of this process of transformation, one might easily suppose that modernity is characterized by a simple rejection of transcendence in favour of immanence, meaning the pure self-sufficiency of the finite world to itself. Yet although the shift to immanentism was certainly crucial, the re-conceptualization of transcendence as sublimity was of equal importance: either in tension with, or else as a complement to this shift. What was the nature of the re-conceptualization? At its heart lay a new thinking of the transcendent as the absolutely unknowable void, upon whose brink we finite beings must dizzily hover, as opposed to an older notion of a supra-hierarchical summit which we may gradually hope to scale.

This reconstrual has persisted from the relatively modern through to the relatively postmodern epoch, although it has undergone significant shifts. Throughout these transformations however, it has nonetheless remained fundamentally enabled by a supposedly crucial aesthetic distinction between the sublime on the one hand and the beautiful on the other. In the postmodern version of this distinction, beauty becomes a purely banal, ideological, or even impossible instance, leaving the aesthetic field free for an art entirely reduced to the effecting of sublime shock and rupture.

In what follows, I shall question whether this is, after all, a truly critical distinction. Since this distinction alone upholds the reconfiguration of transcendence as sublimity, this will lead to a questioning also of the critical character of this transformation.

The enthusiasm for Longinus amongst Boileau and other French theorists of a "classicist" aesthetic was contemporary with the first influence of Cartesian philosophy in France, a philosophy which completes metaphysics as epistemology and therefore achieves a so-called "turn to the subject." The treatise *On the Sublime* in its own way also foregrounds the subjective. However, it does so in a fashion that can involve the interest, today, of "postmodern" thinkers preoccupied with a dislocated and unstable subjectivity. For already, with Longinus, the discourse on the sublime was concerned not only with the manifestation of the singular individual, but with the elevation of this individual above himself, often in circumstances which pose a threat to his own survival. Thus the sublime experience characteristically mediates between an indeterminate interiority and an equally indeterminate object which threatens to overwhelm the subject and indeed provokes and reveals his subjective depths. Because it still concerns at the limit a subject representing an object, the sublime can best be defined as that *within* representation which nonetheless *exceeds* the possibility of representation. And since thereby it invokes at once the subjective as such, as the unrepresentable ground of representation, and yet also the subject as on the brink of collapsing its distinction from the represented object, it can be said that "the sublime experience" is at once modern and postmodern in a way which problematizes this very divide. It is notable, in this regard, that a "post-structuralist" concern with the sublime is combined with the view that we cannot consistently maintain a step outside the illusion of a secure identity, a secure subjectivity, but have always to return to this apparently stable ground—just as the sublime gesture is necessarily on the *brink* of the abyss without completely succumbing to it. Equally, however, the post-structuralist reading of the sublime (especially with Lacoue-Labarthe) insists that the indeterminate abyss not only *undoes* the subjective, but also gives rise to it, since a constitutive openness is precisely what renders it not an object.[2]

The discourse on sublimity, therefore, tends to open up a necessary continuity between the turn to the subject and the dissolution of the subject. But it has a third characteristic, and this is its continued echo of the idea that the transcendent or the unrepresentable creator God is the paradigmatic instance of the sublime. However, where once the sublime God was *also* beautiful, also regarded as the eminent infinite reality of every mode of harmonious proportion and value, modernity and postmodernity tend strictly to *substitute* sublimity for transcendence. This means that all that persists of transcendence is sheer unknowability or its quality of non-representability and non-depictability. Hence Kierkegaard, in his journals, defined the sublime as merely an "aesthetic accounting" for transcendence.[3]

Now, what must be asked at this point is whether the modern and postmodern sundering of the sublime from the beautiful and consequent substitution of sublimity for transcendence is an authentic critical gesture. *Is* it truly reason that grounds the representation of the unrepresentable as the void, as the univocal, as the indifferent? Or is this elevation of the sublime without beauty *itself* merely a contingent gesture towards the unknown, a gesture which absolutizes the unknown simply *as* the emptiness of that gesture? This is all the more a crucial question because it would then be that same mere gesture which ensures that the subject remains opposed to and indifferent to the object, whether, as for modernity, because it is over-against the object, or else as for postmodernity, because the subject is nothing other than the inevitable substitution of one indifferent object for another.

To substantiate this notion that the substitution of the sublime for transcendence is but an arbitrary gesture, rendering the subject unnecessarily empty and unmediated by objectivity, I want, in what follows, to trace a genealogy of the sundering of the sublime from the beautiful, and to show how this development was not genuinely critical, but determined both by an impoverished theology and by political economic theory.

II

In the Patristic and Medieval eras, "the beautiful" was not an autonomous subject of discussion, since the infinite truth was deemed to shine forth in due proportion in every aspect of the created world and so to attract those of good disposition towards it. Beauty was so implicitly omnipresent in knowledge and practice that, to echo Eric Gill, she "took care of herself." If "sublimity" was mentioned at all, then this concerned the "elevation" of the soul through a certain sequence of ordered form towards that which is unlimited, and exceeds our sense of order. There was certainly a wounding, a shock and a rupture involved here, and yet not a total rupture, since the unlimited was held to be, in its simplicity, an unimaginable infinite fullness of beautiful form, not its negation.[4]

Now when one turns to consider the French classicist interpreters of Longinus, who mostly moved in an Augustinian theological milieu, it is clear that in many respects they retain this Medieval perspective. In so far as they diverge from it, then, this is because they inherit the general Baroque concern not just with *finding* analogies for God, but rather with *performing* them, either in the guise of "spiritual exercises" or else in theatrical works of art. In fact Baroque aesthetics had become so concerned with originality of performance as denoting openness to the divine, that it tended to identify the beautiful as such with the ingenious and surprising.[5] Boileau, despite his classicism, embraced Longinus essentially under this Baroque aegis; hence for him the sublime discloses the beautiful as the *je ne sais quoi*, such that it is impossible to have a *theory* of the sublime, and the only way to explain it is to exemplify it.[6]

However, Boileau deploys Longinus to veer away from the Baroque in two significant respects. First of all, the more elaborate Baroque conceits are seen as collapsing under the weight of their own artifice—sublime figures of speech, by contrast, are not usually elaborate. On the contrary they are ideally such as not to appear figurative at all, though precisely for this reason, says Boileau, they are all the more successfully figurative—just as nature only appears to us "natural" because she is supremely good at concealing her own artifice. Examples of sublime figures include, for Longinus and Boileau, repetition, inversion of word order, and abrupt switch of addressees.[7] Compared with Baroque conceits therefore, they are less to do with content and more with *force of expression* (repetition, word order) or else they depend entirely upon *circumstance*: as when an orator makes what he is saying about a third party suddenly redound upon his immediate audience.

If sublime figures are more simple then, it is this concern with context which marks their second divergence from Baroque rhetoric and poetics. The latter, in its sole concern with elocution, had tended to lose all contact with the two prior rhetorical moments of determination and disposition of a subject matter, thereby reducing its political relevance to that of propagandistic mass manipulation, first perfected within the Baroque era.[8] By contrast, the sublime helps Boileau to reintroduce an ethical and "civic humanist" political context for poetics, since he regards an ingenious and surprising utterance as only truly sublime in relation to its attendant circumstances: *non quid sit, sed quo loco sit.*[9] Sometimes this concerns the invocation of the strength and nobility of the speaking subject which can be suggested but not represented. To cite Boileau's example, Parmenio says: "Were I Alexander, I would accept the offer from Darius King of Persia of one half of my kingdom in return for marriage to his daughter." To which Alexander replies: "So would I, were I Parmenio."[10] Or, again, context may assume that a sheerly verbal performance can negate objective disaster. To cite an example of Longinus: when Demosthenes, after the Athenians' defeat at the battle of Chaeroneia at the hands of Philip of Macedon, invokes "those who fought in the battle at Marathon and those who fought aboard ship at the battle of Salamis" in order to raise their spirits, this is sublimely figurative and not literal utterance. Taken literally, the mention of past victories might provoke present shame. But the sublime force of this invocation is to suggest that by fighting at all at Chaeronia, the Athenians have achieved the same symbolic victory on behalf of the cause of political freedom as in their literal victories of the past.[11]

The invocation of Longinus, therefore, served to re-ethicize the political context for the consideration of ingenious utterance. And just because of this embedding in an interpersonal context, sublime suggestions of the inconceivable and excessive were not yet divorced from specific beautiful form. Rather they were only effective if they were somehow conjoined to such form, a conjunction often achieved by a reduction to simplicity. But use of "complex metaphors" could *also* be an instance of the sublime, since the sublime conjoins an invocation of the unknown with the utterance of the completely unexpected and yet superlatively apt phrase. Were it not for this metaphorical effect, "the sublime" would no longer remain a figure of rhetoric, even though, according to Longinus and Boileau, it exceeds the rhetorical by "transporting" rather than merely "persuading."

If one were to ask here, just what is it that mediates between the obscure hinterland of that which is merely conjured up and the clear foreground or utterance, then the answer is precisely verbal performance. That is to say, words which *do* something and therefore suggest a surprising and indeterminable—even indeterminate—force in the speaker. For Boileau as for Longinus this is supremely the case with God; here the Mosaic oracular repetition concerning the existence of light corresponds to a divine transition from word to deed, such that we know that God's will is (incomprehensibly) identical with his power or capacity.[12] However, the sublime does not reside in the obscure divine background alone; it is also the manifest, sudden and unbearable light. This light, although intolerable and excessive, is nonetheless visible and clarifying. Hence in Boileau as for Longinus, it remains the case that the sublime concerns non-representability in a double sense: first, in an "aesthetic" register it is the non-representability of that which cannot be made to appear; second in a "rhetorical" register it is the non-representability of that which arises as a unique moment through speech, and cannot be identically repeated. The performed event is itself sublime: here, as Lyotard implies, Boileau anticipates a non-mimetic and avant-garde view of art as event, which the spectators must judge acceptable or otherwise, yet without being able to subordinate it to pre-established criteria of what is acceptable.[13] However, Lyotard suppresses the fact that for Boileau this sublime event has not ceased to belong to the realm of the beautiful, precisely because of its ethico-political connotations: that is to say, to be sublime it must be universally and politically acceptable and therefore must succeed in blending with other established instances of social beauty.

III

By contrast, during the course of the eighteenth century, and emphatically with the work of Edmund Burke, the beautiful and the sublime—or, one might say, the relatively determinate and the relatively indeterminate—became dualistically separated from each other. And it may be contended that both German Romanticism *and* recent "post-structuralism" remain confined in this dualism, despite its questionability. I would now like to insinuate precisely wherein this questionability might lie, by suggesting that, despite the fact that the sub-lime/beautiful dichotomy can be read as one way of constructing the secular, it nonetheless has paradoxically a twofold *theological* genealogy. This genealogy is to be located, first of all, in Protestant attitudes to the language of the Bible and to the imagistic in general; second, in mystical traditions which recom-mended "indifference" with respect to the love of God, or a love of God that took no account of one's own ultimate happiness.

First of all, the question of Biblical language. By the time one gets to Burke and Rousseau, the context of discourse about the sublime has mainly shifted from rhetoric to aesthetics. No longer is sublimity construed as something to which one gives voice: instead it is something which one regards, or rather (for both subjective and objective reasons) endeavors to regard but cannot regard. What caused this shift? At least in part the answer would appear to lie in the realm of attitudes to the language of the Bible. Boileau engaged in a polemic with the Protestant Jean Le Clerc and the Catholic Bishop Daniel Huet, con-cerning Longinus's attribution of sublimity to the Biblical text. Le Clerc and Huet argued that Longinus, knowing nothing of Hebrew, simply mistook or-dinary Hebrew usage of parallelism for a figure of speech.[14] Furthermore, they claimed that eloquence was inappropriately attributed to the Bible when it is describing plain "fact," albeit theological fact, and that while one might find rhetorical sublimity in the psalms, it was not to be located in the book of Gen-esis.[15] To the first objection, Boileau replied that Le Clerc and Huet had missed the point: for he had not been talking about a definable "sublime style," but a sublimity whose figurative character depended on *occasion*, such that paral-lelism, for example, could still be used to remarkable effect, however banal custom might have rendered it.[16] To the second point, which argued that the purportedly "plain speech" of Genesis was more appropriate to the solemn proclamation of a theological fact, Boileau replied that remote, lofty, sublime matters required all the more to be spoken of in a sublime fashion.[17] This amounts to the claim that something inherently inconceivable is not repre-sentable in denotative language, but rather can only be gestured towards, or in some fashion *performed* by language that in a small way repeats and echoes the passage from creator to creation. There can be no "plain" discourse about the creator in his infinity, but there can be a certain sort of figured language which invokes his bringing about of the finite, through which act alone the infinite comes to be known by us in some measure.

As a counterpart to their subordination of sublimity *within* language, Le Clerc and Huet also insisted that one could speak of sublimity *outside* of lan-guage, or apart from rhetorical performance. First of all, they argued, it was God himself, the act of creation, and the sight of creation by us that were sub-lime, rather than the textual citations of these things.[18] This essentially Protes-tant insistence then becomes one source of the view expressed by, among others, the British writer on the sublime, John Baillie, that there is no need to say much concerning the sublime in words, as such words merely *represent* the sublime in nature.[19] This point of view should, however, by no means be taken as entirely dominant within British aesthetics of the eighteenth century: for, by contrast, early in the century the aesthetician John Dennis, and later the highly influential Anglican Bishop Robert Lowth, perpetuated and extended in a proto-romantic direction the French classicist interest in uncovering a *rhetoric* of sublimity within the Bible and especially in poetic parallelism. For Lowth the sublimity of nature is not so much something represented in language as something which irrupts *through* language as an expressive event: a figurative expression which is also in itself sublime.[20] Here, also, a contrast of the sublime with the beautiful does not seem to be relevant: sublimity is rather construed as the highest intensity of rhetorical expression and of figurative beauty, an intensity that is "Hebrew" rather than "classical." (Just the same new respect for a "Hebrew aesthetic" forms part of the background to Handel's Biblical oratorios.)[21]

Nonetheless, while much Anglican thought by no means succumbed to the "Protestant" removal of sublimity from language, the position exemplified by Baillie was widespread in Britain, and blended seamlessly with a Lockean empiricist attitude to language which regards words as standing for signs which "represent" external facts. Within the perspective of Boileau or Lowth, the sublime as rhetorical event is at once "external" and "inward" and indeed is the emotive as well as intellectual event of the manifestation of the first in the second, such that the distance between them is nonetheless preserved. By contrast, for an empiricist outlook there arose a problem as to how an external massiveness and indeterminacy, registered as mere objective fact, nonetheless gives rise to feelings of awe and fear within. As Peter de Bolla intimates, this was a pseudo-problem, for empiricism overlooks the truth that the externally mighty and indeterminate is only so for a subjective apprehension—which from the outset is as much emotive as intellectual—in the first place.[22] Now although Kant and the later German idealists clearly were apprised of this ineliminability of the subjective and feeling-imbued moment in the apprehension of the sublime, they nonetheless remained still somewhat captivated by the primacy of *representation*, and therefore the idea that the sublime resides at the extreme paradoxical limits of conceptual capacity: it is a nowhere-somewhere to be (not) represented. Within their fuller carrying out of an epistemological realization of the ambition of ontology to represent, they failed to recover the sense that the unknown is not simply that which cannot be represented, but is *also* that which arrives, which ceaselessly but imperfectly makes itself known again in every new event. Thus for Kant what is sublime in subjectivity is not the actual performed deeds of each individual (as it might well be for Boileau), but rather the abstract fact of his possession of an indeterminate freedom. The consequences of this failure within idealism to recover the rhetorical perspective on sublimity will be returned to presently.

The second element of theological genealogy for the eventual separation of the sublime from the beautiful concerns the idea of the "disinterested" love of

God. As Hans Urs von Balthasar and others have shown, in the early modern period spiritual writers became more and more obsessed with the idea of loving God for himself alone, quite apart from any questions of one's own salvific destiny and the regard of God towards oneself.[23] Although much in this attitude is in keeping with Christian tradition, there are perhaps two main reasons why its earlier proponents had on the whole earlier drawn back from such an extreme conclusion. First of all, as Balthasar remarks, if our relation to God has ceased to be in any sense a matter of hope—since of course God himself is not in need of hope—then has not this relationship become strikingly depersonalized? For to claim to acknowledge God in abstraction from our own hopes and fears may indicate a self-obliteration in the face of otherness, but it *also*—and paradoxically—indicates a hubristic identification with this otherness, and an impossible crossing of the creator-created divide. The second reason concerns the problem of exactly what constitutes God's loveability, if we love him for his own sake alone? For every charm, every attractive feature of anything radiates outwards, rendering things apprehensible and thereby specifically loveable only in the measure that they affect the state of the observer in a positive fashion. By a second paradox it therefore follows that to love anything *purely* for itself, in abstraction from the quality of its influence upon oneself, is not at all to love that thing in its specificity, but rather to love it for that mere abstract quality of "being" that it shares with anything else whatsoever. In the case of persons, the qualifier "free" may be adjoined to the ontic term, but the same abstractness, non-specificity, and generality remains. In the case of God it follows that "to love him purely for his own sake" turns out to mean, not only to overidentify with him, but also to overidentify with a mere cipher, a mere void, or at best a hovering will.

Hence the mystical discourse on indifference tended to determine the essence of the unknown as empty freedom or even, incipiently, the void. In this respect it appears to have something in common with the aesthetic discourse on sublimity. Did the two discourses ever, historically, converge? There is evidence that they did, and particularly in the person of Fénelon, who was concerned with both poetics and spiritual mediation, and who sees both aesthetic sublimity and spiritual self-forgetting as manifest in the "naïve" moment when language expresses a noble subjectivity in an entirely unselfconscious fashion.[24] However, by the time we reach Kant, such convergence is quite manifest: the aesthetic sublime is now a mere pointer to the true *ethical* sublime whose essence is freedom, and which we are to love utterly for its own sake.[25] For us this true sublime is wholly without attraction, without reward, without any link to our own happiness. The influence of the spiritual discourse on disinterestedness, in this case mediated by pietism, is here quite undeniable. And it therefore follows that it is an association of "the sublime" with the quality of disinterested love for the good or for duty which in Kant's case has helped to wrench the sublime away from the emanating attractiveness of the beautiful, and to ensure its exclusive association with painful shock and rupture: that is to say, a break with our natural pursuit of happiness and tranquillity. For Kant, the element of displeasure within the sublime experience is a sign of the necessary *sacrifice* of the pleasurable, which is the only possible mode of access to the purely moral domain.

However, this was only one relevant effect of the tradition concerning "disinterested love" within aesthetics. For not only did it help to prise apart the sublime and the beautiful, it also helped to *sublimate* the beautiful itself. Platonic and Neo-Platonic discussions of the beautiful, as inherited by the whole western tradition, had linked it closely with *eros*: creaturely and especially human beauty was deemed to lead one to a higher *eros* for the true intellectual beauty. And the later irruption of subjectivity and "personality" into this ultimate principle (through Biblical influence) means that certain Jewish, Islamic, and Christian writers insist yet more upon the importance of a passionate component in our relationship to a God who himself draws us by the force of his own desire. At the same time, the Christian insistence on the persistence of a horizontal society into the most ineffable depths—love of God as always manifest in love of neighbor—allowed Dante to conceive of an erotic love for one woman as persisting in a transfigured mode into the heart of the beatific vision, whereas for Plato the initial love for an individual is something later to be "left behind."[26] (Although this perspective is already surpassed in the *Phaedrus*.) In the case of Christianity, it is only relatively modern writers, in the wake of the Reformation, who have argued, in contrast to the Church fathers, for an exclusion of all *eros* from *agape*, regarded as a purely other-regarding and self-giving love.[27] And this supposed rigor, far from preserving Christianity from Greek metaphysical contamination, has had precisely the opposite effect, in a fashion analogous to the paradoxes of indifference as outlined above. For a person, or even a God who exercises a merely agapeic love towards others is locked within a needless self-sufficiency which renders him simply uncharacterizable. This position cannot therefore even allow that God desires without lack in ceaselessly attaining to his own beatitude. Hence it makes subjectivity collapse back into substance, ignoring specifically Biblical erotic metaphors for God's relationship to humanity and to his own inner emanations (of Son and Spirit). A God who would offer only a "cold love" is thereby paradoxically "objectified," just as if he is the object only of *our* "cold love" he is rendered abstract and empty.

Hence modern spiritual discourse had tended to distance *eros* from the absolute, both in the sense that it denied it to the absolute itself, and in the sense that it denied it to our attainment of the absolute, and *even* to our aspiration towards it. But since for antiquity and the Middle Ages beauty is associated with the absolute and with consummation, it is not surprising that this same attitude should encourage a sundering of *eros* from the beautiful. By whatever precise historical routes this occurred, the transfer is evident in the case of Kant: now the beautiful can only be a sign of the moral if it is purged of contamination by desire. Hence even though, for Kant, the beautiful is a sign of the moral *blending* of material happiness with spiritual freedom,[28] whereas the sublime is a sign of the latter alone, nonetheless all the more social and rhetorical aspects of "beauty" are relegated beneath the level of the genuinely aesthetic. Hence the observer's delight in fine painting is taken as paradigmatic of the aesthetic experience, whereas "the use" of beauty in rhetorical persuasion, sexual seduction, bodily adornment, cuisine, and architecture is systematically disparaged. Tellingly, he declares that the tattooing of the body as practiced by the benighted Caribs and Iroquois is a "misuse of the decorative." This is because true beauty is held *not* to incite desire, and to be quite above the merely "charming." It is rather a matter of a disinterested delight in form for its own sake.[29] Now by making "art" instead of "God" the object of a disinterested contemplation, Kant has placed himself at a double remove from previous Christian tradition: first of all art has become a secular end in itself, no longer an erotic incitement to our higher desire for God. Second, *as* an end in itself, it nonetheless appropriates the new de-eroticized mystical conception of our relationship to God. Hence not only does Kant's category of the sublime echo a previous disassociation of God from *eros*, his category of the beautiful does so also.

What does this circumstance really betoken? It shows that, just as a reduction of language to representation helps to sunder the sublime from the beautiful, so, likewise, does a refusal of an erotic path of access to transcendence. This follows, because if a God loved purely for himself is a sublime void voiding our desires, and if our desire in consequence no longer leads through and beyond immanence, then it becomes natural to conceive of this world also, in its formed beauty, as a *terminus* for desire, and as something for which we must acquire a "disinterested" feeling. If desire is not regarded as a cognitive probe that is revelatory of the other, it will tend to be defined as a mere lack, which is therefore effaced by arrival at a goal. Hence a refusal of the mediation of finite with infinite through *eros* ensures that we are suspended between a disinterestedness as regards indeterminate freedom, *and* a secondary disinterestedness as regards the sensible *phenomena* which for Kant constitute finitude.

However, there is one further element to be noted: in Kant (and perhaps necessarily) the gulf between the sublime and the beautiful is only constituted in terms of the hierarchical superiority of the former. Were this not the case, then the beautiful, as that which synthesizes happiness with freedom, would so permeate freedom with happiness, that freedom would be accessible only in a specific harmonious arrangement. But conversely such synthesis would also suggest a "depth" to immanence, a transcendent background which would be the manifestation of the sublime in, through, and as the beautiful itself. Therefore, the phenomenon "beauty" would itself always involve a manifestation of "more" than what is given *in* what is given, an excess coincident with a registration of desire. Again the latter element correlates with the sublime, since a beauty only registered by desire is also terrible, is also painful and piercing, drawing us towards an unknown background which is given precisely *in* the mysterious perspective which confronts us. Against Kant one should therefore argue that there is no beautiful which is not also sublime, whereas his distinction of the sublime from the beautiful leaves us with the residue of the "merely" beautiful, without terror. But in denying that there exists any such extra-erotic, disinterested beauty, one can also see that there is no sublime terminus except that which is opened up by a beautiful approach. What mountain is sublime merely because of its size? Surely its grandeur is rather a matter of the way its specific form suggests the uniquely overwhelming, and the way it both is and is not in continuity with a harmonious, beautiful approach towards it, or the *picturesqueness* of a vista (to avert to another eighteenth-century aesthetic category). Or again, in Bach's *St. John's Passion*, sudden switches to chromatic atonality are only "sublime" as temporary suspensions of tonal intervals which they both interrupt and yet somehow mediate. In fact one can say that Kant's own recognition that the occurrence of beautiful proportion always coincides with an absolutely unique judgment not subordinate to any already constructed categories or criteria,[30] itself shows that the acuteness and surprise of specifically aesthetic harmony (as opposed, say, to geometric tedium) depends upon the risk of a sublime interruption of our expectations, which nonetheless our judgments can accept. Thus, it can be contended, the sublime is only sublime as a rupture in *this* or *that* context, or of this or that beautiful proportion, but this is precisely because the beautiful is itself only a continuity sustained despite sublime discontinuity. It is true that certain experiences are relatively more beautiful and others relatively more sublime, yet neither can be entirely the one without something of the other.

It follows that, were Kant to have made the beautiful as significant as the sublime, he would have had to construe the beautiful as the mediation of beauty with sublimity, and that in consequence both the hierarchy and the distinction would have been abolished. Likewise, as we shall shortly see, the distinction and hierarchy between happiness and freedom: for with the supremacy of the mediation of beauty through desire would follow also the co-supremacy of the pursuit of happiness along with freedom, and the idea that we are only truly free when we attain to a genuine social beatitude. But since, to the contrary, it is the sublime, not the beautiful, which for Kant leads from the aesthetic to the superior ethical realm—the latter hierarchization being but one aspect of the same dubious complex of ideas I am criticizing—it is unsurprising that the beautiful should be seen as possessing the same essential characteristic as the sublime, namely disinterestedness, but in an inferior degree. Inferior, because one more fully sustains disinterest when nothing meets the sight to please, just as it is the case that while the beautiful represents the instantiation of the moral virtues and the ethical harmony which results, only the sublime discloses their principle and ground, namely the upholding of the autonomous freedom of "self-possession" which exceeds specific form.

Nevertheless, the hierarchical sundering of the Sublime from the Beautiful did not, in the eighteenth century, always take the de-eroticized form exemplified by Kant. The latter inherits the distinction from Edmund Burke, and yet in Burke it is established in a distinctively different fashion which rather than placing the Sublime over the Beautiful by removing the role of *eros*, instead achieves the same thing by *dividing the erotic itself*.[31] In this scheme the beautiful is by no means sublimated, but rather arises as an emotive effect of whatever happens to please the physical senses. It is to be explained at once in theological and functionalist terms: God has placed this response within us in order to promote erotic union and social cohesion. However, the mere charm of the beautiful is, for Burke (in this respect like Kant) less poetically compelling than the awe of the sublime, which arises not from any attraction, but rather from pain, or the threat of death either temporally postponed or held at a spatial distance. The true opposite of the beautiful, which is a static, empirical registration of pleasure, is *not* in fact the sublime, but rather equally static pain; sublimity concerns rather a dynamic invocation and yet retreat from pain, and so its opposite is mourning or *melancholy*, the equally dynamic loss of beauty or the pleasurable.[32] But where melancholy is actively relation-seeking, since it concerns the loss of something or someone desired, sublimity concerns simply self-preservation in the face of a threatened dissolution of self. Yet it is the latter, for Burke's male, martial tastes, which is the more overwhelming and influential. The explicit articulation of this preference again involves a fusion of theology with a utilitarian functionalism. God, as most clearly portrayed in the Old Testament, is seen by Burke to be most fundamentally invoked by human beings as an object of fear, and concomitantly Burke conceives God as ensuring social order *primarily* through the drive to self-preservation and the fear of the other, rather than through the drives of sympathy and shared pleasure. As with Kant, the hierarchical elevation and distinction of the sublime undergirds the primacy of individual self-autonomy over social bonding in the constitution of the social order. What is truly *exchangeable*, what truly constitutes a public currency, is the universally substitutive value of fear-for-self-warded-off. By contrast the explicit *investment* of this value in that which diverts and delights within the bounds of safety, is a strictly private matter. The main difference from Kant and other Germans, as Howard Caygill has explained, is that whereas providence in Burke and in other British writers as a matter of empirical fact coordinates diverse freedoms through the marketplace (like Adam Smith's hidden hand) for the Germans such divine coordinating is mediated by the *a priori* of human reason which is also the centralized "police" procedure of the state.[33]

In this Burkean scheme it would seem that the erotic is not banished twice, as with Kant, but only once, in relation to transcendence, since it is allowed to flourish in the immanent realm of the beautiful as the motor of our blind strivings which God must coordinate "behind our backs" through the empirical miracle of the marketplace. However, at a deeper level, the erotic is surely accepted twice, since the *frisson* of delight in pain and death withheld is not ethicized by Burke as by Kant into a solemn cold acknowledgment of the unknown as freedom. The uncontaminated *frisson* can only be erotic, and therefore it follows that Burke has split the erotic between the *lesser* heterosocial play of quiet charms furthering procreation, and a higher homoerotic thrill of male combat and male confrontation of danger deemed to "frame" society more fundamentally than the business of heterosocial eroticized beauty.[34] But of course it goes without saying that this construction is entirely questionable: the "heterosocial," "beautiful" aspect could be held equally to "frame," and its division from sublime, relatively sado-masochistic elements is also unsustainable. (While of course it might be argued that all these constructions are arbitrarily essentializing.)

Yet what is to be noticed here is that the whole framework is upheld by a certain deviant theology: a theology which construes God as abstract will without transcendental goodness, truth, and beauty, and which regards him, not fundamentally as the author of being, but rather idolatrously as an actor in our plot, manipulating fear to produce order. The same loss of erotic mediation of finite with infinite as observed in Kant follows from this starting point: but whereas Kant abandons erotics, Burke produces a pseudo-erotics in which *on the one hand* the (male subject) desires not the *other* (female) body but rather death which is also the (male) same (since what is most proper to oneself is that one is to die), and hence necrophilia is the most perfect autoeroticism; while *on the other hand* this archetypally male subject desires the female other without reference to his or her death, so without reference to the loss, sacrifice, self-giving, and thrill of fear of the other which traverses any possible erotic relationship. Eventually I shall suggest that in this questionable dualism one has *in nuce* the structure of that Bataillean erotics which undergirds the whole of "post-structuralism" and "post-modernism": love of death standing above love of the living other which is subordinated as an illusory and yet necessary moment.

However, today we see that alongside an eroticizing of the sublime void, stands—less as an alternative and more as another aspect of the same thought-complex—also an *ethicizing* of the void (Levinas, Marion, Derrida).[35] And where the former has an anticipation in Burke, the later has an anticipation in Kant. Implausibly, the German philosopher sought to spiritualize Burke's divine utilitarian regulation of a primordial violence into mutual recognition of freedom by noumenal selves. Implausibly, since freedom is only more than a fictional supposition when it is enacted, and as soon as it is enacted must impose upon the other as violence, unless there are norms for legitimate giving and receiving over and above those for the preservation of freedom.

Such norms over and above freedom would *either* have to impose the rigid stratifications of a traditional society, or *else* would belong to an emergent social harmony arising from a shared but constantly re-expressed sense of the beautiful, or of legitimate give-and-take. The latter would represent a radical rather than reactionary alternative to a formal liberalism that is merely a mask for the violence of state and marketplace. Now what is extraordinary and truly striking is that in a sense *the entire effort* of German philosophy from the Kant of the Third Critique through the idealists concerns the search for just such an alternative, and that this search is always and with necessity construed as an attempt to resurrect the role of the beautiful and of *eros* in the face of the dominance of the sublime. Therefore, it can be said to be characterized by a yearning for transcendence *rather than* sublimity, since the former construes the beautiful as itself sublime through the mediation of finite and infinite by an *agape* that is itself *eros*.[36]

As I shall now show, this attempt to embrace transcendence nonetheless failed, and the hierarchical differentiation of the sublime was always reinstated. Since the so-called "postmodern" version of the sublime repeats this same construction, it will also be suggested that the gap between post-structuralism and idealism is exaggerated, and the incipient nihilism of the latter overlooked.

IV

In the case of Kant himself, first of all, the supremacy of the sublime is not unambiguous. In the most fundamental principle of his philosophy, namely the supremacy of practical (not theoretical, nor aesthetic) reason, it does, indeed, appear to be affirmed. For the ascent from the beautiful to the sublime is but an interlude mediating a more fundamental ascent from that "purposiveness-without-purpose" which characterizes the aesthetic as such, to the pure capacity of freedom as the *source* of all purpose. Yet the judgment of beauty involves, for Kant, a harmonious blending without prior rules of reason and intuition, according to a "free play" of the faculties in which one can no longer, as in theoretical reason, assign the relative contributions of schematizing concepts and schematized sensory input.[37] This construal of aesthetic feeling depends upon the abolition of the hierarchy of the noumenal activity of reason over sensible receptivity of the phenomenal. And yet, as Caygill and Jean-Luc Nancy in different fashions have indicated,[38] if the supremacy of the sublime leads one back to the priority of the noumenal, then this must secretly be already at work in the judgment of the beautiful, such that the apparently harmonious coincidence of reason and intuition—which is like an event of "grace"[39]—is in fact an arbitrary construct, and the violent, arbitrary imposition of a certain freely-chosen form by noumenal reason acting with priority. Therefore it follows that a supremacy of duty over a virtue integrating duty with happiness deconstructs the integrity of virtue. (This is what needs to be said against the shallowness of Onora O'Neill's defence of Kantian virtue against Alasdair Macintyre.) [40]

The only way to save Kant from such an immanent deconstruction would be to develop hints in his work towards an overthrow of hierarchy, and a reverse prioritization of the beautiful which would draw back the sublime within its sway; hints most apparent whenever he invokes the theological. Thus in *Religion within the Limits of Reason Alone* Kant transgresses the purity of the categorical imperative which concerns only duty, by adding that there is also an imperative to add happiness to freedom.[41] And for Kant every *actual* moral act always involves such addition, and can therefore never be purely situated in the noumenal kingdom of ends. Thus he consistently links the possibility of a genuine social harmony with the idea of that imprescribable aesthetic judgment of the beautiful which exceeds the theoretical bringing of intuitions under an *a priori* categorical organization.[42] And he further links the possibility of such harmony to divine grace, and our belief in its possibility to our having trust in the advent of such grace. That such harmony is possible, and that we should believe it to be possible Kant further links to divine grace and faith in God respectively.[43] I do not at all mean by this that Kant encourages a certain secularizing substitution of "artistic grace" for "religious grace." On the contrary, it is rather that the admission by Kant that one cannot bring the aesthetic under the determinate judgment of either reason or the senses ensures that it retains the character of an event disclosing a transcendent depth which had been lost both to principles of reason and to sensory experience since at least the time of Descartes. The aesthetic is here no "modern equivalent for the religious," but rather in its integrity bears the theological ineliminably within its heart, remembering that the aesthetic is only *judged* with a kind of faith, and unpredictably *arrives* through a kind of grace.

However, despite these hints which would point to a reversal of his whole philosophy, and a prioritization of feeling over theory and practice which would subsume them both (as the beautiful would subsume the sublime), Kant does not consistently develop them. Instead, he holds that aesthetic feeling concerns only a kind of surplus expressive enjoyment of the transcendental adaptation of the rational categorical capacity in general to the power of sensory intuiting in general, and points to no real theoretical truth.[44] This precisely corresponds to a reduction of the divine blending of freedom and happiness—and of nature and subject, phenomena and noumena, "regulatory" invocation of God with actual "postulation" of God[45]—to a mere extrinsic rewarding of genuine freedom with an empirical experience of happiness, within time or at the "last judgment."[46] Here happiness does not require to be judged, and does not admit of degrees of authenticity which would disclose the authenticity of the freedom in question. Just as the aesthetic reveals no truth, but is only a surplus pleasurable adjunct, so also happiness does not truly guide us to the good. And since both the true and the good are deemed to exceed the pleasurable, Kant cannot finally allow that an interpersonal search for consensus and "mutual placement" might define ethical endeavor, but instead retreats to a modern reworking of the antique (pre-Christian) concentration on a private war of reason with the passions, in which sacrificial pain is the mark of authenticity. Conversely, the aesthetic constitution of the interpersonal is in fact confined by Kant to a transcendentally grounded agreement concerning such archetypally *private* experiences as the contemplation of a picture in an art gallery. He never dared fully to entertain an alternative autonomy-within-heteronomy of a reason which is *throughout* an aesthetic as well as a theoretical and practical reason, and which therefore operates *only* on the ground of intersubjective acceptance of a judgment of harmony without reasons other than those of its own subjective occurrence.

But after Kant, Schiller moved somewhat in this direction, which for Hegel in his *Aesthetics* defines precisely what he means by the Absolute Idea.[47] Here *all* truth has become "aesthetic" in the sense that truth unfolds or performs itself, such that freedom and necessity perfectly coincide: freedom chooses what it should choose, yet this compulsion is apparent *only* for freedom. However, the Absolute Idea did not succeed in remaining within the bounds of the aesthetic judgment of the beautiful, and this *precisely* because of the continuing hierarchized duality between the beautiful and the sublime. Even for Schiller, the categorical imperative based solely on freedom remains the highest quality: this is "dignity" (*Würde*) or Venus in her naked beauty without her girdle of aesthetic charm (*Anmut*), even if Juno's stealing of the girdle in order to seduce Jupiter indicates the need to complete dignity with grace.[48] But there is a twofold problem with Schiller's categorization. First of all, his graceful beauty is not really a gift of *divine* grace, but a feature of a purely immanent reality; in consequence it tends to be downgraded to an instance of a fateful necessity.[49] Secondly, the dignity of freedom still retains its superiority, and that hierarchy leaves one only two ways to construe the charm of beauty which is the concretized social harmony of established custom (*Sittlichkeit*). Either, as with the deconstruction of Kant, charm is secretly an arbitrary and violent ruse, or else one must seek to derive charm from dignity, or beauty from freedom, as a logical requirement of the outworking of freedom itself. And this is the course taken by Hegel.

While it would seem, on the face of it, that Hegel's entire endeavor is an effort to reconcile the sublime with the beautiful, or freedom with *Sittlichkeit*, all he in fact succeeds in doing, as Slavoj Zizek has demonstrated, is to establish a more radical philosophy of sublimity.[50] For while it is true that, in Hegel, the Absolute Idea includes a moment in which the divine Notion expresses itself in the finite created order—such that the sublimely indeterminate is in itself self-determining as beauty—this negation of the infinite is itself negated. Again, while it is true that the Absolute certainly involves *both* moments, such that it affirms *both* the identity of identity and non-identity, *and* the non-identity of identity and non-identity, this however by no means allows the resumption of the concrete contents of finite order into divinity.[51] There is no analogical "eminence" in Hegel, as with Aquinas, since in the moment of identity, particularity is simply sublated as freedom, while in the (admittedly retained within the absolute) moment of non-identity, these concrete contents remain alien to infinite freedom in terms of their finite freedom, accidentality, and contingency. The problem with Hegel, from a theological point of view, is in part the opposite from what it is usually taken it to be: instead of a genuine providence he offers not just a fateful necessity but also too much sheer surd autonomous chance and freedom in the finite realm. Thus in the moment of sublated freedom, finite "beautiful" contexts are left behind in their sheer accidentality: all that is resumed is the need for spirit to express itself in *some* such contingent fashion in order for it to establish itself as freedom at all, and for it to become a more than quasi-finite individual freedom. In like manner, state and corporation reinterpret the self-interested economic motivations of the marketplace as a necessary concretization of freedom, which alone ensures that many freedoms will harmoniously blend: yet they are also thereby resigned to the sheer self-interested pleasure-seeking and fear-avoiding character of this moment.

This ontology and this politics both correlate with—and perhaps are reducible to—Hegel's notion of a "Christian" or "romantic" aesthetic. For Hegel, it is antique classical art which represents "the beautiful," or a perfect, indivisible union of free form with essential content. This is contrasted with a sublime, "symbolic" art of more primitive eras, not concerned with the embodying of human grace, but with the invocation of something superhuman and monstrous. However, "romantic" art which arises in the Christian era revives, in a higher mode, a sublime and symbolic art.[52] This new sublimity on the one hand permits a greater artistic realism in the depiction of the purely secular and contingent, and yet on the other hand negates *all* form—in which spirit cannot truly fulfill itself—in order to point back towards a purely noetic spiritual fulfillment.[53] In this economy, and not in bodily incorporation, lies for Hegel the truth of the Incarnation, such that for him the crucifixion represents a kind of necessary completion of incarnation in disincarnation, rather than a moment independent of incarnation, which exposes the essence of sin to be the impulse to destroy God as the gift of Being itself.[54] In a similar fashion, for Hegel the eating of the eucharistic elements betokens a sacrificial cancelling of their materiality, and not, as for Catholic tradition, the paradoxical transformation of us *into* the divine body which we are consuming.[55] In all these three instances—romantic art in general, the Incarnation, the eucharist—the sublime and the beautiful are conjoined merely in the sense that first, the sublime is only real in its self-negation as the beautiful, and yet second, the *truth* of the beautiful resides only in its negation of the negation to establish a sublimity which as noetic will be "in and for itself."

Hence Zizek is right: Hegel's philosophy is a more exclusive "sublimatics" as opposed to "aesthetics," when compared with that of Kant, and he is further right to say that this is precisely because he does *not* hypostasize the sublime abyss by gesturing towards it as a kind of hidden noumenal "something." Let us see how this is the case. There is, for Hegel, no real, inert abyss of freedom "to begin with," lying beyond the margins of formed, beautiful finality. Instead, the noumenal, the freely indeterminate, only first exists in the moment where it *exercises* its freedom and therefore negates its indeterminate essence in determining it as something or other. Sublimity is for this reason first manifest along with the beautiful, or rather it only resides in the instance of beauty in so far as it is a sign which symbolizes something overwhelmingly more than itself. However, in a second instance one eliminates, or rather leaves to its pure residue of contingency, the specific form of the beautiful in order to grasp it *only* as symbol, and in this moment one comprehends that while freedom must express itself in order to be, such particular enactment never corresponds to the indeterminate essence of freedom. Consequently, only the sublime remains: it is no longer that real beyond to which we gesture, but rather the ultimate emptiness of all our gestures, reducing their "beautiful" content to an empirical residue. Hegel *effaces* the beautiful in favor of the sublime.

It follows that the Kojèvian construal of Hegel as an incipient nihilist is essentially right, and that the mode of his "theology" confirms rather than negates this. And Kojève's successors, Bataille and Lacan through to other poststructuralists, especially Derrida, can indeed be read as expounding an extension of Hegelian logic, when they take the absolute to be a sublime void present only when a-voided in difference, and re-voided only in re-differentiation, in ceaseless oscillation. The true alternative to nihilism cannot be the Hegelian sublimation of the aesthetic, but only a drastically subverted Kantianism which extends aesthetic judgment to the whole field of knowledge and holds the sublime and the beautiful together in harmonious suspense, allowing merely a relative distinction between the two. Only such a conception of the aesthetic as the unpredictable advent of grace saves it, along with knowledge and practice, from the imputation of either violent arbitrariness (the ungroundedness of a free judgment if not referred to a transcendent standard) or logical necessity (the reduction of such freedom to immanent necessity, in order to avoid an incomprehensible dualism).

And yet, despite this "Kantian" preference, there remains something distinctive to be learned from Hegel. Like Schiller, Hegel rejected the possibility of a return to classical beauty, or to the "aesthetic state" of the Athenian *polis*, on the grounds that this imposed from the center a single fixed order, and took too little account of human freedom.[56] Judgment of the beautiful without a sublime moment too much suggests the autonomous unfolding of a single organism through time. It does not allow sufficiently for the spatial confrontation of different individuals who do not truly compose one single subjectivity. Unfortunately, as we have seen, Schiller and Hegel's proposals at this point fail to transcend the bounds of political economy: only a formal mediation of freedom is entertained, such that actual human choices in their content seem so much dross, contributing nothing to an unfolding idea of the human. Thus Hegel finally abandoned classical political hope for aesthetic consensus in favor of a logic of sublimity. Nevertheless, if one is to avoid organicist illusions it would appear to be true that the beautiful must be construed as also sublime, or that aesthetic judgment demands of itself to be constantly *suspended* in order to allow for the non-representable perspective of the other—"object" or "subject"—for its, his, or her regard of *us*, and for such judgment's inherent non-completion or promise. Indeed since the beautiful, as I have argued, is itself the arrival of surprising harmony, even "our own" art is only the impinging upon our own perspective of the perspective of the other also. Hence beyond the Kantian construal of the beautiful as the free determination of the object by the subject—which is also the manifestation of the object to the subject—must be added the notion of an ineliminable co-determination by the freedom of "the other." This is most crucial of course in the collective art of a human society, but one can allow that even non-conscious things manifest a certain "subjective" spontaneity, which is the aesthetic impact of the particular, unpredictable by scientific laws of causal necessity. Hence not only does the aesthetic blend person with person, it only does so in a mode which retains the otherness of the other, and *through* form manifests an ecstatic reaching towards the other in excess of form. In this case the other does not reside at Burke's *melancholic* distance, since it is not a distance of loss, but of presence: a disclosing and therefore sublime distance which reveals through withholding and suspension. But neither is a sublime which discloses the beautiful a withholding of pain; instead terror is here converted by trust into the thrill of promise.

Such a view blends well with a refusal of the aesthetic as pure disinterested contemplation, and with a re-instatement of its link with desire. This does not, of course, mean that the beautiful can be possessed, but that by opening a hidden depth it exposes also sublime or ethical dimensions of both gift and promise. The beautiful appears as a distance in which it in part consists, and consummation resides in the *remaining* of this distance, the persistence of a certain delightful longing, not in the cancellation of a lack. This implies that any aesthetic work is in a radical sense incomplete—not in the sense that it only exists in part, but in the sense that every element in its completion is also a concrete mode of incompletion: hence it is always a new, specific theme in music which calls out to be developed further; hence also it is the truly original individual work that tends to give rise to an entire new genre. For, as J-L Nancy points out, the firmer the boundary the more the suggestion of something beyond that boundary;[57] yet I would add, not of a mere abyss, rather of something *in analogical continuity* with what lies within the boundary.

If every definite work of art or aesthetic experience is for just that reason indefinable and incomplete, then it also follows, on the subjective side, that every true judgment is a *suspended* judgment: not a refusal to judge, nor a judgment taking no form, but a judgment which takes the only possible form of giving to the other—"object" or "subject"—its due, of allowing that it possesses its own standards, its own inner principles, whose future development one cannot altogether anticipate. These alien standards of formation we can *recognize* and can continuously *blend* with our own, yet the moment of recognition includes a dimension of non-control which renders an aesthetic judgement not just an occurrence of reason without criteria, and not just a surrender to the other (though it is both those things) but also a gift towards the other of our own mode of being which we request that she complete in her own particular way. An expression then, is also a gift, but a gift is also a request: a "prayer."

In this mode therefore, one could seek to restore the sublime to the beautiful and close the duality. And the mode discloses that the key to such restoration is once more to construe the beautiful as part of a movement towards desire of the other. Where this is denied, and the sublime is sundered from the beautiful—eventually, as in postmodern nihilism to the point of obliterating it—then the passage to the sublime leads not to union with a living other, but to a dispassionate freedom which beckons us beyond encounter, to total fusion. And then *either* this lure of the sublime is the command of absolutely self-sacrificial duty—ethics as our commitment to a future we shall not live to see—or *else* this is a delirious necrophiliac narcissism, in which we are beckoned by that of which we cannot be robbed, our own death, which is yet absolutely other, but only as the *nihil*.[58] In the first case, no one lives to see a salvation in time which is always postponed; in the second case also, salvation is an exit from time and being, and not in any sense participated in by them. In the first case politics (the social body to which the individual surrenders himself) obliterates the individual; in the second case there is no political hope, only a hysterical interruption of the political sphere.

Hence in either case, the distinction and hierarchical elevation of the sublime discloses its secret truth to be *absolute self-sacrifice without return*.[59] By contrast, the re-integration of the sublime with the beautiful does not locate supreme value in self-sacrifice at all. In this re-integration the beautiful leads desire back to an Other only partially disclosed in finite others, to a distance disclosed but always also withheld, but a distance which we trust—have "faith in"—as an always ever greater depth of such harmony; a distance we do not rationalistically construe simply as a shuddering abyss, since this is to render the unknowability of the unknown its ontological essence (in a fashion natural to conceptual reason, yet without adequate conceptual warrants). Through this re-integration we are returned from the sublime to a genuine transcendent, and then, in consequence, enabled to re-think the sacrificial. For if there exists a genuine transcendent, if the finitely beautiful *participates* in an absolute unknown beauty, this absolute *gives* the finite without fall, without rupture, without dissimulation. And then in turn our giving back to the absolute, by which we respire or exist at all, is not a sacrificial self-cancelling, but an equally total giving in order to receive back a being always different, which is only partici-pated by us. But more fundamentally, both our receiving and our counter-giving are but one single movement, namely the passage through us in time of the desired other (which is quite different from Lyotard's account of art as the temporal event of sublime rupture).[60] Through this movement we are com-pleted in our very incompletion, beautiful in our very sublimity. For no longer is this incompletion a source of anxiety, nor of a dark eroticism that is but the inverse face of an absence of physical love, but rather of erotic delight, both in human others and in the divine Other.

Thus, we can conclude: the dualism of sublime and beautiful is the inner se-cret of "critical" philosophy, both "modern" and "postmodern." And yet it turns out to be no transcendental truth whatsoever, but a mere subjective ges-ture, derived from a "Protestant" genealogy, together with an unacknowledged resignation to a capitalist duality of public indifferent value mediating private and meaningless preference. To this I have opposed a different phenomenol-ogy of the beautiful, and appealed to a different mode of experience. Yet it is possible to refuse, deny or reduce this experience, if one insists on making the gesture of *mere* (objectifying) reason, which is ultimately a nihilistic gesture. I can only repond that there remains *another* critical possibility, another possi-ble gesture, a gesture which does not situate indifference over-against formed differentiation as that which both governs and subverts it. Rather, this other gesture incorporates both the sublimely indeterminate and the beautifully determinate within a single manifestation: that of *Kabod*, glory, as the Old Testament describes it. If one asks, what is the (ungroundable) transcendental presupposition of the gesture towards such manifestation, then the answer can only be, a genuine transcendent, or power which is both infinitely free and in-finitely formed, both differentiating and unifying and both in virtue of the other aspect. In consequence this power is deemed to give at once both free-dom and formation. Here is neither moral nor perverse rupture, but only ex-pectancy to increase delight.

Notes

1. Longinus, "On the Sublime" in Aristotle/Horace/Longinus, *Classical Literary Criticism*, trans. T.S. Dorsch (London: Penguin, 1965), 97–158; N. M. Boileau, *A Treatise of the sub-lime, translated from the Greek of Longinus* [English translation of the French] (London, 1712).
2. See J-F. Lyotard, "The Sublime and the Avant-Garde" in *The Lyotard Reader* ed. H. Ben-jamin, 196–212; Lisa Appignanesi ed. *Postmodernism: ICA Documents* (London: Free Asso-ciation, 1989), esp. J-F Lyotard "Defining the Postmodern," 7–10; "Complexity and the sublime," 19–26; Philippe Lacoue-Labarthe, "On the sublime," 11–14. See also Philippe La-coue Labarthe, *Typography* (Cambridge, Mass., Harvard University Press, 1989), 139–208 and J-F Lyotard, *Lessons on the Analytic of the Sublime*, trans. E. Rottenberg (Stanford, Calif.: Stanford University Press, 1994).
3. S. Kierkegaard, *Journals* (London: Oxford University Press, 1938), 346.
4. See Hans Urs von Balthasar, *The Glory of the Lord: A Theological Aesthetics. IV. The Realm of Metaphysics in Antiquity*, trans. Brian McNeil et al. (Edinburgh: T. and T. Clark, 1989), 317–413.

5. See Walter J. Ong, *Ramus: Method and the Decay of Dialogue* (Cambridge, Mass.: Harvard University Press, 1958); Guido Morpurgo Tagliabue in *Retorica barocco*, ed. E. Castelli (Rome: Bocca, 1955), 119–95.

6. N. Boileau "Preface" to *A Treatise of the Sublime* 2; *Posthumous Works of N. Boileau* vol III (London, 1713), "Three new Reflections on Longinus" Reflection X, 52.

7. N. Boileau, "Preface," 7; "Three New Reflections," x, 56, 58 ff.; xl, 71–75, xii, 76; Longinus, "On the sublime," chaps. 16–28; 125–138.

8. See José Luis Maravall, *Culture of the Baroque*, trans. Terry Cochran (Minneapolis: Minnesota, 1986), 207–267.

9. Boileau, "Three New Reflections," x, 61.

10. Boileau, "Three New Reflections," x, 56.

11. Longinus, "On the Sublime," chap. 16; 126.

12. Boileau, "Three New Reflections," x, 59–62; Longinus, chap. 9; 111.

13. J-F Lyotard, "The Sublime and the Avant-Garde."

14. Jean Le Clerc, "Remarks upon Boileau's Tenth Reflection upon Longinus" and Daniel Huet and Jean Le Clerc, "An Examination of the opinion of Longinus upon this passage in Genesis Chap. I verse 3: 'And God said let the light be made and the light was made,' " in Jean Le Clerc, *Bibliothèque Choisie* vol. x, 154–70, 21–50.

15. Le Clerc, "An Examination," 162.

16. Boileau, "Three New Reflections," x, 59–62.

17. Boileau: [one needs words] "whose elegant and majestic obscurity makes us conceive a great many things beyond what they seem to express," "Reflections," x, 59–60. See also 60–65, esp. 64:65: Moses himself did not himself think of graces and niceties of art "but the Divine spirit who inspir'd him, thought of it for him, and made use of 'em accordingly, with so much the more Art, in that no Art at all is perceived."

18. Jean Le Clerc, "Remarks" 164. Huet and Le Clerc, "An Examination," 34, 41–43; "The sublime of Things is the true sublime, the sublime of Nature, the original sublime, the rest are only by Imitation and Art."

19. John Baillie, *An Essay on the Sublime* (London, 1947), 15–16; Peter de Bolla, *The Discourse of the Sublime: History, Aesthetics and the Subject* (Oxford: Basil Blackwell, 1989), 40–42.

20. John Dennis, *The Advancement and Reformation of Modern Poetry* (London, 1701) *The Ground and Criticism in Poetry* (London, 1704); Robert Lowth, *Lectures on the Sacred Poetry of the Hebrews* (London, 1987). On the perpetuation of the "aesthetic" approach to the Old Testament in Wilhelm de Wette, see Sheila Briggs "The Deceit of the Sublime" in *Semeia* 59, 2993, 2–35.

21. Ruth Smith, *Handel's Oratorios in Eighteenth Century Thought* (Cambridge, U.K.: Cambridge University Press, 1995), "The Biblical Sublime," 108–27.

22. De Bolla, *The Discourse on the Sublime*, 40ff.

23. Hans Urs von Balthasar, *The Glory of the Lord V: The Realm of Metaphysics in the Modern Age*, trans. Oliver Davies et al. 124ff, 496–531.

24. Balthasar, loc. cit.

25. Immanuel Kant, *Critique of Judgment*, trans. Werner S. Pluhar (Indianapolis: Hackett, 1987) Part I. 29: 124–43; 31: 143–44; *Opus Postumum* trans. E. Foster and M. Rosen (Cambridge University, 1993), 212, 226.

26. See Catherine Osborne, *Eros Unveiled* (Oxford: Oxford University Press, 1994). Balthasar *The Glory* Vol. V 265–7.

27. See Anders Nygren, *Agape and Eros*.

28. *Critique of Judgment*, Part I, 42: 169: "A lily's white color seems to attune the mind to ideas of innocence and the seven colors [of the spectrum] from red to violet [similarly seen to attune it, respectively, to the ideas of] (1) sublimity, (2) courage, (3) candor, (4) friendliness, (5) modesty, (6) constancy, and (7) tenderness. A bird's song proclaims his joyfulness and contentment with his existence."

29. *Critique of Judgment*, Part I, 16: 76–8; 29: 130; 41: 164; 42: 166–8.

30. *Critique of Judgment*, Part I, 15: 73–5.

31. Edmund Burke, *A Philosophical Enquiry into the Origin of our Ideas of the Sublime and the Beautiful* ed. Adam Phillips (Oxford: Oxford University Press, 1990).

32. Burke, *A Philosophical Enquiry*, Part One, section X; 39–30; Part Two, section V, 59–65; Part Four, section XIX, 131–136.

33. Howard Caygill, *Art of Judgement* (Oxford: Blackwell, 1989), 38–188.

34. Burke, *A Philosophical Enquiry* Part One, section X; 39–40; Part Two, section V, 59–65; Part Four, section XIX, 135–136.

35. See John Milbank, "Can a Gift be Given?" in *Rethinking Metaphysics* ed. L.G. Jones and S.E. Fowl (Oxford: Blackwell, 1995), 119–161.

36. Philippe Lacoue-Labarthe, *Typography*, 208–48, 267–300, "La verité sublime" in *Du Sublime* ed. J.P. Courtine et al. (Paris: Belise, 1988), 97–149.

37. *Critique of Judgment*, Part I, 16–17: 76–84; Part I, 22: 91–95. 131—*sacrifice*.

38. Caygill, *Art of Judgement*, 284–393. But see also "Post-Modernism and Judgment" in *Economy and Society* vol 17 No. I Feb 1988; Jean-Luc Nancy "L'Offrande sublime" in *Du Sublime*, 37–77.

39. See note 43 below.

40. Onora O'Neill, "Kant After Virtue" in *Constructions of Reason* (Cambridge University, 1989), 145–62.

41. Immanuel Kant, *Religion within the Limits of Reason Alone*, trans. T.M. Greene and H.H. Hudson (New York: Harper, 1960), *Preface*, 1–13.

42. *Critique of Judgment*, Part One, 20–27: 87–91. 59: 225–230.

43. *Critique of Judgment*, Part One 59: 229: "In this ability [taste] Judgment does not find itself subjected to a heteronomy from empirical laws, as it does elsewhere in empirical judging—concerning objects of such a pure liking it legislates to itself, just as reason does regarding the power of desire. And because the subject has this possibility within him, while outside him there is also the possibility that nature will harmonize with it, judgment finds itself referred to *something that is neither nature nor freedom* and yet is linked with the basis of freedom, *the supersensible, with which the theoretical and the practicable are in an unknown manner combined and joined into a unity* [my italics]." Since aesthetic judgment is here construed as participating in a divine coordination of nature and freedom which is *unknowable*, it is clearly like an event of grace. Likewise it tends to encourage in us a belief in an orderedness of nature that goes *beyond* mere means-end relation as a "purposiveness without purpose," yet this is not apodictically provable and so requires *faith*. See, further, "Appendix: Methodology of Teleological Judgement" 79–91: 301–369. And see also *Religion Within the Limits of Reason Alone* in which Kant finds room within a "reasoned faith" for an eschatological dimension in terms of the hope for an arrival of a *supplement* of freedom by happiness in the last judgment, which however includes a restoration of happiness here on earth: "The teacher of the Gospel revealed to his disciples the Kingdom of God on earth as in its glorious, soul-elevating moral aspect, namely in terms of the value of citizenship in a divine state, and to this end he informed them what they had to do, not only to achieve it themselves, but to unite with all others of the same mind and, so far as possible, with the entire human race. Concerning happiness, however, which constitutes the other part of what man inevitably wishes, he told them in advance not to count on it in their life on earth . . . yet he added . . . 'Rejoice and be exceeding glad, for great is your reward in heaven.' The supplement, added to the history of the church, dealing with man's future and final destiny, pictures men as ultimately *triumphant*, i.e. as crowned with happiness while still here on earth." *Religion Within the Limits*, 125. See also 4–5, 48–9, 70–71, 179–80. This element of eschatological faith in Kant also takes the form of a belief in a providentially guided process towards a state in which the moral law will increasingly be socially and politically realized and coordinated with happiness (the "supplement"). Thanks to the *cooperation* of "the great artist nature in whose mechanical course is clearly exhibited a predetermining design to make harmony spring from human discord, even against the will of man," I. Kant, *Perpetual Peace*, trans. M. Campbell Smith (London: Swan Sonnenschein, 1903). First supplement, 143.

44. *Critique of Judgment*, Part One, 15: 73–75: 74: "Hence in thinking of beauty, a formal subjective purposiveness, we are not at all thinking of a perfection in the object."

45. See I. Kant *Opus Postumum*, 200–257: 225: "Both *technical practical* and *moral-practical* reason *coincide* in the idea of God and the world, as the *synthetic unity of transcendental philosophy*." In the *O.P.* it is stressed that there is a "technical practical" aspect to theoretical reason, and that our discovery of laws of nature presupposes the *free* operation of mind upon nature, and even a certain "faith" that a rational treatment of nature will go on being possible in the future. Hence "nature and freedom, both of which must be treated theoretically and practically" [my italics]. Theoretical reason seems to require a certain transcendental presupposition of freedom, and yet freedom is only *guaranteed* by moral duty in practical reason (223).

46. *Critique of Judgment*, Part II 87: 339.

47. Friedrich Schiller, *Über Anmut und Würde* (Stuttgart: Philippe Reclam, 1971), 69–171.

48. Schiller, *Über Anmut*, 69 ff.

49. See Hans Urs von Balthasar *The Glory of the Lord* V. 513–46.

50. Slavoj Zizek, "Not only as *substance*, but also as *subject*," in *The Sublime Object of Ideology* (London: Verso, 1989), 201–31. Zizek is here criticizing Yirmiyahu Yovel, *Hegel et la Religion* (Paris, 1982).

51. *Hegel's Logic*, trans. W. Wallace (Oxford: Oxford University Press, 1975), 214: 278, "The Idea is the dialectic which again makes this mass of understanding and diversity understand its finite nature and the pseudo-independence in its productions, and which brings the diversity back to unity. Since this double movement is not separate or distinct in time, nor indeed in any other way . . . *the Idea is the eternal vision of itself in the other, notion which in its objectivity has carried out itself, object which in inward design is essential subjectivity* (my italics). Here the idea *only* is in its self-negation in objectivity, yet the "alien" moment of objectivity (including such contingency) essentially remains, even though it is rooted back in subjectivity. See also 240–44. 242: 295: "The end . . . is consequently the unity in which both of these firsts, the immediate and the real first, are made constituent stages in thought, merged, and at the same time preserved in the unity." Hence the "immediacy" of the "natural," objective world is for Hegel first shown up as illusion in relation to the real mediated work of "spirit," yet finally reclaimed as one essential moment of spirit, even as that through which it alone is, *for all* that it is the very illusion which occludes it. The postmodern logic of "double annihilation" is not very far away. . . . Finally, see the concluding sentences 244: 296: "The Idea does not merely pass over into life, or as finite cognition allow life to show in it: in its own absolute truth it resolves to let the 'moment' of its particularity, or of the first characterization and other-being, the immediate idea, as its reflected image go forth freely as Nature" (i.e., that Idea which "is independent or for itself," the objective, immediate, contingent, merely "given"). By a crucial paradox *Nature*, not *Geist*, is literally Hegel's last word.

52. G.W.F. Hegel, *Aesthetics*, trans. T.M. Knox (Oxford, Oxford University Press, 1975), 75–100, 313, 435–6, 517ff.

53. The sublime is that instant where "the revelation of the content is at the same time the supersession of the revelation," *Aesthetics*, 363. The true content of Romantic Art is "absolute inwardness, stripped of all external relations and processes of nature," 519. The coincidence of "realism" with "symbolism" here—one could say, "Balzac" with "Mallarmé"—which exactly corresponds to the paradoxical finality of *Nature* in the Shorter Logic, is best expressed in the following passage: "God is no bare ideal generated by imagination. . . . On the contrary, he puts himself into the very heart of the finitude and contingency of existence, and yet knows himself there as a divine subject who remains infinite in himself and makes this infinity explicit to himself." In consequence art can now make "the human form and mode of externality in general . . . an expression of the absolute," 520.

54. *Aesthetics*, 534 ff.

55. *Aesthetics*, 104.

56. See *Aesthetics*, 96 ff.

57. See J-L Nancy, "L'Offrande Sublime."

58. See Catherine Pickstock, *After Writing: On the Liturgical Consummation of Philosophy* (Oxford: Blackwell, 1998), 101–105.

59. See John Milbank, "Stories of Sacrifice" in *Modern Theology*, January, 1996.

60. See Hans Urs von Balthasar, *The Glory of the Lord*, in general. I am grateful to Alison Milbank for conversations concerning debates on the sublime in the eighteenth century.

13
The Descent of Transcendence into Immanence, or, Deleuze as a Hegelian

SLAVOJ ZIZEK

If there ever was, in the twentieth century, a philosopher of absolute immanence, it was Gilles Deleuze, with his notion of life as "the immanence of immanence, absolute immanence: it is sheer power, utter beatitude."[1] Deleuze's main reference in this assertion of immanence was Spinoza, whom Deleuze celebrated as the "Christ of philosophers"—so who (or, rather, what) is Spinoza?

He is, effectively, the philosopher of Substance, and this at a precise historical conjuncture: *After* Descartes. For that reason, he was able to draw all (unexpected, for most of us) consequences from it. Substance means, first of all, that there is no mediation between attributes: each attribute (thoughts, bodies, etc.) is infinite in itself; it has no outer limit where it would touch another attribute. "Substance" is the very name for this absolutely neutral medium of the multitude of attributes. The first philosophical consequence of this notion of Substance is the motif on which Deleuze insists so much: the univocity of being. Among other things, this univocity means that the mechanisms of establishing the ontological links described by Spinoza are thoroughly *neutral* with regard to their "good" or "bad" effects. Spinoza thus avoids both traps of the standard approach: he neither dismisses the mechanism which constitutes a multitude as the source of the irrational destructive mob, nor does he celebrate it as the source of altruistic self-overcoming and solidarity. Of course, he was deeply and painfully aware of the destructive potential of the "multitude"—recall *the* big political trauma of his life, a wild mob lynching the de Witt brothers, his political allies. However, he was aware that the noblest collective acts are generated by exactly the same mechanism—in short, democracy and a lynching mob have the same source. It is with regard to this neutrality that the gap which separates Negri and Hardt from Spinoza becomes palpable: in *The Empire*, we find a celebration of multitude as the force of resistance, while, in Spinoza, the concept of multitude *qua* crowd is fundamentally ambiguous: multitude is resistance to the imposing One, but, at the same time, it designates what we call "mob," a wild, "irrational" explosion of violence which, through *imitatio afecti*, feeds on

235

and propels itself. This profound insight of Spinoza gets lost in today's ideology of multitude: the thorough "undecidability" of the crowd—"crowd" designates a certain mechanism which engenders social links, and *this very same* mechanism that supports, say, the enthusiastic formation of social solidarity also supports the explosive spread of racist violence. What the "imitation of affects" introduces is the notion of trans-individual circulation and communication. As Deleuze later developed in a Spinozan vein, affects are not something that belong to a subject and are then passed over to another subject; affects function at the pre-individual level, as free-floating intensities which belong to no one and circulate at a level "beneath" intersubjectivity. This is what is so new about *imitatio afecti*: the idea that affects circulate *directly*, as what psychoanalysis calls "partial objects."

The next philosophical consequence is the thorough rejection of negativity: each entity strives towards its full actualization—every obstacle comes *from outside*. In short, since every entity endeavors to persist in its own being, nothing can be destroyed from within, for all change must come from without. What Spinoza excludes with his rejection of negativity is the very symbolic order, since, as we have learned already from Saussure, the minimal definition of the symbolic order is that every identity is reducible to a bundle (*faisceau*—the same root as in Fascism!) of differences: the identity of the signifier resides solely in its difference(s) from other signifier(s). What this amounts to is that absence can exert a positive causal influence—only within a symbolic universe is the fact that the dog did not bark an event. . . . This is what Spinoza wants to dispense with—all that he admits is a purely positive network of causes and effects in which, by definition, an absence cannot play any positive role. Or, to put it yet another way: Spinoza is not ready to admit into the order of ontology what he himself, in his critique of the anthropomorphic notion of god, describes as a false notion which merely fills in the lacunae within our knowledge—say, an object which, in its very positive existence, just gives body to a lack. For him, any negativity is "imaginary," the result of our anthropomorphic, limited, false knowledge that fails to grasp the actual causal chain. What remains outside his scope is a notion of negativity which would be precisely obfuscated by our imaginary (mis)cognition. While the imaginary (mis)cognition is, of course, focused on lacks, these are always lacks *with regard to some positive measure* (from our imperfection with regard to god, to our incomplete knowledge of nature). What eludes it is a *positive* notion of lack, a "generative" absence.

It is this assertion of the positivity of Being which grounds Spinoza's radical equation of power and right: justice means that every entity is allowed to freely deploy its inherent power-potentials, that is, the amount of justice owed to me equals my power. Spinoza's ultimate thrust is here anti-legalistic: the model of political impotence is for him the reference to an abstract law which ignores the concrete differential network and relationship of forces. A "right" is, for

Spinoza, always a right to "do," to act upon things according to one's nature, not the (judicial) right to "have," to possess things. It is precisely this equation of power and right that, in the very last page of his *Tractatus Politicus*, Spinoza evokes as the key argument for the "natural inferiority" of women:

> . . . if by nature women were equal to men, and were equally distinguished by force of character and ability, in which human power and therefore human right chiefly consist; surely among nations so many and different some would be found, where both sexes rule alike, and others, where men are ruled by women, and so brought up, that they can make less use of their abilities. And since this is nowhere the case, one may assert with perfect propriety, that women have not by nature equal right with men.[2]

However, rather than score easy points with such passages, one should here oppose Spinoza to the standard bourgeois liberal ideology, which publicly guarantees to women the same legal status as to men, while relegating their inferior social status to a legally irrelevant "fact of nature." All great bourgeois anti-feminists from Fichte up to Otto Weininger were always hypocritically careful to emphasize that, "of course" the inequality of the sexes should not be translated into inequality in the eyes of the law.

The final feature in which all the previous ones culminate is Spinoza's radical suspension of any "deontological" dimension, i.e., of what we usually understand by the term "ethical" (norms which proscribe how we should act when we have a choice)—and this in a book called *Ethics*, which is an achievement in itself. In his famous reading of the Fall, Spinoza claims that God had to utter the prohibition "You should not eat the fruit from the Tree of Knowledge!" because our capacity to know the true causal connection was limited. For those who know, one could say, for instance, "Eating from the Tree of Knowledge is dangerous for your health." This complete translation of injunction into cognitive statements again desubjectivizes the universe, implying that true freedom is not the freedom of choice but the accurate insight into the necessities which determine us. Here is the key passage from his *Theologico-Political Treatise*:

> . . . the affirmations and the negations of God always involve necessity or truth; so that, for example, if God said to Adam that He did not wish him to eat of the tree of knowledge of good and evil, it would have involved a contradiction that Adam should have been able to eat of it, and would therefore have been impossible that he should have so eaten, for the Divine command would have involved an eternal necessity and truth. But since Scripture nevertheless narrates that God did give this command to Adam, and yet that none the less Adam ate of the tree, we must perforce say that God revealed to Adam the evil which would surely follow if he should eat of the tree, but did not disclose that such evil would of necessity come to pass. Thus it was that Adam took the revelation to be not an eternal and necessary truth, but a law—that is, an ordinance followed by gain or loss, not depending necessarily on the nature of the act performed, but solely on

the will and absolute power of some potentate, so that the revelation in question was solely in relation to Adam, and *solely through his lack of knowledge* a law, and God was, as it were, a lawgiver and potentate. From the same cause, namely, from lack of knowledge, the Decalogue in relation to the Hebrews was a law. . . . We conclude, therefore, that God is described as a lawgiver or prince, and styled just, merciful, etc., merely in concession to popular understanding, and the imperfection of popular knowledge; that in reality God acts and directs all things simply by the necessity of His nature and perfection, and that His decrees and volitions are eternal truths, and always involve necessity. [3]

Two levels are opposed here, that of imagination/opinions and that of true knowledge. The level of imagination is anthropomorphic: we are dealing with a narrative about agents giving orders that we are free to obey or disobey, etc.; God himself is here the highest prince who dispenses mercy. The true knowledge, on the contrary, delivers the totally non-anthropomorphic causal nexus of impersonal truths. One is tempted to say that Spinoza here out-Jews Jews themselves: he extends iconoclasm to man himself—not only "do not paint god in man's image," but "do not paint man himself in man's image." In other words, Spinoza here moves a step beyond the standard warning not to project onto nature human notions like goal, mercy, good and evil, and so on—we should not use them to conceive man himself. The key words in the quoted passage are: "*solely through the lack of knowledge*"—the whole "anthropomorphic" domain of law, injunction, moral command, etc., is based on our ignorance. What Spinoza thus rejects is the necessity of what Lacan calls "Master Signifier," the reflexive signifier that fills in the very lack of the signifier. Spinoza's own supreme example of "God" is here crucial: when conceived as a mighty person, god merely embodies our ignorance of true causality. One should recall here notions like "phlogiston" or Marx's "Asiatic mode of production" or, as a matter of fact, today's popular "post-industrial society"—notions which, while they appear to designate a positive content, merely signal our ignorance. Spinoza's unheard-of endeavor is to think ethics itself outside the "anthropomorphic" moral categories of intentions, commandments, and the like—what he proposes is *stricto sensu* an *ontological ethics*, an ethics deprived of the deontological dimension, an ethics of "is" without "ought." What, then, is the price paid for this suspension of the ethical dimension of commandment, of the Master Signifier? The psychoanalytic answer is clear: superego. In Spinoza's effort to rid himself of the ethical dimension, he has introduced the superego. Superego is on the side of knowledge; like Kafka's law, it wants nothing from you—it is just there if you come to it. This is the command operative in the warning we see everywhere today: "Smoking may be dangerous to your health." Nothing is prohibited; you are just informed of a causal link. Along the same lines, the injunction "Only have sex if you really enjoy it!" is the best way to sabotage enjoyment. This conclusion may appear strange: in a first approach, if there ever was a philosopher foreign to superego, it is Spinoza—does his thought not display a unique attitude of almost saintly indifference, of the elevation not only above ordinary human passions and interests, but also above all feelings of guilt and moral outrage? Is his universe not that of pure positivity of forces with no life-denying negativity; is his attitude not the one of the joyful assertion of life? However, what if superego is the hidden name of this very indifference and pure assertion of life?

It is at this precise point that Kant, the Kantian break, sets in. What Spinoza and Kant share is the idea that virtue is its own reward and needs no other: they both reject with contempt the popular idea that our good deeds will be remunerated and our bad deeds punished in the afterlife. However, Kant's thesis is that the Spinozan position of knowledge without the deontological dimension of an unconditional Ought is impossible to sustain: there is an irreducible crack in the edifice of Being, and it is through this crack that the "deontological" dimension of "Ought" intervenes—the "Ought" fills in the incompleteness of "Is," of Being. When Kant says that he reduced the domain of knowledge in order to make space for religious faith, he is to be taken quite literally, in a radically anti-Spinozist way: from the Kantian perspective, Spinoza's position appears as a nightmarish vision of subjects reduced to marionettes. What, exactly, does a marionette stand for—as a subjective stance? In Kant, we find the term "marionette" in a mysterious subchapter of his *Critique of Practical Reason* entitled "Of the Wise Adaptation of Man's Cognitive Faculties to His Practical Vocation," in which he endeavors to answer the question of what would happen to us if we were to gain access to the noumenal domain, to the *Ding an sich*:

> . . . instead of the conflict which now the moral disposition has to wage with inclinations and in which, after some defeats, moral strength of mind may be gradually won, God and eternity in their awful majesty would stand unceasingly before our eyes. . . . Thus most actions conforming to the law would be done from fear, few would be done from hope, none from duty. The moral worth of actions, on which alone the worth of the person and even of the world depends in the eyes of supreme wisdom, would not exist at all. The conduct of man, so long as his nature remained as it is now, would be changed into mere mechanism, where, as in a puppet show, everything would gesticulate well but no life would be found in the figures.[4]

So, for Kant, the direct access to the noumenal domain would deprive us of the very "spontaneity" which forms the kernel of transcendental freedom: it would turn us into lifeless automata, or, to put it in today's terms, into "thinking machines." The implication of this passage is much more radical and paradoxical than it may at first appear. If we discard its inconsistency (how could fear and lifeless gesticulation coexist?), the conclusion it imposes is that, at the level of phenomena as well as at the noumenal level, we—humans—are a "mere mechanism" with no autonomy and freedom: as phenomena, we are not free, we are a part of nature, a "mere mechanism," totally submitted to causal links, a part of the nexus of causes and effects, and as noumena, we are again not free, but reduced to a "mere mechanism." (Is what Kant describes as a person which directly knows the noumenal domain not strictly homologous to the utilitarian subject whose acts are fully determined by the calculus of pleasures and pains?) *Our freedom persists only in a space* in between *the phenomenal and the noumenal.* It is therefore not that Kant simply limited causality to the phenomenal domain in order to be able to assert that, at the noumenal level, we are free autonomous agents: we are only free insofar as our horizon is that of the phenomenal, insofar as the noumenal domain remains inaccessible to us. What we encounter here is again the tension between the two notions of the Real, the Real of the inaccessible noumenal Thing and the Real as the pure gap, the interstice between the repetition of the same: the Kantian Real is the noumenal Thing beyond phenomena, while the Hegelian Real is the gap itself between the phenomenal and the noumenal, the gap which sustains freedom.

Is the way out of this predicament to assert that we are free insofar as we *are* noumenally autonomous, *but* our cognitive perspective remains constrained to the phenomenal level? In this case, we *are* "really free" at the noumenal level, but our freedom would be meaningless if we were also to have the cognitive insight into the noumenal domain, since that insight would always determine our choices—who *would* choose evil, when confronted with the fact that the price of doing evil will be the divine punishment? However, does this imagined case not provide us with the only consequent answer to the question "what would a truly free act be?" a free act for a noumenal entity, an act of true *noumenal* freedom? It would be to *know* all the inexorable horrible consequences of choosing the evil, *and nonetheless to choose it.* This would have been a truly non-pathological act, an act of acting with no regard for one's pathological interests.

The basic gesture of Kant's transcendental turn is thus to invert the obstacle into a positive condition. In the standard Leibnizean ontology, we, finite subjects, can act freely *in spite of* our finitude, since freedom is the spark which unites us with the infinite God; in Kant, this finitude, our separation from the Absolute, is the *positive* condition of our freedom. In short, the condition of impossibility is the condition of possibility. In this sense, Susan Neiman is right to remark that, "the worry that fueled debates about the difference between appearance and reality was *not* the fear that the world might not turn out to be the way it seems to us—but rather the fear that it would."[5] This fear is ultimately ethical: the closure of the gap between appearance and reality would deprive us of our freedom and thus of our ethical dignity. What this means is that the gap between noumenal reality and appearance is redoubled: one has to distinguish between noumenal reality "in itself" and the way noumenal reality *appears* within the domain of appearance (say, in our experience of freedom and the moral Law). This tiny edge distinguishing the two is the edge between the sublime and the horrible: God is sublime for us, from our finite perspective—experienced in itself, God would turn into a mortifying horror.

However, one should be very careful not to miss what Kant is aiming at. In a first approach, it may appear that he merely assumes a certain place prefigured by Spinoza: unable to sustain the non-anthropomorphic position of true knowledge, he proclaims the substantial order of Being inaccessible, out of bounds for our reason, and thus opens up the space for morality.[6] However, things are more complex. In his *Les mots et les choses*, Foucault introduced the notion of the "empirico-transcendental doublet": in the modern philosophy of subjectivity, the subject is, by definition, split between an inner-worldly entity (as the empirical person, the object of the positive sciences and political administration) and the transcendental subject, the constitutive agent of the world itself—the problematic enigma is the umbilical cord that links the two in an irreducible way. And, it is against this background that one can measure Heidegger's achievement: he grounded the "transcendental" dimension (*Dasein* as the site of the opening of the world) in the very finitude of man. Mortality is no longer a stain, an index of factual limitation, of the otherwise ideal-eternal Subject; it is the very source of its unique place. There is no longer any place here for the neo-Kantian (Cassirer) assertion of man as inhabiting two realms, the eternal realm of ideal values and the empirical realm of nature; there is no longer any place even for Husserl's morbid imagine of the whole of humanity succumbing to a pestilence and the transcendental ego surviving it. One should insist here on the split between this doublet and the pre-Kantian metaphysical problematic of particular/sensual/animal and universal/rational/divine aspect of man: the Kantian transcendental is irreducibly rooted in the empirical/temporal/finite—it is the trans-phenomenal *as it appears within the finite horizon of temporality*. And, this dimension of the transcendental (specifically as opposed to the noumenal) is what is missing in Spinoza.

What does Hegel bring to this constellation? He is not any kind of "mediator" between the two extremes of Spinoza and Kant. On the contrary, from a truly Hegelian perspective, the problem with Kant is that *he remains all too Spinozean*: the seamless positivity of Being is merely transposed onto the inaccessible In-itself. In other words, from the Hegelian standpoint, this very fascination with the horrible Noumenon in itself is the ultimate lure: the thing to do here is not to rehabilitate the old Leibnizean metaphysics, even in the guise of heroically forcing one's way into the noumenal "heart of darkness" and confronting its horror, but to transpose this absolute gap which separates us from the noumenal Absolute into the Absolute itself. So, when Kant asserts the limitation of our knowledge, Hegel does not answer him by claiming that he can overcome the Kantian gap and thereby gain access to Absolute Knowledge in the style of a pre-critical metaphysics. What he claims is that the Kantian gap already *is* the solution: Being itself is incomplete. *This* is what Hegel's motto "one should conceive the Absolute not only as Substance, but also as Subject" means: "subject" is the name for a crack in the edifice of Being.

This brings us to an unexpected subterranean link between Deleuze and Hegel: *immanence*. If there ever was a philosopher of unconditional immanence, it is Hegel. Is Hegel's elementary procedure not best encapsulated by his motto, from the Introduction to *Phenomenology*, according to which the difference between For-us and In-itself is itself "for us": it is ourselves, in the immanence of our thought, who experience the distinction between the way things appear to us and the way they are in themselves. The distinction between appearance and transcendent reality is itself a fact of our experiential appearance; when we say that a thing is, in itelf, in a certain way, this means it *appears* to us in this mode of being. More generally, absolute immanence also determines the status of Hegel's critique of Kant and the Kantian handling of antinomies/contradictions: far from denying us access to the Thing-in-itself, the antinomic or contradictory character of our experience of a Thing is what brings us into direct contact with it. This is also how Hegel would have approached Kafka: the Castle or Court "in themselves" are just a reified projection of the immanent movement of our thought-experience—it is not the inaccessible Thing-Castle which is refracted inadequately in our inconsistent experience. On the contrary, the specter of the Thing-Castle is the *result* of the inherent-immanent refraction of our experience. And, finally, does the passage from one to another "shape of consciousness" in the *Phenomenology* not also rely on the turn towards absolute immanence? When Hegel refutes asceticism, he does not proclaim it inadequate to the objective state of things; he simply compares it to the immanent *life-practice* of the ascetic subject—it is this practice (in Deleuzian terms: what an ascetic subject "does" with asceticism, on behalf of it) that refutes what asceticism "is."

The wager of Deleuze's concept of the "plane of consistency," which points in the direction of absolute immanence, is that of his insistence on the univocity of being: in his "flat ontology," all heterogeneous entities of an assemblage can be conceived at the same level, without any ontological exceptions or priorities. To refer to the well-known paradoxes of inconsistent classification, the plane of consistency would be something like a mixture of elements thrown together through a multitude of divergent criteria (recall Borges's famous taxonomy: brown dogs, dogs who belong to the emperor, dogs who don't bark, etc.—up to dogs who do not belong to this list). It would be all too easy to counter here that the Lacanian Real is precisely that which resists inclusion within the plane of consistency, the absent Cause of the heterogeneity of the assemblage—is it, rather, not that this "plane of consistency" is what Lacan called the "feminine" non-All set, with no exceptions and, for that very reason, no totalizing agency?[7] When, at the very end of *Seminar XI*, Lacan refers to Spinoza as the philosopher of the universal signifier and, as such, the true antipode of Kant,[8] he makes the same point: Spinoza is the philosopher of feminine *assemblage*, against Kant as the philosopher of the masculine Exception (the moral Law which suspends the imbrication of phenomenal causes and effects). The Spinozan One-Whole is thus a non-totalized Real, bringing us back to Lacan's fundamental thesis: the Real is not simply external to the Symbolic, but, rather, the Symbolic itself deprived of its externality, of its founding exception.

What about Hegel? What if Hegel "feminized" Kant again by way of reducing the Kantian ontological opposition between phenomena and the Thing-in-itself to the absolutely immanent tension inhering within phenomena themselves? It is thus already with Hegel that the logic of Transgression, the idea that, to attain Truth or ultimate Reality, one has to violate the superficial order (with its rules) and force the passage to another dimension hidden beneath, is suspended. Hegel would undoubtedly fully endorse Deleuze's scathing remark about Bataille, the ultimate thinker of Transgression:

> "Transgression," a concept good for seminarists under the law of a Pope or a priest, the tricksters. Georges Bataille is a very French author. He made the little secret the essence of literature, with a mother within, a priest beneath, an eye above.[9]

In a late story by Somerset Maugham, an older Frenchman has a paid young concubine. When he finds her in bed with a young man and she confesses that they really love each other, he proposes a unique solution: the two of them should marry; he will provide them with an apartment and a job for the young man—the price being that, twice a week, while the young man is at work, the old man will visit the young wife and make love to her. The solution is thus the reversal of the usual situation: instead of the young woman living with an old man and cheating on him with a young lover, she will live with the man whom she really loves, and cheat on him with the old, unattractive man. Does this story not provide the clearest staging of the Bataillean transgression? Bataille's ultimate horizon is the tension between homogeneity and its heterogeneous excess—between the profane and the sacred, the domain of exchange and the excess of pure expenditure. (And, insofar as Bataille's opposition of homogeneity and heterogeneity echoes Lacan's couple of S_2 and S_1, the chain of "ordinary" signifiers and the Master-Signifier, this is how one should also read the series of S_1 in Lacan's seminar *Encore*: not as an ordinal series, but as the series of excesses themselves.[10]) Or, to put it in Chesterton's terms: a miracle is no longer the irrational exception which disturbs the rational order, since *everything* becomes a miracle; there is no longer the need to assert excess against normality, since *everything* becomes an excess—excess is everywhere, in an unbearable intensity. Therein resides the true transgression: it occurs when the tension between the ordinary phenomenal reality and the transgressive Excess of the Real Thing is abolished. In other words, the truly subversive agent asserts the univocity of Being, assembling all the heterogeneous elements within the same "plane of consistency." Instead of the ridiculously pathetic fake heroism of forcing the established order towards its transcendent traumatic core, we get a profoundly indifferent enumeration which, without the blink of an eye, puts in the same series ethics and buggery.

This brings us to the basic Hegelian motif of Deleuze, his reversal of the standard relationship between a problem and its solution(s), his affirmation of an irreducible *excess* of the problem over its solution(s), which is the same as the excess of the virtual over its actualizations:

> In Deleuze's approach the relation between well-posed explanatory problems and their true or false solutions is the epistemological counterpart of the ontological relation between the virtual and the actual. Explanatory problems would be the counterpart of virtual multiplicities since, as he says, "the virtual possesses the reality of a task to be performed or a problem to be solved." Individual solutions, on the other hand, would be the counterpart of actual individual beings: "An organism is nothing if not the solution to a problem, as are each of its differentiated organs, such as the eye which solves a light problem."[11]

The philosophical consequences of this "intimate relation between epistemology and ontology" are crucial: the traditional opposition between epistemology and ontology should be left behind. It is no longer that we, subjects of a scientific investigation engaged in the difficult path of getting to know objective reality by gradually approaching it, formulate and solve problems, while reality just *is* out there, fully constituted and given, unconcerned by our slow progress. In a properly Hegelian way, our painful progress of knowledge, our confusions, our search for solutions—that is to say: precisely that which seems to *separate* us from the way reality really is out there—is already the innermost constituent of reality itself. When we try to establish the function of some organ in an animal, we are thereby repeating the "objective" process itself through which the animal "invented" this organ as the solution of some problem. Our process of approaching constituted objective reality repeats the virtual process of Becoming of this reality itself. The fact that we cannot ever "fully know" reality is thus not a sign of the limitation of our knowledge, but the sign that reality itself is "incomplete," open, an actualization of the underlying virtual process of Becoming.

It is here that we can clearly pinpoint what is arguably Deleuze's crucial misunderstanding of Hegel's move against/beyond Kant: Deleuze continues to read Hegel in a traditional way, as the one who returned from Kant to an absolute metaphysics which articulates the totally self-transparent and fully actualized logical structure of Being. Already in *Difference and Repetition*, Deleuze interprets Kant's transcendental Ideas from the perspective of his notion of "problematicity" as the excess of the question over answers to it: a transcendental Idea designates not an ideal, but a problem, a question, a task, which no answer, no actualization, can fully meet. So, Deleuze can only read the excess of the problem over its solutions as an anti-Hegelian motif, insofar as he perceives Hegel as the one who, as it were, filled in the gaps of the Kantian system and passed from Kant's openness and indeterminacy to the notion's complete actualization/determination. What, however, if Hegel does not *add* any positive content to Kant, does not fill in the gaps—what if he just accomplishes a shift of perspective in and through which the problem already appears as its own solution? What if, for Hegel, "absolute Knowing" is not the absurd position of "knowing everything," but the insight into how the path towards Truth is already Truth itself, into how the Absolute is precisely—to put it in Deleuzean terms—the virtuality of the eternal process of actualization?

We are thereby within the very heart of the problem of *freedom*: the only way to save freedom is through this short circuit between epistemology and ontology—the moment we reduce our process of knowledge to a process external to the thing itself, to an endless approximation to the thing, freedom is lost, because "reality" is conceived of as a completed, positive order of Being, as a full and exhaustive ontological domain. The inconsistency of Kant apropos of freedom is here crucial in its structural necessity. On the one hand, the subject is free in the noumenal sense—its freedom attests to the fact that it does not belong to the realm of the phenomenal enchainment of causes and effects, that it is capable of absolute spontaneity. On the other hand, spontaneity is transcendental, not transcendent: it is the way the subject appears to itself—as we learn in the final paragraphs of the Part I of the *Critique of Practical Reason*, it may well be that, in ourselves at the noumenal level, we are just marionettes in the hands of the all-powerful God. The only solution is here the Hegelo-Deleuzian (sic!) one: to transpose the incompleteness and openness (the surplus of the virtual over the actual, of the problem over its solution(s)) *into the thing itself.*

In what, then, effectively resides the difference between Hegel and Deleuze? Perhaps the difference is not between immanence and transcendence, but between flux and gap: the "ultimate fact" of Deleuze's transcendental empiricism is the absolute immanence of the continuous flux of pure becoming, while the "ultimate fact" of Hegel is the irreducible *rupture* of/in immanence. Here, one should evoke Einstein's passage from special to general theories of relativity: for Hegel, the gap between phenomena and their transcendent Ground is a secondary effect of the *absolutely immanent* gap of/in the phenomena themselves. "Transcendence" is the illusory reflection of the fact that the immanence of phenomena is ruptured, broken, inconsistent. To put it in somewhat simplified terms: it is not that phenomena are broken, that we have multiple partial perspectives, because the transcendent Thing eludes our grasp; on the contrary, the specter of this Thing is the "reified" *effect* of the inconsistency of the phenomena. What if this gap in the immanence (which is not caused by any transcendence, but is itself its own cause) is what Deleuze cannot accept?

Therein resides Hegel's true lesson: immanence generates the specter of transcendence because it is already inconsistent in itself. This movement is best exemplified by the "Christian syllogism," consisting of three judgments/divisions (*Ur-Teile*):

1. The starting point is the experience of transcendence: one begins with positing the radical split between man and transcendent God—as exemplified by the figure of Job, who finds himself perplexed by what God is doing to him.
2. In the second judgment, this split is reflected into God himself, in the guise of the split between God-the-father and Christ: in the figure of Christ dying on the cross, God himself turns into an atheist, experiencing himself as abandoned by God-the-father.
3. Finally, this split falls back into the split between man and man-Christ, the "minimal difference" separating the two. This final figure is the "truth" of the entire movement.

What this syllogism demonstrates is how immanence is not the starting point, but the conclusion: *immanence is not an immediate fact, but the result which occurs when transcendence is sacrificed and falls back into immanence.* Or, to put it in Nietzschean terms: truth is not one perspective, "the true one," against the other, illusory one; it only occurs in the very *passage* from one to another perspective.[12] Rene Girard made the same point apropos of the Book of Job: what makes it so subversive (in short, so *true*) is the very shift from one (divine) to another (Job's) perspective, along with the ultimate incompatibility of the two perspectives.[13] Similarly, immanence only emerges as the shifting of transcendence, that is, at the moment when it suddenly strikes us how the gap that separates us from the transcendent Beyond is just a fetishized misperception-effect of the gap within immanence (the gap between "ordinary" phenomena and the phenomena in which the Beyond "shines through"). The second version of this syllogism would be that of truth itself:

1. First, truth is posited as the inaccessible Beyond, something which can only be approached, something that the subject always misses;
2. Then, the accent shifts to the psychoanalytic notion of truth as intervening in the moments of slips and distortions, in the interstices of "ordinary" discourse: truth erupts when the continuous line of our speech gets interrupted and perturbed;
3. Finally, we arrive at a third position, that of *moi, la verité, je parle.*[14] The shift from subject to object is crucial here: it is not that what the subject says is true—it is truth itself which speaks, which turns from predicate (a qualification of subject's statements) to subject (of enunciation). It is here that Truth turns into an "organ without a body" that starts to speak.

The first two versions share the notion that Truth is an inaccessible beyond, they are precisely two versions of it: since its place is Beyond, the Truth never appears "as such," but always only in a refracted/distorted mode—or, as Lacan put it, *la verité ne peut que se mi-dire*, it can only be half-told. It is only in the third mode that truth as such *can* speak—how? In the guise of a fiction, precisely, or, to put it in another way, in the mode of the fool's (or, rather, buffoon's) discourse—from Paul who designated himself as a buffoon to Nietzsche. (In a closer analysis, one should subdivide the second mode in two: is the refraction/distortion the *effect* of the fact that the Truth persists outside, as an inaccessible noumenal In-itself, or are these refractions "all there is," with no Beyond to cause them?) Is, however, such a position of the one *through whom the Truth directly speaks (or acts)* not the ultimate perverse illusion? Does it not obviously rely on the existence of the big Other (as in the Stalinist "Marxism-Leninism," in which the Party posits itself as the executor of historical Necessity)? This counter-argument involves a crucial misunderstanding: *the "object" which starts to speak is the object that stands for the lack/inconsistency in the big Other, for the fact that the big Other doesn't exist.* "I, truth, speak" does not mean that through me, the big metaphysical Truth itself speaks, but that the inconsistencies and slips of my speech directly connect to the inconsistencies and the non-all of the Truth itself. Lacan's "I, truth, speak" is thus to be read *together with* "la verité ne peut que se mi-dire /truth can only be half-spoken," elaborated in the very opening paragraph of his later *Television*:

> I always speak the truth. Not the whole truth, because there's no way to say it all. Saying it all is literally impossible: words fail. Yet it's through this very impossibility that the truth holds onto the real.[15]

What this means is that the true task of thought is to think together the notion of the "object which speaks" and the inexistence of the big Other. "I, truth, speak" does not involve the magic overcoming of skepticism and uncertainty, but the transposition of this uncertainty into truth itself. (Christ is such an object which speaks, his words are exemplary of "I, truth, speak" which emerges at the very point of the death of big Other *qua* god.) It is here that one should overcome the position of finite subjectivity, that of "we cannot ever get to know Truth itself, we can only get partial glimpses of it, our knowledge is constrained by our subjective position, we cannot ever claim that the truth speaks through us . . . ": what if truth itself is non-all, affected by the real-impossible of an irreducible antagonism?

Notes

1. Gilles Deleuze, "Immanence: une vie . . . ," quoted from John Marks, *Gilles Deleuze*, (London: Pluto Press 1998), 30.
2. Benedict de Spinoza, *A Theologico-Political Treatise and A Political Treatise*, (New York: Dover Publications 1951), 387.
3. Spinoza, op.cit., 63–65.
4. Immanuel Kant, *Critique of Practical Reason*, (New York: Macmillan 1956), 152–153.

5. Susan Neiman, *Evil in Modern Thought*, (Princeton: Princeton University Press 2002), 11.
6. Is the same stance not clearly discernible in today's neo-Kantian reactions to biogenetics? Basically, Habermas is saying: although we now know that our dispositions depend on meaningless genetic contingencies, let us pretend and act as if this is not the case, so that we can maintain our sense of dignity and autonomy—the paradox is here that autonomy can only be maintained by prohibiting access to the blind natural contingency which determines us. That is to say, we maintain our autonomy, paradoxically, by *limiting* our freedom of scientific intervention.
7. See chapter VI of Jacques Lacan, *Le séminaire, livre XX: Encore*, (Paris: Editions du Seuil, 1975).
8. Jacques Lacan, *The Four Fundamental Concepts of Psycho-Analysis*, (New York: Norton 1977), 253.
9. Gilles Deleuze and Claire Parnet, *Dialogues II*, (New York: Columbia University Press, 2002), 47.
10. See chapter XI of Jacques Lacan, *Le séminaire, livre XX: Encore*, (Paris: Editions du Seuil, 1975).
11. Manuel DeLanda, *Intensive Science and Virtual Philosophy*, (New York: Continuum, 2002), 135.
12. Is this not what Lacan was aiming at when, in his *Seminar XX*, he emphasized that the discourse of the analyst emerges briefly in every passage-shift from one to another discourse?
13. See Rene Girard, *Job: the Victim of his People*, (Stanford: Stanford University Press, 1987).
14. "Men, listen, I am telling you the secret. I, truth, speak." Jacques Lacan, *Ecrits*, translated by Bruce Fink, (New York: Norton, 2002), 114.
15. Jacques Lacan, "Television," *October* 40 (Spring 1987), 7.

Contributors

Thomas A. Carlson is Associate Professor in the Department of Religious Studies at the University of California, Santa Barbara. He is author of *Indiscretion: Finitude and the Naming of God* (University of Chicago Press, 1999) and translator of several works by Jean-Luc Marion, including *God without Being* (University of Chicago Press, 1991), *Reduction and Donation: Investigations of Husserl, Heidegger, and Phenomenology* (Northwestern University Press, 1998), and *The Idol and Distance* (Fordham University Press, 2001).

Mladen Dolar held a position of professor in the Department of Philosophy, Faculty of Arts, University of Ljubljana, for twenty years till 2002; now he works as a researcher and an editor for the Society for Theoretical Psychoanalysis, Ljubljana. His publications in Slovene include *The Structure of Fascist Domination* (1982), *Hegel and the Object* (with Slavoj [Žižek, 1985), *Hegel's Phenomenology of Spirit* (2 vols, 1990, 1992), *On Avarice* (2002). In English: *Opera's Second Death* (with Slavoj Žižek, Routledge 2002), *His Master's Voice* will be published by Verso in 2004.

Kevin Hart is Professor of English at the University of Notre Dame. His books include *The Trespass of the Sign*, expanded ed. (New York: Fordham University Press, 2000), *The Dark Gaze: Maurice Blanchot and the Sacred* (University of Chicago, 2004), *The Power of Contestation: Perspectives on Maurice Blanchot*, co-edited with Geoffrey Hartman (The Johns Hopkins University, 2004), *Other Testaments: Derrida and Religion*, co-edited with Yvonne Sherwood (Routledge, 2004) and *Postmodernism: A Beginner's Guide* (Oneworld, 2004). His poetry is gathered in *Flame Tree: Selected Poems* (Bloodaxe, 2003).

Robyn Horner is a lecturer in theology at the Melbourne campus of Australian Catholic University, and is a research associate of Monash University. She is the author of *Rethinking God as Gift: Marion, Derrida and the Limits of Phenomenology* (Fordham University Press, 2001) and the forthcoming *Jean-Luc Marion: An Introduction for Theologians* (Ashgate, 2004), as well as articles on Marion, Levinas, and Derrida. With Vincent Berraud she translated Marion's *In Excess: Studies of Saturated Phenomena* (New York: Fordham, 2002).

Jeffrey L. Kosky is Assistant Professor of Religious Studies at Washington & Lee University. He is the author of *Levinas and the Philosophy of Religion* (Indiana University Press), the translator of Jean-Luc Marion's *Being Given* (Stanford

University Press) and *On Descartes' Metaphysical Prism* (University of Chicago Press), and the co-translator of *Phenomenology and the "Theological Turn"* (Fordham University Press).

Emmanuel Levinas (d. 1995) was Professor of Philosophy at Nanterre, University of Paris, and the Sorbonne, as well as director of the Ecole. His many publications include *De l'existent a l'existence, Existence and Existents* (The Hague, 1978), *En devouvrant l'existence avec Husserl et Heidegger* (Paris, 1967), *Totalité et Infini* (The Hague, 1961)/*Totality and Infinity* (Pittsburgh, 1969), *Difficile Liberté* (Paris, 1963, revised ed., 1976), *Quatre lectures talmudiques* (Paris, 1968), *Humanisme de l'autre homme* (Montpellier, 1972), *Autrement qu'être ou au-dela de l'essence* (The Hague, 1974)/*Otherwise than Being or Beyond Essence* (The Hague, 1981).

Jean-Luc Marion is professeur de métaphysique à l'Université Paris-Sorbonne and J. Nuveen Professor at the University of Chicago. He is also directeur de la collection "Epiméthée" aux Presses Universitaires de France. His publications include *The Idol and Distance* (Fordham, 2001, originally *L'idole et la distance*, Grasset, 1977); *God Without Being* (Chicago, 1991, originally *Dieu sans l'être*, (Fayard, 1982); *The Erotic Phenomenon* (Stanford, forthcoming, originally *Le phénomène érotique*, Grasset, 2003), *Being Given* (Stanford, 2002, originally *Étant donné*, PUF, 1997), *On Descartes' Metaphysical Prism* (Chicago, 1999, originally *Sur le prisme métaphysique de Descartes*), *Reduction and Givenness: Investigations of Husserl, Heidegger, and Phenomenology* (Northwestern, 1998), Cartesian Questions (Chicago, 1999).

John Milbank is Frances Myers Ball Professor of Philosophical Theology at the University of Virginia. His publications include *Being Reconciled* (Routledge, 2003), *The Word Made Strange* (Blackwell, 1997), *Theology and Social Theory* (Blackwell, 1990), and *The Religious Dimension in the Thought of Giambattista Vico* vols 1 and 2 (Edwin Mellen vol 1, 1990, vol 2, 1991). He has co-edited *Radical Orthodoxy* (Routledge, 1999), and co-authored, with Catharine Pickstock, *Truth in Aquinas* (Routledge, 2001).

Regina Schwartz is Professor of English and Religion at Northwestern University. Her publications include *Remembering and Repeating: On Milton's Theology and Poetics* (rpt Chicago, 1992), *The Curse of Cain: The Violent Legacy of Monotheism* (Chicago, 1997), "Freud's God," in *Post-secular Philosophy*, ed. Philip Blond (Blackwell, 1997) and *When God Left the World: The Sacramental and the Secular in Early Modern England* (forthcoming). She is editor of *The Book and the Text: The Bible and Literary Theory* (Blackwell, 1990) and co-editor of *The Postmodern Bible* (Yale, 1995).

Christian Sheppard is co-editor of *Mystics: Presence & Aporia* (University of Chicago Press, 2003) and is finishing his first book *"All So Luscious": Mystical Walt Whitman*. He has written on religion, literature, and culture for *The Chicago Review, The Chicago Tribune, The New York Times,* and *Symposium*. A recent graduate of the University of Chicago Divinity School, he is now Lecturer in the University of Chicago's Basic Program.

Charles Taylor is Board of Trustees Professor of Law and Philosophy at Northwestern University and Professor Emeritus of Philosophy at McGill University. His publications include: *Hegel* (Cambridge, 1975); *Hegel and Modern Society* (Cambridge, 1979); *Philosophical Papers, vol. 1: Human Agency & Language* (Cambridge, 1985); *Philosophical Papers, vol. 2: Philosophy and the Human Sciences* (Cambridge, 1985); *Sources of the Self* (Harvard, 1989); *The Ethics of Authenticity* (Harvard, 1991), "The Politics of Recognition" in *Multiculturalism*, ed. Amy Gutmann (Princeton, 1994); "Nationalism and Modernity" in *The Morality of Nationalism*, eds. Robert McKim & Jeff McMahan (Oxford, 1997).

Graham Ward is Professor of Contextual Theology and Ethics at the University of Manchester and executive editor of *The Journal of Literature and Theology* (Oxford). His publications include *True Religion* (Blackwell, 2002) *Cities of God* (Routledge, 2000), *Theology and Contemporary Critical Theory* (Macmillan, 1998 and 1996), *Barth, Derrida, and the Language of Theology* (Cambridge, 1995), and he is the editor of *The Postmodern God* (Blackwell, 1997), *The Certeau Reader* (Blackwell, 1999), and *The Blackwell Companion to Postmodern Theology* (2001).

Slavoj Zizek is Senior Researcher at the Department of Philosophy, University of Ljubljana. His publications include: *The Fragile Absolute, or Why is the Christian Legacy Worth Fighting For* (Verso, 2000), *On Belief* (Routledge, 2001), *Revolution at the Gates* (Verso, 2002), *Welcome to the Desert of the Real* (Verso, 2002), *The Puppet and the Dwarf* (MIT Press, 2003), and *Organs Without Bodies* (Routledge, 2003).

Index